Publishing Law

Publishing Law is a comprehensive guide to the law as it affects the publishing process. Written by the Copyright Counsel to the Publishers Association and a practising solicitor with many years' experience of the publishing trade, this work will serve as a comprehensive handbook for all those who need a practical understanding of where and how the law may apply, including publishers, authors and agents, and all those involved with published material.

Hugh Jones and Christopher Benson address a range of key legal issues in the publishing process, including:

- copyright, moral rights, commissioning and contracts, including online and e-book issues
- libel and other legal risks such as negligence, privacy and obscenity
- infringement and defences such as fair dealing; trade marks and passing off
- consumer law, data protection, advertising, distribution and export.

This fully updated fourth edition features:

- full coverage of electronic rights and e-commerce issues
- up-to-date coverage of changes in EU and UK legislation, including the Digital Economy Act 2010.

Legal points are explained with reference to important statutes, cases and relevant trade practices. A revised glossary, lists of useful addresses and further reading are also provided.

Hugh Jones is Copyright Counsel to the Publishers Association. A qualified solicitor, he worked in publishing for fifteen years, for law publishers Sweet and Maxwell and reference publishers Macmillan Press, before practising for eight years as a publishing and copyright lawyer at city law firm Taylor Joynson Garrett (now Taylor Wessing). He writes and lectures regularly, and is Treasurer of the British Copyright Council.

Christopher Benson is a solicitor at City law firm Taylor Wessing. He has been practising for over fifteen years as an intellectual property lawyer. He has considerable experience in the fields of publishing and copyright and also advises on all aspects of intellectual property law, both contentious and non-contentious, including copyright protection, trade mark protection and passing off, brand management, licensing, merchandising, sponsorship, franchising and advertising. He is a regular writer and lecturer on intellectual property matters.

Publishing Law

Fourth edition

Hugh Jones
and
Christopher Benson

Routledge
Taylor & Francis Group

LONDON AND NEW YORK

First published 1996
by Routledge
Second edition published 2002
Third edition published 2006

This edition published 2011
by Routledge
2 Park Square, Milton Park, Abingdon, Oxon, OX14 4RN

Simultaneously published in the USA and Canada
by Routledge
711 Third Avenue, New York, NY 10017

Routledge is an imprint of the Taylor & Francis Group, an informa business

Typeset in Goudy by Swales & Willis Ltd, Exeter, Devon
Printed and bound in Great Britain by CPI Antony Rowe, Chippenham, Wiltshire

British Library Cataloguing in Publication Data
A catalogue record for this book is available from the British Library

Library of Congress Cataloging in Publication Data
Jones, Hugh, solicitor.
  Publishing law / Hugh Jones and Christopher Benson.—4th ed.
  p. cm.
  Includes index.
  1. Authors and publishers—Great Britain. 2. Press law—Great Britain.
  3. Copyright—Great Britain. I. Benson, Christopher, solicitor. II. Title.
  KD1340.J66 2011
  343.4109'98—dc22
  2010046667

ISBN: 978–0–415–57513–3 (hbk)
ISBN: 978–0–415–57517–1 (pbk)
ISBN: 978–0–203–83817–4 (ebk)

For Osman

Contents

Preface to the fourth edition   xii

PART I
The law, and original works   1

1   Publishing and the law   3
     UK and international law 3
     EU law 4
     UK law 5

2   Copyright   9
     Original ideas 9
     Introduction to copyright 9
     Copyright and intellectual property 10
     From scrolls to screens: a brief history of copyright 11
     The EU copyright directive 12
     Copyright: the way ahead 14
     Copyright works 15
         Summary checklist: literary works 21
         Summary checklist: artistic works 23
         Summary checklist: copyright works 27
     Ownership of copyright 29
         Summary checklist: copyright ownership 34
     Qualification for copyright protection 34
         Summary checklist: qualifying works 36
     Duration of copyright 37
         Summary checklist: duration of copyright 44

3   Other rights of authors and publishers   45
     Moral rights 45
     The right of paternity 46
         Summary checklist: the right of paternity 49
     The right of integrity 49
         Summary checklist: the right of integrity 52

False attribution 52
The right to privacy of certain photographs or films 53
Remedies for infringement of moral rights 54
Database right 54
Publication right 57
Human rights 58
Public lending right 58
Artist's resale right (droit de suite) 59

PART II
Commissioning: publishing contracts   **61**

4. Author contracts   63
    How a contract is made 63
    Particular contracts and legal capacity 68
        Summary checklist: binding contracts 72
    Author–publisher agreements 72
    The standard author–publisher agreement 73

5. Other contracts   103
    Academic/professional/STM authors 103
    General editors 108
    Contributors (text and illustrations) 111
    Translators 115
    Subsidiary rights contracts 117
    Online access licences 140
    E-book agreements 142
    Aggregator agreements 144
    Other electronic agreements 146
    Agreements between authors and agents 146

PART III
Delivery, editing and obligations on publication   **149**

6. Delivery, editing and obligations on publication   151
    Delivery: acceptance or rejection 151
        Summary checklist: delivery 154
    Editing and alterations 154
        Summary checklist: editing 157
    Permissions 157
    Production and proofs 160
    Obligations on publication 160

PART IV
Publish and be damned   **163**

7. Defamation and other risks   165
    Defamation 165
    What is defamation? 168
    Libel and slander 168
    Defamatory meaning 169
    Social context 171
    Context of the statement 172
    Hidden meaning and innuendoes 172
    The repetition rule 173
    Levels of meaning 173
    Identification 174
    Publication 175
    Defences 177
    Costs 188
    Linking 189
    User-generated content 190
       Summary checklist: defamation 191
    Malicious falsehood 192
    Negligent mis-statement 193
    Obscenity 195
    Blasphemy 201
    Incitement to racial and religious hatred 201
    Contempt of court 202
       Summary checklist: other risks 205

8. Confidentiality and privacy   206
    Introduction 206
    Confidential information 206
    Private information 213
    Remedies for breach of confidence and privacy 217
    Online issues 220
    Official secrets 220
       Summary checklist: confidentiality and privacy 224

9. Copyright infringement   226
    Primary infringement 226
    The Digital Economy Act 233
    Secondary infringement 235
    Permitted acts and other defences 238
       Summary checklist: likeliest possible defences 238
    Civil and criminal remedies in the UK 251

Piracy 260
International copyright protection 261

10. Trade marks and passing off   270
   Trade marks 270
   Passing off 277
   Domain name disputes 279

PART V
Sales and marketing   283

11. Sale of goods and consumer protection   285
   Sale of goods 285
     Summary checklist: legal ownership in sales 290
     Summary checklist: descriptions, and misrepresentation 292
     Summary checklist: satisfactory quality 295
     Summary checklist: fitness for purpose 297
   Consumer protection 301
     Summary checklist: consumer protection 305

12. Advertising   306
   Introduction 306
   Unfair Commercial Practices 307
   Business protection from misleading advertising 311
   Comparative advertising 311
     Summary checklist: advertising 316
   Unsolicited goods and services 316
   Distance selling 317
   Data protection 319
     Summary checklist: promotion and data protection 329

13. Distribution and export   331
   Introduction 331
   Trade and competition 331
   Restraint of trade 332
   EU and UK competition rules 333
   Article 34: free movement of goods 345
   Exhaustion of rights 346
   Recent developments 347
     Summary checklist: competition 350

Appendix A: A to Z glossary of legal terms 351
Appendix B: useful addresses 355
Appendix C: further reading and sources 357
Index 359

Preface to the fourth edition

In the four years since the last edition, publishing has continued to develop rapidly in line with new technologies, media platforms and business partners (such as aggregators), and the law has continued to do its best to keep up (note that it is usually this way round). Some areas – such as copyright – have been under almost constant review, in the UK and EU, and still are – the Gowers review process found that intellectual property law in the UK is still basically fit for purpose in the twenty-first century (albeit with 54 recommendations), but at the time of writing a new Prime Ministerial Review into IP laws was about to start again 'to make them fit for the internet age' (on the assumption, presumably, that they aren't). Despite such regular review, the world's first copyright act, the Statute of Anne, celebrated its 300th birthday this year, so although much has changed, and must of course continue to do so, presumably copyright is doing something right, although new sections on cyber-crime and dealing with peer-to-peer networks under the Digital Economy Act 2010 suggest there is no room for complacency.

In addition, there is a proposed reform of libel laws to protect freedom of speech. A Defamation Bill is to be drafted and introduced into Parliament. There is also to be consultation on proposals of civil litigation funding and the question of costs of civil actions.

Taking account of all this remains a considerable challenge, so this book is increasingly a collaborative effort between specialist media lawyers, and the publishers, authors and others who have to put it all into practice. We owe particular thanks to the following long-suffering friends and colleagues: Olga Martin Sancho, much missed lawyer for the Federation of European Publishers, for commenting on EU material in Chapter 1, Paul Mitchell, of Taylor Wessing and the British Copyright Council, for detailed comments on Chapters 2 and 3, Jim Parker, the Registrar of Public Lending Right for once again providing statistics of the PLR scheme, Gilane Tawadros of the Design and Artists Collecting Society for helping us make (some) sense of Artist's Resale Right, Kate Pool of the Society of Authors and Kevin Stewart, Publishing Contracts Consultant, for their invaluable experience of authors' contracts in Chapter 4, Mark Majurey and William Bowes of Taylor and Francis and Informa respectively, and Sue Joshua and Cliff Morgan of Wiley, for enormous help with online and aggregator agreements in Chapter 5, James Shirras of Film Finances

Ltd, Mark Bide of EDItEUR and Brian Green of Book Industry Communications for continued help with subsidiary and electronic agreements in the same chapter. Mark Seeley of Elsevier once again contributed substantial new material on US copyright law.

Thanks are also due to the following from Taylor Wessing for their invaluable help: Lorna Caddy in relation to defamation, Mark Dennis and Tim Pinto on confidentiality and privacy, Nick Cody and Graham Hann on sale of goods, consumer protection and advertising, Sally Annereau on data protection and Robert Vidal and Louisa Penny on distribution and competition. Thanks also to Catherine Lloyd and Andrew Breeze for preparing the index and Marian Donne for researching the Appendices.

Any errors and inaccuracies are all our own work. As before, it would be helpful to hear of any errors or omissions, or sections which could be clearer, since the main aim of this book is still to make this corner of law understandable to the people it affects most. We have, once again, tried to foresee at least the major likely developments at the date given below, but this remains a fast-moving area of law, and if in doubt after that date it may always be wise to check with a publishing lawyer.

Hugh Jones
Christopher Benson
Brighton and London
16 January 2011

Part I
The law, and original works

Publishing and the law

1

Anyone can be a publisher in the UK. You don't need professional qualifications, or letters after your name, or a practising certificate. All of us 'publish' opinions or other information every time we send an e-mail, or circulate anything that anyone other than the intended recipient may see (although there may be an argument about personal text messaging). Most of this is normal Internet and mobile phone traffic, the lifeblood of twenty-first century communication, and most of it – most of the time – keeps well away from the law. But what if an e-mail you send to a list of friends or colleagues defames someone's reputation? Or what if text or pictures you use on your website infringe someone else's copyright? The law can quickly become involved, even in such apparently domestic transactions, so anyone who is part of the full-scale business of publishing – either as an author, a publisher, or in any other capacity – needs to keep the law in mind all the time. That is what this book is about, and what it is for – a roadmap of publishing, for those who wish to stay within the law.

The rest of this book will broadly follow the chronological sequence of most publishing, so we will start at the beginning, with the author's first idea, and follow the process through copyright and contract, to the legal risks of publication to the outside world (such as libel), and on through sales and marketing to distribution and export (in hard copy or digital form). At every point, we will find that the law has a habit of getting involved. Those of us who are familiar with the law will not find this terribly surprising (although there is a school of thought that some of us should get out more). Those for whom law (especially English law) is an arcane mystery, may need a few more signposts along the way. So even before our author has his (or her) first idea, here is a brief introductory map of the legal system which governs most UK publishing – UK and EU law, linked to foreign laws in many cases via international treaties such as the Berne Convention.

UK AND INTERNATIONAL LAW

One of the most important things to understand about law is that most laws operate on a territorial basis – in other words, they are promulgated by nation-states for their own citizens and to regulate activities within their own territorial boundaries.

They do not generally apply anywhere else. This has strengths and weaknesses – if in the UK you create or publish an original copyright work (like this book) you will have the full protection of UK copyright law, but if you find your copyright is being infringed in, say, Turkey or China, there is nothing UK law itself can do to help you and any legal remedies you may have will largely be dependent on local Turkish or Chinese law and on local courts. As you can imagine, some countries have better laws (and offer better protection) than others. In an Internet age, this worldwide patchwork of very different legal regimes is already proving a challenge. If material which infringes copyright, or libels someone, is created in New Jersey, uploaded to a server there, hosted on a UK website and downloaded in France and Saudi Arabia, whose law should govern the resulting dispute, and whose courts should have jurisdiction to try the case? This is no tiresome technicality – for publishing today, this can matter a great deal, since some laws are relatively liberal while others can be positively restrictive.

Increasingly, of course, the countries of the world have tried to regularise all this by means of **international treaties**, so there is an **International Court of Justice** at The Hague (mainly referred to for war crimes), and a **European Court of Human Rights** in Strasbourg. However, these only operate in certain areas, and (as in the case of the European Court of Human Rights) their judgments may be regional rather than global, and normally enforced against individual member states. There is no truly global International Court, applying global laws. Many think the Internet will eventually require something similar, but it seems we are still a long way away from persuading all governments in the world to agree on what the global laws would be, and who should enforce them. Copyright, however, is comparatively well off, thanks to one of the world's most successful and longest-running treaties, the **Berne Copyright Convention** of 1886, now acceded to by well over 160 countries, which obliges members to apply reciprocal 'national treatment' in their own courts to works of other member states. National treatment means that the UK, for example, is required to give copyright works of other convention countries – such as the USA – the same protection in UK courts as it gives to UK works – and vice versa. The World Trade Organisation's **TRIPS Treaty** also requires member states to enforce copyright effectively (for more on this, see Chapter 9).

EU LAW

The UK is of course a member of the **European Union**, comprising 27 countries at the time of writing (with three more countries currently applying for membership – Croatia, Turkey and Macedonia), and like every other member state the UK participates in its government, with nominated Commissioners holding portfolios at the **Commission** in Brussels, and elects MEPs to the **European Parliament** in Brussels and Strasbourg. Equally, apart from its own domestic laws, it is also subject to EU laws. European legislation derives from the EU Treaties (so-called EU primary legislation), which are agreed voluntarily on joining by all member states. The latest Treaty in force, since December 2009, is the Lisbon Treaty, which aims mainly to increase efficiencies in the decision-making process, give a greater role to the European Parliament and national parliaments, and increase external effectiveness (e.g. with a single Presidency and foreign affairs role). The purpose of much EU law is to harmonise legal regimes across Europe, in pursuit of the famous 'level playing field'. These EU laws can be on a wide variety of topics – from fish farming to intellectual property – and (as so-called secondary legislation) commonly take the form of:

- **Regulations**, which have direct effect in the member states of the EU, or
- **Directives**, which as the name implies are directions to member states to amend their own laws in accordance with given rules.

Both these forms of law take precedence over domestic UK laws. The E-Commerce Directive of 2000 and the Copyright Directive of 2001 are examples of laws which particularly affect publishing in the EU. They are enforced by the **European Court of Justice**, which sits in Luxembourg, with 25 judges drawn from a variety of member states, and an Advocate General. A **General Court** (formerly known as the **Court of First Instance)** was also established in 1988 to help with the case-load problem. In addition, there are **Decisions**, binding on those to whom they are addressed, and **Recommendations** and **Opinions** which have no binding force but which result from references by national courts to the European Court of Justice for interpretation. Such 'soft law' instruments have become the most frequent tools used to develop EU policies in recent years, in particular relating to issues affecting publishing.

HUMAN RIGHTS LAW

The UK has been a signatory to the European Convention for the Protection of Human Rights and Fundamental Freedoms since 1950. However, in October 2000 the Human Rights Act 1998 came into force, thus bringing convention rights such as freedom of expression and privacy more centrally into UK law. When courts now interpret the law, they must do so in a way which is compatible with the Convention. In doing so, they must take account of the decisions of the European Court of Human Rights.

This, then, is the international and European context in which UK law now operates.

UK LAW

'COMMON LAW'

After the Romans departed (taking Roman law with them) the islands now making up the UK were a pretty lawless place. But over the centuries a body of Anglo-Saxon, and then Norman, law developed, based on cases decided by judges, and increasingly following set rules.

This became known as the common law of England (a key part of **English law**) and was administered by common law courts. Separate laws developed in Scotland (**Scots law**) and Northern Ireland. Actions for breach of contract or negligence were (and still are) common law actions. Separate ecclesiastical courts regulated matrimonial law, and Courts of **Equity**, such as the Chancery courts, could be appealed to for remedies (such as injunctions) based less on rules than on basic fairness and justice (hence 'equitable' solutions). The judges, however, played a crucial role. Meanwhile, on the Continent, the codified rules of Roman law continued to be influential, so a separate **civil law** tradition grew up (and still operates, e.g. in France and Germany, based on civil Codes containing general principles, rather than a body of fact-based case law).

STATUTES

Although much of publishing law is still based on common law and equity, nowadays an increasing amount comes from **Acts of Parliament**, passed by Parliament in Westminster (also called **Statutes**), and subsidiary orders or **Regulations** made under those Acts, called **Statutory Instruments** (or S.I.s). Examples of Statutes relevant to publishing law are the Copyright, Designs and Patents Act 1988 (still the primary source of copyright law in the UK), the Trade Marks Act 1994, and the Human Rights Act 1998. Most of this legislation is introduced into Parliament in the form of government **Bills**, usually in the House of Commons, but Bills are sometimes introduced in the Lords, or often appear as Private Members' Bills: the Copyright (Visually Impaired Persons) Act 2002 began life as a backbench MP's Bill.

Often, the legal principles contained in Acts of Parliament need fleshing out in more detail, so may be followed by Regulations, which amplify – and perhaps amend – the original Act. A good example was the wonderfully named Copyright (Librarians and Archivists) (Copying of Copyright Material) Regulations 1989, which followed immediately after the 1988 Copyright Act in order to clarify the permitted extent of library copying.

Here is an example of how the EU and UK legal system works:

- The UK term of copyright under the 1988 Copyright, Designs and Patents Act was 'Life plus 50' (more precisely, 50 years after the end of the year in which the author died).
- In October 1993, the EU Parliament passed EU Directive 93/98/EEC (the Term Directive, sometimes called the Duration Directive), harmonising the term of copyright throughout the EU at 'Life plus 70'. Member states had until July 1995 to increase their copyright terms if necessary.
- This required an amendment to the UK's 1988 Act, so the required changes were introduced by the UK Government in part by a Statutory Instrument called the Duration of Copyright and Rights in Performances Regulations 1995, which came into force (late) on 1 January 1996. From that moment, the UK term of copyright for most works was increased by 20 years, to Life plus 70.

It will be seen from this how Acts of Parliament passed in Westminster come to be amended by laws created in Brussels, and also how important it is to keep track of any amending Regulations, many of which change the law quite dramatically.

CONTRACTS

All this important-sounding government activity should not blind us to the fact that we can make laws too. Or at least, that we can enter into agreements that the law will enforce, called **contracts**. Publishing is crowded with contracts, of course, from **licences**, which permit or authorise us to do things, to more complex agreements such as author contracts, which grant rights in return for a promise to publish and (usually) remuneration, to agreements not to do things at all, such as restrictive covenants. Some contracts need to comply with certain formalities (an exclusive licence needs to be in writing, and signed by the person granting it, for example), but as a general rule contracts do not necessarily need to be written at all. All this is set out in detail in Chapters 4 and 5.

The law will enforce most reasonable contracts, so if one of the parties to a contract fails to comply with significant terms of that contract, the other party may bring a legal action against him (or her) for **breach of contract**. Usually, if the value of a case is £5,000 (£2,000 in Northern Ireland) and less than £15,000, it will generally be allocated either to the **small claims** track or to the **fast track**, which is within the **County Court**. Claims for over £15,000, or complicated claims, are allocated to a 'multi track' and can be heard in the **High Court**, depending on the claimant's choice of court and the nature of the claim. There is an appeal from there to the **Court of Appeal**, and from there in some cases to the **Supreme Court** (formerly the judicial committee of the **House of Lords**). Where cases involve questions of interpretation of EU law, the UK courts can make references to the **European Court of Justice**. Decisions of these court cases are reported and published, and judgments – particularly of the higher courts – are followed by judges in later cases, thus establishing a system of judge-made law, known as **precedent**. So although an increasing amount of our law derives from politicians passing Acts of Parliament, judges still have a very important role in interpreting the law in order to reach decisions in individual cases.

If a breach of contract is proved, claimants are entitled to a remedy sufficient to restore them to the position they would have been in had the breach not occurred.

TORTS

Tort is the French word for wrong, so since Norman times a **tort** has meant a civil wrong (as opposed to a criminal wrong, which is a crime). Examples of torts are libel, negligence, nuisance, copyright and trade mark infringement, breach of confidence, malicious falsehood or passing off – wrongful or harmful acts which we may do to each other, and for which we may take legal action against each other in the civil courts (as with breach of contract, above).

Successful claimants in a tort action are generally entitled to a remedy so far as possible sufficient to restore them to the position they would have been in had the tort not occurred.

CRIMES

Criminal offences, on the other hand, like murder or assault, are regarded as so serious by the state that prevention and punishment are taken out of our hands altogether in order for those concerned to be **prosecuted**, usually by the **Crown Prosecution Service,** or **H.M. Revenue and Customs** (formerly the Inland Revenue and H.M. Customs and Excise). Obscenity, indecency and incitement to racial hatred are criminal offences, all of which may affect publishers (see Chapter 7). Certain activities infringing copyright, such as importing or possessing infringing equipment, are also criminal offences under the 1988 Copyright Act, for which there are set penalties, including **fines**, seizure or destruction of stock, and even **imprisonment**. Offences involving illegal importation are usually the responsibility of H.M. Revenue and Customs. Offences such as selling illegal or bootleg copies, e.g. of books, CDs or DVDs, are usually prosecuted by **Trading Standards Officers**, as are offences under the Trade Descriptions Act. So reputable publishers, as well as more recognisable criminals, may commit criminal offences.

On which happy note, we should perhaps complete our tour of the legal system which governs publishing in the UK, and turn our attention, in the next chapter, to an author starting to write an original work.

Copyright 2

ORIGINAL IDEAS

All published works start with an original idea, and all ideas have an author. *The Oxford English Dictionary* equates author with 'originator': in the classic publishing hierarchy, the inspiration of authors is the beginning, the process starts here. This is the classic blank sheet of paper (or the blank screen) which all authors encounter, in the back bedroom, on the kitchen table, or (in J.K. Rowling's case) in the Edinburgh coffee bar. When – finally – the original idea appears, is it protected at all by the law?

Possibly, but in different ways. A good publishing idea may have immense commercial value – it may generate not only profitable individual works but also entire series of profit-making publications as well as substantial other revenue, for example, from merchandising or film, TV or electronic exploitation. Even if the final finished works were written by others, none of what follows would have happened without the original idea. Despite this, it is not at all easy to protect original ideas as such; as a general rule, there is no copyright in an idea, and the less developed it is, the harder it will be to protect in any other way.

Some possible ways include:

- Trade mark protection – for a new children's character, for example (for more on this, see Chapter 10).
- Confidential information – concepts, plots and other ideas imparted in confidence may be protected by the law of confidence in appropriate circumstances (see Chapter 8).
- Copyright – particularly for material set down and developed beyond the idea stage, perhaps to substantial drafts, sketches or works in progress (see below).

INTRODUCTION TO COPYRIGHT

We saw above that there is no copyright in an idea. However, there might be copyright protection for some kinds of more developed material, once something is put into concrete form or given tangible expression. Copyright law will not protect you just for having a good idea, but it may protect you for doing something positive to express it – in effect, for putting it into a form where it can be shared with the rest of the world. The law recognises that doing this requires an investment of time and effort, and also some skill (quite apart from any financial costs, which may also be involved). It also carries with it a serious risk: once expressed in tangible, physical form, an idea can be copied by others. This has always been true – even before Gutenberg – but it is particularly true in an Internet age. So the law provides protection against copying for those who make that investment and take that risk, and thus an incentive for them to invest their efforts in more ideas in the future. This is one of the most important truths to grasp about copyright, and UK copyright in particular. Although it protects authors and their works – quite rightly – it is not only a reward for authorship, but a protection for investment. This explains why UK copyright law has developed in the way it has over the centuries, and it is unlikely that the UK's worldwide publishing business in its present form could exist without it.

What is copyright then, and why is it so important to publishing?

COPYRIGHT AND INTELLECTUAL PROPERTY

Copyright should, literally, be the right to copy; in fact in legal terms it is better to think of it as the right to *control* copying by others. Put a little more precisely, copyright in the UK is the exclusive statutory right, given (usually) to those who create original works, to exercise control for a specified period of time over the copying and other exploitation of those works. It therefore gives creators two different, but matching rights:

- an exclusive, positive right to copy and exploit their own works, or license other people (such as publishers) to do it for them; and
- a negative right to prevent anyone else from doing so without their consent, coupled with powerful legal remedies for copyright infringement if they do.

Under UK law, the emphasis has been very much on the second, negative, right: UK copyright was primarily a right to prevent other people from doing things. It is important to remember, though, that it is far from being an absolute monopoly, and was never intended to be; as well as a limited duration, after which works revert to the public domain, there are clear exceptions for purposes beneficial to society, such as 'fair dealing' for research and private study, or library and educational exceptions. (We will look at copyright infringement, and the various permitted exceptions under UK law, in Chapter 9.)

Copyright may thus be grouped with the protection given to the owners of patents and the proprietors of trade marks, which (together with registered and unregistered designs, database rights, rights in performances, publication rights, moral rights and confidential information) traditionally make up the area of law known as 'intellectual property'. This term is not very precise, or very accurate (not every right is strictly speaking a right of property, for example), but it is a useful label for the increasingly important legal protection given to products of the mind: intellectual creations which, when applied commercially or industrially, are of some value to society, and worth protecting legally. In today's Internet society, intellectual property (the more scientific rights such as patents are sometimes called 'industrial property') is an increasingly important form of national and international legal protection for trade in all kinds of goods and services; not only for books, e-books, websites and databases, but also for films, DVDs, computer software, distinctive trade brands, new drugs and other inventions. It is a key issue for all trading countries, and for trading blocs such as the EU and the World Trade Organisation, and intellectual property is normally fairly near the top of the agenda in international trade negotiations. Some developing countries, whose lack of infrastructure puts them on the wrong side of a growing 'digital divide', have suggested that intellectual property should be diluted to allow easier access, primarily to generic drugs, but this would harm local authors and publishers, who need copyright protection (for example, against piracy) even more than their colleagues in the West.

Before looking at modern copyright law in detail, it may be helpful to explain how we have got to this point, and how copyright law has developed over the centuries to meet the challenges of a fast-moving technological society.

FROM SCROLLS TO SCREENS: A BRIEF HISTORY OF COPYRIGHT

Although authors had a limited form of copyright and moral rights in the ancient world (plagiarism being punishable in Ancient Greece, for example), and Chinese block-printed books dating from the eleventh-century Song Dynasty have been found with copyright claims, copyright only really started to develop as an organised system of legal protection in Europe when commercial copying first became possible in the fifteenth century with the invention of the printing press. In England the new printing process – introduced here by William Caxton – quickly came under the control of the Stationers Guild as part of a royal licensing system which, by the time of the Catholic Queen Mary, had as much to do with the suppression of heresy as the propagation of literature or learning. Parliament finally refused to renew any further Licensing Acts in 1694 after the Glorious Revolution, and the Stationers therefore lobbied Parliament for a proper statutory form of copyright protection.

The result was the first Copyright Act, the Statute of Anne of 1710. Under that Act, authors were given 'the sole right and liberty' of printing books for a fixed (renewable) term of 14 years, or 21 years for works already in print. Works had to be registered (of course) with the Stationers Company. This provided initially only a brief statutory monopoly, and continuing arguments about common law copyright were only finally resolved in favour of a fixed statutory term for published works in the historic case of *Donaldson* v. *Becket* in 1774. Unpublished works continued to enjoy an indefinite term of protection (now limited to 2039, or life of author plus 70 years, depending on when the work was created). The term was progressively increased through the eighteenth and nineteenth centuries, and extended to other works, such as paintings and photographs, but it remained, as today, a fixed statutory term, although increasingly this varied depending on how long the author lived.

To this developing national protection, the Berne Convention in 1886 added for the first time an international treaty system of reciprocal copyright protection, now (after a hundred years) accepted by over 160 nations. Key elements are:

- fully reciprocal 'national treatment';
- no requirement for formalities, e.g. registration, but works must be 'original';
- minimum protection for life of author plus 50 years.

A watered-down version of these requirements was included in the 1952 Universal Copyright Convention (UCC), established largely to accommodate the two superpowers, the USA and Russia, neither of which had yet joined Berne (they both since have). The UK joined the UCC in 1957.

The twentieth century was otherwise a century of rapid technological change, during which new advances such as films, broadcasts and computer programs were successively given statutory protection. The current UK Act, the Copyright, Designs and Patents Act, was passed in 1988 and came into force on 1 August the following year (referred to throughout the rest of this book as the '1988 Act'). It has already been heavily amended to take account of various EU directives, providing among other things for Rental and Lending Rights, legal protection of databases, and for extension of the term of copyright protection from life plus 50 years to life plus 70 for most works, including most works of EEA origin. Some of the most significant changes came when the UK implemented the EU Copyright Directive, designed to harmonise copyright protection across the expanding EU and enable full accession to the 1996 WIPO Copyright Treaty, bringing the Berne Convention more fully up to date with the digital society.

In addition, the World Trade Organisation has now replaced the old system of GATT trade negotiations, not only adopting Berne as the minimum copyright standard for member states, but also (via the 1994 TRIPS Agreement) requiring member states to provide sufficient and effective copyright enforcement. In an Internet world, this is already proving a challenge.

THE EU COPYRIGHT DIRECTIVE

Directive 2001/29/EC on the harmonisation of certain aspects of copyright and related rights in the information society (generally referred to as the EU Copyright Directive) was finally passed by the EU Council of Ministers on 9 April 2001 after two years of unprecedented lobbying, and implemented in the UK (late) via the Copyright and Related Rights Regulations 2003 (referred to in this book as the 2003 Regulations), which came into force on 31 October the same year. The following summary sets out the basic structure of this key Directive (now fully implemented by all EU member states), together with references to the UK Regulations where appropriate. Further details of copyright enforcement provisions, and new 'non-commercial' wording for many copyright exceptions, are included in Chapter 9.

CORE RIGHTS

Adopting wording drawn directly from the WIPO Copyright Treaty 1996, the Directive required member states to provide the following key rights for authors:

- *Reproduction right* (Article 2). The exclusive right to authorise or prohibit direct or indirect, temporary or permanent reproduction by any means and in any form, in whole or in part. This was largely already covered in the 1988 Act.
- *Right of Communication/making available to the public* (Article 3). The exclusive right to authorise or prohibit any communication to the public of their works, by wire or wireless means, including the making available to the public of their works in such a way that members of the public may access them from a place and at a time individually chosen by them. This was new, and has resulted in changes to sections 16 and 20 of the 1988 Act (set out fully in Chapter 9). Opinion is divided about whether the changes increase the scope of copyright protection already given under UK law.
- *Distribution right* (Article 4). The exclusive right to authorise or prohibit any form of distribution to the public by sale or otherwise (already dealt with under the 1988 Act).

EXCEPTIONS

In addition to new core rights, there are 21 possible exceptions, set out in Article 5. The first (5.1) dealing with temporary copying, is mandatory; the other 20 are optional, forming an à la carte menu from which the 27 member states now required to implement the Directive are inevitably making different selections – thus seriously limiting the chances of any real harmonisation. It is at least an exhaustive list, so that no further exceptions within the EU are possible.

- *Temporary reproduction* (Article 5.1) This exempts from the reproduction right temporary acts of reproduction 'which are transient or incidental and an integral and essential part of a technological process and whose sole purpose is to enable [network transmissions or lawful uses] … which have no independent economic significance'. Since it is the only mandatory exception, and every word was the result of such vigorous argument by all sides, it was included almost verbatim in the UK Regulations (regulation 8), giving a new Permitted Act of 'Making Temporary Copies' under a new section 28A of the 1988 Act (see Chapter 9 for more on this). It is generally felt to be a workable compromise between the interests of rightsholders to protect their works against economically significant misuse, and the legitimate need for intermediaries, users and telecommunications companies to have a workable exception that will enable the Internet to function. There are more general provisions dealing with liability of intermediaries in the E-Commerce Directive.

- *Optional exceptions* There is not space here to set out all 20 optional exceptions, particularly since the UK selected very few, sticking broadly to current 'fair dealing' exceptions, such as criticism or review, or research or private study plus existing educational and library exceptions, many now subject to express 'non-commercial' criteria. However, there was also provision in the Directive for an exception for disabled people, which the UK utilised in passing the Copyright (Visually Impaired Persons) Act 2002, and which now permits making 'accessible' copies by visually impaired people (or on their behalf if no licensing scheme is available). The Act came into force on 31 October 2003, and licensing schemes are now established, including one operated by the Copyright Licensing Agency.
- *The 'three-step test'* One very important proviso applying to all 21 exceptions is contained in Article 5.5. Using wording drawn directly from Article 9(2) of the Berne Convention, it provides that each exception should only be applied 'in certain special cases which do not conflict with a normal exploitation of the work or other subject-matter and do not unreasonably prejudice the legitimate interests of the rightsholder'. This wording now forms part of EU copyright law, and is already proving to be an increasingly important yardstick for future interpretation, in the UK and across the EU.

TECHNOLOGY AND REMEDIES

Articles 6 and 7 required member states to provide protection against circumvention of technological measures, such as encryption, and rights-management information. Both these provisions were implemented in the 2003 Regulations. Article 8 (also implemented) further provided for sanctions and remedies, which must be 'effective, proportionate and dissuasive', including remedies against service-providers which it is hoped will lead to effective Notice and Takedown provisions suitable for the Internet age.

COPYRIGHT: THE WAY AHEAD

In the decade since the 2001 Copyright Directive, copyright has been under almost constant scrutiny in the UK, EU and internationally. Aspects of copyright such as the extent of copyright exceptions in a digital age have received (and, at the time of writing, still receive) particular attention. This is in many ways a good thing, in a fast-moving digital age, with new formats and rapidly developing business models: most commentators agree on the importance of maintaining the essential balance in the UK copyright system, between (1) the need to protect exclusive rights in an age of easy cybercrime, and (2) the legitimate expectations of users and society for reasonable access, increasingly in digital formats.

In 2006, after lengthy consultation, the government-sponsored Gowers Review of intellectual property in the UK reported, finding that the UK IP system was basically

'fit for purpose' in the twenty-first century, but unsurprisingly making 54 recommendations for modernisation and amendment, which are already leading to proposals for legislative change, for example to extend educational exceptions to distance
learning and to permit format shifting by libraries for preservation purposes (likely
to feature in Regulations in 2011). In 2009, the UK government published a policy
document 'Copyright – The Way Ahead', with proposals to tackle the perceived
complexity of copyright, to deal with peer-to-peer downloading (now dealt with
in the Digital Economy Act 2010, see Chapter 9), but also to modernise copyright
licensing and permissions. On several issues, such as format-shifting for personal
copying, the government has deferred to Europe, suggesting that any wider initiative
will need to be European. Elsewhere in Europe, copyright remains a high priority,
with recent Communications and Green Papers consulting on 'fragmented licensing' across the EU, mass digitisation, orphan works and future possibilities such as
Extended Collective Licensing.

Perhaps a broader issue for copyright remains: that of public awareness and
acceptance. Unlike previous generations, the present generation of PC-users and
net-surfers rightly expects quick and easy access to information, and the difference
between (free) public information and (possibly restricted) copyright content is
often a difficult act to sell. As ever, technology itself increasingly has the answer
(for example, in digital rights management), but there is no doubt that much
consultation and negotiation between rightsholders, users and governments lies
ahead.

COPYRIGHT WORKS

INTRODUCTION: TYPES OF WORKS

Initially, as we have seen (above, p. 11), copyright only extended to books and other
printed matter. However, definitions based on traditional packages such as 'books'
are no longer specific or flexible enough for modern content industries like publishing, where individual creations – such as text, graphics, or sound recordings – may
now need to be re-used and adapted in different combinations and in different forms
(such as online services or websites). Each original element may also be created and
owned by quite different people, who may wish to exploit them in different ways; it is
important therefore to identify who owns the rights in each constituent part and deal
with those rights separately. For this reason, it is better to think of books, journals,
CD-ROMs or websites not as 'works' at all but as packages or bundles of works, each
of which may need different treatment.

What copyright works, then, does UK law protect? Not every creation counts as
a work. The works which may currently be protected are set out in section 1(1) of
the Copyright, Designs and Patents Act 1988. These categories were only slightly
altered by the 2003 Regulations, which removed the separate category of cable programmes, now included under broadcasts. Three general categories of works may
now be protected:

(1) original literary, dramatic, musical or artistic works;
(2) sound recordings, films, or broadcasts; and
(3) the typographical arrangement of published editions.

There is now a separate **publication right** in previously unpublished works, and a separate statutory **database right**, both dealt with in Chapter 3. Copyright may still cover some original databases, dealt with below (p. 17).

If you want to secure copyright protection for a work in the UK, therefore, the first thing you will need to do is make sure that it falls into one of the above categories. There are other qualifying criteria which each individual work will also need to fulfil (see below, p. 34), but these three categories are the essential starting point. Many of the categories have been defined quite widely over the years – so that literary works, for example, now include computer programs and compilations – and we will examine each of the categories most relevant to publishing in turn. As will become obvious, a modern publication may contain several different types of copyright works.

LITERARY WORKS

Of all copyright works, literary works are still the most important for authors and publishers, although others (such as artistic works) are important too as we shall see. Under section 3 of the 1988 Act, a 'literary work':

- means any work (other than a dramatic or musical work) which is written, spoken or sung;
- includes a table or compilation (other than a database) and a computer program;
- includes a database which by reason of the selection or arrangement of its contents, constitutes the author's own intellectual creation;
- must be recorded, 'in writing or otherwise'.

'Written, spoken or sung'

A work does not need to be 'literary' in the colloquial sense in order to be a literary work, as long as it is written, spoken or sung. Some very un-'literary' written matter indeed has been given copyright protection in the past, such as business letters, football coupons, trade advertisements and examination papers: indeed, it is possibly more useful to think of 'literary' in the broadest context of sales 'literature' or business 'literature' than as having any necessary connection with Dickens or Proust. It merely needs to be written (or spoken or sung) and recorded, in writing or otherwise (see below). There is no requirement for written matter to be written in any particular language or notation, or even to use words at all: mathematical symbols and equations, scientific formulae or even circuit diagrams will be equally protected. However, a single invented word will not be sufficient to constitute a literary 'work'.

Under section 178 of the 1988 Act 'writing' and 'written' include any form of notation or code, whether by hand or otherwise, and regardless of the method or the
medium used.

Tables and compilations

Tables and compilations have been given copyright protection as literary works since
the 1911 Copyright Act, and may be of considerable commercial value in published
works today – in many cases forming the whole or virtually the whole of the work.
Examples are TV listings, sports fixture lists, professional or trade directories, street
directories, trade catalogues, websites, bulletin boards, or even – given sufficient
originality in the selection (see p. 19 below) – schemes of chapters or sequences
of topics or headings. However, compilations stored electronically are equally protected whether or not printed out or published in written form. UK copyright law
recognises that an original compilation is more than the sum total of individual
entries (which may or may not be literary or other works in their own right) and
protects the selection and arrangement of those items as a separate copyright work.
This new compilation may have value as much for what is omitted, as for what is
included: however, there does need to be some evidence that some skill and judgement has gone into the selection and arrangement – we will consider this below,
and under originality (p. 19). Compilations which are databases now have to satisfy
a more rigorous test of originality to qualify for copyright protection (see below).
This means that many compilations which enjoyed copyright protection in the past
might not do so now. However, there are transitional provisions protecting databases
created on or before 27 March 1996.

Databases

Although databases (however mundane) have traditionally been protected under
UK copyright law as compilations, since the Copyright and Rights in Databases
Regulations 1997 (implementing the EU Database Directive) came into force on 1
January 1998 databases have only been eligible for full copyright protection in the
UK if they bear the hallmark of the author's 'intellectual creation'. With this pro-
viso, they are still protected as literary works, and are now defined widely to include
any collection of independent works, data or other materials which:

(a) are arranged in a systematic or methodical way; and
(b) are individually accessible by electronic or other means.

This broad definition would include not only commercial databases and most
websites, but also newspapers and journals (and even this book) but probably not
films, because of the requirements of individual accessibility at (b). However, none
of these will be given copyright protection unless original, and revised section 3A(2)
of the 1988 Act (inserted by the 1997 Regulations) now provides that:

a literary work consisting of a database is original if, and only if, by reason of the selection or arrangement of the contents of the database, the database constitutes the author's own intellectual creation.

This new intellectual standard was a dramatic change for UK copyright, which had previously protected quite mundane databases, whose authors – unlike their Continental counterparts – had to display not so much 'intellect' as 'sweat of the brow' (see below, p. 20). As a result, many basic, but commercially valuable, databases, such as alphabetical listings or directories, may not now be eligible for full copyright protection, now lasting in most cases for the life of the author plus 70 years. They may not, however, be unprotected if there has been 'substantial investment' in 'obtaining, verifying or presenting' their contents – in which case they may be protected now by a separate statutory Database Right, preventing unauthorised extraction or re-use, and lasting for a much shorter 15-year term, but renewable regularly in appropriate circumstances. There are transitional provisions protecting databases created on or before 27 March 1996 and which were protected by copyright on 31 December 1997. Database right was significantly narrowed by the Court of Appeal in 2005, applying the European Court of Justice's judgment in the *William Hill* case, but the High Court ruled in *Football Dataco Ltd* v. *Brittens Pools and Others* in April 2010 that database copyright can subsist in football fixture lists, particularly where significant labour, skill and judgement has been involved (dealt with fully in Chapter 3).

Computer programs

Computer programs are specifically protected as literary works, having been given statutory protection for the first time by the Copyright (Computer Software) Amendment Act 1985. They are not defined in the 1988 Act, but would probably include any sequence or set of instructions in machine-readable form which are capable of causing a computer to perform a particular task or function. This would extend to programs held in most current forms, as long as they could be said to be held in notation or code and therefore 'written': this would clearly include printouts, but equally computer chips, disks and recordings. Design material created in preparation for computer programs is now also protected as a literary work under the Copyright (Computer Programs) Regulations 1992.

'Computer-generated works' are also protected under the 1988 Act, and are defined as works generated by a computer 'in circumstances such that there is no known author of the work'. This difficult philosophical concept is probably best left to the experts: we will consider who owns such creations at p. 31.

Recorded in writing, or otherwise

A literary work will not be protected unless it is put into some permanent, or material, form or, in the case of electronic information, a retrievable form. The means of recording used is very widely defined: 'in writing, or otherwise' could include almost any form of record, and specifically extends to non-written media. This means that a speech or lecture will be protected as a literary work even if delivered without a text or notes, provided that someone (not necessarily the speaker) makes a record of it at the time; for example, keys it into the memory of a lap-top computer. The same might be true of an interview, provided what was said had enough originality to qualify as a copyright work at all (see below).

It does not matter who makes the recording, and in fact there is no requirement that it should even be made with the speaker's consent. In many cases two quite separate copyrights will be created at the same time – copyright in the spoken (and recorded) words as a literary work, and a separate copyright in the recording, or a transcription of it, either as a new literary work or as a sound recording. Even a verbatim written report of a speech has been given separate copyright protection – in the famous case of *Walter v. Lane* in 1900 – where special skill is needed to write it down. As we shall see later, although such parallel copyrights may be dependent on each other, they may be owned by different people. For example, a photograph taken of a painting may be entitled to copyright protection if sufficient skill is used by the photographer (for example, in choice of angle, cropping or lighting). If the painting is still in copyright, there will then be two separate copyrights, which may well be owned by separate people, the artist and the photographer.

Originality

Copyright protection under the 1988 Act is not given to all literary works, but only to 'original' literary works: dramatic, musical and artistic works must also be original. The requirement does not extend to any other works, but since literary (and artistic) works in particular play such a central role in publishing, establishing originality in appropriate cases is clearly of great importance. So: what is 'original'?

For the purposes of copyright law, all that original means is that the work concerned should originate from the author: in other words, that he or she should not have copied it from anywhere else. Any evidence that you have saved yourself time and effort by copying directly from someone else, without sufficient original input from you, will rob your work of its originality and thus of its copyright protection. However, it does not need to display what we may think of colloquially as original thought, in the sense of unique perception or insight which no one else has contributed to the subject before. It is quite permissible to base your work entirely on common sources and existing material (provided you do not copy them) – as the Court of Appeal recently confirmed in a case involving Dan Brown, author of *The Da Vinci Code*, who (it found) had not infringed copyright in an earlier work *The Holy Blood and The Holy Grail* despite using it as a source of general themes ('generalised propositions, at too high a level of abstraction to qualify for copyright protection'), with no actual textual copying.

The originality which is required is not so much original thought as original effort: an independent work which (however mundane or derivative) you have used your own time and effort, and your own faculties and skills, to create. (In America they used to refer to this as 'sweat of the brow' – however, following the 1991 US case of *Feist Publications Inc.* v. *Rural Telephone Service*, mere sweat is not now enough under US law. It will also not now be sufficient to protect databases in the EU – see above.)

On this basis, it is easy to see how English law has granted copyright protection to railway timetables and sports fixture lists, as well as to great works of literature. It also means that two or more very similar – or even identical – works could be created independently by different people, provided that each of them has expended their own skill and effort. Thus two photographers might take virtually identical photographs of the same scene, and two novelists may write strikingly similar stories: provided no copying had taken place, each one may constitute a separate copyright work.

Some copyright works are, by their very nature, bound to be similar, if not identical. Published mathematical tables are the classic example, since any two authors working them out properly are bound (one hopes) to arrive at the same result. A compilation such as a directory of professional names and addresses is bound to be very similar to another directory covering the same profession, but both will be protected if both are the result of independent skill and effort. Copying does occur, of course, and we will consider 'originality' again later on, under infringement of copyright (Chapter 9). Many directory publishers include deliberate minor errors in their databases in order to expose copying: it is stretching coincidence a bit far to claim that, while expending your own skill and effort, you still nevertheless happened to reproduce exactly the same errors as someone else (as confirmed in the 1993 case *Macmillan Publishers* v. *Thomas Reed Publications*).

New editions, and even possibly revised reprints, will often contain enough originality to be protected as separate copyright works, provided that there is sufficient that is new. However, to create a copyright by alterations in the text, these must be extensive and substantial, rather than minor or merely cosmetic.

Abridgements may also be protected, including abstracts of articles (but abstracts may often be copied under section 60 of the 1988 Act).

Adaptations of a book by turning it into a play or a film will create new copyrights, if sufficient skill and judgement is used, even though the original work is reproduced in the new works.

Translations have always been given separate copyright protection in view of the obvious skill involved, even though – by definition – derived entirely from an existing work.

It is very unlikely that the title of a book would have enough originality to be protected as a literary work in its own right – unless it was unusually long. Indeed, it may not be a 'work' at all, and it may also not be a substantial part of another work (see Chapter 9). However, titles may in appropriate cases be protected as registered trade marks, given their necessary distinctiveness, or in some cases by the law of passing off (see Chapter 10).

SUMMARY CHECKLIST: LITERARY WORKS

To summarise briefly so far: in order to be protected under UK copyright law as a literary work, a work must display the following features, among others:

- It must be written, spoken or sung (this includes tables, compilations and computer programs).
- It must be recorded, in writing or otherwise.
- It must be 'original'.

There are other qualifying requirements which apply to all copyright works, as we shall see (below, p. 34) but a work must fulfil at least the above three criteria if it is to be protected as a literary work at all.

ARTISTIC WORKS

Artistic works are defined in section 4(1) of the 1988 Act to mean:

(1) a graphic work, photograph, sculpture or collage, irrespective of artistic quality;
(2) a work of architecture being a building or a model for a building; or
(3) a work of artistic craftsmanship.

'Artistic' is not defined but, like 'literary', it is more a generic grouping than any particular cultural yardstick. As the definition shows, artistic quality is not required at all for graphic works, photographs etc., which are protected 'irrespective of artistic quality', but a specific artistic element does seem to be required for works of artistic craftsmanship: we will look at this further when we consider those works (below, p. 22).

Remember also that artistic works, like literary works, must be 'original' in order to be protected under the 1988 Act: a direct copy would be unlikely to be given copyright protection. It is arguable, however, that a professional (or at least a skilful) copy of a painting might constitute a new copyright work, even though it was an exact replica, and re-origination of old illustrations by a new computer process might also create new copyrights if sufficient skill and judgement were involved.

The artistic works most relevant to publishing are graphic works, photographs and works of artistic craftsmanship.

Graphic works

Graphic works are defined in section 4(2) of the Act as including:

- paintings, drawings, diagrams, maps, charts or plans;
- engravings, etchings, lithographs, woodcuts or similar works.

All such works are protected irrespective of artistic quality, so judges (fortunately, one may think) are not required to make value judgments about 'art'.

Together with photographs, this wide definition of graphic works must cover most if not all illustrations which may currently be contained in published or accessible works, or which are relevant to publishing; for example, the design of a new typeface. Note also that diagrams and charts are included, so that small and relatively mundane technical illustrations within the text or website, such as graphs, may be given copyright protection as artistic works just as much as more obvious pictures, provided they display sufficient originality.

Strangely, unlike many other works, there is no express requirement under the 1988 Act that graphic works should be fixed in any permanent (or retrievable) physical form, although this is almost certainly implied. Artistic works are defined in the 1988 Act in such a way that they would have to exist in a material form to fall within the definition and thus be protected. In the case of a painting, there is also some authority for saying that it must be put on to some permanent (or at least fairly fixed) surface.

As from 1 January 2006, artists who have created original works of graphic (or plastic) art have been entitled to an **artist's resale right** (or *droit de suite*) to a percentage share of the sale price every time their work is resold (e.g. by a gallery). For more on this, see Chapter 3.

Photographs

Section 4(2) of the 1988 Act defines a photograph as:

> a recording of light or other radiation on any medium on which an image is produced or from which an image may by any means be produced, and which is not part of a film.

Films are separately protected, and a single frame of a film would therefore now be protected as part of a film and not as a photograph, although the position was different before the 1956 Copyright Act came into force: the date the photograph was taken may therefore be highly relevant, to ownership, to whether or not any 'originality' is required, and also to how long copyright protection lasts (see p. 41).

The 1988 Act makes no distinction between negatives and positive prints: negatives, as the master copy, would certainly be protected, and prints may well be protected separately if they displayed sufficient originality. However, a straightforward photocopy would not qualify as an original copyright work.

Works of artistic craftsmanship

Original works of craftsmanship, such as furniture or ceramics, may be protected as registered designs under the Registered Designs Act 1949, or (since the 1988 Act) as unregistered designs: however, they may also in some circumstances be entitled to copyright protection as works of artistic craftsmanship if they are more than merely functional and display some 'artistic' element. It is not clear how significant this artistic element needs to be, or what relationship it needs to bear (if any) to the function of the item in question. A prototype for a suite of mass-produced furniture, and the arrangement of objects and the members of the pop group Oasis from an album cover, have both been denied copyright protection on this basis, but works with a more obvious artistic element, such as hand-painted ceramics, inlaid cabinets, stained glass, specialised printing and hand-tooled bookbinding would almost certainly be protected.

SUMMARY CHECKLIST: ARTISTIC WORKS

To be protected under UK copyright law:

- All artistic works must be 'original'.
- Graphic works (paintings, drawings etc.) and photographs must be original, but need not display any particular artistic quality.
- Paintings must be fixed on to a surface.
- Works of artistic craftsmanship must have an 'artistic' element.

DRAMATIC AND MUSICAL WORKS

Dramatic works

When dramatic works were first given separate statutory protection under UK law, in the Dramatic Copyright Act 1833, they were defined as including 'any tragedy, comedy, play, opera, farce or other dramatic piece of entertainment'. Now, under the 1988 Act, they are not defined at all, other than to specify (in section 3(1)) that they include a work of dance or mime. A dramatic work probably, however, needs to be capable not only of being performed in some way, but also of being acted, and hence needs to have an essential and coherent dramatic structure of its own. The cases of *Fraser v. Thames TV* (1983) and *De Maudsley v. Palumbo* (1995) confirmed that, to be protected, a dramatic work must be 'clearly identifiable and potentially realisable', and 'capable of being realised as a finished product'. Similarly, a singer giving a recital in the Wigmore Hall, although clearly performing, would be unlikely to be performing a dramatic work, unless a significant amount of action was involved.

The case of *Norowzian v. Arks Ltd (No 2)* (2000) decided that a film could be a dramatic work for the purposes of the 1988 Act. The Court of Appeal held that the ordinary and natural meaning of a 'dramatic work' was a 'work of action, with or without words or music, which was capable of being performed before an audience'. A film would often, though not always, be a work of action and it would be capable of being performed before an audience. In making this finding the Court of Appeal recognised that cartoons could now be classed as dramatic works and as such receive protection under UK copyright law. They would still be protected as films, and the underlying drawings would also be protected as artistic works. Perhaps the most puzzling example of a dramatic work given by the courts is a film made using particular editing techniques (which was later used in a Guinness advertising campaign) because film works are already entitled to their own copyright protection under section 5B of the 1988 Act (see later).

Like literary and musical works, dramatic works must be recorded 'in writing, or otherwise'. They must also be 'original'.

Musical works

The 1988 Act, at section 3(1), helpfully defines a musical work as 'a work consisting of music'; it does however go on to tell us that such a work is distinct from any words or action intended to be sung, spoken or performed with it. Thus, lyrics of a song or the libretto of an opera would not be part of the musical work itself, but would normally be separate literary works, and choreography or other action would be a dramatic work: quite often these works would have been created and thus will be owned by different people.

Musical works, to be protected by copyright, must be recorded, in writing or otherwise – this may be by means of written scores or by being recorded on to CDs, or by being fixed by any other means. The recording itself will be a separate copyright work (probably either a literary work or a sound recording).

The Court of Appeal recently observed that the essence of musical work is combining sounds to listen to, in a way intended to produce effects on the listener's emotions and intellect – it is more than mere noise. The resulting sounds are protected by copyright, provided they are recorded in material form.

Finally, as with other copyright works in this group, all musical works must be 'original'. As has been seen with literary and artistic works, this implies no more than some significant creative effort and skill, and an absence of copying: it is not necessary to be Mozart. However, an original musical work must be more than a mere interpretation.

SOUND RECORDINGS, FILMS, BROADCASTS OR INTERNET TRANSMISSIONS

Sound recordings

Sound recordings were given separate copyright protection under UK law by the 1911 Copyright Act, as a response to the growing sale of phonographs and perforated rolls. The recording industry is now a major international industry and the opportunities for digital as well as mechanical copying are considerably more sophisticated, as the *Napster* and *Grokster* litigation in the USA showed – involving not only unauthorised copying but also systematic uploading and peer-to-peer file-swapping. The US Supreme Court found that the filesharing activities of Grokster were illegal and infringed copyright, but the recent *Pirate Bay* litigation in Sweden showed that the opportunities for cybercrime are still very real.

Sound recordings continue to be protected in the UK as separate copyright works under the 1988 Act, and are now defined (in section 5A(1)) as meaning:

(a) a recording of sounds, from which the sounds may be reproduced; or

(b) a recording of the whole or any part of a literary, dramatic or musical work, from which sounds reproducing the work or part may be produced,

regardless of the medium on which the recording is made or the method by which the sounds are reproduced or produced.

Thus, two separate kinds of sound recording are protected – those which are recordings of pure sounds (such as birdsong), and those which are recordings of other copyright works, such as recordings of famous actors reading books (literary works), or reciting plays (dramatic works), as well as – of course – recordings of music.

Modern film soundtracks are now protected not only as part of the films which they accompany (under section 5B(2)) but also as sound recordings separately from the films themselves (although the position may be different for soundtracks created before 1989).

In addition to copyright, the 1988 Act also introduced a limited rental right for sound recordings (and for films and computer programs) – we will deal with this later, when we look at the restricted acts which only a copyright owner may do (Chapter 9). There is, as yet, no blank tape levy in the UK.

There is no requirement that a sound recording should be original (unlike literary, dramatic, musical or artistic works). However, copyright will not protect a sound recording which is merely a copy of a previous sound recording (section 5A(2)).

Films

A film is a separate copyright work, defined in section 5B(1) of the 1988 Act as meaning 'a recording on any medium from which a moving image may by any means be produced'. This definition is wide enough to cover DVDs, film downloads and some aspects of computer games. Film soundtracks are now protected both as part of the films concerned, and independently as sound recordings (see above). In addition, a typical film will include many other copyright works, and the relevant rights will need to be acquired (or licensed) from the respective owners in order to make the film: these rights are collectively referred to in the film business as the 'underlying rights'. These might include, for example, the screenplay and the book or script (dramatic and literary works), the score (a musical work), graphics, cartoons or set designs (artistic works), as well as the soundtrack (sound recording). Individual frames or stills from a film are protected as part of the film, and not as photographs (see above, p. 22). This may be significant, since (for example) a photograph (as an artistic work) must be original, whereas the film need not be. Films, like sound recordings, do not need to be original; however, section 5B(4) of the 1988 Act provides that a film which is merely a copy of a previous film will not be protected by copyright.

Broadcasts

Broadcasts include not only traditional radio and TV broadcasts and cable transmissions, but also (since the Cable and Broadcasting Act 1984) direct broadcasting by satellite. The wide definition of broadcasts (in section 6 of the 1988 Act, as amended by the 2003 Regulations) effectively includes all transmissions including those sent via fixed, land-based routes (such as cable): broadcast means 'an electronic transmission of visual images, sounds or other information' which can lawfully be received by the public or which is sent for public presentation. Note: (1) that broadcasts may consist not only of pictures and sound but also of 'other information' – such as teletext; and (2) that an encrypted transmission is only regarded as being lawfully received by the public if they have access to authorised decoding equipment.

Broadcasts do not include Internet transmissions unless they fall into one of three categories:

(a) transmissions taking place simultaneously on the Internet and by other means;
(b) concurrent transmissions of a live event; or
(c) transmissions of recorded moving images or sounds forming part of a [scheduled] programme service offered by the person responsible for making the transmission.

These categories of transmission on the Internet will be treated as broadcasts. Other Internet transmissions will fall within the new section 20 of the 1988 Act. This deals with communication to the public, which includes both broadcasting and making a work available to the public. It is this latter right which will cover most Internet activities. Making a work available to the public is defined in section 20(2)(b) of the 1988 Act as 'the making available to the public of the work by electronic transmission in such a way that members of the public may access it from a place and at a time individually chosen by them'. This can clearly be distinguished from broadcasting, where the public does not determine the time of the broadcast.

Internet transmissions

It is interesting that there is now no specific category of copyright work which relates to transmissions on the Internet which are not included in the category of 'broadcast'. Under the previous law, such a transmission would have been protected as a cable programme. That separate category of work has been abolished by the 2003 changes in the law. Cable programmes are now protected as a type of broadcast. Under the new law, works transmitted on the Internet are protected by the communication to the public and making available rights, but the transmission itself is not protected as such, unless it falls within the new definition of a broadcast, which excludes many types of Internet transmission.

TYPOGRAPHICAL ARRANGEMENTS

There is a separate copyright in the UK in typographical arrangements of published editions. It lasts only for 25 years from the end of the year of publication, and is owned by the publisher: the purpose is to protect the publisher's skill and investment in the composition and typesetting, so a separate copyright is given to the visual appearance of the printed page itself as well as to its contents. This means that, on a typical printed page there are likely to be several copyrights: a literary copyright in the text, and possibly in any compilation, artistic copyright in any photographs, charts or illustrations, and a separate typographical copyright, owned by the publishers, in the arrangement of the page itself. This protects a publisher of a public domain edition, say of Shakespeare or Milton: although the text is long since out of copyright, there may still be an enforceable copyright in the publisher's edition.

It seems likely that this protection would also be available to the creator of a website or an e-book. However, it seems equally possible that a conventional book, or similar text, might be reproduced via those media, and typographical copyright in the original edition might be infringed depending on the way it was reproduced.

A substantial part of the *whole* 'published edition' does, however, need to be copied. This is clear from the decision of the House of Lords in *Newspaper Licensing Agency Ltd* v. *Marks & Spencer PLC* (2001), where the NLA failed in a claim that Marks & Spencer had infringed typographical copyright in newspapers by operating an unlicensed cuttings service which circulated cuttings of individual articles to members of its staff, usually mounted as single items on plain sheets of paper. Was a single article, taken out of context, a substantial part of the typographical arrangement of the whole published edition? The Lords thought not, and Lord Hoffmann spoke for the majority view when he said 'I find it difficult to think of the skill and labour which has gone into the typographical arrangement of a newspaper being expressed, in anything less than a full page'. For more on the need to copy a substantial part, see Chapter 9.

Typographical arrangements do not need to be 'original' as such (unlike the artistic copyright which may exist in a new typeface) but they will not be protected if they merely reproduce the typographical arrangement of a previous edition. A publisher cannot therefore perpetually extend typographical copyright beyond 25 years simply by re-issuing the last edition. Typographical copyright was not affected by UK implementation of the EU Copyright Directive, other than by the introduction of a new wide-ranging exception for temporary copies, under new section 28A (see p. 13 above).

SUMMARY CHECKLIST: COPYRIGHT WORKS

It should be clear by now that a modern publication such as an e-book or a CD is unlikely to be a single copyright work, but a bundle of several different works. Before we go on to consider who *owns* each copyright, it may be useful to remind ourselves which works may most often be relevant.

Books and e-books

May contain:

- original text (literary work). The plot – if any – may be a dramatic work;
- quoted text from other sources (separate literary works);
- index, prelims, tables or compilations (literary works);
- illustrations/photographs (artistic works);
- overall compilation (particularly in the case of collective works such as encyclopaedias (literary works);
- databases (literary works and/or database right works);
- typographical arrangement (typographical copyright);
- jacket text and illustrations (literary and artistic works);
- computer programs/software (literary works), in the case of e-books.

CD-ROMs

May contain:

- original and quoted text (literary and possibly dramatic works);
- tables or compilations (literary works);
- illustrations/photographs (artistic works);
- overall compilation (literary work);
- databases (literary works and/or database right works);
- computer programs/software (literary work);
- accompanying manual/booklet (literary and artistic work and typographical copyright).

Digital publications (such as a website)

May contain:

- some or all works in a CD-ROM (see above);
- animations/graphics/cartoons (artistic works);
- video and film (films);
- music (musical work);
- lyrics (literary works);
- drama/plays (dramatic works);
- recordings of music, speech or other sounds (sound recordings);
- performances of works (rights in performances);
- broadcasts (insofar as a website is broadcasting).

Moral rights of authors may also now be relevant in relation to many of the above works – on moral rights generally, see Chapter 3.

OWNERSHIP OF COPYRIGHT

Who owns all these different copyrights, and connected rights? Given the variety of copyright works which UK law protects, it might be thought that working out who owns which rights would be a complete nightmare – but in fact, in most cases, the underlying principle of copyright ownership is very simple. There are (of course) some exceptions (such as employee works) which we will come to, but, subject to those, the general rule is stated in section 11(1) of the 1988 Act: 'The author of a work is the first owner of any copyright in it, . . .'

The search for a copyright owner is therefore in most cases the search for the author. And who, then, is the 'author'? Section 9(1) tells us: the author is the person who creates the work. As a general rule, therefore, the creator of a work usually owns the copyright in it.

It should not be forgotten that the rules governing who is the author of a work and who owns copyright in it vary according to when the work was made. In the notes which follow, we will focus on the current law, but for pre-August 1989 works it will often be necessary to refer back to the 1956 or 1911 Copyright Acts, or even earlier.

Ownership of copyright is unaffected by the EU Copyright Directive, or by the 2003 Regulations.

'AUTHORS'

As we saw in Chapter 1, there is no copyright in ideas, so the author or creator of a novel or a play is not necessarily the person who had the original idea, but the person who first put that idea into concrete form. These may be one and the same person, of course, or they may have worked on the project together (in which case they may be joint authors), but they may also be completely different people. The law tries to find the real creator – the person who actually executed the work, the person who made it. This may vary according to the type of work. For example, the creators of a film will be more than one type of person, such as the producer and the principal director.

Someone who was merely putting a literary (or artistic) work on to paper at the instruction of someone else – a secretary writing a letter, or an amanuensis helping to take down a book, for example – would not be regarded as the author of that work. But where the work is not merely dictated, but is ghost-written, then the ghost-writer will own the copyright, because it is the ghost writer who has created the work which appears on the page. Appropriately enough (for ghosts) this was held in a 1927 case to protect the writings of a spiritualist medium, despite claims that the real 'author' resided in another world. And, in the same way, a reporter writing up a report of a speech (even, in one famous case, a verbatim report) would probably be regarded as the 'author' of that report and would own the copyright in it (although copyright in the speech itself would still be owned by the speaker).

Joint authors

In some cases, it may simply not be possible to identify separate copyright works, and say that X wrote this bit and Y wrote that. Where it is possible (for example where contributors write distinct chapters of a book or entries in an encyclopaedia) each one will own a separate copyright. Where it is *not* possible, but more than one person clearly contributed (as, for example, where a scientific research team publishes their findings) they are treated as joint authors.

In many cases, it will be a question of degree as to whether what is created is a collection of separate works, or whether it is truly a joint work. Under the 1988 Act (section 10(1)) a work of joint authorship is:

a work produced by the collaboration of two or more authors in which the contribution of each author is not distinct from that of the other author or authors.

Each of them must be authors, however: someone who contributed ideas and suggestions, but took no part in the actual writing, would be unlikely to be considered a joint author (although this is not completely impossible). This would be the case even if they made minor revisions, unless their revisions were unusually original. For example, members of the pop group Spandau Ballet failed in one case to prove that they made a significant and original contribution to the group's songs and, therefore, were not entitled to joint authorship in the songs with Gary Kemp, the main songwriter and lyricist. Contributions such as a saxophone improvisation in the song 'True' were held to be only examples of a performance (that any accomplished musician would make) rather than of the joint creator of a work.

Joint authors usually own the copyright as 'tenants in common' – under section 173(2) of the 1988 Act, no single joint copyright owner can publish or license the work without the consent of the others, and when a joint copyright owner dies the same rights and duties will pass to his or her heirs.

Collective works

In a collective work such as an encyclopaedia or dictionary, there is likely to be a copyright not only in the individual entries – normally owned by the respective authors – but also in the overall compilation of the collective work as a whole. The 'author' of that compilation is usually taken to be the person who was responsible for assembling it, and whose selection and arrangement it is. This might be one person, such as a General Editor, or one or more of the contributors (who may then be joint authors of the compilation) or quite possibly the publisher.

Photographs

Under the 1988 Act, the author of a photograph is the person who creates it – usually the photographer. This means that copyright in all photographs taken after 1 August 1989 will be owned by the photographer, unless there is an agreement to the contrary or one of the exceptions applies (see below). For photographs taken between 1 June 1957 and 1 August 1989, however, the 1956 Copyright Act defined the author as the person who, at the relevant time, owned the material on which the photograph was taken – it may therefore be important to find out when the photographs were taken, in order to find out who owns the copyright. Commissioned photographs were also treated differently in some circumstances under the 1956 Act (see below, p. 32) and also under the 1911 Act.

Software and computer-generated works

Copyright in a computer program which is created by an identifiable human being will normally be owned by that person, as with any other literary work. In a case of a computer-generated work, however – generated in circumstances such that there is no human author – section 9(3) of the 1988 Act provides that the 'author' is the person who undertook the arrangements necessary for the creation of the work.

Typographical arrangements

Copyright in typographical arrangements of published editions is owned by the publisher.

Sound recordings and films

Under the 1988 Act, the author of a sound recording or a film is the person by whom the necessary arrangements for making it were made. In many cases this might be several people, but is most likely to be a record or film production company. In the case of a film, the principal director is also an author. Additionally, in the case of a film, the Duration Directive, and 1995 Regulations made under it (see p. 42), have specified that copyright protection shall be calculated from the death of one of four possible categories of persons, but this does not change the position that the authors of a film are the producer and the principal director.

The soundtrack of a film is now not only treated as part of the film concerned but is also protected as a separate copyright work (as a sound recording) and copyright may thus be separately owned.

As pointed out at the beginning of this section, pre-1989 ownership may be different, and the complex provisions are beyond the scope of this book. In cases of doubt, specialist legal advice should be sought.

Broadcasts

The author of a broadcast under the 1988 Act is the person who makes the broadcast (provided he or she has at least some responsibility for its contents, and is not – like BT – simply a common carrier). Where more than one person is involved in making the broadcast, the broadcast may be a work of joint authorship.

Where a broadcast is relayed, the original broadcaster is the author, rather than the person making the relay.

Commissioned works

Unlike US provisions regarding Works for Hire (where the commissioner may own copyright in certain commissioned work), there are no special provisions in the 1988 Act relating to copyright in commissioned works in the UK, so for works created after 1 August 1989 the general rule of copyright ownership applies, and the author will normally own the copyright, not the commissioner (unless there is a contract providing otherwise, or a contract term which may be implied in appropriate circumstances). In fact (despite popular beliefs to the contrary) even before 1989 there has never been any general rule of law that if you commissioned a work you would automatically own the copyright in it. There were three very limited exceptions under the 1956 Copyright Act, covering certain kinds of commissioned artistic works, but these never extended to literary or other works. The exceptions were:

- commissioned photographs;
- commissioned portraits (painted or drawn);
- commissioned engravings.

A person commissioning such works after 1 June 1957 but before 1 August 1989 might own the copyright, if the work was made in response to the commission, and if he or she paid for it (or at least agreed to). There were somewhat similar provisions under the 1911 Copyright Act. Otherwise, subject to the rules set out above, the artist or photographer, like authors of literary works, would probably own the copyright in the normal way. For most commissioned works, therefore, unless one of the limited exceptions above applies, or unless there is an agreement to the contrary, it is likely that the author or artist, not the commissioner, will own the copyright.

WORKS BY EMPLOYEES

There is one major exception to the general rule that authors own copyright in their works, and that concerns works created by employees. Under section 11(2) of the 1988 Act:

> where a literary, dramatic, musical or artistic work or a film is made by an employee in the course of his employment, his employer is the first owner of any copyright in the work subject to any agreement to the contrary.

The position was broadly the same (save in relation to films) under the 1956 and 1911 Acts. There are two particular points to note.

'Employees'

The terms 'employee' and 'employment' refer to employment under what the law calls a contract of service or apprenticeship – in other words, someone employed under a contract of employment, rather than a self-employed person such as a free-lancer. The contract of employment does not need to be full-time, or permanent, so part-time and temporary employees would be covered, but as Lord Denning said in one case, the person concerned does need to be 'employed as part of the business'. One traditional test, in cases of doubt, used to be the degree of control exercised by the employer – if the people concerned have little or no discretion over the way the work is done they are probably employees (although there are exceptions: directors, for example, may have considerable discretion but might still be regarded as employees for copyright purposes). It is usually reasonably easy to tell: in the 1916 case of *University of London Press Limited* v. *University Tutorial Press Limited* two external examiners were held *not* to be employees of London University, since they were not exclusively employed by London University, and prepared the papers in their own time, for a one-off fee: they therefore owned the copyright, not the university. In the more recent case of *Beloff* v. *Pressdram Ltd* (1993), Nora Beloff, the lobby correspondent of the *Observer* was held to be an employee on the basis, amongst other things, that she worked full time at the *Observer* and did not use her own capital for the job, and would be paid her salary whether or not the paper made a profit.

'In the course of his employment'

For the employer to own the copyright, the employee must have created it *in the course of* that employment, not merely while employed. A night security guard who wrote a novel while on duty would probably therefore own the copyright in it, since writing novels would be unlikely to feature anywhere in his (or her) job description. In other cases, such as lecturers preparing teaching manuals, or academic or scientific researchers publishing research papers, the position may be less clear-cut, and there is considerable pressure from some academic institutions for copyright in works created by their staff to be owned by the institutions, if the institution's facilities were used, even without any agreement or assignment. This is highly debatable under English law, but even where the work is done outside official working hours, it may still be in the course of employment. Ideally, such issues should be covered clearly in employment contracts.

Before 1989, under the 1956 Copyright Act (and earlier law) employers might also have owned the copyright (or part of it) in works of their employees. In the case of works created by employees of a newspaper, magazine or similar periodical which were created for publication in that newspaper, magazine or periodical, the owner would own part of the copyright in the works. This only applies, however, to pre-1989 works.

MANUSCRIPTS AND ARTWORK

Before we leave the subject of ownership, it is important to remember that ownership of copyright in something is not the same as physical ownership of the documents or artwork, or other materials such as disks, on which it is recorded. Although ownership of physical materials might still be relevant to establish authorship of some older works – such as photographs created before 1989 – for most purposes now the two things are completely separate. An author delivering a manuscript, print-out or disks, or an artist delivering original artwork or photographs, will therefore continue to own those physical materials, and be entitled to their (reasonably) safe return, even if he or she does not own the copyright or subsequently assigns it to someone else. In the case of most artistic works, the artist has, since 1 January 2006, been entitled to an **artist's resale right** of up to 4 per cent of *any* subsequent sales (see Chapter 3). Since busy publishing offices are not always the best places to store valuable materials, many publishers in the delivery clauses of their contracts expressly disclaim any liability for loss or damage to manuscripts and other materials submitted to them; however, publishers are probably under a general duty at least to take reasonable care of an author's or artist's materials.

SUMMARY CHECKLIST: COPYRIGHT OWNERSHIP

- As a general rule, for modern works, the author of a work owns the copyright in it.
- Is the person concerned really the 'author'?
- Are there joint authors? If so, do all the copyright owners agree?
- Is there a separate copyright in any compilation, or a database right in any database?
- Have any computer-generated works, sound recordings or films been created? If so, who made the necessary arrangements, and who is the principal director of the film?
- Were any photographs taken before or after August 1989?
- Were any commissioned photographs, portraits or engravings created before August 1989?
- Was the author an employee?
- Did the author create the work in the course of that employment?

QUALIFICATION FOR COPYRIGHT PROTECTION

Although it is no longer necessary to register copyrights at Stationers Hall (or anywhere else), the work will not qualify for copyright protection under UK law unless it meets certain qualifying criteria. Works may qualify by virtue of:

- the author; or
- the country in which the work was first published.

These two 'points of attachment' for copyright protection are common to most Berne member countries: it does not matter whether it is the author or the place of first publication which qualifies for copyright protection, but one or other of them must. Often, of course, a work will qualify on both counts.

QUALIFICATION BY REFERENCE TO THE AUTHOR

A work qualifies for copyright protection in the UK if the author was at the material time a 'qualifying person'. A qualifying person is defined in section 154 of the 1988 Act and includes:

- a British citizen or a citizen of a British Dependent Territory;
- a British National (Overseas) or a British Overseas Citizen;
- a British subject or a British protected person;
- a person domiciled or resident in the UK (or another country to which the 1988 Act extends or has been applied);
- a body incorporated under UK law (or the law of another country to which the Act extends or has been applied);
- a citizen or subject of a foreign country to which the 1988 Act has been applied or extended by Order in Council (or who is domiciled or resident there).

Most of these terms are defined further in the British Nationality Act 1981. For most practical purposes, an author will qualify, at least as 'resident', if at the material time he or she lived at a home address in the UK or the relevant foreign country. Foreign countries are periodically added by Order in Council, in accordance with the UK's Berne, UCC and other treaty obligations (see Chapter 9).

The 'material time' is:

- for unpublished works, when the work was made;
- for published works, the date of first publication.

(If the author dies before publication, the material time is immediately before his or her death.)

COUNTRY OF FIRST PUBLICATION

If for some reason copyright protection does not attach to a work by virtue of the author's nationality or other qualifying status, it may still do so if it was first published in the UK, or another qualifying country to which the 1988 Act extends or is applied.

What is 'first publication'? Indeed, what is 'publication'?

Publication

Publication, under the 1988 Act, takes place when copies of the work are issued to the public with the licence of the copyright owner. This would cover most publishing, but not for example the delivery of a speech or lecture, or the exhibition of a painting (unless copies were subsequently issued). Note that copies, in the plural, must be issued, although making the work available to the public via the Internet will count as publication in the case of literary, dramatic, musical and artistic works. A local intranet might be sufficient if access to it was sufficiently wide. It is not necessary that works should be issued for commercial sale: private or free circulation would probably count as publication. The work will not be 'published', however, if publication is a purely token gesture and 'not intended to satisfy the reasonable requirements of the public' – what the 1988 Act describes as 'merely colourable'.

First and simultaneous publication

First publication, although not defined, simply means what it says: the first time authorised copies are issued to the public. So if a copyright owner, or his or her licensee, first issues copies of a work to the public in the UK, that work will qualify for copyright protection under UK law, irrespective of the nationality of the author. Works of (say) US authors would therefore have qualified for copyright protection under UK law if they were first published here, even before the USA joined the UCC or Berne Conventions.

Publication also counts as first publication, even if simultaneous publication takes place somewhere else: 'simultaneous publication' for these purposes means publication within 30 days. So a US work simultaneously published in New York and London with a gap of no more than 30 days between publication dates would count as first published in the UK. (Under the 1911 Copyright Act, the simultaneous publication period was only 14 days – this shorter period continues to apply to works first published before 1 June 1957.)

SUMMARY CHECKLIST: QUALIFYING WORKS

- Was the author a qualifying person at the material time?
- If the author does not have a relevant British qualification (such as nationality or residence) is the author a citizen or subject of a qualifying foreign country?
- For a published work, did the author qualify at the date of first publication?
- For unpublished works, did the author qualify when the work was made?
- If the author is not a qualifying person, was the work first published in the UK (or another country to which the 1988 Act applies)?
- If not first publication, was there 'simultaneous' publication within 30 days?
- Did publication satisfy the reasonable expectations of the public?

DURATION OF COPYRIGHT

AUTHORS' LIVES

As we have seen, copyright in the UK is primarily a statutory right, and ever since the first Copyright Act of 1710 it has had a fixed term, or duration. After that, it expires and the protection ends. Although the first statutory copyrights only lasted for 14 years, they could be renewed for a second term if the author was still alive at the end of the first one, so from the outset the length of copyright protection has been linked to how long the author managed to stay alive. After various increases, the Berne Convention countries agreed each to adopt the same minimum term of copyright protection for literary and artistic works, starting from the moment of creation of the work and lasting until 50 years after the death of the author (sometimes referred to as 50 years 'post mortem auctoris', or '50 years pma'). At the time of the 1911 Act this was thought sufficient to protect two generations of the author's heirs (on the assumption – presumably – that each generation produces an heir at the average age of 25) and seemed a suitable compromise between those who argued that free access to literature required a shorter fixed term and those who felt that copyright should benefit the author's estate in perpetuity. It is not a perfect formula, but during the course of the twentieth century the Berne period gained widespread international acceptance. Countries belonging to the Universal Copyright Convention (see Chapter 9), adopted a shorter minimum period of 25 years pma, but the Berne period of 50 years is now the minimum period adopted by most countries.

For convenience and certainty, since the exact date of authors' deaths is often hard to prove, the 50-year period of copyright is deemed to run, not exactly from the 50th anniversary of the author's death but 50 years from the end of the calendar year in which the author died. So if an author died on 1 July 1945, copyright in the author's works would expire on 31 December 1995. It is important to remember this: for authors who die in January this can mean virtually a whole year's extra copyright protection.

REVERSION OF RIGHTS UNDER THE 1911 ACT

While dealing with authors' lives, it is important not to forget one small but important detail of the 1911 Act, which provided for reversion of many rights to authors after 25 years. The 1911 Act considerably increased the term of copyright from life plus seven years (or 42 years, whichever was longer) to life plus 50 years. Perhaps by way of a counter-balance, a provision (section 5(2)) was included in the 1911 Act under which copyright rights assigned or granted by authors would, in some specified circumstances, revert to them or their estates exactly 25 years from their death. This applied irrespective of any agreement to the contrary. It applied only where the author was the first owner of the copyright (so did not apply to employee works or certain commissioned works). It also did not apply to assignments made by will, or to collective works. The provision was repealed by the 1956 Act, so applied automatically to all such rights assigned or granted between the coming into effect of the 1911 and 1956 Acts (respectively 16 December 1911 and 1 June 1957). People often forget this, since it only applies to old titles, but it can be a significant limitation on publishers' rights. There are similar provisions in the laws of some Commonwealth countries and the USA has its own version of reversionary rights called termination rights.

It is worth bearing in mind that it was possible for an author or his estate to enter into a fresh assignment on or after 1 June 1957 which would be effective to assign the reversionary rights (even if he or she had previously retained them in any wider assignment, for example to a publisher).

EU HARMONISATION: LIFE PLUS 70

The Berne 50-year standard did not, however, provide a level enough playing field for the European Commission, since it only provided a minimum, and some EU member states (such as Germany and Spain) provided longer terms. In addition, some countries like France gave longer protection to certain works, and, in certain cases, to account for the war years of both world wars.

The EU attempted to deal with this lack of harmony in 1993 by Directive 93/98/EEC – variously called the Duration Directive, or the Term Directive – which provided for the copyright term for literary, artistic and other works to be harmonised upwards to 70 years pma throughout the EU and EEA. Member states were required to implement the necessary changes to their domestic laws by 1 July 1995, and the increased term now applies to all EEA-origin works which were protected in at least one member state on that date. The UK implemented the Directive (late) by means of the Duration of Copyright and Rights in Performances Regulations (1995). The USA has also now increased its own term of protection to life plus 70 years under the Sonny Bono Term Extension Act of 1998 (see Chapter 9).

THE 1995 REGULATIONS

Because the Duration Directive extended protection for works protected at 1 July 1995 'in at least one member state', each member state's implementing measures had to provide not only for *extensions* of copyright periods which were still running, but also for *revivals* of copyright in works which had gone into the public domain in their own country during the previous 20 years, but which might still be protected in, for example, Germany or Spain. Following the *Phil Collins* decision of the European Court of Justice in 1993, this was especially true if the author was (or would have been) an EU national. In the UK, this means that works by authors such as Thomas Hardy, John Buchan or Rudyard Kipling will have come back into copyright, having previously been in the public domain. The needless confusion and uncertainty caused by this retrospective law may continue for several years to come. In addition, the much-vaunted harmonisation is unlikely to result for some time, since it was left to each member state to decide several crucial questions, each in their own way:

- Who should own the revived or extended copyright?
- What – if any – royalties would the new owners be entitled to?
- What protection or compensation would be available for those publishers (and others) who had exploited previously public domain works in good faith?

The UK's 1995 Regulations came into force on 1 January 1996. As well as longer protection for newly created works, they provided for:

(1) *extensions of copyright* for relevant works in which copyright still subsisted in the UK at 31 December 1995; and
(2) *revivals of copyright* for works whose terms of copyright expired before 31 December 1995 in the UK but which were still protected by copyright in another EEA member state on 1 July 1995.

The 1995 provisions did not apply to Crown or Parliamentary copyright, or to computer-generated works.

Extensions

The owner of an extended copyright is generally the person who owned the copyright immediately before commencement (1 January 1996).

In addition, any copyright licence, any term or condition of a copyright agreement, or any waiver or assertion of moral rights which existed immediately before commencement, and which was for the (then) full period of copyright, will continue to apply during the period of extended copyright (subject to any agreement to the contrary).

Revivals

Following the *Phil Collins* decision of the European Court of Justice (see above), this is now likely to cover the works of all EU and EEA authors who died between 1925 and 1945, provided they were protected in another EEA state (most probably Germany) at 1 July 1995. Depending on the year of the author's death, the revived copyright may last for anything from a year or so to an extra 20 years.

The new owner of any revived copyright is generally the person who owned copyright immediately before it expired. This is at least even-handed between publishers and authors: the last owner may have been a publisher, or equally a literary estate. If the former owner has died (or, in the event of a company, ceased to exist) the author or his or her estate will acquire the right; however, there may be some problems in tracing rights ownership.

Any waiver or assertion of moral rights in force immediately before copyright expired will continue to apply during the period of revived copyright: there are now detailed provisions for exercise of moral rights after an author's death.

Acquired rights

The Directive required member states to protect acquired rights of third parties: although it was not entirely clear exactly what this meant, it was the only express provision protecting those, like publishers, who had invested in good faith in editions of public domain works, only to find themselves potentially infringing a new, revived copyright. The 1995 Regulations protect such publishers in relation to revived copyrights in two ways:

(1) *Non-infringing acts.* After commencement (1 January 1996), it is not an infringement of any revived copyright to do anything in pursuance of 'arrangements made' before 1 January 1995, or to issue to the public copies of the work made before 1 July 1995 (in both cases, at a time when the work was in the public domain). There are similar provisions relating to anthologies or adaptations, although these are slightly unclear.

(2) *Licences of right.* There is considerable comfort for publishers of previously public domain works: 'any acts' (including copying, or issuing copies to the public) will be treated as licensed by the new owner of the revived copyright, subject only to payment of 'such reasonable royalty or other remuneration as may be agreed' (or, in the absence of agreement, arbitrated by the Copyright Tribunal). The acts will be treated as licensed from the outset (even though any royalty is not agreed or arbitrated until later), but the publisher must give reasonable notice to the new copyright owner of an intention to do the acts concerned (before the publisher does any of them).

Previous exclusive licensees will find that they may be in competition with any number of non-exclusive licensees of right under the above provisions, but on the other hand there does seem to be a reasonable basis for protection for those who seek to exploit (or continue to exploit) previously public domain works in good faith. The requirement to give notice may, however, cause publishers some difficulty, particularly where the identity of the new copyright owner is not immediately obvious. At the time of writing it seems that most publishers, authors and agents are setting reasonable rates between themselves (bearing in mind that all licences of right are by definition non-exclusive).

Works not of EEA origin

Section 12(6) of the 1988 Act (inserted by the 1995 Regulations) provides that when the country of origin of a work is not an EEA state and the author is not an EEA national, the duration of copyright is that to which the work is entitled in its country of origin, subject to two provisos:

• the work cannot have a longer term of protection in the UK than it would have had if it had been of EEA origin;

- (for works in existence on 1 January 1996 and protected by copyright in the UK on 31 December 1995) this provision would not reduce the period of copyright protection which the work enjoyed under the old law.

The overall effect of this is that works not of EEA origin may also enjoy the extension (or part of it) and in appropriate cases revival of copyright where the term of protection in their country of origin exceeds that granted in the UK prior to 1 January 1996.

DURATION OF COPYRIGHT IN INDIVIDUAL WORKS

In addition to harmonising – or attempting to – the period of copyright protection for literary and artistic works, the Duration Directive also contained important provisions for duration of copyright in other works such as films, and for certain neighbouring rights. We shall deal with these and the relevant UK provisions in turn below, when we look briefly at each kind of work.

Literary, artistic, musical and dramatic works

The term of copyright was previously 50 years pma: it was increased in the UK from 1 January 1996 to 70 years pma (that is 70 years from the end of the calendar year in which the author died (see above, p. 37)). Photographs benefit from the 20-year extension, like other artistic works: this is a double extension for pre-1989 and pre-1957 photographs which were calculated for a fixed period from the year of first publication, and from the year the photograph was taken, respectively: for all photographs the term is now 70 years from the end of the year of the photographer's death.

Works of joint authorship

The Duration Directive and the 1995 Regulations reinforced the existing UK position, under which the term of copyright (now increased to 70 years pma) is calculated from the year in which the last surviving (known) author dies.

Anonymous and pseudonymous works

Under the 1995 Regulations the term is increased to 70 years from the year it was made, or (if it was published during that period) 70 years from the end of the year in which the work is made available to the public. However, this only applies when the author is truly unknown – when the pseudonym adopted leaves no doubt as to the author's identity (or the author's identity is revealed) the term of copyright will be 70 years pma, as in literary, artistic, musical and dramatic works above.

Computer-generated works

The 1995 Regulations exclude computer-generated works from the provisions of the Duration Directive: the term of copyright in the UK is still the term provided in the 1988 Act; that is, 50 years from the end of the calendar year in which the work was made.

Posthumously published works, and publication right

Under the 1956 Copyright Act, copyright in posthumous literary and artistic works ran for 50 years from the year of first publication. With effect from 1 August 1989, the 1988 Act provided a fixed period of 50 years from 1 January 1990 for unpublished works in existence at 31 July 1989. These periods are unchanged by the 1995 Regulations. However, if the new provisions would give a longer period of protection (e.g. life plus 70) to a work unpublished at 31 July 1989, the longer period of protection will apply. Works created on or after 1 August 1989 enjoy the normal copyright period (e.g. life plus 70), calculated in relation to the author's life, whether they are published or not.

Where posthumous first publication in the UK or elsewhere in the EEA took place after the then period of copyright protection had expired, Article 4 of the Duration Directive provided for a new publication right. This right is owned by the first publisher of the work, and lasts for 25 years from the end of the year in which the work is first made available to the public. The UK implemented these provisions in the Copyright and Related Rights Regulations 1996 (see Chapter 3).

Unpublished works

Unpublished works were at one time protected in the UK by a perpetual common law copyright, but this was abolished by the 1911 Copyright Act. The transitional provisions of the 1988 Act provided that works which were still unpublished when the 1988 Act came into force (1 August 1989) should be protected for 50 years from the end of that year – that is, until 31 December 2039. They still are, unless the period of protection given by the new provisions would give a longer period of protection, in which case the longer period will apply.

Typographical arrangements

Copyright in the typographical arrangement of published editions is unaffected by the 1995 Regulations, and continues to last for 25 years from the end of the year in which the edition was first published.

Sound recordings and films

Under the 1988 Act, copyright in both sound recordings and films expired 50 years from the end of the year in which they were made (or, if they were released before then, 50 years from the year of release). Following the Duration and Copyright Directives and the 1995 and 2003 Regulations, there are two significant changes:

(1) for sound recordings, the 50-year period remains the same, but the definition of 'release' is now replaced by 'publication', which now includes any (authorised) making available to the public (by being played in public or communicated to the public);

(2) for films, the period of copyright is increased dramatically to 70 years from the end of the year in which the last known of four persons connected with the films dies:

   (a) the principal director;
   (b) the author of the screenplay;
   (c) the author of the dialogue;
   (d) the composer of the music (if it was created specifically for the film, and actually used).

If the identity of *none* of these people is known, copyright expires 70 years from the year the film was made, or (if it was made available to the public before then) 70 years from the year it was made available.

In the (unlikely) event that no one falls into the categories (a)–(d) above, then the Regulations (and section 13B(9) of the 1988 Act) provide that the extension will not apply and copyright will expire 50 years from the year the film was made. It is possible that the Duration Directive will be amended in the not too distant future to extend the term of sound recordings to 70 years from making or publication, as applicable.

Broadcasts and cable programmes

Copyright – owned by the relevant broadcasting organisations – continues to last 50 years from the end of the year in which the first transmission was made, whether by wire or over the air, by cable or satellite.

Copyright in a repeat broadcast or cable programme expires at the same time as copyright in the original broadcast or cable programme.

Crown and Parliamentary copyright

The Crown claims copyright in every Act of Parliament, and in all works created either by the Queen personally, or by an officer or servant of the Crown in the course of his or her duties: this is called 'Crown Copyright', which is administered by the Office of Public Sector Information (OPSI). Under the 1988 Act (unchanged by the 1995 Regulations) Crown Copyright lasts for 125 years from the year the work was made, if the work remains unpublished commercially. Official papers are often never published commercially, but simply made available for inspection after 30 or more years. If the work is published commercially within 75 years of its making, copyright lasts 50 years from the year of first publication.

Parliamentary copyright exists in Bills and other works made under the direction or control of either House: it lasts for 50 years from the end of the year in which the work was made. A similar copyright is owned by certain international organisations. These also are unaffected by the 1995 Regulations.

Universities' copyright

The universities of Oxford, Cambridge, Edinburgh, Glasgow, St Andrews and Aberdeen, and the Colleges of Eton, Westminster and Winchester secured perpetual copyright in 1775 in works printed by them, in which they had been given or bequeathed the copyright. This perpetual copyright was limited by the 1988 Act, and any such copyrights will now expire at the end of 2039. The works concerned may of course qualify for copyright protection on other grounds, in which case longer terms of protection may apply.

Peter Pan

J.M. Barrie's famous play went out of copyright at the end of 1987, but the 1988 Act contained special provisions to enable the trustees of the Great Ormond Street Hospital to continue to collect royalties in perpetuity in respect of certain uses of the play. Following the 1995 Regulations, it is likely that all Barrie's works, including *Peter Pan*, came back into copyright in the UK as from 1 January 1996, and continued in copyright until the end of 2007: presumably the hospital has continued to receive royalties during this period (unless some other arrangement was agreed) and since 2007 the provisions of the 1988 Act have continued.

SUMMARY CHECKLIST: DURATION OF COPYRIGHT

- UK copyright is a statutory right, and now always has a fixed term of years.
- That term may vary, depending on the work, and it may be calculated in relation to the date of the author's death, or in relation to creation or first publication of the work, or to the year it was 'released' or first made available to the public.
- The Berne Convention international minimum for literary and artistic works is 50 years from the end of the year in which the author died.
- Within the EU, the term of copyright in literary, artistic, musical and dramatic works has been harmonised upwards by the Duration Directive to 70 years pma.
- The 70-year term applies to all EEA-origin works which were protected in at least one member state on 1 July 1995.
- The 70-year term (or part of it) also applies to certain works not of EEA origin, depending on the term of protection for those works in their country of origin.
- Within the UK, this meant that some existing copyrights were extended, but also that some works will have come back into copyright, having previously been in the public domain.
- For the current UK position, it is necessary to check the relevant provisions of the 1995, 1996 and 2003 Regulations (and the 1988 Act, as now amended).

Other rights of authors and publishers

3

MORAL RIGHTS

INTRODUCTION

In addition to copyright, authors now have in the UK personal statutory rights relating to their works and their reputations, called moral rights. They are quite separate from the copyright itself, and remain attached to the author personally, or the author's estate, even if the copyright is later assigned to someone else, such as a publisher. They cannot be sold or assigned to anyone else (although they can be inherited) but they can be waived: we will consider waiver further, below.

The idea of authors having personal moral rights is (relatively) new to UK law, although *droit moral* has been well-established in France, and elsewhere in Europe, for some time: indeed, the Continental view of copyright itself is primarily as an author's right (*droit d'auteur*) – quite different from the pragmatic economic right which has developed in the UK. With our different mercantile traditions, some in the UK initially regarded moral rights as dangerously romantic and suspiciously foreign, but they have been a (Berne) Treaty obligation of the UK for some time, and are now included in the 1988 Act.

Moral rights are unaffected by the EU Copyright Directive, and are specifically stated (Recital 19) to be outside its scope. There have been suggestions of an EU Moral Rights Directive, but although at the time of writing this seems unlikely, the UK government has been discussing possible amendments to strengthen the UK's moral rights regime.

Article 6 *bis* of Berne

Moral rights as a species come in all shapes and sizes: consider, for example, the thought-provoking *droit de repentir*, which in countries where it applies (not the UK) allows an author to have second thoughts entirely and insist on withdrawing a work, even after publication (there is usually provision for compensation). Only two moral rights, however, are specifically written into the Berne Convention (at Article 6 *bis*): the right to claim authorship of the work (**the right of paternity**), and the right to object to distortions, mutilations or other derogatory treatments of the work which would prejudice the author's honour or reputation (**the right of integrity**). All member countries are obliged to provide for protection of these two key rights.

The 1988 Act

The 1988 Copyright, Designs and Patents Act now provides for four statutory moral rights in the UK:

- the right of paternity;
- the right of integrity;
- the right to prevent false attribution;
- the right to privacy of certain photographs or films.

They are, however, severely hedged about with restrictions, as we shall see.

THE RIGHT OF PATERNITY

Section 77 of the 1988 Act gives the author of a copyright literary, dramatic, musical or artistic work, and the director of a copyright film, the right to be identified as the author or director of the work whenever the work is published commercially, performed in public, or communicated to the public, or issued to the public as part of a film or sound recording (or, in the case of an artistic work, exhibited in public, or a visual image of it communicated to the public). Given that communication to the public includes making available to the public on the Internet, the **paternity right** has considerable relevance to Internet exploitation. In the case of commercial publication, this means that the author has the right to be identified in (or on) each copy or, if that is not appropriate, in some other way 'likely to bring his identity to the notice of a person acquiring a copy'. This might require careful consideration if the information is only available online, or as part of a website. The identification must be 'clear and reasonably prominent'. The author may specify a pseudonym, or some other form of preferred identification (for example, initials). The right lasts for as long as the work remains in copyright.

In a recent case, the claimant claimed that his moral rights had been contravened by a number of articles not attributed to him which he claimed 'exploited' a number of articles written by him. While he accepted he was not the author of the other work, he argued that he was entitled to be identified as the author under section 77 of the 1988 Act, as he was the originator of the ideas. The court found that the moral right contained in section 77 is, in relation to a literary work, concerned with the authorship of a written paper and not with crediting the originator of the ideas embodied in the paper. The claim was accordingly struck out.

Although this new statutory right now complies with the UK's Berne obligations, it is accompanied by a number of restrictions, some of them quite significant.

THE WORK MUST BE IN COPYRIGHT

The paternity right only applies to 'copyright' works: the works must meet the various criteria for copyright protection in the UK (see Chapter 2), and the period of copyright must still be running. It also only applies to copyright literary, musical, dramatic or artistic works, or films – sound recordings, broadcasts and typographical arrangements are not covered.

PUBLICATION MUST BE COMMERCIAL

In the case of a book or similar publication containing literary and/or artistic works, the author's right of paternity operates to give the author the right to be identified when certain acts take place. These include 'commercial' publication, performance in public or communication to the public or inclusion in copies of a film or sound recording issued to the public. This therefore rules out token or nominal publication, or anything that is not intended to satisfy the reasonable requirements of the public. By implication, the book must be reasonably widely advertised to its intended market, and be available in quantities capable of fulfilling a likely minimum of orders. In the case of communication to the public, including transmissions on the Internet, the requirement that the act is done commercially does not apply. Care needs to be taken, therefore, with Internet uses.

THE RIGHT MUST BE ASSERTED

The right of paternity is the only moral right that needs to be expressly 'asserted' by the author before it can be enforced (section 78). Joint authors must each assert independently. The UK government consulted in 2009 on a proposal to abolish this requirement, but abolition did not appear to promise significant savings, and at the time of writing the requirement seems likely to remain.

The assertion may be included:

- in an assignment of copyright (which must be in writing); or
- via some other written document signed by the author.

The former method binds not only the person to whom copyright is assigned but also all those whose claims stem from theirs – whether they personally knew about the assertion or not. The latter method binds only those 'to whose notice the assertion is brought', which is why many author contracts now provide not only that the publishers themselves will credit the author but also that a similar contractual obligation will be written into any sub-licences. It also explains why notice of assertion appears in most books published in the UK.

The author must therefore assert his or her right positively and in writing. For print and e-book editions, a form of assertion is usually included on the reverse title page of each edition of the work, next to the copyright and bibliographic details.

For publications only available online, an equivalent method of public notice would need to be found. Note that it is *only* the paternity right which needs to be asserted: all-embracing phrases such as 'the author's moral rights are hereby asserted' go further than is strictly necessary.

Assertion is not retrospective, so if an author allows a work to be published without asserting his or her right of paternity, and later decides to assert, the publisher cannot be sued in respect of sales already made. Once the publisher is on notice of the author's assertion, however, all copies subsequently sold must identify the author in accordance with the Act.

THE RIGHT DOES NOT APPLY TO EVERY WORK

No right of paternity attaches to authors of certain works. The following are the most important:

- computer programs, computer-generated works, or typeface designs;
- works created in the course of employment (where the copyright is originally owned by the employer and the employer has authorised the publication complained of);
- works made for the purpose of reporting current events;
- works written for publication and published in a newspaper, magazine or similar periodical;
- works written for publication and published in a 'collective work' such as an encyclopaedia, dictionary or year book.

The last exception seems at first sight to cover all major (even multi-volume) works of reference, but it must surely be a question of degree. Where individual articles or entries are significant contributions to the literature in their own right, it will probably still be advisable to identify the author in accordance with the Act – unless one of the restrictions applies (for example, that the right has not been asserted, or has been waived).

THE AUTHOR MAY CONSENT, OR WAIVE THE RIGHT ALTOGETHER

Under section 87 of the 1988 Act, none of the author's moral rights will be infringed if he or she consented to the acts concerned. This is perhaps only reasonable; however, section 87 also goes much further and provides that all the author's moral rights, including the right of paternity, may also be *waived*, partially or completely. This is in sharp contrast to the Continental position – in France, for example, the author's *droit moral* is 'perpetual, inalienable and imprescriptible' – and has been strongly criticised as a further serious weakening of the author's rights in the UK.

Under the 1988 Act a waiver may be general and unconditional, or it may be limited in some way: it may apply only to certain works, or kinds of works, or it may apply only in certain circumstances, for example, as in some contracts, only in so far as necessary to exploit subsidiary rights, such as film or tv rights. It may also be conditional, and it may be made subject to revocation.

Waivers do not have to be in writing, and section 87(4) specifically allows for informal waivers (implied by the author's conduct, for example) under general common law principles. However, such implied or informal waivers may be difficult to prove, and if a reliable waiver is needed it is probably advisable to take the hint in section 87(2) that moral rights 'may be' waived by a written document signed by the author.

SUMMARY CHECKLIST: THE RIGHT OF PATERNITY

- Is the work a relevant copyright work? Is it one of the excluded categories of works?
- Has it been published commercially, or otherwise exploited?
- Has the right been asserted?
- Has the author consented, or waived the right?

THE RIGHT OF INTEGRITY

If the right of paternity is the Berne Convention's primary moral right of authors, the second key right enshrined in Article 6 *bis* is almost as important: the right of authors to object to 'derogatory treatment' of their work. This is usually referred to informally as the **right of integrity**. The right is set out in section 80 of the 1988 Act, which provides that authors of copyright literary, dramatic, musical or artistic works, and directors of copyright films, have the right, in specified circumstances, not to have their work subjected to derogatory treatment. Like the paternity right, the right of integrity lasts for as long as the work remains in copyright.

DEROGATORY TREATMENT

What, one may ask, is 'derogatory treatment'? Does it cover what publishing contracts often refer to as reasonable editorial changes?

There are in fact two separate questions:

- Do the particular acts complained of amount to a 'treatment' at all?
- If so, is that treatment 'derogatory'?

'Treatment'

The 1988 Act defines treatment to include any of the following things done to a work:

- adding to it;
- deleting from it;
- altering it;
- adapting it.

Specifically excluded from this list, however, are translations, or musical arrangements or transcriptions which amount to no more than a change of key or register. The exclusion of translations might seem hard to justify, given their frequency, but contractual remedies are usually available in such circumstances, under the translation rights contract (see Chapter 5).

What if the work is entirely untouched and unchanged, but is placed in an unflattering or unfortunate context (perhaps included in a website next to racist or indecent material)? Under the 1988 Act if none of the four positive acts listed above had occurred, the placing of the work in that context would not amount to a 'treatment' at all, and could not therefore infringe the integrity right. So a composer whose music was faithfully played and recorded could not complain of a breach of the integrity right if that recording then featured in the sound track of a documentary film condemning the political regime under which the composer lived and worked (as Shostakovich and a number of other Soviet composers found in a celebrated US case after the Second World War).

'Derogatory'

The 1988 Act (section 80) provides that:

> The treatment of a work is derogatory if it amounts to distortion or mutilation of the work or is otherwise prejudicial to the honour or reputation of the author or director.

'Distortion' and 'mutilation' are strong words. 'Prejudicial to . . . honour or reputation' also implies an objective standard, similar in strength to the various definitions of defamation (see Chapter 7). It seems likely, therefore, that it will not be the author's opinion (or injured feelings) alone which will provide the yardstick for what is or is not prejudicial to their honour or reputation: authors will have to produce objective evidence that their honour or reputations have actually suffered, or are likely to.

Derogatory treatment will clearly include complete mutilation or emasculation of a work, or a complete misrepresentation of the author's real views or philosophy. Indeed, if the treatment is that serious there would probably also have been an action for defamation anyway.

Editorial 'improvements' in general are therefore highly unsafe, particularly where the risk of breaching the author's right of integrity is accompanied by the risk of defamation, or breach of contract. In the case of breach of contract this will particularly be so where the contract is an informal one, with no express provisions allowing the publishers to make 'reasonable' (or any other) changes.

In a more standard publishing agreement, it is likely that there will be some provision for reasonable alterations, and if the alterations made broadly comply with the terms of the contract it is unlikely that a claim of derogatory treatment will succeed, since the author will have consented – via the contract – to the changes made (see below).

Where alterations go *beyond* any contract, however, an action for breach of contract may well succeed and there may also now be derogatory treatment. There might also be an issue of false attribution.

'Bad Boys Megamix'

Although a music case, the injunction granted to George Michael in 1991 is still instructive as one of the few reported occasions so far, since the 1988 Act, on which an issue of derogatory treatment was considered by the UK courts. Michael complained that five of his early tracks, recorded in the days when he was a performer with Wham!, had been used without his consent in a 'Megamix' medley: the tracks (he alleged) had been edited, some words had been changed, and fill-in music from elsewhere had been added. Clearly, a 'treatment' of the works had taken place, since there were both deletions and alterations (and possibly additions also – although 'filler' music linking separate tracks might not strictly speaking 'add' to the tracks themselves) – but was the treatment 'derogatory'? Michael argued that the megamix 'completely alters the character of the original compositions'. The judge, adopting a somewhat cautious approach, first pointed out that:

> It is not, in my judgment, self-evident that taking parts of five different works and putting them together necessarily involves a change of character or modification.

However, on the arguments before him he took the view that it was at least arguable that such treatment amounts to distortion or mutilation within section 80(2)(b) of the 1988 Act, and therefore granted Michael's application for an injunction.

That particular case went no further, and there have been few cases since: in one of the most recent (*Confetti Records* v. *Warner Music UK Ltd* (2003)), it was decided that the addition of a rap line to a sound recording did not in itself amount to derogatory treatment of the musical work recorded. There was no evidence that rapping of the kind added was prejudicial to the honour or reputation of the author.

LIMITATIONS ON THE RIGHT OF INTEGRITY

As with the right of paternity, the author's right of integrity will only apply if:

- the work is a copyright work;
- the work is published commercially (other uses may also suffice: see p. 47 above).

The integrity right does *not*, however, need to be 'asserted'. The right does not apply to the following works, among others:

- computer programs or computer-generated works;
- works made for the purpose of reporting current events;

- works written or made available with the consent of the author for publication and published in a newspaper, magazine or similar periodical;
- works written or made available with the consent of the author for publication and published in a 'collective work' such as an encyclopaedia, dictionary or year book;
- works created in the course of employment (where the employer owns the copyright, authorises the treatment concerned and – where the author is identified – provides a 'sufficient disclaimer').

Most of the above exceptions are similar to the list of exceptions to the right of paternity (see above, p. 48), apart from the provision for a disclaimer in employee works, and the omission of typeface designs from the list – the paternity right does not apply to such designs, but the right of integrity *does*.

The right of integrity also does not apply to anything done to avoid the commission of an offence, or complying with a statutory duty, or (as with the BBC or possibly organisations such as the Internet Watch Foundation) to avoid anything which offends against 'good taste or decency or which is likely to encourage or incite to crime or lead to disorder or to be offensive to public feeling'. This last exception now provides a let-out for the BBC even where alterations are significant structural changes. While the deletion even of a few (crucial) words from a play could be 'structural', it would not amount to derogatory treatment if the BBC's cuts were motivated by a desire not to offend public feeling. As with employee works, however, there must be a 'sufficient disclaimer' (if the author is identified).

Finally the right of integrity will not apply:

- to anything done with the author's consent; or
- if the author has fully waived the right.

SUMMARY CHECKLIST: THE RIGHT OF INTEGRITY

- Is the work a relevant copyright work? Is it one of the excluded categories of works?
- Has it been published commercially, or otherwise exploited?
- Has any 'treatment' of the work taken place?
- Has the work been added to, deleted from, altered or adapted (except by translation)?
- If so, was the treatment 'derogatory'?
- Did it distort or mutilate the work?
- Was it otherwise prejudicial to the author's honour or reputation?
- Did the author consent, or waive the right?

FALSE ATTRIBUTION

Authors not only have a moral right of paternity – to be credited as the author – but also have its converse: the right *not* to be credited with things they did *not* write. This is known as the **right to prevent false attribution**, and is contained in section 84 of the 1988 Act. Of the four moral rights contained in the 1988 Act, it is the only one to have existed before in statutory form: there was a very similar right in section 43 of the 1956 Copyright Act.

The right applies to literary, dramatic, musical and artistic works, and to films and (unlike the paternity and integrity rights) can be exercised by any 'person' – they do not have to be authors.

The attribution complained of may be express or implied, and the right will be infringed wherever a false attribution:

- is included in copies of a work issued to the public; or
- is in (or on) an artistic work exhibited to the public.

In the case of *Alan Clark* v. *Associated Newspapers*, the MP Alan Clark brought an action for false attribution against the publishers of the *Evening Standard* newspaper. One of the *Standard's* journalists wrote a regular column entitled 'Alan Clark's Secret Election Diary' (together with a picture of Mr Clark) which was intended to be a parody of Mr Clark's well-known diaries. The court used a similar test under section 84 as in the law of defamation, namely that it was necessary to determine what single meaning was conveyed to the reasonable reader. Since the articles contained clear and unequivocal false statements attributing authorship to Mr Clark, he therefore proved his false attribution claim.

The right may also be infringed by false attributions contained in public performances or showings, or communications to the public, but only where the person concerned knew or had reason to believe that the attribution was false. There are also secondary offences of possession, or dealing with, copies of works containing such attributions, but again where the presence of the attribution was known, and was known to be false.

The right is an entirely personal right, allied to a person's reputation rather than to any copyright works he or she may have created – it does not therefore last for the full term of copyright, like other moral rights, but only for 20 years after the person's death.

As with other moral rights, it often overlaps with other legal remedies – in this case with the existing laws of defamation and passing off. (Alan Clark also succeeded in proving passing off against the *Evening Standard* because he had a substantial reputation as a diarist which would have been important to the readers in deciding whether to read the articles, because the readers were misled and he suffered loss.) Indeed, where other, more traditional, remedies exist it may well be that judges will prefer to use those and will pay less attention to specific statutory moral rights.

THE RIGHT TO PRIVACY OF CERTAIN PHOTOGRAPHS OR FILMS

Some countries – the USA for example – have significant and substantial laws protecting personal privacy, but a general privacy law is still in the process of developing in the UK under the Human Rights Act 1998, particularly following the *Naomi Campbell* and *Michael Douglas* cases (see Chapter 8). This limited moral **right to privacy**, contained in section 85 of the 1988 Act, is not really a moral right at all, and applies only to certain photographs and films which are commissioned for private and domestic purposes (such as wedding photos).

Under the 1956 Act, the person who commissioned such photos (usually the happy couple) owned the copyright in them, and could thus control the use made of them. Under the 1988 Act, however, this rule was changed (see p. 32) and the author (that is, the photographer) now owns the copyright. This would have meant that professional photographers could make unlimited copies of wedding photos they had taken and could, for example, sell them to national newspapers if the bride or groom subsequently became newsworthy. It was to prevent this limited, but very real, danger that section 85 was passed. Those commissioning such photos or films can now prevent:

- copies being issued to the public;
- the works being exhibited or shown in public; or
- the works being communicated to the public.

The right lasts for as long as the work concerned remains in copyright.

REMEDIES FOR INFRINGEMENT OF MORAL RIGHTS

Section 103 of the 1988 Act provides that an infringement of a moral right:

Is actionable as a breach of statutory duty owed to the person entitled to the right.

Damages may be awarded, and an injunction may be granted in appropriate cases. There is also express provision for a disclaimer, to be approved by the court, 'dissociating the author or director from the treatment of the work'.

DATABASE RIGHT

There are two possible intellectual property rights that can protect databases:

(1) Copyright – some databases will qualify for copyright protection, provided that they are original, which they will be (section 3A of the 1988 Act) 'if, and only if, by reason of the selection or arrangement of the contents of the database, the database constitutes the author's own intellectual creation' (as opposed to the content itself). See also the 2010 *Football Dataco* case, below.
(2) Database right, as provided for in the Copyright and Rights in Databases Regulations 1997.

Database right is the right to prevent unauthorised extraction or re-use and was provided for by the EU Database Directive. The right was implemented here by the Copyright and Rights in Databases Regulations 1997. The Regulations came into force on 1 January 1998.

Under the Regulations, there may be a database right 'if there has been a substantial investment in obtaining, verifying or presenting the contents of the database'. Following the *William Hill* case (below), and the European Court of Justice's ruling in that case, the question of where the investment has been made is key (particularly whether it was truly in 'obtaining' the data).

'Substantial' is a test of quality as well as quantity (provided, again, that the investment is in obtaining (etc.), rather than creating, the data). 'Investment' includes any investment, whether of financial, human or technical resources, and 'database' is widely defined to mean any 'collection of independent works, data or other materials arranged in a systematic or methodical way and individually accessible by electronic or other means'. Whether there has been 'substantial investment' involves an assessment of the resources used to locate the constituent materials, to collate them, verify them and present them. Any investment relating to the *creation* of the materials (as opposed to obtaining them) is irrelevant to the question of whether there will be database right for the database in which they are contained.

The right is owned by the 'maker' of the database, who is defined as the person whose initiative is responsible for the relevant obtaining, verifying or presenting, and who assumes the risk of the necessary investment. As with ownership of copyright itself, however, this general rule of ownership does not apply to databases made by employees in the course of their employment: these will be owned by the employer. There will be no database right unless the maker was at the material time (usually when the database was made) an EEA national or resident, or a body incorporated or based in the EEA (including partnerships or other unincorporated bodies).

The database right lasts for 15 years from the end of the year in which the database is completed. This term can be effectively renewed if substantial new investment can be demonstrated as a result of 'substantial change', including the accumulation of successive additions, deletions or alterations – in other words, a significant new edition or re-origination but not a mere reprint.

Under Regulation 16 'a person infringes database right if, without the consent of the owner of the right, he extracts or re-utilises all or a substantial part of the contents of the database'. Repeated and systematic use of insubstantial parts may amount to use of 'a substantial part', provided (following the *William Hill* case) that the sum total of what was taken would enable the defendant to reconstitute and re-publish a substantial part of the whole database, in a way which would conflict with normal exploitation of the database. Extracts can be permanent or temporary, and by any means or in any form. 'Re-utilisation', however, must involve making the contents available to the public, albeit by any means.

There are two exceptions for certain limited purposes. Fair dealing by a lawful user 'for the purpose of illustration for teaching or research' will not infringe a database right as long as the source is indicated. Use may also be permitted where it is not possible 'by reasonable inquiry' to identify the maker and it is reasonable to assume that the 15-year term has expired.

It is clear from all of the above that UK database right is a distinct and individual statutory right whose operation depends on close consideration of a number of key definitions, some of which are now narrowly defined. Was there a 'substantial investment' initially, was it in *obtaining*, as opposed to creating, the data, and was 'a substantial part' extracted or re-utilised? In *British Horseracing Board* v. *William Hill Organisation Ltd* (2005), the Court of Appeal reversed an earlier decision of the High Court that William Hill had 'extracted' a substantial part of the BHB horseracing database by taking information from its daily data supply and loading it on to computers for the purpose of making it available on its own website, and the later transmission and loading of that data on to its website for access to the public was a 're-utilisation'. Interestingly, this was despite the fact that the BHB database was a single database in a constant (daily) state of updating and refinement. In the judge's view, this meant that 'as new data are added, so the database's term of protection is constantly being renewed'. The Court of Appeal referred several questions to the European Court of Justice, which delivered its ruling in November 2004 (along with rulings in a group of similar sports fixture cases). The Court of Appeal followed this ruling, with William Hill succeeding in its appeal. The decision and rulings make it clear that the database right is concerned with obtaining (verifying and presenting) data and not the creation of the data itself. 'Obtaining' in this sense does not include the act of selecting and arranging fixtures. Instead, the right is concerned with the promotion and protection of investment in data storage and processing systems.

This is a narrow distinction in many cases. Many databases are comprised of relatively simple data with most of the resources being ploughed into sorting through that data. Where the obtaining of the content, the verification and the presentation do not involve much investment beyond creating the data, the right will not apply. In creating most databases, there is often a single process that involves creation of data, its obtaining, verification and presentation, and it may be difficult – if not impossible – to separate these processes one from another. There is some hope, however. Even though the database does not attract the database right, the database owner may still be entitled to copyright protection in respect of the content, i.e. the data itself, provided that the data passes the test for protection as a literary work and provided that the database owner is also the owner of the copyright in that data. Where the database shows signs of 'the author's own intellectual creation', the database may well attract copyright protection and the owner can take advantage of a longer term of protection. This intellectual standard may prove a difficult test for straightforward listings or alphabetical directories. However, in April 2010, the High Court ruled in the case of *Football Dataco Ltd and Others* v. *Britten Pools and Others* that database copyright can subsist in football fixture lists. In his judgment, the judge explained that there are a great many steps involved in preparing English FA Premier League and Scottish Premier League football fixture lists (e.g. ensuring that two teams from the same town were not playing at home at the same time, and that international fixtures had been taken into consideration). He found that creation of these fixture lists 'involved very significant labour and skill in satisfying the multitude of often competing requirements of those involved. The process is not therefore one where everyone would come up with the same answer . . . Judgments have to be taken.'

It is unclear how much intellectual creation has to be involved before copyright subsists in a database. We know from the recitals to the Database Directive that the compilation of tracks on a CD is not sufficient for copyright to subsist. However, it remains to be seen whether there will be copyright protection for other sporting fixture lists that can be created with far less skill and effort.

PUBLICATION RIGHT

Publication right was introduced by the Copyright and Related Rights Regulations 1996. It protects people who publish for the first time in the EEA original literary, dramatic, musical and artistic works and films in which copyright has expired, but which were never previously published during their copyright terms anywhere in the world. To qualify for the right, the publisher of the work must, at the time of first publication, be a national of an EEA member state.

The right will benefit many editions of previously unpublished works in EU and EEA member states, which do not have typographical copyright, but in the UK it will overlap extensively with existing rights; both typographical copyright and the final stages of perpetual copyright in unpublished works (which is not due to expire finally in most cases until 2039). Many unpublished works in the UK continued to have perpetual copyright under the 1911 and 1956 Copyright Acts, until the 1988 Act ended that arrangement for good by providing that works of deceased authors remaining unpublished when it came into force (1989) would enjoy a maximum of a further 50 years' protection – i.e. until 2039. So some such unpublished works may still be protected by copyright until 2039, and the key requirement of publication right (that copyright must have expired) may often not apply until then. The extension of copyright to life plus 70 years means that unpublished works created in the 20 years prior to 1989 may continue to be protected until the expiry of the 70 year period.

Publication right may benefit any 'person' who satisfies the criteria set out in the Regulations, and 'publication' is given a very wide meaning (including any (authorised) communication to the public, such as making available via electronic retrieval systems, rental or lending, performance, exhibition or broadcast) so if ancient manuscripts, diaries or pictures which seem to have some publishing potential are found in the attic, it may be advisable to exercise some caution before they are given or lent to anyone else, or even displayed in a museum or library. However, the criteria are fairly exacting:

- the work must have been protected by copyright;
- copyright must have expired without the work being published;
- the work must still be unpublished;
- the person publishing the work must be an EEA national and must first publish the work in the EEA.

For most unpublished works of deceased authors in the UK, at least the second of these criteria may not be satisfied until 2039 or later, as (described above) in the case of authors who died before 1989. For those who died later, copyright in their unpublished works will continue for 70 years after their death. For works which do qualify, though, publication right may prove a valuable right, effectively conferring all the rights of a copyright owner. The right lasts for 25 years from the end of the year of first publication. It goes without saying that the unpublished works of living authors are still in copyright.

HUMAN RIGHTS

Following the coming into force of the Human Rights Act 1998, and a number of key judicial decisions, a general right of privacy seems to be developing as part of UK domestic law. For a fuller treatment of this, and some early decided cases, see Chapter 8.

PUBLIC LENDING RIGHT

After vigorous lobbying by authors such as Maureen Duffy and Brigid Brophy, a **public lending right** for authors (PLR) was established in the UK by the Public Lending Right Act 1979, and came into effect in 1982. The first payments were made in 1984, and payments have been made annually ever since: payment is entirely out of central government funds. The scheme is administered by a Registrar of Public Lending Right and a small staff, supported by an advisory committee representing interested bodies, including the responsible government department, the Department of Culture, Media and Sport.

The PLR scheme provides for authors (and others, such as illustrators) throughout the EEA to receive payments in proportion to the number of times their books are borrowed from public libraries in the UK: borrowings are recorded from a sample of 30 library authorities around the UK and the results grossed up annually to arrive at an estimate of the national loans of each book. Over £75 million has been distributed to authors since the scheme started.

No author may currently get more than £6,600 per annum: 250 authors received the maximum amount in the financial year 2009/10, and 6,000 got more than £100. The total government funding for the PLR scheme in 2009/10 was £7.58 million, of which £6.76 million was distributed in payments to 23,241 authors – working out at a rate per loan of exactly 6.29p.

In order to participate in the PLR scheme, and benefit from any modest annual payments which may be on offer, it is necessary to register with the PLR Registrar (his address is set out at Appendix B). Those entitled to register include not only authors, but also other persons who have contributed to the text or illustration of a published book: this would include illustrators, photographers, editors and translators, who will receive a share of any PLR payment generated by loan of the book. Those registering must be resident in the EEA, and there are reciprocal arrangements with a number of EU member states including Germany, France and Spain, although implementation of the 1992 Rental and Lending Right Directive elsewhere in the EU (especially Eastern Europe) is less good.

Payment continues for 70 years after the death of the author or contributor, in line with of the term of copyright.

PLR was extended to audiobooks and e-books under section 43 of the Digital Economy Act 2010, although at the time of writing the relevant provisions have not been brought into effect. The definitions of 'book', 'lent out', 'loan' and 'borrowed' in the Public Lending Right Act were to be amended accordingly in order to cover cases in which public libraries make audio or e-books available on the premises to members of the public, for use away from the premises for limited periods of time. The definition of 'author' was also to be amended to include producers and narrators. However, ministerial undertakings were given that digital lending would be restricted to one loan per reader for each copy of the work held by the library, and that PLR would not extend to making works available online via remote downloads or communication to the public off library premises. It is not clear at the time of writing when, and how far, the section 43 provisions will be brought into effect.

ARTIST'S RESALE RIGHT (*DROIT DE SUITE*)

Although not strictly speaking an author's right, **artist's resale right** is of considerable importance to many artists. It provides for artists or their heirs within the EEA, or a listed country, to receive a percentage of the sale price of their works of art when they are re-sold by auctioneers, dealers or galleries (often at vastly inflated prices). The idea is written into the Berne Convention and the legislation of most EU member states (France has had *droit de suite* since 1920), but it took a long time for the Resale Right Directive 2001 to be passed, and then only after a protracted conciliation procedure between the EU Parliament and Council, during which the UK, among others, objected that such a right would seriously damage the London art market. In the end, the UK finally implemented the Directive on 13 February 2006, under the Artist's Resale Right Regulations 2006, which apply to all sales on or after 14 February 2006 for living artists. For deceased artists whose works are still in copyright, the implementation date is not until 1 January 2012, under a derogation in the Directive (see below).

Key elements of the Regulations are:

- the right is limited to genuine re-sales, rather than first sales;
- the work must still be protected by copyright;
- private sales (as opposed to gallery, auction or other commercial sales) are excluded;
- the right may not be assigned or waived (although it may be bequeathed, but only to a human being or a charity. However, the UK secured a derogation whereby any beneficiaries under a will would not inherit until 2012, despite overwhelming public opposition to this delay);

- The right may only be administered collectively, via a collecting society such as DACS.

Under the UK Regulations, the works covered include any work of graphic or plastic art such as a picture, a collage, a painting, a drawing, an engraving, a print, a lithograph, a sculpture, a tapestry, a ceramic, an item of glassware or a photograph. Artist's resale right applies to all sales of €1,000 or more. Payment is jointly and severally due from the seller or his agent, or the buyer.

The UK Regulations provide for a sliding scale of royalty rates as follows:

- 4 per cent for the bottom band up to €50,000
- 3 per cent from €50,000 to €200,000
- 1 per cent from €200,000 to €350,000
- 0.5 per cent from €350,000 to €500,000
- 0.25 per cent for any amount over €500,000

The maximum an artist can receive in resale right on any single sale is €12,500.

As explained above, the UK Regulations do not yet apply to work of deceased artists but will do so at the beginning of 2012.

Part II
Commissioning: publishing contracts

Author contracts

4

HOW A CONTRACT IS MADE

In this chapter we will look at contracts generally – what they are, legally, and how they are made – and then examine in some detail the contract which is in many ways the most important contract in publishing – the publisher's initial contract with the author. Whether publication is to be in print on paper or in digital form, or for a book or journal article, or for other web-based content, this will raise a number of important issues, such as ownership and control of rights, which we will need to come back to again and again, so we will spend some time on these. In Chapter 5, we will go on to look at some other key publishing contracts, such as contracts with contributors, and co-publishing and subsidiary rights deals, including electronic rights.

WHAT IS A CONTRACT?

A contract is an agreement that the law will enforce. That sounds rather simple, and it is: contracts are in essence very simple things. You do not need to sign a 20-clause standard form document in order to have a binding contract with someone – indeed in most cases you do not need any writing at all. The 20-clause document may be important later on, in granting rights and confirming your agreement on a number of detailed points, and we will look at such important details in the second half of this chapter. But you may well find you have an agreement that the law will enforce long before you get to that stage. There are two separate elements to consider:

(1) '*An agreement*'. There must actually be an agreement between the parties concerned; all that this means is that the parties:

- must have reached a clear agreement on a specific matter; and
- must have intended 'to enter into legal relations' – intended, in other words, to make a binding legal commitment to each other on the matter.

(2) '*That the law will enforce*'. The agreement must be legally enforceable – so the parties must be capable of entering into binding contracts (which will not, for

example, be declared void because one of them is under age, insane or incapable through drink), the bargain must not itself be illegal or contrary to public policy, and must either be under seal or in writing (for certain types of contract) or – more usually – must be supported by some 'consideration': something (almost anything) of value must be given or promised in return for the promises made.

We will look at these various criteria below, but assuming that most authors and publishers are over 18, not insane or (completely) drunk, and that their agreement is (on the whole) legal and decent, the most important requirements for an enforceable publishing contract are likely to be these:

- a clear agreement;
- an intention to be legally bound by it;
- some valuable consideration to seal the bargain.

We now know, following the 1991 decision of the Court of Appeal in *Malcolm* v. *OUP* (see below, p. 66) that these simple key requirements can be met long before a formal written contract is signed, or even discussed, and that a publisher may become bound contractually to publish a book, even during what have traditionally been thought of as mere 'pre-contract negotiations'.

CLEAR AGREEMENTS: OFFER AND ACCEPTANCE

For a contract to exist, a clear agreement must be reached, with no significant misunderstandings: the parties must not be at cross-purposes. One side must make an offer in clear terms, and the other side must accept that offer on basically the same terms, otherwise no contract can come about. Let us suppose that Routledge makes an offer to two authors (who shall be nameless) to publish at a (fairly) reasonable royalty a fourth edition of a 350-page book by them on publishing law, to be delivered by 1 October 2010. That is a fairly clear 'offer'. If accepted, they clearly intend it to be legally binding, and the provision for a royalty means there will be valuable 'consideration'. Suppose then, however, that the authors reply: 'Thank you for your offer; we are happy to confirm that we will write a 1,288-page loose-leaf text, including precedents, on publishing law on the terms you have set out.' Is there a contract? No – because the offer, to publish a 350-page book, has not been accepted: what has happened is that the authors have made a counter-offer, to deliver something altogether different and more ambitious. Routledge may like this new offer, and decide to accept it, or the parties may continue negotiating, and reach agreement sooner or later, either on the original terms or on revised terms, but until the offer and acceptance match each other no contract exists.

Acceptance by conduct, and offers to treat

Silence does not imply acceptance (even if the offer attempts to provide that it will) but offers may be accepted by *conduct* as well as by written or spoken words.

Suppose that an author and publisher are discussing a draft contract but for one reason or another never actually sign it. The basic terms of the offer contained in the proposed contract may still be accepted or confirmed by either or them if they start to act on the basis of those terms – for example, by delivering the book on time, or by commencing production. If publisher and author both continue to 'perform' the terms of the contract, even though it was never signed, it will increasingly bind them, on those terms. However, if it is left unsigned, and there is no separate agreement on these points, the publisher may well find that it has no more than an implied licence to publish (and perhaps deal with certain subsidiary rights) on a non-exclusive basis, and would not have been granted an assignment of copyright, or any exclusive publishing licence (both of which must be in writing, and signed).

Does a bookshop make an offer when it displays a book in the window at a certain price? Suppose the price label is out of date: can a customer 'accept' the offer and claim there is a binding contract at the old price? No – because shops in those circumstances are not making binding offers, but merely offers to come in and enter into negotiations – what the law calls 'offers to treat'. So if our canny customer takes the book to the till and offers the old price, it is then open to the bookseller to reject that offer and instead make a counter-offer to sell it at the correct price.

INTENTION TO BE LEGALLY BOUND

Both parties must intend to enter into legal relations, and intend that their agreement will bind them legally. An agreement to meet in the Festival Hall Bar at 7 p.m. is *not* usually intended to be legally binding, and if one party is late and as a result they both miss the first half of the concert (because the late one has the tickets) there may be a serious row but there will be no breach of any contract. An agreement by an office syndicate to share in National Lottery winnings, however, or an agreement by an author to deliver a manuscript on disk to a publisher by a specified date *are* both normally intended to be contractually binding. It will be a question of fact in each case.

If one or other party wishes to negotiate but avoid any binding legal commitment for the time being, it is possible to achieve this by marking all correspondence 'Subject to Contract', so that it is clear that the necessary intention to conclude a contract is not yet present.

CONSIDERATION

So that there is no doubt that the parties mean what they say, an agreement is not generally binding under English law unless:

- it is signed and witnessed as a Deed, or made under seal (for some formal assignments, or certain transactions involving land); or
- it is supported by some valuable 'consideration'.

For most publishing contracts therefore – even informal, verbal ones – this means that there must be consideration – either consideration now, or a promise of future consideration to come. An upfront fee or an advance would be present consideration – an undertaking to pay future royalties would count as future consideration. Sometimes of course both exist, but both are equally valid in the eyes of the law.

Although money normally features somewhere, 'consideration' does not actually need to be in the form of convertible currency, provided it is of some economic value. It also does not have to represent an adequate commercial price – it can be purely nominal, for example £1. A promise by a magazine publisher to publish in book form articles by the athletes Harold Abrahams and Eric Liddell (later made famous in the film, *Chariots of Fire*) for a payment of '4d per copy' was held by the Court of Appeal in 1922 to be sufficient consideration to form the basis of a binding publishing contract, even though virtually no other details had been settled. Despite the reservations of the Court ('I cannot but wonder that publishers and authors enter into agreements as indefinite as this'), '4d per copy' is perfectly clear, and sufficient, consideration.

Mutual promises can be good consideration for each other, provided that both of them have an economic value to the party to whom they are made: arguably, a publishing agreement which is not signed as a Deed and which makes no mention of fees or royalties or anything else of economic value – even free author's copies or offprints – might well lack the necessary consideration to be binding, even if it contains a firm commitment to publish, since although the act of publishing will cost the publisher money it may not in itself convey anything of economic value to the author (except perhaps for academics whose promotion or even tenure may depend on it). Most publishing agreements, however, are quite clearly of economic value to the author.

VERBAL CONTRACTS

A publishing agreement does not need to be in writing (although it helps) and a publisher can be bound by even a purely verbal agreement, provided it has the necessary ingredients listed above. This has been clear since the case of *Malcolm v. OUP* in 1991, when a number of verbal assurances, made over the telephone to an author, Mr Malcolm, by OUP's then editor, Mr Hardy, were held by the Court of Appeal to constitute a binding contract.

Mr Malcolm submitted a manuscript to Oxford University Press. Their in-house editor, a Mr Hardy, and an outside reader, both liked it, but thought it too long, and Mr Hardy suggested substantial cuts. Now, Mr Malcolm had had a number of unsatisfactory experiences with other publishers at this 'pre-contract discussion' stage, and made it clear to Mr Hardy he was looking for a firm publishing commitment before embarking on any more revisions, which he estimated could well take up to six months' work. There followed two telephone conversations, both of which Mr Malcolm – with unusual foresight – tape recorded. In the second telephone conversation Mr Hardy made some crucial remarks, which should be required reading in every editorial department:

. . . we would like to do it. That is to say, I mean I know you want a commitment sufficient to take you through the last stage of revision and that's what I am offering.

It seems to me that because it's such a risky venture I am not going to be terribly generous financially, erm . . . I mean what I think we should agree is that you have a fair royalty.

The Court of Appeal – reversing an earlier decision by the High Court – found that in these circumstances all the necessary elements were present to create a binding contract, and therefore found that OUP's refusal to publish after all was indeed a breach of contract.

The Court made a number of important findings:

- No special formalities are required for publishing contracts, and it does not matter if contract details such as exact royalty terms, print number or format are all left to be agreed later; an agreement is not incomplete in law simply because it calls for further agreement on some key points later on, as long as the parties have settled the essential elements of the bargain.
- In this case, there was a clear agreement – that Mr Malcolm would deliver, and OUP would publish, a specific book (indeed the author was busily revising it to OUP's own specifications).
- There was a sufficiently clear intention on both sides to enter into legal relations: Mr Malcolm had made clear his determination to have a firm commitment before doing any more work and Mr Hardy had offered that commitment. As Lord Justice Leggatt put it: 'It is difficult to know what was meant by "a firm commitment" other than an intention to create legal relations . . . to suggest that Mr Hardy intended to induce Mr Malcolm to revise the book by giving him a valueless assurance would be tantamount to an imputation of fraud.'
- There was also sufficient 'consideration' for the contract, in the shape of Mr Hardy's promise to pay a 'fair royalty'. This vague phrase is not a recommended method of settling consideration for a publishing contract, but it is (just) sufficient in law. '4d per copy' was sufficient consideration in 1922 (see above p. 66) and 'a fair royalty' appears to be equally sufficient today.

On this basis Lord Justice Leggatt and a majority of the Court concluded that OUP did enter into a binding contract to publish Mr Malcolm's book, for a fair royalty ('it follows that in my judgment when Mr Hardy used the expressions "commitment" and "a fair royalty" he did in fact mean what he said and I venture to think it would take a lawyer to arrive at any other conclusion').

A final – equally important – finding by the court was that specific performance of a publishing contract might be ordered in appropriate cases – in other words, that the publisher should be ordered to publish the book – and it is important to bear this in mind. In most cases, however, courts will avoid making such orders, since they will be difficult, if not impossible, for the court to enforce. If (as here) an award of damages for breach of contract is a viable alternative, courts will normally prefer to award damages (on damages generally, see Chapter 9).

In the more recent case of *Sadler* v. *Reynolds* (2005), involving a verbal agreement with a ghost-writer for an autobiography, the High Court similarly found that a prominent football chairman who told a well-known sports reporter that he wanted him to write his autobiography, for a 50:50 split of a £70,000 advance which the reporter had negotiated, was in breach of contract when he subsequently gave the ghost-writing contract to someone else. The Court awarded the reporter his £35,000 half of the deal by way of damages, plus a further £1,000 for loss of opportunity. Many publishers and agents now use 'deal memos', which may go into some detail on rights to be offered, but which are marked 'subject to contract' specifically to avoid a binding contract being inadvertently created before the parties intend it to.

PARTICULAR CONTRACTS AND LEGAL CAPACITY

CONTRACTS WHICH NEED WRITING

Although verbal contracts are binding in most publishing situations, there are some kinds of contracts which must be in writing. Others do not need to be in writing themselves, but some written evidence must exist to support them. In addition, some specific assignments or grants or licences must be written.

Contracts which must be in writing

- Bills of exchange, promissory notes, and bills of sale;
- Regulated consumer credit agreements;
- Hire purchase and consumer hire agreements.

Contracts for which written evidence must exist

- Marine insurance contracts;
- Contracts of guarantee;
- Contracts for the sale (or other disposition) of an interest in land.

Assignments or grants which must be written

- Assignments of copyright (under section 90(3) of the 1988 Act);
- Grants of Exclusive Licences (under section 92 of the 1988 Act).

In both of these last two cases, the assignment or grant must not only be in writing, but also *signed* by, or on behalf of, the copyright owner. If it is not, it will be unenforceable as a legal right (although an equitable interest may in some cases exist). Note that under the Electronic Communications Act 2000 electronic signatures will be recognised as valid evidence of authenticity.

ILLEGALITY

The law will not enforce a contract to do something which is legally wrong, such as the commission of a crime, or a tort (such as a libel), or which is otherwise contrary to public policy. Thus contracts which promote sexual immorality or which pervert the course of justice are void and unenforceable, as are certain kinds of gaming and wagering contracts. Contracts to finance other people's litigation in return for a share in the proceeds (formerly an offence known as 'champerty') are unenforceable (although at the time of writing conditional fee arrangements are still permitted in the UK for libel cases, despite their undoubted chilling effect on freedom of speech). Also illegal are contracts in restraint of trade, and contracts the purpose of which is to procure the breach of an existing contract: so that publisher B, wishing to entice an author away from publisher A, cannot sign the author up to a more attractive deal knowing it to involve the breach of the author's existing contract – the new contract will be unenforceable, and publisher B will probably be liable to an action in tort from publisher A for procuring a breach of contract.

INCAPACITY OF THE PARTIES

Not everyone is legally capable of entering into binding contracts. Those who might *not* have the necessary legal capacity at the relevant times, and whose contracts would therefore be liable to be declared voidable (i.e. where the parties have the power to avoid the legal relationship by invalidating the contract or to avoid the contract and continue), include the following.

Minors

The age of legal capacity was reduced from 21 to 18 by the Family Law Reform Act 1969. Until people have reached their eighteenth birthday, they are not fully capable of entering into binding legal contracts – they are known as minors (previously 'infants'). This is designed to protect the young from unwise contracts – particularly from contracts which (as in the case of many young pop singers or sports stars) might involve very large sums of money and which would significantly restrict their future freedom. On the other hand, those who do business with minors in good faith may also need protection – if for example they supply valuable goods to them on credit, or pay them advances. In order to balance these two objectives, the law will as a general rule uphold minors' contracts if they are for 'necessaries', or are otherwise – on the whole – for the minors' benefit. In a well-known publishing case in 1966 (*Chaplin v. Leslie Frewin (Publishers) Limited*) Charlie Chaplin's son – who was then a minor – was held to be bound by a book publishing contract under which he had already been paid significant advances, since the contract was itself for his benefit and also enabled him to make a start as an author; equally, it would have been unfair to deprive the publisher of the opportunity to recoup his advances.

Mental patients

If you are insane, you are considered by the law to be 'incapable of intelligent consent'. However, insanity is not always a permanent state and those suffering from insanity often have lucid intervals during which they are quite capable of entering into rational agreements. A contract made by a mental patient is therefore not void from the outset, but may be declared void by the patient later if it is not for his or her benefit, particularly if the other party knew of the insanity and took advantage of it. Equally, a beneficial contract made while insane can be *affirmed* later on.

Drunkards and drug abusers

Rather like the insane, those who enter into contracts while their faculties are completely incapacitated through drink (or, by analogy, drugs) may plead their extreme drunkenness or incapacity as a defence in any subsequent actions under those contracts. But they may do this only if:

- their condition completely prevented them from understanding the transaction; and
- the other party knew this.

Most publishing lunches nowadays would be unlikely to have the necessary effect. In any event, if the drunkard ratifies the contract later on, when sober, he or she will become liable in the normal way.

Convicted prisoners

There seems no reason why a convicted criminal should not be as capable of entering into a binding contract as anyone else, but following the Coroners and Justice Act 2009, in order to prevent criminals 'profiting from the proceeds of crime', any profits (such as fees or royalties) derived from memoirs or other publications by criminals convicted of serious crimes may be recovered from them via Exploitation Proceeds Orders. It is understood that these will be directed exclusively at the assets of the prisoner concerned, without imposing any liability on the publisher

Those acting beyond their authority

Companies which enter into contracts for activities which are not within the company's objects as set out in its Memorandum and Articles of Association may well be acting *ultra vires*, or beyond their authority, and such contracts may be open to challenge, for example by the shareholders. For this reason, most Memoranda and Articles are drafted as widely as possible, but something clearly *ultra vires* may still be declared void. One way of avoiding this risk is to provide that the object of the company is to carry on business as 'a general commercial company' – since 1991 this authorises a company 'to carry on any trade or business whatsoever'.

Similarly, partners may not always have authority to bind a partnership in contracts unconnected with the partnership – such contracts may need to be ratified later on.

Employees who are allowed regularly to negotiate contracts such as publishing directors, or commissioning editors may, however, often be considered to have apparent authority to do so, and a contract made in good faith with such employees may well bind the company. Publishers should therefore bear in mind that if they give employees business cards describing them as 'Publisher' or 'Commissioning Editor' and send them off to the Frankfurt and Bologna book fairs and on commissioning tours around universities, they may well be bound by any apparently reasonable contract they may make (however strenuously the board or publishing committee may object later on).

Similarly, agents – such as commercial or literary agents – may in some circumstances also go beyond the scope of their authority, but (depending on their particular terms of appointment) most agents will have considerable implied authority to enter into reasonable contracts on behalf of their principals.

Finally, contracts entered into by bankrupts may not always be enforceable, unless affirmed by their trustee in bankruptcy. However, a contract – such as a royalty agreement – which produced *income* for a bankrupt (or his or her creditors) would almost certainly be affirmed.

THIRD PARTIES

Until November 1999, there was an established legal doctrine (known as privity of contract) that contracts could not be enforced against or enforced by third parties (those not party to the contract). Therefore, pre-1999, if a publisher contractually agreed with an author to pay all royalties to a friend of the author, the friend could not compel the publisher to pay the royalties to him, because he was not a party to the contract. These rules were the subject of much criticism.

Dissatisfaction about the situation led to the introduction of the Contracts (Rights of Third Parties) Act 1999, which created a wide-ranging exception to the doctrine of privity of contract. It provided (subject to exemptions such as employment contracts) that a third party could acquire rights under a contract, if, and to the extent that, the parties to the contract so intend.

The Act states that a third party will be able to enforce a term of the contract if:

- the contract expressly provides that he or she can do so; or
- it clearly identifies him or her (by name, description or class of persons) and the benefit conferred.

The effect of this legislation is that the 'friend' in the example above could use the Act to enforce his or her contractual right to payment against the publisher, as could any other third party promised a contractual benefit. This would clearly apply to literary agents who are entitled to a percentage of earnings in any publishing contract, although most agents have their own contracts under which they benefit directly as parties.

SUMMARY CHECKLIST: BINDING CONTRACTS

- Are both parties legally capable of entering into contracts?
- Has a clear agreement been reached between them?
- Has a specific offer been accepted (in substantially the same terms)?
- Did both parties intend the agreement to bind them legally?
- Is there valuable 'consideration' (however nominal)?
- Is the contract one which needs to be in writing (for example, if it is to include an assignment of copyright)?
- Might it be illegal, or against public policy?
- Might it be voidable, for example if entered into by a minor or someone acting beyond their authority?
- Is a specified third party entitled to a benefit under the contract, and, if so, is this what the contractual parties intended?

AUTHOR–PUBLISHER AGREEMENTS

STANDARD FORM AGREEMENTS

After all the discussions and pre-contract negotiations (and, possibly, the lunch) there will come a point of decision, yes or no: either the author or the publisher (or both) will decide they do not wish to take the idea any further after all, or both of them will decide that they are ready and willing to go ahead, and to commit themselves to do so by signing a formal publishing contract. They may already have agreed the basis of a deal (indeed, as we have seen above, they may already have a binding contract) but now they will want to confirm in legally binding terms what they have already agreed, and settle a number of other detailed matters at the same time. They will want an agreement that enables them to do two key things:

- to make mutual undertakings to each other ('I will write the book or supply the content if you publish it');
- to acquire rights (in the publisher's case, all the rights it needs to publish and exploit the work, and in the author's case the right – amongst other things – to a reasonable share in the proceeds).

Most publishers with any experience will have some kind of standard author agreement; in the case of a large publishing company it is likely to be a detailed printed or word-processed document of 20 or more clauses. It will, however, reflect that publisher's own experience: every clause will be there for a good reason, but it will – of course – be drafted from the publisher's point of view. This does not necessarily mean that it is unfair or unreasonable, but authors need to bear its origins in mind, and also the possibility that it was not drafted for the particular work (or even type of work) concerned. The Publishers Association maintains a Code of Practice on Author Contracts, which contains useful guidelines for book publishers (see below). Equally, most major literary agencies have their own standard author–publisher contracts, which not surprisingly are drafted much more with the author's interest in mind: for example, fewer rights are normally granted to the publisher, and the financial terms to the author are usually better. Whose version is used depends entirely on the relative negotiating strengths of the parties. A literary agent representing a successful author is likely to be in a strong position to deal on its own standard terms, whereas a publisher taking the risk of publishing an unknown author will prefer to use its own standard contract initially.

Dealing on the other side's standard terms can still represent a serious negotiating disadvantage, especially if detailed terms are not properly explained or understood. If in doubt, ask. If no satisfactory explanation is forthcoming, get a second opinion from your professional body, or from an independent lawyer with experience of publishing contracts. And, when dealing with any standard form contract, bear the following points always in mind:

- The law will enforce most reasonable agreements which reflect what both parties want (for the few exceptions, see above, p. 68).
- From a legal point of view, most clauses of most contracts are therefore fully negotiable.

THE STANDARD AUTHOR–PUBLISHER AGREEMENT

Most good publishing contracts deal with the same basic points, although sometimes in a different order and sometimes (as we have seen) from very different points of view. Some academic (particularly journal) authors prefer to license their works on 'Open Access' terms, using Creative Commons licences in use since 2002 which grant more liberal rights of 'non-commercial' use and re-use, and some UK and US academic and funding institutions demand that funded articles should be published, or made available via repositories, on primarily Open Access terms, at least initially. Needless to say, this may have a significant effect on the publisher's commercial market, although there is sometimes room for initial embargoes. Some scientific, technical and medical (STM) publishers now offer 'hybrid' agreements, with Open Access elements, with authors paying to make their work more widely accessible than usual, although the take-up of Open Access licences as a whole has been relatively small.

In the rest of this chapter we will follow the sequence of topics in the standard author–publisher agreement which is probably in most widespread use, the first precedent in Charles Clark's admirable source book, *Publishing Agreements* (eighth edition, 2010). Comparisons with other versions, such as agent's contracts, will be made as we go along. You may find it useful to refer to your own version at the same time. The latest edition of the Publishers Association Code of Practice on Author Contracts (2010) also deals with a number of e-publishing issues.

THE PREAMBLE: THE PARTIES AND THE WORK

It may sound rather obvious, but it is a good idea to say clearly right at the beginning of any publishing contract who you are and which precise publication you are talking about. Both sides are taking on significant legal obligations, so it is necessary to know who it is exactly who will be bound by those obligations. It is also essential to know how far those responsibilities extend, so 'the Work' needs to be clearly defined; whether it is a traditional book or journal, e-book or online service, it is often sensible to set out a precise specification (content, format, number of illustrations, etc.) in a separate appendix to the contract. Finally, although strictly speaking it is not legally necessary, if the contract is not already pre-dated it is highly desirable if the last person to sign the contract also *dates* it clearly so that everyone knows when the rights and obligations start to run (and, in some cases, when they finish). There might be difficult problems of evidence later on, otherwise.

The parties

The parties need to be carefully defined. In the case of 'the Author' (sometimes the 'Proprietor'; for example, where there is a literary estate) it is normal for the term to be defined to include the author's executors and (sometimes) administrators, where the author dies or becomes incapacitated, and also his or her 'assigns': we will deal with assignments below.

In the case of 'the Publisher' it is customary to include the publisher's successors in business, should the company be taken over (as has been known) and often also other related publishing imprints, so that a publisher will retain the option to publish the work under another imprint if that seems more appropriate at the time, but limited (usually) to subsidiaries, or imprints elsewhere in the same group.

'Assigns' and assignment

The parties are often defined to include their respective 'assigns'. As a general rule of law, either party to a contract may freely assign their rights under that contract (unless there is a specific provision in it to the contrary) but not their *duties*. The person to whom the rights are assigned (called 'the Assignee') may take over the entire benefit of the contract from the person doing the assigning ('the Assignor'): it is also possible, of course, to assign specific rights separately, such as the copyright. The author may wish to assign the benefit of the contract to a spouse or relative, or to a separate company (perhaps for tax reasons). Equally, the publisher may wish to assign copyrights or publishing licences under individual contracts, or whole lists of contracts, as part of a sale to another publisher in due course. If this is envisaged – or might be – it is important to make sure that the wording of the contract allows for this: the definition of both parties should include their respective 'assigns', and there should be no ban or undue restriction on assignments later on in the contract, unless this is what both parties want. A separate clause permitting (or prohibiting) assignment may often be the clearest solution.

Any continuing *duties* and obligations of either party may *not* generally be assigned without at least the implied consent of the other – particularly in a contract involving continuing skill and judgement on both sides, as with many publishing contracts. Either party may quite justifiably have reservations about the possibility of future assignment of continuing obligations by the other. The publisher may be unhappy about the author assigning any remaining personal obligations – for example, to take part in publicity or serial interviews, or to keep a reference work up to date – to a third party, or a company, less able to meet these obligations, and may require a letter of inducement from the author beforehand by way of reassurance. The author may have equal fears that any continuing obligations of the publisher – to promote and exploit the work effectively, for example, and pay royalties – may be assigned to a different company altogether, with less feel for the market or the work concerned and about which the author quite possibly has strong views. Where such personal obligations remain, it is always advisable (and may be essential) to obtain the express consent of the other party before any assignment, if this is possible. In many cases – such as the sale of a list – it is usually advisable to arrange for relevant contracts to be 'novated' (newly executed, and signed by the new parties), so that:

- the relevant rights are re-affirmed;
- the new publisher clearly takes over both the benefit and the burden of the contract.

Some agents' contracts include non-assignment clauses, usually towards the end of the contract, banning assignment by the publisher without the prior written consent of the author, sometimes with a proviso that such consent shall not unreasonably be withheld. This can make sense, but both parties should think carefully whether such restrictions on their future activities are in their long-term interests, particularly if the proposed restriction is not mutual, but affects only one side.

Acquisition of an entire company – usually by a purchase of shares – will not normally involve any individual assignments, and will therefore probably not be prevented by non-assignment clauses in individual author contracts.

RIGHTS GRANTED

From a publisher's point of view, one of the main objectives of an author contract is to acquire rights. By far the greatest part of a typical publisher's business consists in exploiting other people's copyright works, and that exploitation may cover many languages, forms and media and involve publishing activities in all corners of the globe: it is essential therefore that it should all be clearly licensed by the copyright owner. Every author contract should therefore make it clear who owns the copyright (is it the author, or the author's employer?), what publishing rights that owner grants to the publisher, which may be freely sub-licensed (there may be arguments, for example, about print on demand or e-books), and which formats (such as audio) may be subject to reversions if not exercised within a set period. Ownership of digital publishing rights, including Internet rights, is very important today, even if at first sight the work may not appear to have much immediate scope for digital exploitation, even as part of a larger database. It is prudent to consider at the outset who will be best placed to exploit such rights in due course, together with other key rights. Whether they are granted to the publisher, or reserved by the author or agent, the contract should make the position as clear as possible. This will ensure:

- that author and publisher (and the rest of the world) clearly know who controls which rights;
- that the publisher can safely sub-license individual rights to others;
- that rights can effectively be assigned or transferred;
- that all licensed activities can be protected legally against copyright infringers (around the world if necessary).

There are two ways for a publisher to acquire the publishing rights it needs:

(1) by obtaining an assignment of the entire copyright from the copyright owner; or
(2) by being granted a publishing licence – in terms wide enough to cover all the publishing 'activities' envisaged.

Full copyright or a licence?

It is more common for authors to retain their copyrights and for publishers to be their exclusive licensees, but there may be areas of publishing where an assignment of the full copyright makes sense if both sides agree – such as major works of reference, multimedia works or journals, often with hundreds of different contributors, where the publisher will want to retain overall long-term control. It may also be an issue in some territories in protecting the work against international piracy. In most other cases, however, a sole and exclusive publishing licence, drafted in wide terms if necessary (including a very robust clause allowing the publisher to take legal action if necessary), will probably meet most publishers' needs. It has been likened by a number of commentators to taking a lease of a house rather than buying the freehold – a long lease for all practical purposes will probably be just as valuable. Although the image is helpful, the analogy is not entirely accurate, since a freehold should last forever whereas copyright in most cases expires 70 years after the author's death. While the copyright lasts, however, a full assignment of it is the closest to a freehold a purchaser can get. And an assignment is generally irrevocable, while a licence can usually be revoked (for example for breach of its terms).

If a full assignment of copyright is needed, remember that in order to be effective under the 1988 Act it must be *in writing*, and *signed* by or on behalf of the copyright owner. Do not assume that just because an assignment letter has been sent off to the author a valid assignment has somehow magically taken place – it hasn't. Copyright will not be assigned until the author or their representative actually signs.

Sole and exclusive licences

If you grant someone the 'sole' right and licence to do something you are undertaking not to grant a similar licence to anyone else, but you are not necessarily ruling out the possibility that you may continue to do it yourself (although this has usually been implied). An 'exclusive' licence, on the other hand, is defined under the 1988 Act and clearly excludes not only other potential licensees but also the person granting the licence. An author granting both a sole and an exclusive licence to a publisher is therefore granting complete control of all the publishing activities listed. It is by far the most powerful right to have, short of a complete assignment, and under the 1988 Act gives such licensees in the UK the same rights and remedies against copyright infringers as if they were full assignees (we will look at remedies further in Chapter 9). Like assignments, however, exclusive licences must be in writing and signed by or on behalf of the licensor.

Scope of the licence

The activities licensed

In the process of publishing, the publisher will need to do a number of things which UK law treats as 'restricted acts', and which may only be done with the copyright owner's licence or permission. We will look at restricted acts more fully in Chapter 9, but – in due course – bearing in mind the 2001 EU Copyright Directive, a publishing licence now probably needs to include:

- the right to reproduce (which would cover copying);
- the right to communicate and make available to the public (which would include online access);
- the right to distribute (in hard copy form); and
- the right to license others to do the same.

Arguably, the traditional grant of rights to 'produce and publish' would cover at least the first and third of these, but in the light of recent case-law there may be some doubt about whether the second was fully included. If the parties wish, it may avoid uncertainty in due course to adopt updated wording similar to that above, which reflects not only the EU copyright regime, but also the international standards adopted by the WIPO Copyright Treaty 1996. It may be advisable to adopt a belt and braces approach and grant 'the right to reproduce, publish and distribute, communicate and make available to the public'. (Alternatively, if appropriate, the right to communicate and make available to the public could be left to a separate grant of subsidiary rights later on, and subject to different terms – see below.)

The right to make an 'adaptation' in forms specifically licensed may also be needed if, for example, translation rights are included. It is important that the licence should cover not only the work as a whole, but also any 'substantial part' of the work to be used, for example, in catalogues, advertising or on websites, since otherwise this may also be a copyright infringement. Again, we will discuss this more fully in Chapter 9.

There are other restricted acts, such as public performance of the work and rental right which are normally covered – if appropriate – under subsidiary rights (see below, p. 90).

Formats

The licence may cover 'all forms and media', which although not very specific at least makes the intention clear, or it may be restricted to 'volume' form or 'print rights' only (excluding audio or e-books, for example). 'Volume' rights normally include all the publisher's own hardback and paperback editions, including promotional, mail order and premium sales and book club sales, together with royalty-inclusive export sales of bound copies or sheets. Although there is no unanimously agreed definition of volume rights, the term quite probably also includes anthology, digest book and condensation rights, and may include other rights too which relate to exploitation of the verbatim text of the work as a whole (but see next paragraph).

All this must now be considered in the light of alternative methods of digital delivery, such as downloadable text or hand-held devices such as e-books and mobile phone apps. If the complete verbatim text is published or made available in this form, such exploitation might arguably be considered as part of the main volume rights, but publishers, authors and agents generally agree nowadays that it is necessary in such cases to have an express grant of rights, and even then perhaps only for a limited term. This is very likely to be an issue if the publisher wishes to license audio downloads, or to make the work available for online searching via Amazon's Search Inside or Google – this may be highly beneficial for both author and publisher, but it is very unlikely that such use (often involving digital access to the entire text) would fall under 'volume rights'.

At the time of writing, there have been no UK cases on this point, although two US cases may be instructive. In *Tasini v. The New York Times* (2001) the US Supreme Court held that publishers of 'collective works', such as newspapers and magazines who were publishing articles by freelance writers – usually without any signed contract or grant of rights – did not have the right to go on to exploit those articles in electronic databases. And in *Random House v. Rosetta Books* (2001), even where the publisher did have exclusive rights to publish a number of long-established authors 'in book form' it was held that this did not give exclusive rights over e-book exploitation of the same text.

Volume rights do not include other subsidiary rights such as audio or serial rights or film rights, but these, like electronic rights, are often the subject of additional specific grants of rights under the royalties and subsidiary rights sections (see below, pp. 88 and 90). It is absolutely crucial to make sure that all the forms and media in which publication is envisaged are included somewhere and that the parties agree who has the right to exploit the work in which formats; translation rights may be vital to travel books, for example, and merchandising rights to children's books – neither of these are included in volume rights. Publishers with experienced rights managers may be quite capable of exploiting such rights, but many agents prefer to retain them; it will be for the parties to decide who is best placed to control these rights. If in doubt, seek advice, or refer to Lynette Owen's indispensable guide: *Selling Rights*.

Languages

Licences often cover the English language only, but sometimes include all languages. The restriction to English only would deprive the publisher of the right to publish (or more likely to license) translations, unless translation rights are granted later on (see below, p. 93). Avoid confusing terms such as 'French rights' (which may be understood to mean France only) if what you want are (worldwide) French language rights. As in the section on Formats above, this should be clearly agreed.

Territories

Licences may be granted to publish worldwide (or even 'throughout the Universe', in order to remove any doubts about satellite broadcasting). Alternatively, they are often limited to specific territories of the world (ideally listed individually in a Schedule), but in some cases, of course, Internet publication may transcend such market divisions and worldwide licences may be more appropriate or even unavoidable. It is entirely for the parties to agree who is best placed to exploit the work in each part of the world – many publishers will have the capacity to exploit internationally, either online via the net or in hard copy, or the author or agent may prefer to retain some rights (for example North American or US rights) for themselves. Note, now, that exclusive UK rights are no longer exclusive if the rest of Europe (specifically, the EU and EEA) are open territories shared with other publishers: under the Free Movement of Goods Provisions in Article 28 of the Treaty of Amsterdam (see Chapter 13) a US edition lawfully on sale in (say) Belgium cannot be prevented from entering the UK. There may be other territories whose local copyright laws may make exclusivity difficult to enforce, such as Australia or New Zealand: if these territories are likely to be important to you, it may be worth taking further advice.

Duration

Finally, it is very important to specify clearly for how long the licence granted lasts. Many publishers will seek a licence for the full term of copyright (now, in the EU and USA, increased to 70 years after the author's death), and in the case of some works, especially textbooks or major reference works, the publishers may well need the life of several editions before the work will truly come into profit. If the full term of copyright is agreed, it is advisable to include not only the current term, but also any extensions, renewals and revivals (on Duration generally, see Chapter 2).

Some contracts provide for reviews after a specified term, but any comparisons or yardsticks should be clear. It will be for the parties to agree what suits them (and that particular work) best, but a publisher accepting a licence for a limited period should be aware of the risks of investing heavily in establishing a work (and perhaps an author) only to find that the licence, or part of it such as the paperback rights, terminates after 10 or 20 years.

DELIVERY, APPROVAL AND ACCEPTANCE

Delivery of the work is the author's primary responsibility under the contract, so the publisher will want to make sure:

- that it is actually delivered, in the required format and more or less on time;
- that, when it arrives, it accords with the contract;
- that any necessary revisions and improvements can be made, or – failing that – the contract can be terminated on a reasonable basis.

Equally, the author will want to see a fairly clear commitment to publish the work (and possibly within a given timetable) if it is delivered substantially as per contract, and that if things do go wrong there is a reasonable agreement about any advances and monies due and, particularly, that the rights can be reclaimed.

There are a number of other important considerations to bear in mind: not least, what amendments might be 'reasonable' in the light of what was agreed, and the author's moral rights, and how both author and publisher can disentangle themselves from the contract if the work as originally agreed clearly isn't going to happen. We will explore all these tricky issues – and some possible solutions – in more detail in Chapter 6, but when considering the contract wording itself, these are the points to bear in mind:

- In the event of a dispute, it is the wording of the contract which will prevail – so make it as clear and unambiguous as possible.
- Agree clearly the time and method of delivery (for example on disk) and what happens if it is late.
- If time is of the essence, say so: otherwise it is unlikely the publisher will be able to terminate the contract simply because the work is not in bang on time.
- Agree in advance any acceptance criteria. Refer if possible to known yardsticks: a requirement that the work 'shall conform to a reasonable extent to the specifications set out in the Appendix' (or possibly the synopsis) is fairly easy to pin down in any subsequent dispute, but beware generalised phrases like 'of a standard which might reasonably be expected' (by whom?), or other question-begging adjectives such as 'acceptable' or 'satisfactory'.
- Agree a specific procedure and a timetable for any revisions, and do not forget that the author will usually have a moral right of integrity (see Chapter 3).

- Consider the effects of termination: will the publisher retain an option, and will the author keep any advance (particularly if termination was not their fault)? The circumstances may be different, depending on whether the work was commissioned or not, and how much work in progress exists. It is also advisable to make it clear if (and how) the rights are to revert to the author; reversion is implied when a contract containing a licence is terminated, but the rights will not necessarily revert where there was an assignment, unless there is clear provision for this (probably by means of a formal re-assignment).

COMPETING WORKS

Many publishers' contracts contain non-competition clauses under which the author promises as long as the contract lasts not to undertake any other works which might reasonably be considered either to compete directly with the contract work or to 'affect prejudicially' its sales or other exploitation. These are often expressed to cover not only directly competing works, but also abridgements or expansions of the same material, if done without the publisher's consent. Such restrictions may be an obvious way of protecting the publisher's investment, particularly in the case of STM or professional content (less so for fiction or children's books), but they must be drafted tightly and not so widely that they would amount to a total ban on any further writing in the area: that would almost certainly be an unreasonable restraint of trade (see Chapter 13), which the courts might refuse to enforce (particularly if the publisher already had the option of suing for breach of an exclusive licence). This will particularly be the case where the author is an acknowledged expert in the area concerned: such a ban might prevent the author not only from developing his or her reputation and career, but quite possibly from earning a living. Many contracts get round this problem by specifically allowing authors to use their material for professional purposes, e.g. for training or seminars, or similarly for academics in their own teaching.

WARRANTIES AND INDEMNITIES

In publishing a work, a publisher takes a number of significant legal risks. If the work contains statements defamatory of other people, the publisher will be liable legally for publishing them just as much as the author; equally, if any material is obscene, it is the publisher who will be prosecuted, for publishing an obscene article. The wider the publication, the greater the risk, so a website or bulletin board accessible worldwide may require special vigilance. There are a number of other legal risks, which we will discuss fully in Chapters 7 and 9, and for this reason the publisher will normally require certain warranties and indemnities from the author to protect against them. This does not mean that the publisher should become complacent about the need for in-house vigilance and, if necessary, outside legal advice (such as libel reading), or the need for adequate insurance cover, but it is generally thought to be reasonable that the author (who after all knows the work better than anyone else) should either disclose any known risks or else warrant that the work is safe to publish.

Which warranties are sought, and which are given, is of course a matter for the parties to agree. Many publishers' standard contracts contain full lists of warranties – an agent's contract may contain only one or two. However few or however many there are, they should all be taken seriously. Breach of a warranty will probably not entitle the publisher to terminate the contract altogether (see p. 85), but it will provide an action for damages, so together with the indemnities which are usually required each warranty should give the author pause for thought.

The warranties most commonly given are these:

That the Author has full power to make the agreement

Not everyone has full legal capacity to enter into binding contracts – for example the mentally ill, children under 18, or those acting beyond their authority (for a full treatment see above, p. 70). The author's warranty on this point will give the publisher some protection against the risk of the contract subsequently being declared void.

That the Author is a qualifying person

Following the 1988 Act it is now common to seek a warranty that the author is at the material time a 'qualifying person' under section 154 of the Act. As we saw in Chapter 2 the work may qualify for copyright protection in the UK either on the basis of first publication here or in another qualifying country, or alternatively on the basis of the author's nationality or other status. Clearly, the place of publication is outside the author's control, but the author may be able to warrant that he or she is (for example) a British citizen or British subject, or domiciled or resident here, or a citizen of another EU member state: the full list of nationality and status qualifications is set out in Chapter 2.

That the Author is the sole author of the Work and owns the rights granted

It is important for a publisher that the author owns all the relevant rights, and that there are no rival claimants such as employers or joint authors. As a general rule, you cannot grant rights you do not own.

That the Work is original to the Author

A literary or artistic work will not be protected as a copyright work unless it is 'original'. Under UK law the standard of originality required is not very high (see Chapter 2), but there must be some evidence of skill and judgement, and individual effort. The author will not own the copyright unless that effort is his or her own effort – if anyone else's effort is involved there may be joint authors, or possibly a claim for copyright infringement (see below).

That the Work has not previously been published, or any of the rights previously assigned or licensed

As we saw in Chapter 2, first publication can be one basis for copyright protection and also, as we saw in Chapter 3, a claim for publication right, so it is important to know that there will be no rival claims from any previous publications. The warranty against previous publication is usually limited to the exclusive territories covered by the agreement, and often to the specific formats covered (such as volume form) although sometimes it covers any forms. It may be particularly important for the publisher to be reassured that the work has not already appeared on the Internet, or perhaps under Open Access conditions required by a research funding agency, or even within a local intranet, or is not about to: for many STM or academic works, such prior publication, particularly if free of charge, might significantly reduce any commercial market.

It will also be important to the publisher to know that an assignment or exclusive licence has not previously been diluted by the grant of some particular rights elsewhere: for example US rights or French language rights. Such previous grants or licences will normally survive any new agreement, and the new publisher's licence will be subject to them. So if it turns out that US rights have already been granted elsewhere, the new publisher will not have worldwide rights after all, but only worldwide rights minus the US rights previously granted. Authors (and agents) are usually therefore asked to warrant that no such previous grants have taken place.

That the Work does not infringe any existing copyright or other right

Since printing and issuing copies of a work to the public may be just as much a copyright infringement as copying, the publisher will be just as much at risk of any legal action as the author: this is therefore a fairly crucial warranty to seek. Ideally it should cover not only copyright infringement as such but also infringements of any other rights of third parties, which would include for example any breaches of the terms of any previous licence, or contract, or any breaches of confidentiality, or moral rights, or database right or any trade mark infringement. For some specialised works, such as medical textbooks, there may be a need for specific warranties relating to the moral right of privacy in certain private photographs or films, or in some cases (particularly where US photographs are involved) that necessary consents or clearances or patient releases have been obtained. Don't forget that there is now a developing law of privacy in the UK, and that there may be obligations of confidentiality, not just for revelations in celebrity books (ghost-written or otherwise) but also applicable more widely, e.g. to educational or academic authors. For more on this see Chapter 8.

That the Work contains nothing defamatory (or libellous)

This is a key warranty, and possibly now the most important of all, if only because of substantial damages awarded for libel by some juries (see Chapter 7). As with copyright infringement, the publisher will be equally at risk with the author for publishing any defamatory statement, and so might anyone else involved in the publication, such as editors, printers and distributors, as well as Internet service providers (although there may be defences of innocent dissemination, or temporary and transient copying). Defamation (which includes libel) is therefore a very serious risk indeed and should be actively borne in mind at all stages by author and publisher alike. A sober reading of Chapter 7 might be a useful starting point. Above all, if either of them has any reason to suspect that a particular passage may be defamatory – the author when writing, or the editor when editing – it cannot be stressed too strongly that the safest policy is to *tell someone*. If there is any doubt, it may make sense to have some passages (or the whole work) read for libel by a lawyer who knows about such things, and share the cost if appropriate. It is *infinitely* better to do this at an early stage than to run the risk of going ahead regardless and hoping no one will notice. Even though authors may rightly be concerned about the costs of libel reading, a good libel read is infinitely cheaper than the damages (and costs) risked by a libel action.

Is it reasonable that the author should bear the risk? The author knows better than anyone else whether (and where) there might be defamatory passages and is in the best possible position to do something about them. If they are not disclosed at the outset then it seems fair for the author to bear the resulting legal risk. Some agents' agreements seek to limit the author's liability to passages 'unknown to the publishers' – this very significantly dilutes the value of the author's warranty, and rather begs the question: 'When?'. There might well be an argument for sharing the risk if a libel is disclosed during the course of writing, or at least between delivery and proofs – when it still might be said the publisher has a realistic opportunity to do something about it – but if a libel only comes to light after the work has gone for press it may be thought that the author, not the publisher, should bear the risk.

It is, of course, possible to insure against the risk of libel (and other associated risks such as malicious falsehood), and many publishers now have comprehensive libel policies. It is also possible in some cases to add specific authors to the policy as coinsured. However, insurance premiums are increasingly expensive, and the level of cover is usually subject to a substantial excess and may not cover the largest awards. It seems likely that an author's warranty will be required for some time to come.

That it contains no obscene, blasphemous or otherwise unlawful material

Obscenity, like defamation, is a real risk in publishing and is not solely restricted to illustrated sex manuals: text can be obscene if it encourages drugs, or violence, for example, and the criminal penalties, including fines and imprisonment, can be severe (see Chapter 7). Consider also the risk of publishing 'indecent' material, particularly photographs of children. Blasphemy was until recently still an offence – although it is in the process of being abolished– and there are other possible offences such as seditious libels, incitement to racial hatred, or offences under the Official Secrets Acts which may well pose a serious legal threat to a published work. All these topics are dealt with fully in Chapter 7.

That all statements are true and that no formula, recipe or instruction will harm the user

This is a fairly wide-ranging warranty, but is particularly common in contracts relating to STM and consumer books. The warranty is normally restricted to all statements 'purporting to be facts' but is still quite a wide guarantee; authors often insert a proviso 'to the best of their knowledge and belief'. This may be acceptable in some circumstances: it still gives the publisher some reassurance that the author will at least have checked. Similarly, there is often a proviso that the warranty will only apply to recipes, formulae or instructions 'if followed accurately' (and perhaps also 'reasonably').

Indemnities

In most contracts, apart perhaps from those where a publisher commissions an author for what is known to be a high-risk venture, the warranties given are normally accompanied by an indemnity, under which the author undertakes to indemnify the publisher against any legal actions or claims, including associated costs and expenses, caused by breach of any of the warranties given (indeed, there is often a separate warranty that the book has not been and is not the subject of any claim, complaint or proceeding). Many contracts also provide for costs associated with claimed (as opposed to actual, or proved) breaches, which may equally involve significant costs and possibly out-of-court settlements. This may require some discussion between authors and publishers, since there may be cases where credible *prima facie* claims are made – but not proved – which the author may wish strenuously to resist but which the publisher (who has a publication to get out) will want to settle as quickly and cheaply as possible. It may also be a condition of some insurance policies – such as libel insurance – that the underwriter's views on whether to settle should prevail. Authors may feel that their publishers should defend them – and their honour – to the hilt in such circumstances, but sooner or later more commercial considerations may well prevail. It is usually wise to make express provision for alterations to be made on the advice of the publisher's legal advisers.

Finally, it is important that any warranties and indemnities should last for as long as the legal risks may continue to exist – which may be long after the book has gone out of print or the agreement itself has terminated. A sentence or a clause to the effect that 'the warranties and indemnities shall survive the termination of this agreement' will achieve this.

THE PUBLISHER'S RESPONSIBILITY TO PUBLISH

If the author's main responsibility under the contract is to deliver the work, the publisher's is to publish it (at the publisher's expense). A legal commitment to publish may arise even out of an informal, verbal contract (see *Malcolm* v. *OUP* above, p. 66) and a failure to publish may lead to an action for breach of contract. Most authors, for obvious reasons, will look for a written commitment before signing a publishing contract, although there may be circumstances in which author and publisher agree that the work will be delivered but not considered for publication until some later date – such agreements are probably not publishing agreements at all, but merely options.

Where a firm undertaking to publish is given, it is normal to include a proviso that this shall be unless prevented by circumstances beyond the publisher's control. A contract for a tie-in publication linked to a specific event, such as a TV series or a royal wedding, might also have a proviso giving the publisher the option not to publish if the event is called off – the payment clause, including the terms of any advances, will need to provide for this. It is also advisable to specify whether publication depends on timely delivery and what happens if the author fails to deliver on time. Many contracts nowadays specify initial formats, such as hardback and paperback, unless otherwise agreed.

A crucial issue may be whether the publisher undertakes to publish within a particular time-scale, and if so when. Topicality may be a key issue not only for current affairs publications but also for many professional or scientific texts, where the area covered is constantly changing (the law is a good example). On the other hand, the publisher will want some reasonable flexibility to launch new works at optimum times, and also to allow for necessary changes to the publishing programme. Twelve or 18 months from delivery (and perhaps 'acceptance' – see above) are both common undertakings, sometimes with a maximum period running from the date of the contract. Phrases not linked to any specific timetable, such as 'with reasonable promptitude' or (worse) 'within a reasonable period of acceptance' are not generally of very much effect, and it may be advisable to include a provision for the author to put the publisher on notice to publish after the author considers a 'reasonable period' has elapsed and terminate the contract and reclaim the rights if publication does not then take place within, say, six to nine months.

PERMISSIONS, ILLUSTRATIONS AND INDEX

Most publishing contracts contain provisions covering the inclusion of necessary extra materials, such as quoted extracts or illustrations, which the author may have taken from elsewhere and copyright in which is likely to be owned by other people. It is absolutely essential to make sure that copyright permission to reproduce such material is obtained before publication, and preferably before the work is delivered (if a realistic amount of time for the necessary – and frequently delayed – correspondence has been allowed), otherwise there may be a serious risk of copyright infringement. Note, however, that defences such as fair dealing may sometimes be available for quoted extracts (see Chapter 9).

It is equally important to ensure that the permission given actually covers all the formats, territories and languages in which the publisher intends to exploit the work, particularly online – the wording of any permission obtained should therefore follow as closely as possible the wording of the author's own grant of rights to the publisher (see above). With some copyright owners, this may require some negotiation, so allow plenty of time. If the permission offered falls short of what is required – a picture agency may only be prepared to grant rights to reproduce their image of a painting or a photograph in certain territories or language editions, for example, and there may also be a hire fee – then both author and publisher may need to reconsider whether that material can be used at all. It is not enough to write off to the copyright owners and then simply assume that permission will be given in due course: copyright owners are not obliged to license their material for use by others if they do not wish to. Bear in mind also that many permissions may extend only to one edition of the work – if a second edition, or e-book version, is planned, it may be necessary to renew the permissions. Note, finally, that adapting a copyright work, e.g. re-drawing 'after X's picture', is also likely to require permission.

Responsibility for arranging, and sometimes paying for, permissions is almost always the author's, although this is entirely a matter for agreement, and in appropriate cases (such as major works, anthologies or highly illustrated works) the publisher will often share the cost or sometimes take over the responsibility altogether. This may be particularly necessary if the publisher wants to acquire permission for electronic use, where the negotiations may be harder (and more expensive).

What, however, do you do if, despite the most diligent search, you cannot find the copyright owner to grant the permission you need? The strict legal answer currently is that you cannot use the material concerned (unless your use may count as fair dealing, dealt with in Chapter 9). This is not exactly helpful, and publishers, librarians and licensing bodies have been discussing possible solutions for this problem of 'orphan works' with the UK government and the EU Commission for some time. There have been suggestions for an overall copyright exception for orphan works, but at the time of writing it seems more likely that approved orphan works licences will be established, based on diligent search, and operated by existing licensing bodies.

As to indexes, some authors prefer to do their own, but good indexing is a professional skill in itself, and a tired author is not always the best indexer. Where the index is particularly important to the success of the work (as for example with a major work of reference) the contract should provide expressly for the kind of index required, when it should be supplied and who should do the work (and – if an outside indexer is required – who should pay their fee).

PRODUCTION, PROMOTION AND PROOFS

All matters relating to physical production, promotion and sale of the work are normally reserved for the publisher's sole discretion and control, although in many cases a publisher will be willing to consult authors on matters of taste or style such as illustrations or jacket design. If the contract includes specific author promotion commitments, often for a set number of days, expenses are normally met by the publisher. The key commercial issue of the price is usually for the publisher alone to decide, although the author may wish to be consulted on this as well as on the publication date itself, perhaps with a provision that the publisher's decision shall be final or that consent will not unreasonably be withheld.

Editorial changes to the work itself (beyond 'house-style' amendments already agreed, or specified in the contract) may not normally be made without the author's consent, particularly if they might amount to derogatory treatment and thus infringe the author's moral right of integrity (see Chapter 3). Where individual authors do not have the final say over editing (e.g. as part of a multi-author team) it will be advisable for the publisher (or, more likely, the work's editor) to make sure each author is credited appropriately (for more on these moral rights issues, see Chapter 3). Publishers will usually provide proofs, but will want an undertaking from the author that they will be returned within a reasonable time (14 or 21 days are typical) and, if not (if the author is away, or ill, for example), that the publishers may pass them for press themselves.

Alterations to proofs made by the author above an agreed level (usually 10 to 15 per cent of the cost of composition) are usually charged to the author or deducted from royalties.

ROYALTIES AND ADVANCES

As we have seen, unless a contract is made under seal, or executed as a Deed, it must be supported by valuable 'consideration' (see above, p. 65). Although the publisher's undertaking to publish may in some circumstances count as adequate consideration, the consideration most authors want to see is money. This may be in the form of a one-off fee but is more often expressed as a royalty on sales. This has the advantage for the publisher of minimising the upfront risk (if no sales are made, no royalties will be paid) and it has the potential advantage for the author of a direct financial link with any success the work might have: the better it sells, the greater the rewards the author will get (particularly if the royalty rate itself increases, via a sliding scale). There is often provision for a payment on account, in the form of an advance.

Needless to say, money can be a fertile source of author–publisher disputes (particularly where the contract is not as clear as it should be) but it is beyond the scope of a book like this to suggest financial terms; such commercial issues are matters for the parties to negotiate, in circumstances which may vary widely. From a purely legal point of view, there are perhaps only two golden rules:

- Be sure both sides fully understand all the terms being proposed (including the likely effect of discounts, and the meaning of phrases like 'net receipts').
- Be absolutely clear about what is finally agreed.

For good specialist commentaries see Clark's *Publishing Agreements* or Lynette Owen's *Selling Rights*. Issues which tend to crop up most frequently include the following.

Advances

Publishers are not legally obliged to give advances (unless they have contracted to do so, of course) but many do. Advances are normally regarded as payments on account of all future royalty earnings (royalty and subsidiary rights), and are recoupable from the author's royalty account in due course; a large advance may therefore take some time to be earned back, before positive royalties start being paid – 50 per cent of the author's anticipated royalty earnings from the publisher's first printing is not untypical, although of course advances vary widely depending on the type of publication, the status of the author and the presence or absence of a literary agent.

It is advisable to make it clear in the agreement whether outstanding advances already paid are to be repaid by the author if, for example, the work is never delivered (or is delivered but rejected) or, in some cases, as a prerequisite to reversion of rights.

The editions and sales avenues covered

Make sure *all* likely editions and routes to market are covered somewhere. The most common categories for volume sales are:

- *'Home' full-price hardback*: the publisher's own hardback. 'Home' may mean the UK and Ireland, or possibly now the EU and EEA (see Chapter 13). This is the 'base royalty' and is often calculated on a sliding scale.
- *Home cheap hardback*: a publisher's hardback at two-thirds or less of the full price: usually with a lower royalty.
- *Home trade paperback*: the publisher's own paperback: royalties are normally lower, but print-runs can be much higher. Again, sliding scales might apply.
- *Home mass-market paperback*: either issued by the publishers or licensed to a paperback house – smaller format, lower price, and even lower royalties – but even bigger print-runs. The author's consent may be required for this kind of sale, perhaps not unreasonably to be withheld.
- *Export editions*: export versions of all four home categories above – usually based on net receipts, often sold at discounts of 60 per cent or more, and with correspondingly lower royalty rates.
- *Small reprints*: usually 1,000 to 1,500 or less (or 5,000 to 7,500 for paperbacks). Since small reprints are often uneconomic, the publisher often reserves the right to offer a lower royalty – often the lowest of the above rates. In order to prevent regular small reprinting, some contracts provide that the publisher may only do this once in any 12-month period, and not less than two years after publication. However, modern print-on-demand technology is making small reprints less necessary or reasonable, although issues are already arising between authors and publishers about appropriate royalties for print-on-demand sales, and what relation the price should bear to the main editions.
- *Promotional and premium sales*: special editions, often under a different imprint, as part of someone else's promotion or special offer: this could mean cornflake packets, so the quantities may be high but royalties will be at low rates. The author may have strong views about this kind of sale: prior consent is advisable.

- *Book club sales:* normally regarded as 'volume' sales, although not usually in the publisher's imprint. Discounts given to book clubs can be very high indeed, but they are generally felt to be a positive extension to the publisher's own market. Authors may well have views about book club editions, and consent (or at least prior consultation) is often written into the contract.
- *E-book sales:* sales in e-book format are now dealt with under volume rights, involving delivery of the complete verbatim text via a website to an individual purchaser in digital form, downloadable on to a PC or a handheld device. It is wise for any contract to define what is or is not an e-book sale. They should be contrasted, for example, with e-versions (such as adaptations), which are usually not like for like reproductions. Royalties are under continuing discussion in the industry. For other digital exploitation, see subsidiary rights, below.

The basis of royalty calculation

It is essential to be clear in the contract how each given royalty percentage is calculated: are home hardback sales at 10 per cent (say) based on the UK published price, or are they 10 per cent of the net receipts (which normally means income actually received, or recommended retail price less any discount)? This can make a large difference to the sums the author will get if a significant proportion of the publisher's sales are likely to be at high discounts. Export sales are often at 60 per cent to 70 per cent discounts: bear this in mind if, say, the US market is going to be important. Equally important: is Europe home or export? Home sales may often also be at comparatively high discounts, if via major chains of bookshops: 50 per cent to 60 per cent is not unusual. Mail-order sales are sometimes at discount, but often at a heavily reduced retail price.

Both publisher and author need to be clear about the likely markets and the probable basis of sales to each; it is infinitely better to sit down and talk about it, and eliminate any misunderstanding, at the outset, rather than wait for unpleasant surprises in the first royalty statement.

Free copies

Royalties are not usually paid on copies given away in the interests of promoting the work (such as review copies), or lost or damaged copies. It may be necessary to seek author consent for copies sold at cost or less in the first year, and copyright owners often ask for a voucher copy.

SUBSIDIARY RIGHTS

What are they?

Non-volume rights, such as TV or merchandising rights, are usually grouped together in a publishing contract under the generic heading of '**subsidiary rights**'. A typical full list is given below. The division is not very precise, and many of the rights (such as electronic and book club rights) may appear confusingly under both volume and subsidiary rights: perhaps the most useful distinction to keep in mind is that, generally speaking:

- Volume rights license the publisher's own publishing (usually in return for royalties).
- Subsidiary rights give the publisher the right to sub-license exploitation by others (for a share of proceeds).

So in the case of electronic rights, the publisher might want both: the right to sell its own e-book or online versions, and also the right to license digital use by others, for example as part of a database, or to be accessed as part of search engines such as Amazon and Google. In all such cases, express author consent is very likely to be needed.

The grant of rights

As with the main grant of rights clause (see above), the first and most important thing to check in a subsidiary rights clause is: does it actually grant the rights required? This may be crucial, because the main *grant* of rights clause may cover volume rights only, and may make no mention of subsidiary rights – so unless the particular rights the publisher wants are separately granted here, the publisher may not get them. The actual words 'the Author hereby grants' (the rights concerned) should ideally appear, preferably shortly followed by 'to the Publisher'. Simply listing some subsidiary rights, with some agreed percentages, may not be enough (although a limited grant of rights may be implied).

Ensure that the rights are granted in the correct terms – so that they cover the required formats, territories, languages (where appropriate) and period of time, and (crucially) that they are expressly stated to be 'exclusive' if that is what author and publisher want. A grant of rights will be regarded as non-exclusive unless it is expressly stated to be exclusive (and signed by the author).

Authors' consent

Some grants of subsidiary rights may be conditional upon the publisher first securing the author's consent before exploitation can take place, or at least consulting him or her; this may apply to the whole list of rights, or be a specific requirement of certain rights only – electronic rights, book club, digest and condensation rights are frequent examples. To get round the publisher's need to do some deals quickly in the author's absence, some contracts require consent only 'wherever practicable'; in other cases, where the author is available but they can't agree, there may be a provision that the author's consent 'shall not unreasonably be withheld'. Ultimately, it is a question of bargaining position, and who wants to retain effective control – and who is best qualified to use it, particularly where the whole or majority of the text is involved. Author consent is not normally required for low-income exploitation, such as anthology and quotation use, or use by print-handicapped people (see later).

Waivers of moral rights

Contracts now often include a conditional waiver of the author's moral right of integrity (or an agreement to waive it in the future), insofar as it may be required in order to exploit the subsidiary rights. Film and TV deals often require this flexibility. On moral rights generally, see Chapter 3.

The list of rights

Subsidiary rights most frequently dealt with include the following:

- *First serial rights:* the right to publish an extract or series of extracts in a newspaper or magazine on or before (or commencing on or before) publication – these can be extremely valuable, both to sales of the work and to the circulations of the periodicals concerned, and are often optioned. If a newspaper wishes to offer access to the work via its website the terms – and timing – for this should be specifically agreed.
- *Second and subsequent serial rights:* serial rights exercised *after* publication has taken place – these are normally less valuable (whenever the licence was signed).
- *Anthology and quotation rights:* some quotations may count as fair dealing for the purposes of criticism and review, if accompanied by sufficient acknowledgement, and copyright permission need not therefore be sought (see Chapter 9) – these rights cover all other substantial quotations and extracts.
- *Digest rights/digest book condensation rights:* these are, respectively, the right to publish an abridgement of the work in a single issue of a newspaper or periodical, and the right to publish an abridgement in separate volume form. They are sometimes grouped together under 'condensation rights', for both magazines and books.
- *One-shot periodical rights:* the right to publish the complete work in a single issue of a newspaper or periodical. These are also now regarded as part of volume rights, following *Jonathan Cape Ltd* v. *Consolidated Press Ltd* (1954).
- *Licensed paperback rights:* for paperback editions sub-licensed to another publisher.
- *Hardcover and educational reprint rights:* the rights to publish straight hardback reprints (in someone else's library series, for example) and educational reprints, usually annotated.
- *Book club rights:* for dealings with book clubs, see Chapter 5.
- *US rights:* the USA may be a major market: these rights may be sold directly or via an agent. They will usually take the form of a straightforward licence to

publish, for a royalty on the US price plus – usually – an advance, or will accompany a sale of bound stock or sheets (or a co-edition) and be dealt with under volume rights (see p. 78). Permissions may need to be re-cleared for US editions.

- *Strip cartoon rights (also known as picturisation rights):* the right to make such visual adaptations may be highly valuable, particularly for children's books and for Manga adaptations (graphic novels).
- *Translation rights:* these may be licensed separately, or accompany a co-edition deal for bound copies in the foreign language concerned: in either case, the foreign publisher will be responsible for arranging a translation of a satisfactory standard, and will normally pay an advance and a royalty (see Chapter 5). Note that the territories covered should be made clear: a Portuguese translation may sell more copies in Brazil than in Portugal.
- *Dramatisation and documentary rights:* usually cover theatrical, radio and TV rights to the work in dramatised form.
- *Single-voice readings:* the right to read extracts directly from the work, either on radio or TV or as part of other public performances. A *Book at Bedtime* is a good example. These rights may need to be cleared separately with the author.
- *Film rights:* if Hollywood is likely to be interested, it is important to ensure that these rights are effectively exploited. If the publisher is not best placed to do this, the author or agent may wish to reserve these rights themselves (for exploitation of film rights, see Chapter 5).
- *Audio and video rights:* audio cassettes or CDs, often spoken by famous actors, are a growing market. Video rights were often dealt with separately from the film rights. These rights used to be combined under the heading 'mechanical reproduction rights' and included CDs, analogue and digital tapes but nowadays more often refer to licensed downloads. Given the speed with which formats are replaced nowadays, such clauses now usually extend the right not only to formats known at the time but also to 'those hereafter invented'.
- *Merchandising rights:* the right to exploit titles or characters from a successful work can be as profitable, if not more profitable, than the work itself. It is therefore worth making sure that these rights are included if required, particularly for children's books, although agents may often prefer to withhold these. They are often associated with film rights; indeed, merchandising rights achieved some kind of apotheosis in the film of *Jurassic Park* when the T-shirts and other merchandise actually featured in the film itself. On the exploitation of merchandising rights, see Chapter 5. Titles, logos and characters with merchandising potential should also normally be registered as registered trade marks (see Chapter 10).
- *Electronic publishing rights:* it is important to distinguish between the publisher's own electronic exploitation of the work (for example, as an e-book) and other, sub-licensed, exploitation (such as an e-version). Older contracts may not make this distinction, and may group 'electronic rights' together (although that phrase has little meaning today). Until recently, the publisher's own e-book exploitation of the verbatim text of the complete work might have been dealt

with under volume rights (on this, see the section on Formats, above), while digital exploitation, use or access sublicensed to others such as via an online database, aggregator or research engine, or access via a site licence might fall under subsidiary rights. It is likely now that in both cases author consent will be highly desirable, and possibly essential. At the time of writing, there have been few (if any) UK cases on this issue, although two interesting US cases are noted in the section on Formats, above.

Exploitation and uses which may need to be considered separately are set out in Chapter 5. Whatever form of digital use or access is required, or envisaged, it cannot be stressed too strongly that there is no substitute for a clear grant of specific rights each time. The author's, or agent's, consent is likely to be required (or at least be strongly advisable) for some forms of exploitation, particularly digital, and care should be taken to ensure that the author's moral rights are not infringed. Some electronic rights may only be available for limited terms, or may require renegotiation after, say, three years. Financial terms currently vary widely.

- *Reprographic reproduction rights:* photocopying is still a fertile source of copyright infringement in the UK, but collective licensing schemes run by bodies such as the Copyright Licensing Agency are now more widely available, and are beginning to include digital rights. Collective licensing is also likely to provide solutions in areas such as orphan works (see p. 87).
- *Non-commercial rights for the print-handicapped:* Braille, or tape (or computer) recorded copies for the Royal National Institute for the Blind and other registered blind users have usually been licensed free of charge by the publisher. A licensing scheme for organisations representing visually impaired people (such as the RNIB) to make 'accessible copies' on their behalf was established by the Copyright Licensing Agency in 2003 following the Copyright (Visually Impaired Persons) Act 2002. Joint scoping and pilot schemes are under discussion between RNIB and rightsholders to find a secure and viable method of using publishers' own digital files to provide quicker accessible copies of the titles visually impaired people most often need, and if possible distribution of copies to other EU member states (and perhaps internationally) via trusted intermediaries.

All other rights are reserved

Any rights not expressly set out in the agreement are normally taken to be retained by the author: there is often an express provision making this clear. This used to include public lending right, which under the Public Lending Right Act 1979 is given solely to the author (on PLR generally, see Chapter 3), but since PLR was extended to audio and e-book versions under the Digital Economy Act 2010 such use, and any conflict with the publisher's own audio and e-book sales, may now need discussion.

SALES STATEMENTS, ACCOUNTING AND VAT

Publishers' royalty statements have been the subject of grim humour for as long as anyone can remember, but most publishers now have computerised royalty systems to keep track of royalties and other rights revenue, and many now pay their authors twice a year rather than the traditional annual payment. Educational and academic publishers still tend to pay annually, however, as do some professional imprints. Payment – when it comes – should normally be no longer than three months after the relevant accounting date (usually 30 June and/or 31 December).

Small credits, say £50 or less, are often carried over to the next accounting period. It is also common for the publisher to keep a reserve against returns on the first account – stock apparently sold to bookshops, but then returned under normal sale or return terms later on. The publisher normally then evens out the account on the third or fourth account. Ten per cent to 25 per cent for hardbacks and 15 per cent for audio is not unusual, and some reserves (usually for paperbacks) can be as high as 30 per cent, but returns are lower in children's publishing. However, there is often provision, particularly in agents' contracts , that any significant subsidiary rights revenue should be paid out as agreed to the author within 30 days of receipt, provided any advance has been earned back. This may be subject to a minimum, such as £200, and may be dependent on request.

Royalty statements themselves should be as clear and informative (and accurate) as possible: avoid (hopefully, ironic) contracts that say 'The Publisher will make up statements of sales'. With the best will in the world, however, computer errors can still occur (as anyone who has a bank account will know) so most contracts provide that the author – or his or her appointed representative – may examine the publisher's accounts in person during normal business hours. Who bears the costs of this normally depends on whether, and to what extent, errors are actually found. Five per cent is normally the maximum error allowable.

Authors who are registered for VAT will be required to notify the publishers and supply them with their VAT number: by agreement with Customs and Excise (which collects VAT), royalty statements can be treated as the author's tax invoices and VAT is added in the normal way.

There is sometimes provision for interest to be payable to the author on late payment by the publisher – it is worth bearing in mind now that interest is often specified by the Payment of Commercial Debts (Interest) Act 1998.

COPYRIGHT

Where the author assigns the full copyright to the publisher, this should be set out in clear wording under the main grant of rights clause (see above). But even where the author retains the copyright, this should still be made clear here, and some special words are still advisable. As we have seen (above) the Berne Convention forbids formal registration requirements of any kind, but it is still advisable for copyright protection under the Universal Copyright Convention (UCC) that a copyright claim should be printed on all copies of the work, and all licensed editions, containing the following information:

- The letter C in a circle (©) now a worldwide copyright symbol;
- The name of the copyright owner;
- The year of first publication.

There is no stipulation in the UCC that the information should be printed in any particular order but it is customary to print it thus:

© Hugh Jones and Christopher Benson 2011

The word 'copyright' is sometimes also printed before the ©, although this is not strictly necessary.

UK works have carried the UCC symbol for many years, because prior to its joining the Berne Convention in 1989 the USA belonged to the UCC but not Berne: the printed notice above was therefore essential to secure copyright protection in the USA. Since 1989 this has no longer been necessary for US protection, but there are still some countries which belong only to the UCC, and UK works should therefore keep the notice. It is also convenient to combine it with any assertion of the author's moral right of paternity (see Chapter 3), and a contractual undertaking to print such an assertion is now common. For the fullest protection of the right of paternity it is also advisable to include a term to the effect that such assertions will also be a condition of any sub-licences, together with the copyright notice itself.

COPYRIGHT INFRINGEMENT

We will deal with this more fully in Chapter 9: suffice it to say here that the publisher will necessarily bear the burden of protecting the work, once published, against pirates and other copyright infringers around the world, and where the author retains the copyright the publisher will therefore need clear authority from the author, as copyright owner, to do so. Exclusive licensees under the 1988 Act have the right to take legal action and join the copyright owner as a party to any action in the UK (on giving an indemnity against costs), but it is still advisable to confirm this in the contract. It also gives the author and publisher the opportunity to agree on the practical control of any such legal action (including the terms of any compromise or settlement), whether the author is required in any way to contribute to the costs and, if so, whether the author will receive a corresponding share of any net damages.

AUTHOR'S COPIES

Most publishers will give authors at least six personal copies of their works, plus one or two copies of each sub-licensed edition (such as translations or US editions).

Different arrangements may apply for audio and e-books. Some are more generous than others; it is usually a question of publishing economics. Additional copies, not for resale, are usually available at a discount (but like any trade customer, the author may need to haggle over these). Agents may also require copies.

REVISION OF THE WORK

With some kinds of works, such as educational, professional and reference texts, keeping the work up to date once published is almost as important as publishing it in the first place. In such cases author contracts will usually contain a clause requiring the author to prepare new editions when they become necessary. Some works may also require one-off updates, for example on publication of a paperback edition of an autobiography, in which specific agreement will need to be reached on this. It may be appropriate to provide for a fresh advance to be agreed at that time. It is prudent also to give the publisher the option of commissioning some other (competent) person to do the work of updating, should the author be unwilling or unable to do so (for example, through illness or death). The fees payable to such persons will then be deducted from the royalties payable to the author, or the author's estate – quite reasonably. It may be worth considering alternative revisers, if time – and cost – allow.

Who decides when new editions are required? This may be an important issue, and it is worth checking the wording of the contract to see what it says. Often the decision is for the publisher alone to make, or sometimes dependent upon mutual agreement – the author is unlikely to be in a position to insist. This perhaps is fair enough (it would be unreasonable to force a publisher to publish against its will and arguably unenforceable anyway), but if more regular new editions (or a more flexible system) are likely to be needed this should be agreed at the outset.

REMAINDERS

Remaindering is a sensitive issue, but most publishers know when a book has ceased to have any further sales potential and may want the power to remainder their remaining stock. Some agents' contracts forbid this within a specified period without the author's prior written consent: where this is not practicable it may be equally effective to ensure that, while the publisher retains the option to remainder, the author will at least have (say) 30 days' notice, and the right to purchase part or all of the remaining stock at the expected remainder price (which will probably be fairly low, as will any royalty). Publishers should bear in mind that such a clause is fully enforceable, like any other clause of the contract, so if they fail to notify the author and remainder the book regardless they may face an action for damages for breach of contract. This was confirmed in one case, where a lecturer won damages against Cassell for breach of such a clause, on the grounds that she had been deprived of the (very real) chance to sell the books cheaply herself to her own students.

TERMINATION OF THE CONTRACT, AND REVERSION OF RIGHTS

Just as it is essential that rights granted should be granted for a specific period of time, so it is equally important that any grounds for early termination should be clearly set out. In the early clauses governing delivery and acceptance (see above) the publisher is normally given grounds for termination of the contract if the work does not come in at all, or is unacceptable when it does – it is therefore in the author's interests to have similar grounds for termination if the *publisher* breaches any terms of the contract later on – for example, by not paying royalties on time, or allowing the work to go out of print.

All rights granted should revert to the author. However, termination of the head contract, and reversion of rights, are usually without prejudice to any sub-licences or other contracts properly entered into while the agreement was in force, or any outstanding claims or monies owing. It may seem reasonable for the publisher to continue to benefit from remaining sub-licensing income where termination results from the work going out of print, but less so where termination results from breach of key terms such as royalty payment.

The most common grounds for termination and reversion are:

- Material breach by the publishers of any terms of the contract (such as failure to publish), and failure to remedy the breach within a specified period (one to three months is normal).
- Insolvency of the publisher's business (or a substantial part of it) – including administration, receivership, winding-up and (in some cases) arrangements with creditors.
- Failure by the publishers to keep the work from going out of print (and failure to reprint after a given period of notice). It is important to agree what 'out of print' means – does this refer only to the publisher's hard copy edition? With print-on-demand technology, works may effectively be available and 'in print' for ever. For some specialist, slow-moving works this may suit both parties well; in other cases it may be advisable to consider termination and reversion of rights when sales fall below a certain level (for, say, two successive years).

OPTIONS

There is a school of thought that no option clause is enforceable. This is not strictly true – but a future option for no fixed consideration ('on terms to be agreed', for example) may be difficult to enforce. Generally speaking, the more specific the option, the easier it will be to enforce legally. A sweeping option over the author's next six works may be extremely difficult to enforce, and may well be in restraint of trade if it unduly restricts the author's future writing (see above), but an option on the next one or two defined works (of fiction, say, or for children) and on specified terms (such as 'the same terms', or 'terms no less favourable') may well be enforceable and bind the author.

It makes sense to provide a clear timetable for the publishers to exercise the option, and provide for the author's freedom to go elsewhere if they do not (or if they cannot agree terms).

MORAL RIGHTS

This may be a suitable place to include an assertion of the author's moral right of paternity, as required under section 78 of the 1988 Act. The paternity right – the right to be credited as the author – is the only moral right which needs to be asserted (in writing) under UK law before it can be enforced: on this generally, see Chapter 3. The author's right of integrity – to prevent derogatory treatment – must also be borne in mind when arranging abridgments or adaptations, and prior consent may be advisable, in the absence of a waiver.

AGENCY

Where an author is represented by a literary agent, the agent's standard contract will usually contain a clause authorising the agent to receive all monies payable under the contract on behalf of the author. Even if an agent's contract is not used (under which the agent will normally be a party) it is still possible for agents to benefit under author–publisher contracts, following the Contracts (Rights of Third Parties) Act 1999. Since authors and agents do occasionally fall out, any contract should also specifically provide that payment to the agent would be a good and valid discharge of the debt – so that the publisher, having paid royalties to the agent in good faith, will not then get embroiled in arguments about payment of the agent's commission later on. It is not generally necessary or advisable to sign an irrevocable appointment or authorisation: if an author wishes to revoke that particular payment arrangement, and be paid direct, he or she should be perfectly entitled to do so. There may then be a separate contractual dispute between author and agent about the agent's commission, but there is no reason why the publisher should become involved in that. There is a long-standing trade practice among literary agents that an agent will expect commission on *all* monies payable to the author under contracts which that agent negotiated – even long after the agent's appointment has been terminated. Such matters are entirely dependent on the author's contract with the agent: see Chapter 5.

RESERVATION OF TITLE

Although this is implied, it is advisable to make it clear that no rights or licences or other interests are granted to the publisher other than those specifically set out and granted in the contract. A provision to this effect is often usefully included at the end of subsidiary rights clauses.

ASSIGNMENT OR NON-ASSIGNMENT

Many agents' contracts contain non-assignment clauses, which forbid any assignment of the benefit and burden of the contract to any third party without the author's consent: sometimes the objection is waived in the case of third parties who are at the same time acquiring the whole or a substantial part of the publisher's business. Non-assignment clauses may seriously restrict the future value of the rights granted and the publisher's capacity to deal with them commercially, and should be carefully considered. The (significant) implications are discussed above.

ARBITRATION

Many publishing contracts contain provisions for arbitration in the event of any disputes. It is important to recognise that because such provisions are deemed to be distinct and separate from the main contract (even if they are contained in a clause embedded in the contract), generally such clauses will survive the termination of the contract. Therefore, both author and publisher will continue to be bound by an arbitration clause, even after the contract itself has come to an end. If one party unilaterally terminates the contract, the other party may (equally unilaterally) invoke the arbitration clause. Both parties should therefore consider how they would actually want any disputes to be resolved before agreeing to such a clause.

The Arbitration Act 1996 has consolidated the previous legislation (Acts of 1950 and 1979) and applies to all arbitration proceedings commenced after 31 January 1997. References to arbitration are of two kinds: conventional (where the parties agree to refer any dispute to a mutually agreeable tribunal and not to a court) and statutory (where the Act lays down default provisions where the parties have not decided on the mechanics of the arbitration procedure). The Act encourages the former approach and generally will not interfere where the parties make their own arrangements by written agreement.

There are a number of arbitration methods. In some cases each party will appoint their own arbitrator, and agree to be bound by the decision of those two people, or (if they cannot agree either) a third arbitrator who they appoint (called their 'referee' or 'umpire'). Where the dispute can be reduced to written submissions, without any (or much) need for oral hearings, such arbitrations can be relatively quick and inexpensive. A full-scale arbitration including hearings with lawyers on both sides, can however be just as expensive as a High Court action – indeed, more so, since the parties will have to pay for the arbitrators whereas judges are free. Following the civil justice reforms under Lord Woolf, even High Court actions are now expedited so that there is more pressure on the parties to settle, and small claims in the County Court can be relatively straightforward

The Publishers Association offers a confidential Informal Arbitration Procedure, where both parties agree, which can be quick and inexpensive, except in very complex cases, but there is as yet no industry-wide arbitration scheme for publishing as a whole.

GOVERNING LAW AND JURISDICTION

It is essential to make it clear which country's laws will govern the interpretation and enforcement of the contract. For most UK publishing contracts it will be advisable for this to be English law: note that Scots law is a separate legal system and may require separate advice.

Bear in mind that a contract offered by a foreign publisher is likely to specify their law as the applicable law – in the case of a US co-edition, for example, this may mean that the relevant state law (such as Delaware, or New York) will govern the contract, and any disputes arising under it.

If no applicable law is specified in the contract itself, there are statutory rules which UK courts will apply. As a general rule, they will apply the law with which the contract is most closely connected: in the context of publishing contracts this will usually mean the law of the party who is primarily to perform the contract. In the case of contracts entered into since 1991, if the contract is entered into in the course of a trade or profession, it is presumed that it is most closely connected with the country where the party who is to effect the performance which is characteristic of the contract has, at the time of conclusion of the contract, [its] . . . principal place of business (or, if the contract is to be effected through a secondary place of business, *that* place of business). If the contract is for a UK-based publisher to (say) supply sheet stock to New York, UK law will prevail. If it is for the New York based publisher to perform, New York State law will apply.

It is important to note that whose law applies is a different issue from whose courts have jurisdiction to hear the case. UK courts regularly hear cases involving issues of New York or other foreign laws. A good contract should always therefore provide for whose courts will have jurisdiction; in most cases, preferably UK (or English) courts.

In the absence of any express provision, there are complex rules governing the right of UK courts to assume jurisdiction over a dispute. These vary, depending among other things on whether the defendant is based inside or outside the EU.

The Brussels Convention on Jurisdiction (which was not binding Community law) was replaced in December 2000 with a binding EU Regulation on Jurisdiction, Recognition and Enforcement to ensure that rules of jurisdiction and enforcement of judgments are dealt with consistently in the EU. The Regulation broadly confirmed the 'country of origin' principle embodied in the E-Commerce Directive that persons (including companies) domiciled in member states must be sued in their own courts. However, this was subject to certain exceptions. For example, in contracts for the sale of goods or delivery of services (including website services), consumers (or others) could sue in the courts of the place of performance of the contract. This would usually be in their home courts in a sale of goods case (place of performance is deemed to be where the goods were or should have been delivered). The same will probably apply in a provision of services case (place of performance is deemed to be where the services were or should have been provided). The issues of jurisdiction and applicable law have been under discussion by the European Parliament for some time, and various amendments to the relevant Conventions have been debated. It seems likely that discussions will continue for some time. For more on this highly complex question, see Chapter 11.

STAMP DUTY

Until the Chancellor's Budget of March 2000, intellectual property rights were considered to be types of 'property' for stamp duty purposes and therefore transfers attracted stamp duty. From 28 March 2000, transactions in intellectual property are exempted from stamp duty, in order to foster an environment in which innovation and invention are encouraged. The exemption applies to transfers and licences of patents, trade marks, registered designs and copyrights.

Note that where property sold under a transfer instrument for more than (currently) £60,000 consists partly of intellectual property (IP) and partly of other property chargeable to duty, an apportionment of the sale price will be made to determine the amount chargeable to duty. If the value of the transaction (involving both IP and non-IP transfers) is below £60,000, it is necessary to include at the end of the contract a clause in approved form saying so.

Other contracts   5

ACADEMIC/PROFESSIONAL/STM AUTHORS

CONTRACTS FOR SPECIALISTS

Some trade authors write for a living; specialist authors more often earn their living primarily doing other things, but can sometimes be encouraged to write on topics connected with their work or their research. They are often experts in their fields, with established (often international) reputations, and their names as authors, or as members of an editorial team, will sell all kinds of publications and services to what are often highly profitable specialist markets. The works they create tend to have distinctive features, and these need to be reflected in the publishing contracts which they sign. We will highlight these features in this section: bear in mind, however, that most of the general legal principles set out in Chapter 4 will still apply as well.

For convenience, we will use the abbreviation 'specialist works' throughout this section to refer to all academic, professional or STM works, and we will call their authors 'specialist authors'.

PUBLISHING IN A DIGITAL AGE

While publishing as a whole is increasingly digital, with new platforms such as iPads and mobile phone apps, and sales of e-books on Amazon at the time of writing now overtaking sales of hardbacks, e-book sales in the general UK market were initially slow to pick up. Sales of specialist publications, such as STM journals, however, have been primarily digital and online for many years. This has important implications for contracts for specialist authors, where conditions for making content available online, authorised users and access restrictions, often assume greater importance. It also often involves licensing aggregators to distribute content and make it available on the publisher's behalf, which involves new contractual relationships and licensing terms (on which see the end of this chapter).

COPYRIGHT: TEAMS AND INSTITUTIONS

Specialist works are often highly detailed and complex, and may require contributions from several different authors: indeed, a major work may need hundreds of contributors all over the world and an international editorial board. More straightforwardly, two colleagues may co-author a text, or co-host a website, or jointly write up some research. At both ends of the scale, it is equally important:

- to ensure that *all* those involved in the project are under contract;
- to be clear who is doing what;
- to agree who owns the copyright (and other rights) in all the work(s) which result;
- to make sure that the publishing activities envisaged are fully licensed by all those owners.

To make absolutely sure, a publisher investing in a major project may wish to seek a full assignment of copyright from all the contributors involved (including editors): such assignments will give the publisher complete control of the material, but they must be in writing and signed by or on behalf of each contributor (see Chapter 4). The contributors may in most cases be allowed to re-use their material elsewhere, such as within a university intranet, or on their own websites or for professional lecturing purposes, but it is advisable to confirm the details of this. In other cases a sole and exclusive publishing licence may be sufficient (provided it is wide enough to cover all forms of exploitation envisaged, including making available and online access), but it is still essential to make sure that all the relevant copyrights and other rights are covered by the licence(s) given, so that no rights will be infringed.

Copyright

Depending on the publication, a number of different copyright works might be created, including a range of literary, artistic and other works: for the full list, see Chapter 2. As well as the obvious ones, such as text and illustrations, do not forget copyright in any overall compilation or database, and also – if it is available in digital form – copyright in any computer software. All these copyrights will probably be owned by the people who created the works, but with specialist writing or research teams there may be joint authors to consider – in which case, if there is a risk they might fall out, it may be advisable to legislate for this in the contract since, as joint authors, neither will have the right to publish (or license) the work without the consent of the other. Also, it may well be that some employee authors will have created the works in the course of their employment, in which case their employer (which may be their university or company) might own copyright in the works they create, not them (Chapter 2). They might also have been persuaded to assign their copyright to the institution or company concerned, and some institutions such as universities are increasingly requiring this.

Other rights

Many collective works nowadays might amount to a database (for the conditions, see Chapter 3). Assuming – as is likely – that the publisher, or other 'maker', of the database has made a 'substantial investment in obtaining, verifying or presenting the contents of the database', that person will be entitled to a statutory **database right** to prevent unauthorised extraction or re-utilisation. It is highly advisable to make it clear in each case whether the right is to be owned by the publisher, or any other 'maker' of the database concerned. The right lasts for 15 years, but is renewable thereafter. For more on this see Chapter 3.

With collaborative works, there may also be issues of confidentiality to consider – if draft research findings (say) are circulated confidentially, it may be a breach of a duty of confidence to publish them without consent (see Chapter 8). Such a duty might be owed to a fellow researcher, or to an institute or other employer.

Also, for material created after 1 August 1989, do not overlook authors' moral rights, which are likely to be more than usually significant for specialist writing, where academic or professional reputations are at stake. Moral rights may not apply to certain 'collective works' such as dictionaries and encyclopaedias (see Chapter 3), but if they do there will be at least three moral rights to consider:

- the right for each author to be identified (this right must at present be specifically asserted);
- their right to object to derogatory treatment of their work (especially if editorial changes are planned);
- the right to prevent false attribution.

(For moral rights generally, see Chapter 3.) These rights may not apply to any acts done with the author's (or in some cases, the copyright owner's) consent, and will also not apply where the rights have been waived. For smaller contributions or for major works, complete waivers may be appropriate; for others, it may be necessary to rely on partial waivers or contractual consents.

WARRANTIES

For specialist works, warranties may need to be revised to take account of joint authorship, or limiting to the author's particular contributions to the work, rather than applying to the work as a whole – clearly, a specialist author cannot be expected to make warranties about other people's work. However, the personal warranty against plagiarism which amounts to copyright infringement may be particularly important in an academic work, and the warranty against libel may prove useful to protect the publisher against academic vendettas carried on in the footnotes. This is particularly true if the work is going to be made available worldwide on the net. The usual warranty against previous publication is particularly important today, given the damage to normal sales and exploitation that can be done by undeclared prior publication or making available of the work (or a version of it) via the net or even a restricted intranet – such things should always be declared at the outset, so that whatever commercial market is left can be assessed properly. This includes any requirement by academic institutions that material produced by their staff – which could include research reports, articles or data sets - should be available on open access terms, often in designated repositories.

The warranties should ideally also include negligent mis-statement (although negligence will be hard to prove – see Chapter 7) and should cover statements of fact, and the reliability and safety of formulae or instructions. It may also be advisable to require the author to provide for safety warnings, to put users on notice of any hazards arising out of dangerous experiments or procedures, and refer to any appropriate safety precautions or standards or codes of practice.

Some specialist authors may only feel able to warrant that statements of fact are true 'to the best of their knowledge' – the publisher may be willing to accept this risk, particularly if adequate insurance is in place. On warranties generally, see Chapter 4.

QUOTATIONS, ILLUSTRATIONS AND PERMISSIONS

These are likely to be important in all specialist works, particularly source books or anthologies. Some textual quotations may freely be used, for example if they count as fair dealing for the purposes of criticism or review (see Chapter 9), but otherwise permission to reproduce all quoted extracts and illustrations must be obtained from the copyright owners. Most publishers will place responsibility for this – including, where appropriate, paying any permissions fees – on the author, but for a major project where permissions are likely to be a significant item, the publishers may be willing (in fact, may prefer) to arrange this themselves, and in some cases may set the cost of any fees against author royalties.

Where the author is responsible for permissions, it may be advisable to specify an agreed financial limit. It is also advisable for the publisher to have copies of any permissions correspondence, for future reference. Where the rights owner cannot be found in order to grant permission, even after diligent search, the legal position at the time of writing is that the work concerned probably cannot be used, other than under normal copyright exceptions, but it is possible that limited licences to use such 'orphan works' may become available under new UK legislation (for more on this, see Chapter 4)

CORRECTIONS

In specialist works, last-minute corrections may be essential to take account of recent research or knowledge, or legal or technical changes. The work may be unsaleable without them, if it becomes dangerously unreliable or out of date. It is advisable for the publisher to be alerted well in advance if there is a risk of significant corrections. It is also important to agree who will pay for them; otherwise, the authors may find themselves paying substantial sums for dealing with changes which the book needs, but which were totally outside their control.

ROYALTIES AND FEES

One-off fees may be more appropriate for a multi-author work, or where the copyright is assigned: many specialist authors are happy to write for money upfront (or at least on delivery and acceptance), especially where there is some academic or professional kudos involved as well. The timing of the fee payment may be crucial – most contributors will prefer to be paid when they have delivered their own work, and not wait until the last (and slowest) contribution comes in, still less until publication. Advance payments may get round this problem. There should also be provision for fee payments if for some reason the project collapses and the work is never published.

Consider, also, any reprints or further exploitation of the work, including digital exploitation and whether further fees or royalties may be appropriate then, if the contribution is a significant proportion of the whole work (or the part of it to be exploited). If the material later proves suitable for digital exploitation, such as inclusion in an online database, or for website or search engine access or local site licensing, the contract will need to allow room for a suitable new payment structure for such use in due course, including aggregator or subscription services. Ideally, this should allow for exploitation by the publishers themselves, as well as any exploitation or access sub-licensed to others (see further, on this, p. 140).

Another factor to consider in contracts for specialist works is the need to phase out royalty payments in a realistic manner where an original author or editor retires or dies. In order to keep the work up to date, and maintain its reputation against rivals, it will be necessary for co-authors to take over, or for new editors to be brought in, and to be paid at realistic rates. As they prune old text and contribute new original material of their own, each edition or update for which they are responsible will contain a smaller and smaller proportion of the original author's copyright material, so it is reasonable that the royalty rates payable to the author or author's estate should decline also. Many specialist contracts now provide for the original author's royalties to continue for one, or perhaps two, further editions but then to cease; an alternative method is to agree a gradually declining percentage, perhaps over a longer period. Where use of the initial author's name remains valuable (such as Grove's dictionary of music, or Wisden), it may be justifiable to pay a continuing share of the royalty to the author or the author's estate.

REVISIONS

A publisher who has taken full assignments of copyright will normally have complete freedom to revise and update a work, although in many cases the publisher will still prefer to give the author first option to make any revisions. The fact that the publisher owns the copyright will normally mean that the author's moral right of integrity will also not apply to any changes the publisher authorises unless the author is identified, and even then not if there is a sufficient disclaimer. In the case of a publishing licence, however, this will probably not be the case, and provision should be made in the contract for revised editions. In any event, many specialist authors will want to retain at least a first option to make any required revisions themselves.

COMPETING WORKS

Non-competition clauses may have particular significance for specialist authors whose reputations often depend on their writing. They must not be drafted so widely as to amount to an unreasonable restraint of trade (see Chapter 4) and specialist authors must not be so prevented from writing in their own field that they cannot develop their work properly or earn a living. If such clauses are to be enforceable, it is advisable to be as clear as possible about the level of competition restricted: a blanket ban on a whole subject is unlikely to be upheld, but directly competing works at the same level in the same market may well be prevented. To avoid any doubt, it may help to list some or all of the activities which *may* be undertaken, such as limited website or intranet access, journal articles, conference papers or anthologies.

REMAINDERS

As we saw in Chapter 4, the courts are willing to enforce an author's contractual right to be consulted before any remaindering. Where the contract contains such a right, damages may be payable to an academic author (for example) who could have sold the remaining copies to students had he or she known the remaindering was about to take place.

GENERAL EDITORS

DON'T FORGET THE EDITOR

As we saw in the last section, major projects often require whole teams of contributors, and the General Editor – there usually is one – will probably be a contributor too. He or she will probably need a quite different type of contract from that of the typical contributor, however, because there are two quite different legal matters to sort out:

- the Editor's practical duties and responsibilities in relation to the team and the project as a whole;
- the Editor's rights (including copyright) in the material produced, and any associated warranties or liabilities.

COMMISSIONING AND DELIVERY

It is essential that the Publisher and the Editor should agree on the scope of the Editor's role, and set this out as clearly as possible in their contract. Does the Editor commission the work – and the contributors – from scratch, or is the publisher doing this? If the Editor does it, it will be advisable for the agreement to settle:

- the overall scope of the work, including length and schedule;
- the management of contributors, and responsibility for ensuring each of them is put under contract with the Publisher;
- any responsibility the Editor has for negotiating fees or other payments and budgets for these;
- who is responsible for clearing and paying for permissions;
- the Editor's duty to review and edit each contribution, and powers of acceptance, amendment or rejection;
- who decides on any extra text (is this entirely at the editor's discretion, or only as necessary in the Publisher's opinion?).

The schedule itself is (of course) usually crucial – note that time will not normally be regarded as being of the essence unless the Editor's contract (and those of contributors) expressly makes it so.

COPYRIGHT AND MORAL RIGHTS

The Editor is likely to own copyright in:

- his or her own contributions as a contributor;
- any other original material he or she creates (such as introductions, forewords and so forth);
- the overall scheme and plan of the work as a whole, as a compilation.

If the Editor does the work, and creates the works, in the scope of employment (by a university or research institute, for example) it may well be that the employer will own the copyright – in which case any publishing contract should be with them (but preferably including the editor in his or her personal capacity too). The Publisher may wish to secure a full assignment of all the relevant copyrights – in which case this should be in writing and signed by or on behalf of the assignor – or may seek a sole and exclusive licence in terms wide enough to cover all forms and media envisaged.

If the work amounts to a database (see Chapter 3) it is likely that the Publisher or 'maker' will have a database right to prevent unauthorised extraction or re-use, for 15 years.

The Editor is likely to have the same statutory moral rights as individual contributors over his or her work. These are likely to include the right to be credited as the editor, the right to object to derogatory treatment and the right to prevent false attribution. On moral rights generally, see Chapter 3.

If the Editor is responsible for procuring assignments of copyright and waivers of moral rights from contributors, the contract should make this clear, although it will probably be more appropriate for the Publisher to negotiate for these.

WARRANTIES

The Publisher will want the usual warranties (see Chapter 4), covering at least the Editor's own contributions and (crucially) any amendments, alterations or additions which are made to the contributor's text or other material. It is important that there should be no gaps in libel cover (for example) – libels can be introduced just as much by editorial additions (or deletions) as by original text.

CORRECTIONS

Does the Editor get an extra correction allowance, or is there one overall percentage? Ideally, the Editor will share with the Publisher the responsibility for keeping corrections under control.

BUDGET, FEES AND EXPENSES

All fees and other expenses payable to the Editor, or on his or her behalf, should be settled at the outset. These may include royalty payments (and any advances) or fees, and also any honorarium. In particular, a budget for expenses such as travel and any overheads such as secretarial support should be agreed.

It may be advisable to clarify in the agreement whether the Editor has any responsibility at all for negotiating fees with contributors (or even paying them) and, if not, to confirm that the Publisher will do this and hold the editor harmless against any liability for such payments.

REVISIONS AND NEW EDITIONS

It is desirable to agree who initiates **revisions and new editions**, and what happens if Publisher and Editor cannot agree. If the Editor is unwilling or unable to edit a revision or new edition, the Publisher will need the right to bring in someone else and pay them for the work they do out of any royalties or fees which might otherwise have been paid to the Editor, or the Editor's estate.

Remember that any moral right of integrity (to object to derogatory treatment) the Editor might have, and which has not been waived, will last for as long as the work remains in copyright, as will the Editor's right of paternity (to be credited as the editor). In the event of a dispute, the converse right – to prevent false attribution – might also be important, and may stop the Publisher putting out a new edition under the Editor's name if it contains substantial amounts of material which the Editor did not write or of which the Editor disapproves. This right lasts for 20 years after the Editor's death.

Finally, remember that any substantial investment of time, skill or money in a database will trigger a renewed 15-year term of database right (owned by the publisher or other 'maker').

CONTRIBUTORS (TEXT AND ILLUSTRATIONS)

COMMISSIONED WORKS

Commissioned work (literary or artistic) has distinctive features which any contract will need to reflect, but it is otherwise substantially the same as any other original work. Contrary to what many people think, the copyright position in the UK is also now fundamentally the same, so that the author, artist or photographer usually owns the copyright (but see below on the US position). Much of what was said in Chapter 4 about author–publisher agreements will thus apply here too, as will the comments about specialist authors at the beginning of this chapter.

The illustrations in some works can be more valuable than the words – indeed some publications (children's books, for example) may consist almost entirely of pictures. In such cases the illustrator will for contractual purposes become the primary author. In others, the publisher will probably need two separate contracts, with author and illustrator, reflecting the contribution the illustrator has made and granting the publisher the necessary rights in what the illustrator has produced. For the important issue of ownership of the artwork (and **resale right**) see below.

DELIVERY AND ACCEPTANCE

Where a project depends on many contributions, the schedule and delivery requirements for each one are likely to be much less flexible. Time may well be of the essence – if so, this must be expressly stated, so that if the work doesn't come in the publisher will have the option of cancelling the contributor's contract and re-commissioning the work from someone else.

There should be provision for what happens if the contribution is delivered but is unacceptable. For text, most General Editors will want considerable freedom to require alterations, or reject the contribution altogether – this should be agreed in advance, and set out in the contract. It is common in contributors' contracts for hard-copy works for the contribution – if it comes in at all – to be accepted for one edition only. For digital or online works, a more realistic future timetable may be necessary. If a contributor is dropped, there should of course be appropriate arrangements for reversion or reassignment of his or her rights.

Since so many decisions about illustrations are matters of suitability and taste, most delivery schedules allow for submission and approval of roughs, as well as finished artwork.

It also makes sense to provide for the possibility that illustrations will not be felt to be suitable after all. A termination fee (known as a 'kill fee') is usually agreed in advance to cover such an eventuality. If rights are to revert to the illustrator, this should be made clear as well.

EDITORIAL CHANGES AND MORAL RIGHTS

For text, it is important to agree in the contract whether and how far the publisher, and any editor, can make the editorial changes which they may consider necessary, since these may well involve quite heavy revisions in the interests of uniformity or overall style. Although for some projects it may be appropriate to have a proviso that no substantial alterations may be made without the contributor's prior written approval, it is probably more usual for the editor to be given a free hand.

In these circumstances it is essential either to secure a full or partial waiver of the contributor's moral right of integrity, or at least to include a clear consent to such alterations in the contract (since moral rights will not apply to any acts which are done with the author's consent).

Otherwise, there will be a danger that significant editorial changes to the contribution may amount to derogatory treatment, and thus infringe the contributor's moral rights (unless one of the 'collective work' exceptions applies – on all this generally, see Chapter 3).

COPYRIGHT

Generally speaking, in the UK the fact that work is commissioned makes no difference to copyright ownership (which is normally vested in the author). However, the position is different for 'Works for Hire' in the USA, where the commissioner may own copyright provided there is a signed document making clear that this is the intention of the parties. There were some limited provisions in the UK relating to commissioned photographs, portraits or engravings prior to 1989 but these have never extended to literary works. So a UK contributor of commissioned literary or artistic work will almost certainly own the copyright, unless:

- there are joint authors; or
- the contributor is an employee, and wrote the work in the course of that employment.

These exceptions, and copyright generally, are dealt with fully in Chapter 2, and Chapter 9. Whoever owns the copyright, the publisher will want to secure a sufficient grant of exclusive publishing rights to cover all likely exploitation of the work, including digital and online access, and possibly – in the case of commissioned text – a full assignment of the copyright. Full copyright assignments must be in writing and signed by or on behalf of the copyright owner in order to be effective.

Not all contributors will be willing to assign copyright in their work, so a publisher embarking on a major project would be well advised to raise the question with each contributor at an early stage and not, for example, leave exchange of formal commissioning letters until right at the end, when it may be too late to re-commission someone else. Without a signed written assignment, the publisher will not acquire the copyright, and indeed if there is no agreement at all the best that the publisher will get is an implied non-exclusive publishing licence, probably for one edition only.

If a contributor is unwilling to assign his or her copyright, the publisher will need to decide whether that particular contributor is crucial to the project, and if so whether a sole and exclusive licence will suffice. In that case, it will be highly desirable for the publisher to obtain an undertaking that the contributor will not assign the copyright elsewhere without giving the assignee written notice of the publisher's exclusive licence.

With illustrations (particularly of characters), bear in mind any merchandising potential including sale of photographs as posters, animated cartoon, film and TV rights, and any possible digital or mobile phone exploitation, including apps.

Bear in mind also the desirability of registering characters and logos with merchandising potential as registered trade marks – and consider who should be the proprietor of the marks. For more on trade marks, see Chapter 10.

OWNERSHIP OF ARTWORK

Do not forget that ownership of copyright in something is quite different from ownership of the physical material on which it is recorded. An illustrator may assign copyright in illustrations but still own the original artwork – which may of course have a substantial value of its own, for resale or exhibition purposes (particularly in view now of the **artist's resale right** – see below). When completed artwork or photographs are delivered, therefore, the publisher should remember that they are probably someone else's (valuable) property (unless of course the publisher already owned them, or has purchased them separately) and take reasonable care of them. It is also probably useful for publishers and illustrators to agree on a reasonable level of mutual access, so that the publisher can have access to the material for publicity or promotion purposes, even after it has been returned, and the artist can include the work if required in exhibitions. Particularly valuable artwork, or negatives, may need to be specially insured while under the publisher's control: if so, it will be necessary to agree a valuation, and decide who is paying the premium or whether this is to be shared.

ARTIST'S RESALE RIGHT (DROIT DE SUITE)

From 1 January 2006, there has been an artist's resale right in the UK and in most countries throughout the EU, giving artists a percentage royalty of between 4 and 5 per cent and 0.25 per cent on all subsequent commercial sales of their works above a value of €3,000. For more on this, see Chapter 3.

WARRANTIES

The usual warranties will be needed (see Chapter 4) but relating of course only to that contributor's particular contribution(s). The warranties that the work is original, has not been published or made available before and contains nothing defamatory are particularly important for text. In the case of scientific or technical material, the warranties may also need to cover safety warnings and refer to appropriate codes and standards. Where recognisable likenesses of identifiable human beings are included, it may be advisable (as in many medical texts) to block out faces, or to ask an artist or photographer for an undertaking that they will secure a form of release, or written consent, from any such identifiable people. The UK has a rapidly developing law of privacy (on which see Chapter 8).

ILLUSTRATIONS AND PERMISSIONS

In the case of contributors writing text to order, so to speak, it is important to be clear about any other, non-text, material which may also be required and which the contributor might wrongly assume is being commissioned by the publisher from somewhere else. This would include not only quoted text, illustrations and photographs, but also charts, graphs, diagrams and maps. If these are not created by the contributor, and they are still in copyright, then permission to reproduce them will be needed from the copyright owners, and the contract will need to specify who is responsible for getting those permissions and who pays for them.

PROOFS

It is not uncommon for the contract to give the editor the right to correct and pass text proofs on the contributor's behalf if the schedule requires this.

FEES AND EXPENSES

It is customary for a one-off fee payment to cover all uses of the work, and all future exploitation, but it is advisable to check this. If an older contract refers to 'existing' (i.e. pre-digital) formats and media only, or is not clear on the point, it will probably be necessary to agree additional fees for any digital exploitation, including site licence or website access licensed by the publisher, as well as online search, aggregator or subscription services.

For artistic works, if the agreed fee does not clearly cover exploitation in all forms and media, it may be necessary to agree additional fees for some kinds of exploitation, such as merchandising or digital (including mobile phone) exploitation. It is also desirable to agree in advance how any extra payments are to be split between the author and illustrator if (as is likely) the words and illustrations are exploited together.

Expenses should also be clarified – for a major commissioned work the publisher may be willing to meet (allowed) expenses, but in general artists and illustrators are expected to meet the costs of materials and roughs, and photographers are expected to pay for their own developing, printing and enlarging, and also for the hire of any studios, props or other equipment, as well as assistants and staff. If separate budgets need to be fixed for these items, this should be clearly agreed.

TRANSLATORS

TRANSLATORS AND TRANSLATIONS

There is a substantial international trade in translation rights – for physics and computing textbooks as much as great literature. We shall look at translation rights contracts later, p. 126: in this section we will look first at the equally important contract with the translator (whose skill – or lack of it – can make or break a work).

COPYRIGHT AND TRANSLATIONS

Under UK law, if you translate someone's work into another language you are making an adaptation of that work. Since adaptation is one of the restricted acts which only copyright owners can do or authorise (see Chapter 9) you will need the copyright owner's permission; otherwise, you will be in danger of infringing their copyright (for this reason, a translator might need some assurance that the publisher actually has the relevant translation rights, and may seek a warranty to cover this risk – see below).

At the same time, creating a translation (even an unauthorised one) creates a new original copyright work, and as with most copyright works – apart from employee works – the copyright in that is owned by the person who created it: in this case, the translator. A publisher commissioning a translation will not own the copyright simply by virtue of having commissioned the work – if the publisher wants to own the copyright, it will have to be assigned by the translator in a written, signed document. Publishers often do seek a full assignment of copyright, particularly for reference or STM works; alternatively, they will need an exclusive licence in terms at least as wide as the translation rights deal, including any digital or online exploitation.

Whether or not the translator retains the copyright, there will need to be two separate copyright claims on the title pages: one relating to the original work, the other covering the translation.

MORAL RIGHTS

Even if copyright has been assigned, it is important to remember that the translator may still have statutory moral rights of paternity (to be credited) and integrity (to object to derogatory treatment) – and so, indeed, may the original author. See generally, on all this, Chapter 3, but note that section 80 of the 1988 Act expressly excludes translations from the definition of a 'treatment', so by definition even the most appalling translation cannot be a derogatory treatment of the original work under UK law (because it is not a treatment at all).

DELIVERY AND ACCEPTANCE

One of the key undertakings a translator will be asked to make is to render a 'faithful and accurate' translation, not only in reasonably good and accurate English but also true to the style, spirit and character of the original work. This is usually accompanied by a specific undertaking to translate the whole work, and not to make any alterations, additions or omissions without the publisher's (and probably the original author's) consent.

Since the publisher is often required under the translation rights contract to submit the translation, or specimen sections of it, to the original foreign publisher for approval, there is usually a requirement to this effect in the translator's contract too. Given the difficulties of checking work in another language, the material may only be given a fairly cursory structural check, but the original author may be entitled under the contract (or under a more informal agreement resulting from the licensing correspondence) to examine the work, and it is therefore advisable to allow a reasonable period of time for approval. Needless to say, it is also advisable to provide for what happens if amendments are required, and who pays for them, and also what happens if the translation for some reason is rejected altogether – specifically, do the rights in that particular translation revert to the translator (see below), and is he or she paid a proportion of the agreed fee, or merely allowed to keep any advances? All this should be spelt out as clearly as possible.

WARRANTIES

The publisher will want a warranty that the translator will not introduce any objectionable new material, particularly nothing that is misleading, defamatory, in breach of privacy or otherwise illegal, and nothing that infringes the copyright or other rights of anyone else (which may result from inaccurate translation as much as any new material). In return, the translator may often seek a counter-warranty and indemnity from the publisher that the original work being translated does not itself carry any such legal risks, since these would put the translator at risk too.

Since the work is not the publisher's own, any such warranties are unlikely to go beyond those given by the original publisher of the work, and the best warranty the publisher of the translation may feel able to give is 'to the best of the publisher's knowledge and belief'.

FEES

Fees – normally at a rate per thousand words – are more common than royalties, but translators are increasingly being regarded as secondary authors and in some cases a royalty may be more appropriate. Payment of fees is usually preferred on delivery – for obvious reasons – although the publisher may wish to hold some instalments of the payment back until final approval or even publication. Some payments might be made to the translator on signature of the contract, some on delivery and acceptance, and some on publication.

TERMINATION

Normal termination provisions will usually apply – on rejection, breach or insolvency, for example (see Chapter 4) – but it is important to make clear what rights, if any, will revert to the translator in these circumstances. Since the publisher is likely to have exclusive translation rights for that work in a relevant language, then as long as those rights are still in force the publisher is not going to want the translator to publish or exploit the original translation or any part of it without its consent (particularly if it was rejected and the publisher has had to go to the trouble and expense of commissioning a new one).

SUBSIDIARY RIGHTS CONTRACTS

RIGHTS DEALS

As we saw in the last chapter, it may be important for a publisher to have the right not only to produce and publish the work itself, but also to sub-license others in different areas to do so too. There may be a market for digital or online exploitation or a Russian translation, or a film or TV version, in which case the relevant subsidiary rights will need to be licensed (see below). Indeed, the revenue from rights deals may well mean the difference between overall profit and loss for a publisher, and may even exceed that derived from the publisher's own publishing. Some authors and agents will prefer to retain and exploit subsidiary rights – or some of them – themselves; in other cases a publisher with an experienced rights manager will probably prefer to control such exploitation itself (in which case the publisher must make sure it *has* the rights in the first place – see Chapter 4). Whoever ends up doing it would be well advised first to consult Lynette Owen's indispensable guide to *Selling Rights* (sixth edition, 2010).

In the rest of this section we will concentrate on the legal issues arising out of agreements for some of the key subsidiary rights.

PAPERBACK RIGHTS

In these days of 'vertical publishing', it is increasingly common for one publisher to undertake both hardback and paperback editions (although mass-market paperback rights may still be licensed to a separate paperback house). Not all publishers are in a position to undertake both, however, and sub-licensing paperback rights to another publisher is still often done, at Frankfurt and elsewhere. In the case of authors with proven sales records, there may be some competition for the paperback rights, with considerable sums changing hands by way of advance.

Grant of rights

As with the original publisher's main grant of rights from the author (which must be checked, see above), it is essential that the rights then granted by the original publisher to others – and their limitations – are clearly spelt out. The roles are of course reversed for such sub-licensing: the original publisher, having up until now been the author's (and others') licensee of the head rights, now becomes a licensor of individual subsidiary rights to others. The original publisher will usually now become 'the Grantor', and 'the Publisher' will now be the paperback publisher acquiring the rights.

The Publisher will almost certainly want exclusive rights to produce and publish the work in all paperback formats: if this is not possible, the Publisher will at least want to know which other paperback editions already exist, or are planned. Has the Grantor already published its own trade or educational paperback, or e-book, or is the work available online? Is any book club edition (paperback or otherwise) licensed, or being planned? If any competing paperbacks exist (or may), a licence for 'all paperback editions' will not be possible and it will be advisable to specify as clearly as possible exactly which paperback rights are being granted. It may be necessary to refer to markets (such as mass-market) or to specific formats (such as A or B format). In the case of book club paperbacks, the Publisher may wish to avoid possible conflict by seeking an undertaking from the Grantor that it will not license any such book club editions without the publisher's prior consent. Similar considerations may apply to low-cost editions or reprints for major export markets such as India or (increasingly) China.

Although it is unlikely that a paperback publisher would acquire translation rights, the grant of rights should also specify the language(s) covered (English-language only, or in other, or all languages) and the territories included – specific territories (such as the USA), lists of territories (such as the EU or EEA, which should be clearly set out, preferably in a Schedule) or the whole world. Any 'open' territories should also be carefully considered, bearing in mind the EU's free movement of goods rules within Europe (see Chapter 13).

Duration and timing

Paperback licences are normally granted for a limited term rather than for the full term of copyright; it is therefore essential to specify what the term is going to be. Eight years from the date of the contract is the most common period: in some cases, such as an encyclopaedia or dictionary or other non-fiction title which is likely to be revised regularly, paperback rights are granted edition by edition. There is usually provision for renewal of the licence thereafter, on terms to be agreed.

It is also advisable to agree well in advance – and as clearly as possible – what the *timing* of the licensed paperback edition is going to be. Since the appearance of a cheaper paperback is bound to affect sales of the hardback and other existing editions, it is normal to provide a breathing space of at least six months or a year before the paperback may be published: earliest and latest dates are often specified. There may also be external events to consider, such as film or TV tie-ins which may be a reason to allow for early release of the paperback with a tie-in cover.

Timing may be particularly crucial in the case of US paperback editions, whose larger home markets and print-runs may lead to highly competitive prices in a number of open markets around the world. Beware, in particular, of leaving Europe (specifically the EU and EEA) as an 'open' territory if you wish to retain UK exclusivity (see Chapter 13) and, equally, the problems of parallel importation into territories such as Australia: it may be worth the original publisher considering a simultaneous (or earlier) export edition of its own in order not to lose some open markets completely. US publishers increasingly seek exclusivity in other world markets, such as India, Australia and Singapore, in return for complete exclusivity in Europe.

Finally, the timing of an English-language paperback may be highly relevant to markets which are already (or may be) served by a foreign-language translation. A Dutch or Swedish translation (for example) could be killed stone dead by the untimely appearance of an English paperback in either territory, since in both places there are substantial English-language markets.

Warranties

Any warranties given by the Grantor should ideally match those it has itself received from the author, although the new Publisher will usually require a warranty that the work has not previously been published in a particular format in the territory concerned. If any new or additional warranties are required the Grantor should carefully consider whether it is willing (or able) to bear the risk.

Alterations and permissions

Given that the author (probably) has a moral right of integrity, it is now even more important to keep amendments to the work itself under control; to be on the safe side, no abridgements, expansions or alterations to the work should be allowed without at least the Grantor's consent, and the author's consent (or waiver) may also be necessary in order to avoid any claim of derogatory treatment (see Chapter 7). Exceptions are sometimes allowed for alterations made on the advice of the paperback publisher's lawyers, on giving due notice to the Grantor (the Grantor – and its own lawyers – will then need to consider whether its own editions are at risk).

The Grantor is more likely to supply duplicates rather than originals of artwork or prints, or other supplementary material, but it is vital to check that any original copyright permissions granted for this do actually extend to paperback publication by a licensee rather than the original publisher in the territories covered: it may well be necessary to renew many (or even all) of the permissions if they do not include the re-use of the material in sub-licensed editions (for example, under different imprints or in different formats).

Copyright and credits

The Grantor will want to ensure that its original copyright claim, including its name and the date of first publication, are included in all subsequent paperback editions (for UCC copyright notices, see Chapter 4). This is also an opportunity to ensure that the author's name appears in its customary form with due prominence, and (if necessary) to include an assertion of the author's moral right of paternity, to be identified as the author (for the wording of assertions, see Chapter 3). The Grantor usually supplies duplicate production material to cover this.

Royalties and accounts

The normal considerations will apply (see Chapter 4), although royalties under paperback licences are usually paid twice a year. A percentage of this (normally 50 per cent or more), although different percentages may apply to home and export sales, will of course go to the author. It is common for a paperback publisher to wish to make some reserve against returns, and there may be a small reprint clause (although this may make less sense in an age of print on demand).

Termination and reversion

Apart from the normal termination provisions – for breach or insolvency, for example – the Grantor will want the right to terminate the licence if the Publisher allows the paperback edition to go out of print or fails to put it back on the market within, say, 9 or 12 months of formal notice to do so. Conversely, when the licence expires or comes to an end for other reasons, the Publisher will probably want a reasonable sell-off period to clear remaining stocks.

BOOK CLUB RIGHTS

Britain, like the USA, has a substantial book club market, with clubs such as Book Club Associates (BCA) claiming well over a million members, although there is now greater competition from discount retailers such as supermarkets. BCA contains a number of individual clubs, and there are also many other independent clubs: some of them are general book clubs such as the Folio Society, and others specialise in particular areas, such as the History Guild (BCA). All of them operate primarily by mail order. Members are regularly recruited via national press advertising, often being induced to join with loss-leading 'premium' offers of the 'four books for £1' variety, with in most cases a modest annual purchasing obligation thereafter.

Although the larger clubs will demand substantial discounts, there can be significant economies of scale on both sides: not only to the club's members, in reduced prices, but also to the licensing publisher, in increased print-runs and lower unit costs.

Such a large, distinct market, dominated by one or two major players, has obvious competition law implications (see Chapter 13) and indeed BCA and Leisure Circle were the subject of a Monopolies and Mergers Commission report in January 1988. The clubs have, however, by and large managed so far to remain within UK competition law by agreeing a measure of self-regulation. Prior to the demise of the Net Book Agreement, this was under the Book Club Regulations and a Concordat supervised under the auspices of the Publishers Association. When the Net Book Agreement died in 1997, the Book Club Regulations died with it, since they applied only to net books.

Licensing book club rights

Selling bound copies

Despite the considerable degree of self-regulation which surrounds book clubs in the UK, the larger clubs still undoubtedly occupy a pre-eminent position and can command discounts from licensing publishers of well over 60 per cent – often as high as 80 per cent. However, publishers are not always negotiating at a disadvantage. The following licensing points should be borne in mind:

(1) It is advisable for publishers to deal only with recognised clubs.
(2) If the club is to have an exclusive licence, a minimum order such as 3,500 copies is common.
(3) No exclusive licence would usually last for longer than three years (with four years for a non-exclusive licence).
(4) Timing may very well be crucial: in which case time should be clearly stated to be of the essence. Publishers will normally be required to specify their own publication date, and any plans for a low-cost or paperback edition of their own. Any penalties for late delivery should be spelt out, and it should also be made clear at what point – if at all – the club has the right to cancel the order altogether.
(5) The normal warranties and indemnities will apply (no copyright infringement, or defamation, for example) and the publisher must therefore make sure it has the necessary book club rights itself, has matching warranties from the author and has re-cleared any permissions which do not already cover book club editions.
(6) The licence should normally provide for termination if the club exhausts its stock within the licence period and does not re-order (it is common for both parties to be prevented from remaindering without prior consent).

BCA now operates on the basis of one master contract with each supplying publisher, supplemented with individual purchase orders. The other clubs may operate on purchase orders only.

Reprint licences

Clubs may seek exclusive reprint licences for longer-term deals, giving them the right to print their own copies, with control of printing costs and delivery timetables. Such licences usually last, once again, for three years, possibly with a further year's non-exclusive extension. As above, it is important for the licensing publisher to check that warranties match, that the rights already acquired extend to book club publication, and that it controls all the necessary markets worldwide.

SAME LANGUAGE RIGHTS: CO-EDITIONS AND JOINT VENTURES

As we have seen, even in the English language, there may be forms and media of exploitation which publishers, authors or agents cannot develop alone; there may also be key English-language markets (such as the USA) where the market may require local promotion and distribution and may best be serviced by a local publisher with daily hands-on contact and goodwill. In many such cases, a straightforward licensing deal may be sufficient, but in others a more collaborative co-edition agreement may be preferred. For newer or more complex products, a formal division of functions, responsibilities and profits (or losses) may be necessary, usually best set out in a co-publication or joint venture agreement.

Co-editions

Unlike a standard licence, where the proprietor simply grants a publisher a licence to print its own local edition in return (usually) for a royalty on sales, a co-edition normally features a combined printing operation in which the local publisher will buy copies (or sheets) in its own imprint at an agreed price per copy. This requires more of an upfront payment from the local publisher, but can give a realistic price – provided exchange rates are not adverse - and provides economies of scale to the proprietor, who can print more copies and thereby reduce the unit cost. It also gives the proprietor more control over the production process which is often an important factor, for example for illustrated or children's books using four-colour printing.

Whoever's standard terms are used – a US co-publisher will often propose its own version – the following points should be covered.

Rights granted and territories

Local publishers will normally want exclusive rights in their home territory, but that territory will usually need careful definition, as will any 'open markets' in which either publisher's edition may sell, particularly Europe. The European Union's rules on free movement of goods (see Chapter 13) mean that an open market edition lawfully on sale in any EU or EEA member state cannot be prevented from entering the UK, despite licensing terms to the contrary – so that making the UK an 'exclusive' territory may in effect be unenforceable if, say, Belgium or Germany are open. Of particular importance is whether the proprietor or local publisher is to make the work available digitally, and if so how – either downloadable as an e-book, or accessible in some other form – and when. The parties should be very clear about this, since any such exploitation may have a dramatic effect on sales expectations.

The other forms and media in which territorial rights may be exploited also need careful definition: are only volume rights granted, or may the local publisher sell digital versions in that territory, or exploit subsidiary rights such as film, TV, paperback, serial and book club rights? Can the rights be sub-licensed or assigned? (Not normally without consent, but if so this must be stated.) It is advisable for the proprietor to reserve all rights not expressly granted.

Term of licence

A US licensee may expect to be granted a licence for the full duration of copyright. However, this may sometimes be resisted if inappropriate (or impossible, if the UK publisher only has a limited term of rights from the author), in which case a five- or seven-year licence is more usual, or perhaps a restriction to the number of copies supplied, with termination to take place when copies are exhausted. For major educational and academic works, it is often preferable to limit licences to the life of a single edition. It is customary to provide for the term to be extended, if required, by mutual agreement, together with an option to take further copies of a reprint or new edition.

Delivery and timing

If time is of the essence, say so – equally, specify any mutually agreed publication dates. The proprietor will be expected to undertake shipment of the publisher's copies by a certain date – often in agreed stages – but this may need to be conditional upon the publisher's timely supply of film or digital files for any permitted local amendments: both sets of dates should be clearly set out. Final delivery details will also need to be specified: which shipping agent, who will supply documentation, whether advance copies by air are required, and time limits for any complaints.

The price

Payment should be in an agreed currency, if necessary at an agreed exchange rate, (perhaps providing for a 5 per cent or other fluctuation either way, any excess to be borne equally). The price is often held for a limited period only. Payment is often staged, for example with one-third payable on signature, one-third on delivery, and one-third 30 or 60 days later. Is there an advance? Is the price royalty-inclusive or royalty-exclusive? Does it include freight and insurance, and are the terms ex works, CIF or FOB, or delivered to the licensee's warehouse? (See Glossary in Appendix A.)

Even though the price may be a royalty-inclusive price per copy, it may still make sense to specify annual sales statements and accounting and the usual provisions for audit, if only to monitor any subsidiary rights exploitation and be forewarned of any need to re-order or reprint.

Local alterations

Where the proprietor is producing copies, the publisher will usually be required to provide film or digital files of any permitted amendments or alterations (in good time within the schedule). Consider carefully any substantial amendments proposed, and bear in mind the author's moral right of integrity (see Chapter 3), and the similar rights of illustrators and other contributors: ideally, no amendments should be permitted without consent.

Permissions

It is crucial to check that any copyright permissions apply to *all* the territories and media to be exploited: some may need to be re-cleared if the original clearance was restricted to publication in the original language, for a limited market, and/or under the original publisher's imprint. For a major reference or illustrated work permissions can be very expensive indeed, so it is best to agree as early as possible who will undertake the task of securing necessary permissions, and also who will pay, or how costs will be shared.

Copyright notice and credits

The proprietor will need to ensure that its own copyright credit appears and any assertion of the author's right of paternity. It is also advisable to require the publisher to take all necessary and reasonable steps to protect the copyrights (and any trade marks) locally, including local registration where required.

Warranties and indemnities

Make sure that any warranties match those already given by the author, or (if not) that it is safe or reasonable for the proprietor to give them. Often this may be a matter for the insurers on either side – it may not be possible for a UK publisher, for example, to warrant with any certainty that nothing in a book will infringe US law (although a warranty about UK law may be perfectly reasonable). It is normal to limit warranties to the licensor's own national law.

Termination

As with all licences, any co-edition agreement should provide clearly for termination under specified conditions: normally breach, insolvency or change of control, or allowing the work to go out of print (with no reprint order in hand with the proprietor). It may be advisable to provide for arbitration in the event of any dispute – particularly if the applicable law is not English law.

Joint ventures

For more ambitious or elaborate projects (such as a large series of illustrated books or a major multimedia product), one publisher may not have all the skills – or finance – necessary. It may make sense in such circumstances to enter into a formal joint venture agreement with another publisher or with a film or TV company or software house – there may often be several parties involved. Joint venture agreements may be entered into at the outset, with all participants sitting down well in advance to plan the contributions – and profit shares – each will make, or sometimes relatively late in a project's development, for example to bring in extra finance, or distribution skills. As a general rule however, the earlier such agreements can be reached the better.

There are a number of key points to watch.

Define the product

It may be a single book such as an encyclopaedia or a series or online database or a multimedia product involving several partners: however many partners are involved, agree as soon as possible on your mutual aims, on the form and the scope of the enterprise, and define any product(s) as clearly as you can, including delivery media. A detailed specification for the product attached as a schedule might be advisable. Include any agreed details such as a General Editor or particular contributors, or intended price or format.

Decide who does what

Agree what each of you brings to the party – be it text, illustrations, other copyright material, software or simply finance, and how the various publishing functions will be split up – how any research will be tackled, who will undertake editorial, design and production, who will be responsible for clearing permissions and underlying rights, who will do the promotion, marketing and distribution and who will account for the proceeds and distribute any profits (or losses).

Timing

If there are specific launch targets, write them in. Agree in particular when the joint venture agreement starts to run and, if it has a fixed term, when it will terminate.

Budget

Budget – and re-budget – carefully, bearing in mind that for a new project in an unfamiliar medium cashflow may be crucial. Agree on allowable costs – what each party may claim back from the project before any profits are shared out. Include any administrative overheads if necessary (such as subsidiary rights management), and distribution costs such as freight and insurance. Needless to say, agree clearly how any profits will be shared out and what will happen in the event of losses.

Ownership of rights

Assuming all necessary permissions have been granted and underlying rights secured, it is important to specify clearly who owns which copyrights and also how any new copyrights which are created – for example in a new compilation or database – are owned: it may be necessary for a joint venture company to acquire the rights. Do not forget other key rights, such as trade marks in any names or logos: will these be registered, and who will be the proprietor and licensed users?

Termination

Don't forget to provide a get-out route in case it all goes horribly wrong, and allow for individual opt-outs if necessary. Agree initial terms, grounds for early termination and suitable notice periods, with arbitration provisions if necessary. Most importantly, agree who will own which rights post-termination in the joint venture product itself, including work in progress, roughs and artwork. Agree the applicable law which will govern any disputes which cannot be settled by arbitration and which country's courts will have jurisdiction (see Chapter 4).

TRANSLATION RIGHTS

Not all works have the potential to sell in translation, but many UK works do – non-fiction as well as fiction. For most UK publishers and agents, selling translation rights can therefore be a major source of revenue and a significant way of extending the market for an author's work. It can also be an effective way of combating unauthorised translations (including those given compulsory licences under some local copyright laws) and piracy of the English edition, in the territory concerned.

Not surprisingly, most publishers and agents who regularly sell translation rights will have one or more standard-form contracts, either for a straightforward sale of rights, or for a co-edition deal. We will deal here with sales of translation rights: co-edition deals are dealt with above, p. 121.

Rights granted

Before translation rights are granted to others, it is highly advisable to check that the person who wants to grant them – usually the publisher, or the agent on the author's behalf – owns or controls them in the first place. You cannot legally give what you do not have. Publishers in particular often assume that they control foreign language translation rights when in fact their publishing licence from the author covers English-language volume rights only. If this happens, any accidental omissions can usually be remedied by a quick phone call to the author or agent and a simple exchange of letters, but this is not always possible. The author or agent may well have plans of their own, and indeed may already have sold the relevant rights to someone else. If in doubt, check.

Once the rights are secured, they will normally be sub-licensed to individual foreign publishers for separate languages and territories. Most local publishers will want exclusive rights in their territory; this is usually acceptable, provided that (within Europe) it does not fall foul of EU competition law (see Chapter 13), and provided that the territory, formats covered and the length of time the licence lasts are clearly defined. Should a Portuguese translation licence cover the whole world (so that it may therefore sell in Brazil, and former colonies like Macau), or just Portugal itself? Licensees should not as a rule be granted territories which they have no facilities to handle. Does it cover hardbacks only, or paperback and book club editions, and even perhaps other forms of exploitation in that language such as digital access or online use? Most importantly, how long does the licence last? Five to eight years from signature is fairly common, depending on the work and the local publisher's plans; licences are normally renewable thereafter. In the case of major reference works and non-fiction works which are likely to be revised, a grant of rights may extend to one edition only, rather than a fixed term of years. All rights not expressly granted should be reserved to the Proprietor.

Publisher's responsibility to publish

Once the rights are granted, the Proprietor will want to ensure that an accurate translation appears reasonably promptly. The local publisher is normally required to undertake that it will commission a faithful and accurate translation by a competent translator (from the original language, based on the latest edition, and with no unauthorised alterations, omissions or additions – see above) and will publish it at its own risk and expense within a specified number of months. If publication does not take place within the given time-scale, the licence will normally terminate and the rights revert, so it is advisable to allow reasonable time for the translation itself (especially if approval is required) as well as local production. The Proprietor will normally wish to be informed of the actual publication date. To assist with production (and accuracy) the Proprietor may supply film or digital files, or otherwise may wish to see samples of any illustrations to be reproduced directly from the original edition in order to assess their quality.

Warranties

The local publisher will normally seek the standard English law warranties from the Proprietor: that the work is not, for example, an infringement of someone else's copyright and has not previously been published or made available in that territory before – any warranties outside the Proprietor's own control should ideally match, and not exceed, those originally given by the author (see Chapter 4). The publisher may want the right (on notifying the Proprietor) to remove passages which on local legal advice may be actionable in the territory concerned.

Permissions and illustrations

Copyright permissions for extracts and illustrations may need to be re-sought for foreign language editions; it is important to agree who is going to undertake this (and who will pay any new fees). For a major work, it may be a complex and time-consuming task, and the Proprietor may prefer to arrange it and charge the publisher the cost plus an administration fee. If the local publisher is going to do it, it may be advisable for the Proprietor to ask for written proof that it has been done.

Illustrations may present unique problems for foreign translations of children's books: pictures that are perfect for one country may not be acceptable in another (for example, on grounds of racial mix, or on moral, social or religious grounds). Some pictures may need to be omitted or replaced; in some cases, a complete set of fresh illustrations better adapted to the local market may need to be commissioned by the local publisher, in which case they will need to be costed in.

Copyright notice

As the making of a translation creates a new copyright work (see above) there will normally be two separate copyright lines – one for the original author, or whoever now owns copyright in the original work, and one for the translator, or whoever owns copyright in the translation. The Proprietor will also probably require details to be included of the Proprietor's original edition, so that it is clear the translation is an authorised arrangement.

In some territories, there may be local registration or other legal formalities before copyrights can be protected; the local publisher should be obliged to make the necessary arrangements, and also undertake to comply with any local copyright regulations.

Advance and royalties

Sometimes a lump sum fee is agreed for a limited print-run, but royalties are probably more common. It is important to be clear what price is to be used as the basis for calculation – local selling price, retail or recommended retail price (minus any VAT) or average wholesale price (used in most central and East European countries). An advance is normally required, with part at least of the payment due immediately on signature of the agreement; there is often a provision that if the agreement is not signed, and the first tranche of the advance paid, within a given period (such as 60 days of the contract date), the licence will terminate and the rights revert to the Proprietor.

The usual detailed accounting information should be required (see above), and it is also wise to agree the currency in which royalties are to be paid; not all local currencies are fully convertible, and payments in blocked currencies which cannot be sent outside the country concerned are of limited use to foreign rights owners (although they may be better than nothing).

Publishers in most countries without fully convertible currencies now find it easier to hold hard currency accounts or to purchase hard currency in order to make licence payments.

Updates/new editions

The publisher will normally want an option on any new or revised editions, on the understanding that all changes notified will be incorporated. The licensor would normally require a new contract to cover any new edition.

Termination and reversion of rights

The normal provisions for termination of the licence will apply, for example for insolvency or breach (see Chapter 4), but special attention may need to be paid to the terms on which rights may revert if a translation goes out of print. Does 'out of print' mean only in the local publisher's home territory, or in all territories (so that a Spanish edition, say, might still be 'in print' if it is available in South America)? Consider also what the position will be if the bound stock is exhausted but the publisher wishes to keep the translation available via print on demand. There may also be a need for a provision that the licence will terminate and rights will revert if sales of the translation fall below a certain minimum level, or generate a certain minimum revenue, in any single accounting period (or perhaps any two periods in succession).

MERCHANDISING RIGHTS

Some publications – particularly children's books – may contain names, characters, designs or illustrations which are popular enough in their own right to be exploited not only via the medium of books but also on T-shirts, stationery, mugs and other merchandise (hence the label 'merchandising rights'). Film and TV exposure usually helps. The characters of Beatrix Potter were early examples of successful merchandising, widely licensed now for a range of merchandise such as children's crockery and other nursery goods; other examples are A.A. Milne's Winnie the Pooh, Harry Potter and Batman. If handled properly, such exploitation, across a wide range of goods, can add very considerably to the earning potential of the original work (and in some cases exceed it).

Where a work has merchandising potential, the author or agent may grant the merchandising rights to the publisher, together with other publishing rights, or they may retain them for separate exploitation. They may be a key element, for example, of film or TV deals. Exploitation may be bit by bit, product by product, in which case the publisher or agent may end up dealing with multiple licences for a whole range of goods; alternatively (and increasingly nowadays), the rights might be licensed in one go to a specialist merchandising company which, in return for a commission on revenue, will then take on the task of seeking out, and sub-licensing, suitable manufacturers and products. Whoever handles the rights, there are a number of key points to bear in mind, two of the most important of which are:

- protection of rights;
- quality control.

Grant of rights

You can't grant merchandising rights if you don't own them or control them yourself. So the first and most essential thing to do is check the contract. If you are a publisher, check your author contract to see that it contains a specific grant of rights, or a clearly inclusive grant of rights such as 'all subsidiary rights' or 'any other rights'. If an author or agent, make sure that merchandising rights have not already been granted elsewhere. And if you want to use original illustrations as well as names of characters, make sure that the illustrator, or other rights owner, has granted you merchandising rights in them too (otherwise – if agreement cannot be reached – you may need to recommission new illustrations).

Assuming – subject to all the above – that you do have the relevant rights, you will need to consider the terms on which you are going to sub-license them (or some of them) to others.

In particular:

- Will the rights granted be exclusive or non-exclusive? (This may depend on your view of the market, and the status of the particular licensee.)
- Will the licence cover the world, or a specific territory or territories? (Merchandising rights are often licensed country by country.) Will it cover Internet or other digital exploitation?
- How long will the licence last? (Three- or five-year terms are common, usually renewable, and often with a sell-off period at the end.)

Product specifications and approval

Unless an overall licence is being granted, the products on which the names or images may be exploited by that licensee must be clearly specified and described in as much detail as possible (for example, T-shirts or different sizes of greetings card or items of breakfast crockery). They are usually set out in an appendix. Any products that the licensor wishes to exploit itself (such as DVDs, or digital publishing, games and apps) should be expressly reserved.

The licensee should have a clear obligation to seek out (actively) potential sub-licensees and, in some cases, distributors and propose the most suitable ones for particular products to the licensor; once selected, the licensee should be responsible for their regular supervision and control. All sub-licences should be in a form approved by the licensor, and should not exceed the term of the original licence. If there is not already an agreed plan, it is advisable in the interests of quality control to set out a regular procedure for submission and approval of product proposals, within set timetables. It should be clear that the products selected should in no way reflect adversely on the image, reputation or goodwill of the licensor, and the licensor should at all times retain a right of rejection or veto. This quality control should not only apply to initial prototypes or mock-ups and packaging, but also continue after the products have been launched, with regular samples submitted for approval, either at random or on demand. The licensor needs to be satisfied at all times that the products are suitable in themselves, and manufactured to a high enough standard. They must also be safe; the licensee must take legal responsibility for any product liability, for example for defective goods, or for breach of any safety standards (and insure where necessary). Needless to say, once approved, there should be no changes without consent.

Promotion and marketing

The licence will normally specify merchandise to be on the market within a given timetable. There is often a launch deadline, within a given number of months or by a particular deadline (for example to tie in with a film or TV series). Thereafter, the licensee should undertake to continue advertising, marketing and distributing the licensed products within the agreed territory. All packaging and promotional material should conform to samples – the licensor may also wish to specify the choice of media used. It is customary for the licensee to undertake to sell only to reputable wholesalers or retail outlets, and the licensor may exclude certain kinds of sales (for example premium sales, or door to door) and retain the right to order the suspension of sales to any particular outlet of which it disapproves.

There will usually be agreed sales targets: quarterly targets are common. If targets are not met (sometimes two or more in succession) the licence will normally terminate, and the rights revert to the licensor.

Copyright and trade marks

The names, characters or illustrations being merchandised will probably be copyright works and quite possibly registered trade marks too (for more on trade marks, see Chapter 10). It is essential in any merchandising licence that all these copyrights and trade marks should be expressly acknowledged and recognised by the licensee and on the products themselves. A copyright claim in agreed form, with the name of the copyright owner (see Chapter 4), should normally appear on all relevant products and packaging, and a trade mark notice, in the UK usually ® or ™, next to all words, phrases or logos which are registered trade marks. If the merchandising licence is for an overseas territory, it may be necessary to make the licensee responsible for registering any copyrights or trade marks locally – this should be done in the licensor's name, not the licensee's. The licensee may, however, need to be recorded as a licensee at the Trade Marks Registry and the parties may need to supply details of the licensing agreement.

In addition, of course, it is very likely that the product itself will constitute a new copyright work, in which case it will be desirable in order to avoid any conflict for the new copyright to be acquired from the manufacturer or designer and assigned back to the licensor; it will normally be the licensee's responsibility to see that this is done.

Infringements and insurance

It is customary to require the licensee to exercise vigilance on the licensor's or proprietor's behalf against any unauthorised copying or use, and notify them of any infringements at once so that any necessary legal action may be taken. The licensor will normally indemnify the licensee against any legal risks and costs arising from permitted use, provided any claims are notified at once, and the licensee will normally give a corresponding indemnity to the licensor for any activities outside the terms of the agreement. The licensee is normally well advised to arrange general liability insurance of its own, although mutual insurance, to spread the risk, is sometimes agreed.

Moral rights

Bear in mind that an illustrator might not only own copyright in original illustrations but also have personal moral rights in them, particularly a right of paternity – to be credited as the illustrator - and a right of integrity – to object to derogatory treatment (see Chapter 3). If the illustrator agrees, these rights may be waived, either unconditionally or insofar as necessary to exploit the particular merchandising rights concerned.

Royalties and commissions

There may be an initial one-off fee for permission to test the market over, say, a one-year trial. Thereafter fees or royalties entirely depend on the popularity and marketability of the character, design or name being licensed: the range is normally between 5 per cent and 15 per cent of the invoice price, but higher commissions – up to 45 per cent – are not unknown for major licensees with a proven track record. Any percentage commission should cease with the end of the licence agreement.

Quarterly sales figures and accounts are usual – the normal requirements to keep accurate accounts, and to allow inspection for errors, should apply. Payments should be made for all sales in the period, irrespective of whether the licensee has yet been paid.

Non-assignment and key men

A merchandising licence is normally non-transferable and non-assignable without the licensor's prior consent in writing. There is also often a stipulation (called a '**Key Man**' clause) that the licence will end, and the rights revert, if any key individual within the licensee's organisation departs, or at least giving the licensor the option to terminate if this happens.

Termination

Termination is usually on the normal terms, for example, for breach or insolvency; merchandising licences may also terminate if a key man leaves the licensee, or if there is any other unacceptable change in the control or management of the licensee.

On termination, the licensee should arrange the termination of any sub-licences, with due notice, and arrange for any samples, artwork or other materials to be returned and any unsold stock to be delivered up (usually at cost) or certified as destroyed. Manufacturing equipment, such as moulds, may need to be destroyed. Needless to say, any outstanding payments should be paid forthwith.

FILM AND TV RIGHTS

Making a feature film or TV series is an immensely complex – and expensive – business, and negotiating rights with film and TV companies is not a recommended pastime for the faint hearted. For the right literary 'property', however, it can be a highly lucrative form of exploitation, not only in fees and royalties from the film itself but also in increased exposure and sales of the book. Sometimes film rights are optioned before the property is published, as happened in the case of the first Harry Potter book and the film adaptation of Lynne Barber's memoir *An Education*. In other cases the film might appear many years after publication of the book, the most obvious recent example being *The Lord of the Rings* trilogy directed by Peter Jackson, which appeared more than 40 years after the publications of J.R.R. Tolkien's novels, although the author had sold the film rights before his death in 1973 and an animated film had appeared in 1978. Film and TV rights often therefore need long-term management and, since the media involved are so different, control of them is often retained by the author's agent rather than granted to the publisher of the book.

Underlying rights

A film or TV producer or production company wishing to make a film based on a book which is still in copyright will need to clear the 'underlying' literary rights at the outset (and, equally, any artistic, musical, dramatic and other rights which may be involved). Initially, as a rule, clearing the rights does not involve actually acquiring them outright; at this stage the film is still an idea only and may never be made, so they may never be needed. What happens first almost invariably is that the producer will seek to secure an option.

Options

The advantage of an option, rather than an outright purchase of rights, is that it enables the film producer to reserve the underlying rights for a (comparatively) modest upfront fee whilst spending anything up to two years preparing a script, finding investors, putting together the necessary film finance, and finding a director, leading actors and suitable locations. It also limits the copyright owner's risk, by avoiding a full grant of rights until it is certain that the film will actually be made and that the producer is able to pay for the rights.

Unless the subject is very topical, options are normally granted initially for a year or 18 months, for a non-returnable fee which is usually not more than 10 per cent of the total intended purchase price (for low-budget films, it may be lower). The option is usually extendable for one or two further 6- or 12-month periods, in case developing a satisfactory script and putting together the finance proves harder than expected (it often does). During the option period, the producer will need the right to make certain uses of the literary work concerned; specifically, to copy extracts and make an adaptation in the form of a screenplay to show potential investors, or even to make a pilot if TV rights are being acquired.

The exact rights (and media) over which the option is granted should be set out clearly: the usual way of doing this is to cross-refer to the intended final Acquisition document (see below) and attach it as an appendix to the option.

If the project falls through, and the option is not exercised within the option period, the rights owner should ideally have the right to buy back any new copyrights created in (for example) the screenplay or any other adaptations of the work – although a producer who does not own the underlying rights, and whose option has expired, will not be able to do much with scripts or other material without infringing existing rights.

Acquisition and assignment

If and when the option is exercised, the Acquisition agreement may then be signed, under which the balance of the purchase price is paid, and in which the necessary film rights are finally granted. This may be via an assignment of the copyright, but now often takes the form of a sole and exclusive licence of (specified) film rights, usually for the full term of copyright, although the period of exclusivity may be limited to 10 or 15 years, for example for made-for-TV films. 'Quitclaims' are often required at the same time, under which the relevant (usually English-language) publishers confirm that they have no conflicting interest in the film rights.

It is essential to set out clearly what rights are included (and which are not), and particularly whether TV rights are included. The definition of 'film' in the 1988 Act would normally include TV programmes, so it is important to be clear about this: if it is not the intention to grant TV rights, a narrower definition of films should be used, such as 'theatrical feature films'. Most producers will want both the film and TV rights, for obvious reasons – a TV channel will, not surprisingly, usually seek to acquire unlimited film and TV rights, but even if the film is being made primarily for theatrical (that is, cinema) exploitation, the producer will still usually wish to show it on television. If, despite this, TV rights are not available the producer may require a 'hold back' clause, restricting the proprietor's own exploitation of TV rights for an agreed number of years.

The rights granted will normally include most or all of the following:

- the right to make one or more films (including all forms of television) plus remakes, prequels, and sequels;
- the right to show the work in public;
- the right to broadcast the work (including excerpts or trailers, and including all forms of television, satellite, cable, high definition and whatever else);
- the right to make adaptations of the work (such as dramatisations and screenplays);
- the right to issue copies to the public (including DVD and Blu-ray rental);
- the right to distribute the work online;
- 'publicity rights': to create written synopses (usually of up to 5,000 or 10,000 words), and broadcast and publish extracts;

- the right to compose music to accompany the work, and the right to make sound recordings;
- the right to use the author's name, likeness and biographical details for promotional purposes;
- the right to publish a 'book of the film' (often withheld by the rights owner);
- associated merchandising rights.

If the film is not made within a specified number of years (for example, five) the Acquisition agreement should provide that the rights revert to the owner, perhaps upon payment of an agreed sum. This is often calculated by reference to the sum originally paid by the producer and also possibly the further amounts the producer has spent in developing the project. During that period it is advisable for the rights owner to specify that the film rights should not be assigned without its consent, at least not without a full novation (see Chapter 4).

There will normally be warranties and indemnities on both sides: the producer will want the usual warranties covering the original work (see Chapter 4), and the owner will often seek a specific indemnity covering any liability arising out of changes made in the film.

Producers and production companies will normally insist on a full waiver of the author's moral rights – at least insofar as they relate to film exploitation form. The right of paternity is not likely to be infringed, since specific on-screen credits are usually agreed in the Acquisition agreement, but the author's right of integrity (to object to derogatory treatment) may become an issue unless the author is willing to consent to 'treatments', as defined in the 1988 Act, being made.

Payment of fees or royalties depends on the status of the author, and the nature of the adaptation. Usually, the purchase price will be a fixed sum, possibly with a further sum on top calculated by reference to a percentage of the film's budget, up to a cap. Most rights owners will also be entitled to a share of the 'net profits'. It is, however, essential to define 'profits' clearly – after deducting the cost of production, financing, distribution and deferments, there may not be very much 'profit' left at all. On top of this, there should be repeat fees, and additional revenue from any re-makes, prequels and sequels. Payments in respect of TV exploitation are normally triggered by the first broadcast or transmission.

DVD and Blu-ray distribution and the like may in some (perhaps rare) cases entitle the rights owner to additional specific payments, but it is more likely that revenues from these sources will simply go into the general revenue stream, and, if the author is lucky, contribute to 'profits' in due course. Under the Copyright and Related Rights Regulations 1996, implementing the EU Directive on rental and lending rights, authors and screenwriters who have transferred their rental rights in films to the relevant producers have an unwaivable right to 'equitable remuneration' from any such rental exploitation, although this is normally bought out under the contract as part of the general payments receivable.

ELECTRONIC RIGHTS

Electronic rights is a somewhat dated and increasingly unhelpful term used in older publishing contracts, often used to cover two quite separate (and very different) rights:

- E-book rights, usually meaning exploitation by the original publisher of the whole verbatim text via the medium of a handheld device or iPad (and often treated as part of volume rights)
- E-version rights, usually meaning subsidiary e-rights or other forms of digital exploitation, often sub-licensed to someone else.

Publishers are increasingly licensing their works directly online, as e-books via platforms such as the Apple iPad, Sony reader or Amazon Kindle, via agreements with aggregators (see below), or often, in the case of journals, to groups of authorised users via site licences (e.g. for academic institutions, or library consortia). This latter raises specific access and security issues (see the following section on online access licences).

Acquiring electronic rights

As explained above, in order to license electronic rights (however that phrase may be defined) you first need to own them or acquire them. From the publisher's point of view, this means acquiring a specific grant of the necessary rights from the copyright owner, usually the author. However, most publishing contracts more than 20 or so years old make no mention of electronic rights, and even more recent agreements may be somewhat vague on the two key issues of:

- what rights exactly are granted; and
- what will be paid for them.

(Often the second of these is left 'to be agreed', although arguably this reduces the 'grant' to a mere option.)

The golden rule is: *never assume*. A publishing contract decades old, which granted 'all rights', or 'publishing rights' (even 'including all subsidiary rights') at a time when the relevant type of digital exploitation – such as e-books – could not possibly have been in the minds of the parties, cannot safely be assumed to grant those specific digital exploitation rights now. A slightly more recent phrase such as volume rights (or even 'electronic rights') might be sufficient to cover straightforward exploitation of the verbatim text in digital form, but it might not be specific enough to license more general Internet use or access. In today's online world, it cannot be stressed strongly enough that a specific platform for e-publication must be supported by an equally specific grant of rights – especially if (as is often the case) substantial investment is proposed. If it isn't clearly provided for in the contract already, it is highly advisable to secure an additional, specific, grant of rights from the rights owner(s). (There may be more than one – in the case of a children's book, for example, a fresh grant of rights may well be required from the illustrator as well as the author. A simple exchange of letters will normally suffice.)

The initial grant of rights: author–publisher licensing

Some publishers (especially reference and periodical publishers) may be in a sufficiently strong bargaining position with their authors and contributors to be able to insist on a full buy-out of electronic rights, but in other cases the author may want some evidence that the publisher actually intends to *exploit* those rights, and has the skill and capacity to do so. If all the publisher is doing is acquiring rights pre-emptively, just in case they may be needed later on, authors – particularly those with agents – may feel it unwise to do more than grant a first option, reserving the rights generally until a firm proposal can be made which refers to a defined platform and product, and offers specific payment terms. A publisher who controls all other publishing rights in a work, however, will at least want some reassurance by way of undertaking that the author or agent is not going to exploit the work electronically elsewhere without prior consultation.

If electronic rights are granted, it is advisable to specify as far as possible what rights exactly this rather vague and dated phrase includes. There will be particular types of exploitation which the publisher may wish to see expressly included, or which an author equally may wish to withhold. In this context it is important to distinguish and deal separately with the 'products' which can be based on, include or be derived from the text being licensed (such as enhanced e-books), and the 'distribution media' for those products. For example:

Product categories:

- original text in digital form including e-books and journals available online;
- online versions or editions of major works, e.g. OED and the Grove music dictionaries;
- information databases and multimedia products, which include the text;
- entertainment/leisure software (such as computer games, mobile phone apps and DVD) derived from the text or its characters;
- recordings of performances/readings of the text; film based on text.

Distribution media:

- Internet and online access;
- CD-ROM for home or office use;
- broadcast (including digital broadcast)/public performance
- open/closed network distribution rights including site licensing;
- pay-per-view and payment for use.

These distribution media options may vary in relation to each of the various product categories being licensed. Also, of course, the appropriate royalty structure and percentages may vary. It is important to define (and license) each market sector separately, and avoid overlapping (and conflicting) grants of rights.

The following points should generally be borne in mind:

- Is the licence exclusive or non-exclusive?
- Are the rights limited to electronic use of the (unaltered) verbatim text? Does this include e-book and online delivery?
- May the work only be used complete, or may it be condensed or abridged, manipulated or altered?
- May it be used in a compilation with other works? Does this include an interactive/multimedia version?
- Is the licence limited to delivery platforms currently in existence or is the intention to include 'any other devices hereafter invented'?
- Is the licence for all languages (human and machine) and all territories? (Bear in mind that territorial limits may be of limited effect with Internet use.)
- What payment methods are available (fees, payments per use, subscriptions, royalties based on net receipts, or dealer price?) and what proportion will the author/contributor get?
- Does the licence last for the full term of copyright, or only for a limited term of years?
- Do (or should) the rights revert to the author if they are not being exploited (or if a product is launched, but then allowed to go 'out of promotion')?

Major publishers planning (or investing in) ambitious online works may prefer to commission authors, illustrators and other contributors specifically for those projects, and take full assignments of copyright from them in their work – or at least sole and exclusive licences for all such exploitation for the full term of copyright. In other cases, where a full buy-out does not seem appropriate, authors and agents may prefer to grant electronic rights for limited periods at a time (perhaps for as little as three or five years) with provision for the rights to revert if the publisher or other licensee concerned has not exploited them within a given period. Following the EU Rental and Lending Directive, it will also be important to deal with authors' rights to 'equitable remuneration' on the rental of films based on their work.

The author's moral rights – particularly of paternity and integrity (see Chapter 3) should also not be forgotten, where they apply (for exceptions, see Chapter 3). Unless moral rights are going to be completely waived, it will be necessary to make sure that authors who have asserted their paternity rights are credited adequately, and also that the works are not subjected to derogatory treatment, and – ideally – are not subjected to any significant 'treatment' at all, without the author's consent.

Electronic licensing and joint ventures

Owners or licensees of electronic rights – such as publishers – may seek to exploit those rights in a number of different ways. Some will have the experience and resources to develop electronic products themselves in-house – but this may be difficult initially for a smaller publisher. Some will acquire electronic publishing expertise by bolt-ons or buy-ins of existing teams from outside, but again this can be expensive. Most will rely on straightforward licensing or sub-licensing to service providers or aggregators already in the market, or – where more active collaboration is required – joint ventures. As with all such licensing, however, many legal constraints are imposed; at the end of the day it is largely a question of who has (or is perceived to have) the relevant expertise, and who you trust.

Key issues which should be covered in any such licence include the following:

- Is the licence exclusive or non-exclusive? Bear in mind any possible conflict with existing e-rights, or film or TV rights.
- Define the languages (computer as well as human) and the territories (where appropriate) in which exploitation may take place.
- Define the permitted platforms (for example Internet, or CD-ROM, or use on a hand-held device, including not only dedicated e-book readers but also iPads and mobile phone apps) if necessary; in some cases it may be advisable to license only a specific format or product.
- Agree on (and cost in) any necessary back-up facilities, helplines or other support overheads: who will provide for these, and how will any costs be shared, or deducted? Will the author(s) need to be involved in regular revisions or updates, and on what terms?
- If necessary, specify permitted kinds of use, any restrictions on authorised or permitted users and in appropriate cases consider a site licence, restricting use to particular geographical sites (such as offices or university campuses – for more on this, see online access licences, below).
- May the work be altered or adapted in any way, and may it – or parts of it – be 'bundled' with other works? Think seriously about the integrity of the work (including the author's moral rights): will you retain a right of consultation (or even veto) over any changes? With a new product in a new medium, quality control may be crucial – don't leave approval until it's too late. Agree, if necessary, a staged consultation/approval procedure as the product develops, and retain the right to withdraw approval and terminate the licence as and when necessary.
- How long will the licence last (three to five years is common)? Is there a launch deadline or specified release date? Consider the circumstances in which you might wish to terminate the licence early and regain the rights: breach of key terms (such as non-payment, or unauthorised use), unsatisfactory sales performance or failure to meet agreed targets, and the usual termination and reversion provisions, for example, on insolvency.

- Be clear about ownership of all relevant copyrights, and any other relevant intellectual property rights such as any trade marks. In the case of a joint venture, the joint venture company may need to acquire the rights. Do not forget to renew any necessary copyright permissions (and agree who will do this – and pay any fees).

- Provide adequately for any moral rights of all relevant authors, and any required waivers (see Chapter 3). If possible ensure that any sub-licences are also made subject to the author's moral rights. Agree specific credits, not only to the authors but to the licensing publisher, and ensure that this covers advertising and packaging as well as the product itself. Be particularly careful about any permitted use of brand names, logos or trade marks.

- Agree clearly what is to happen about money – who gets what and when. For a compilation or multimedia work, this may involve agreeing on the comparative 'value' of each work included: bear in mind that text occupies far less space on a CD than pictures, yet may be far more valuable in selling the product. Allow for the value of any digital amendments which individual rights owners may need to make, but equally bear in mind the high upfront development costs a software house may incur. Agree a payment system appropriate for the product and medium concerned – this may be a familiar royalty structure, or payments-per-use, or a proportion of agreed profits (as in the film and TV industries). In each case be clear about the method of calculation to be used. It may be wise to provide for a review of financial terms after three to five years, and perhaps minimum revenue in a given period.

ONLINE ACCESS LICENCES

In an online world, many people have effectively become self-publishers, via podcasts, blogs and tweets, and most such 'user-created content' is intended to be freely used and read, with no access or re-use restrictions at all. For authors and publishers, however, access conditions for copyright content usually need more serious thought. Given that 'digital is different', and that digital access enables unlimited perfect copying at the click of a mouse, online licences need considerable care. However, for most publishers the demand for online access represents a major publishing market.

Licences for online access raise a number of key issues. The notes which follow reflect a variety of current experience, including site licences for academic or library use.

THE LICENSEE

Be specific, not just in defining the licensee itself, but also in listing all addresses or sites which the licence is to cover. This may most easily be done in an appendix or schedule to the licence, which can then be updated if necessary without having to amend the main contract. It is useful to require contact details, e.g. of a licence administrator or technical contact.

AUTHORISED USERS

It is important to identify as precisely as possible which categories of users will be entitled to access. In the case of an academic institution, will this cover full-time faculty staff, researchers and librarians only, or include temporary, contract or visiting staff? All students, or only those registered full-time at that institution? Some flexibility is usually needed, e.g. to allow for joint degrees and linked research teams (and even walk-in users, if agreed), provided all those concerned are made subject to the relevant terms and conditions, and can gain access only via the licensee's secure network or intranet, either via designated and supervised terminals or from an authenticated IP address.

LICENSED MATERIAL

Set out clearly what is licensed and what isn't – if necessary title by title, but at least which online services and electronic products, and any other content available (and for which, obviously, the publisher owns or controls the necessary electronic rights). Detailed listings may be done more easily in appendices or schedules.

ACCESS LICENCE AND TERM

Online licences are normally non-exclusive and non-transferable – it is highly advisable to spell this out – and it is clearer if they refer to specific licensed activities or permitted uses, and are made subject to any other terms and conditions (such as payment of the fee). Be clear about the dates on which the licence will commence and end, and what happens at the end of the term – will it automatically terminate (unless renewed) or will it continue from year to year? Many institutions ask for 'perpetual' access to be included in the contract – although some publishers (being realistic about immortality) may find this a difficult obligation to justify in practice, it may be possible to arrive at a form of wording which satisfies both sides, such as 'so far as possible'.

INTELLECTUAL PROPERTY

It is advisable to confirm on both sides that the works licensed are copyright works, and confirm any other intellectual property or other rights, such as trade marks. Licensees are often required to use reasonable endeavours to protect relevant IP rights, or at least to notify any breaches. It is common to reserve to the publisher all rights not specifically granted in the licence, for the avoidance of doubt, and to prohibit removal of, or interference with, authors' names or the publisher's copyright notices or trade marks.

PERMITTED AND PROHIBITED USES

The more clearly these can be set out, the better – two separate lists is the clearest method. Consider what proportion of the licensed material may be stored, viewed, downloaded, copied and printed, and for what purposes. Can it be copied or linked to other authorised users, or even more widely? Commercial use or re-use is usually prohibited, as is uploading to any network other than the designated intranet or secure network – if so, it is wise to be very clear about this.

UNDERTAKINGS AND OBLIGATIONS

These are often stated to be mutual, so that the licensee clearly undertakes not only to pay any fees and charges but also, for example, to make access available only via the secure network, to promote the terms and conditions to all authorised users, to take reasonable steps to terminate any unauthorised access and deal with any copyright infringement reasonably under its control. On the publisher's side, the licensee may look for a continuing (or even 'perpetual') obligation for availability and uninterrupted online access, at least as far as reasonably possible and as far as can be predicted.

TERMINATION

It is usual for either side to have the right to give written notice to terminate, subject to an agreed period of notice, as well as the usual provisions for termination due to insolvency or material breach. It is sensible to specify how long access may continue after termination, and whether any licensed material (e.g. CD-ROMs) should be returned, or whether local files should be destroyed or deleted.

E-BOOK AGREEMENTS

While the trade paperback in printed form is still comparatively popular, user-friendly and cheap, handheld devices are progressively becoming smaller, lighter and cheaper, with easier on-screen reading, and e-book platforms such as the Amazon Kindle and Sony reader, and Apple iPads, are an increasingly user-friendly route to market. Many publishers are entering into contracts with aggregators, suppliers of conversion, storage and distribution services, to make their titles available via this route (see below) but, equally, many publishers are entering into direct e-book licences themselves.

The following notes deal with some of the key issues often raised by such licences. Meanwhile, the Publishers Association is at the time of writing in discussions via a working group with the Joint Information Systems Committee (JISC) on model e-book licences, primarily for the library market, but intended to provide useful guidance on the meaning and interpretation of common terms, and core provisions, for all such e-book licences.

TITLES AND E-VERSIONS

It is important to define carefully:
*   The titles to be included (usually in an appendix, and often with a delivery timetable for key titles); and

- The e-versions to be created, in which formats, and usually for which titles (depending on the particular features of each one), and any approval requirements.

RIGHTS GRANTED

The publisher will need to grant the specific rights necessary for conversion into digital versions, usually using the licensee's own conversion processes and software, incorporating codes and metadata as required, and if necessary to store, sell, distribute, make available and offer access (perhaps including rental) on the publisher's behalf; such grants of rights are normally non-exclusive and non-transferable. The licensee may require confirmation from the publisher that the publisher does actually own or control (or have cleared) the relevant digital rights, not only to each title but also to any third party material included (or, if not, that such material will have been removed).

ACCESS

It is normally wise to limit access to servers controlled by the distributor, with no permanent hosting on any other server without the publisher's prior consent. It is also common to require the distributor to maintain the highest industry standards to protect the e-products from unauthorised access or use, and to notify the publisher promptly if any products are accessed or used without a valid licence agreement. Distributors may also be expected to maintain a helpline for subscribers or customers in the event of software or hardware malfunction. On requests for 'perpetual' access, which may at first sight appear impossible, see the section on Aggregator licences, below.

TERM OF LICENCE

Given the speed at which technology is developing, licences are currently short: three to five years is fairly usual.

COPYRIGHT AND IP RIGHTS

It is advisable to confirm that copyright in the titles concerned (including the final e-versions) rests with the publisher, and there is usually a provision that the licensee should credit the copyright on every version. There may also be a need to make provision for protecting or crediting the authors' moral rights. However, although it is customary to specify that the licensee acquires no copyright rights in the licensed content, or rights in any of the publisher's trade marks, the licensee will often need the right to make use of relevant trade marks, subject usually to a right of approval, and a proviso that no alterations will be made without consent.

CHARGES AND PAYMENTS

There may be conversion charges, or charges for any of the services bought in (which should be set out clearly), but there are normally royalty arrangements for e-versions sold. These may be based on list price or in some cases, net price received, depending on whether, for example, the titles are trade or professional titles. It is advisable to be clear about the timetable for any payments, e.g. quarterly or monthly, and audit arrangements – it is important to ensure that complete and accurate records of sales are kept, and regular sales reports are supplied.

WITHDRAWAL AND TERMINATION

It is sensible to provide for withdrawal of any individual title or titles, on reasonable notice, as well as for termination of the entire licence (on the usual terms, e.g. breach of a material provision, or insolvency), again on reasonable notice. It may be necessary to specify arrangements for return or deletion of any material or files held in digital form.

AGGREGATOR AGREEMENTS

As mentioned above, publishers may license their e-content directly themselves or they may prefer to use the services of intermediary hosters, service providers and distributors with an established place in the e-market, known as aggregators, who (as the name implies) may offer the works of a number of different publishers. Licence agreements with aggregators will have many features in common with other e-publishing agreements, but since they themselves will usually have their own licence agreements with end-users there may be an added layer of access and use to manage.

CONTENT

As with all such agreements, it is essential to be very precise about which of the publisher's titles are included, and which are not – the usual solution is detailed listing in a Schedule or Appendix. Is there to be provision for new titles, or series, to be added later on, usually by mutual consent? An opt-in clause to cover this may be advisable. It may also be appropriate to specify that the aggregator will offer a minimum number of titles (or percentage of the total) at any one time, during the term of the Agreement.

DELIVERY

It is usually necessary to specify the format in which titles should be delivered, and also whether direct to the aggregator or to a specified conversion house.

RIGHTS GRANTED

In return for the usual duty to market the works effectively, the aggregator will need a clear grant of rights, including (usually) a non-exclusive and non-transferable licence to reproduce the content, display, distribute, make available and provide access to it, advertise and sell it (and possibly rent it out), ideally on a designated platform or platforms. It is highly advisable to be specific about the territories in which (and into which) the content may be sold (unless the licence is worldwide). It may be necessary to provide for pay-per-view, as appropriate. They may also need a right to adapt the works, as far as necessary for compatibility in the conversion process, but (usually) not otherwise without prior consent. It is also sensible to specify whether the aggregator may sub-license to authorised agents, re-sellers or affiliates (preferably named), and whether there is any restriction on permitted user groups (e.g. consortia or organisations with more than one site), at least without consent. It may also be wise to specify whether or not (usually *not*) the aggregator is permitted to integrate the licensed content with any other works, or create derivative works based on it, without consent.

ACCESS AND SECURITY

Controlling access in an Internet age is a constant problem, so it is usually advisable to limit access exclusively to servers controlled by the aggregator, and provide that there should be no hosting or access from elsewhere without express consent. An aggregator is usually also expected to provide as much system security as reasonably possible to protect the content from unauthorised access, other than authenticated IP address or password, and to notify the publisher if any unauthorised use or access comes to light.

Some end-users (such as libraries) often demand 'perpetual' access, which may need some thought, since most publishers are not necessarily expecting to exist in perpetuity and may find it hard to justify entering into access obligations for ever, but suitable provisos (such as 'so far as reasonably possible') may suffice.

ROYALTIES AND SALES REPORTING

Financial details are always best set out in a Schedule, and how calculated (e.g. a percentage of online only price). Different royalties may of course apply to different classes of users. Timetable for payment is important, often monthly or quarterly, and if appropriate (for example with some journals) there may be a guaranteed or minimum annual royalty. Timetables – and format – for sales reports should also be detailed, together with any audit provisions (often once per year, during normal business hours), and on what notice.

TERM AND TERMINATION

Most licences are for relatively short periods initially (three or five years is common), or sometimes, for journals, the subscription period. A provision for regular review may be wise, and any renewal terms. Normal termination for breach or insolvency is common, but aggregators may have their own supply contracts with their own customers, so termination provisions will need some care. It is also usual to provide that digital files are deleted or returned on termination of the contract.

EXHAUSTION OF RIGHTS AND PARALLEL IMPORTATION

It is important to recognise that licensing an intermediary to distribute or make available your works may in some circumstances lead to exhaustion of exclusive distribution rights in some territories. It is very important that delivery to aggregators or other retailers should only be done under very clear conditions relating to sales and territories covered, otherwise the necessary 'consent' for putting the works concerned onto the relevant market may not exist. For more on this, see the final section on Exhaustion of Rights in Chapter 13.

OTHER ELECTRONIC AGREEMENTS

Given the developing nature of digital exploitation and licensing in the publishing trade, and the rapid pace of change, it is impossible – and probably invidious – in a book like this to do more than try to highlight a few key principles, which we have tried to do in the preceding sections. Meanwhile, for other kinds of electronic licences in current use, see the growing list of precedents in *Clark's Publishing Agreements* (eighth edition, 2010).

AGREEMENTS BETWEEN AUTHORS AND AGENTS

We looked in some detail in Chapter 4 at literary agents' own standard publishing contracts, in the context of the author–publisher agreement. In the final section of this chapter we will take a quick look at the legal relationship between agents and authors themselves.

Most established literary agencies now enter into some kind of written agreement with authors who they take on, usually in the form of an extended letter. It is possible in some circumstances for an agent to acquire actual or implied authority to represent someone else (called their 'principal') *without* entering into a written agreement, but this is not generally recommended as a long-term business practice, and it is always advisable to record such agreements in writing as soon as possible – if only to confirm the extent of the agent's authority, and (the source of most disputes) what payment or commission they will be entitled to receive.

Where there is an agreement, the terms of that agreement will govern the relationship; there is, however, probably also an overriding obligation on all agents to perform their duties in good faith and with reasonable care and skill. Contracts with all commercial agents within the EU are now regulated by the Commercial Agents Directive, implemented in the UK in the shape of the Commercial Agents (Council Directive) Regulations 1993 (as amended in 1998). Some of the key criteria include the following:

- there should be no conflicts of interest;
- the agent's powers or duties should not be delegated without consent;
- agents should not make secret profits or undeclared commissions;
- agents have a right to be indemnified by their principals when acting within their authority;
- all agents have a right to reasonable remuneration.

The entitlement to reasonable remuneration normally comes to an end straight-away when the agency is terminated, unless the contract provides otherwise. However, although this makes sense for most commercial agencies, it does not allow for agents (such as literary agents) who – apart from a share of any advance – are paid substantially by means of a commission on long-term future earnings. Most literary agency agreements therefore expressly provide that the agent's agreed commission will be paid on *all* future earnings, from all sources, which derive from agreements which that agent actually negotiated (or, in some cases, agreements signed by the author while the agency was in force, even if the agent was not directly involved). If the author accepts this, it means that many agents will continue to be paid commission on their former author's titles long after the agency arrangement itself has been terminated. For this reason, most agents' standard publishing agreements include a clause irrevocably appointing them as the author's authorised recipient for all monies payable on that particular title. Some authors may not be willing to make an irrevocable appointment – there is no legal reason why agency appointments should not be revoked at any time if the author wishes later to be paid direct, or via some other agent, but there will then be a separate contractual issue between the author and the agent about outstanding commission. There is, however, no reason why the publisher should become involved in this: it is entirely a matter between author and agent.

For authors wishing to enter into an agreement with an agent, the Association of Authors' Agents maintains a professional code of conduct. Some general guidance, and comparison of commission rates, may be found in various annual publications such as the *Writers Handbook* and the *Writers and Artists Yearbook*. Carole Blake's book *From Pitch to Publication* has a sample letter.

Part III
Delivery, editing and obligations on publication

Delivery, editing and obligations on publication

6

DELIVERY: ACCEPTANCE OR REJECTION

DELIVERY

The emotional trauma and sheer physical effort of delivering a completed copyright work has often been likened to childbirth (usually by men). It is probably true that few authors – apart from the most experienced – realise quite what they are letting themselves in for when they sign their publishing contracts; first-time authors in particular may underestimate what is required (although a good agent or editor should spot this). In addition, even the best-organised authors may be overtaken by unexpected events, especially if they have any kind of family or social life and a full-time job to hold down too. As a result:

- the work may be delivered late; or
- bits of it – or the whole thing – may not be of the standard expected.

A good publishing contract will foresee both these eventualities and make provision for them (see Chapter 4).

Non-delivery or late delivery

Time will not be regarded as being of the essence unless the contract expressly says that it is (it often does, for example, if the work is a contribution to a major reference project on a tight schedule, or linked into some external event such as a royal wedding). Where time *is* of the essence, non-delivery by the specified date will normally be an automatic ground for termination of the contract, although in many cases – particularly where the author is not to blame – a publisher may retain the option to keep the contract alive a while longer if there seems a reasonable prospect that the work will come in soon and there is in fact a little leeway in the schedule.

Where time is *not* stated to be of the essence, late delivery may still constitute adequate performance of the author's contractual obligation to deliver (indeed, an author may deliver 20 years late and still perform the contract, if the publisher is prepared to wait that long). All other things being equal, two or three months either way would almost certainly be regarded as reasonably acceptable performance, and a publisher might find it difficult to terminate the contract on grounds of non-delivery alone if the author had a reasonable excuse for being late and was ready and willing to deliver in, say, three months time. Beyond that, however, it is probably advisable to confirm any revised schedule in a formal exchange of letters, varying the delivery terms of the original contract; otherwise, the author will be at increasing risk of termination for breach of contract, particularly where the publisher makes it clear (preferably in writing) that continued lateness will not be acceptable. It is important, however, to look at all the surrounding circumstances, and bear in mind any informal meetings or telephone conversations, or any previous dealings between the parties, as well as actual correspondence; a publisher may impliedly extend a delivery deadline by conduct as well as by a formal letter.

Acceptance

If and when the work does finally come in, the publisher will want to check as soon as possible whether it conforms to the publishing contract – whether it is, in fact, the thing contracted for. Any specified formats and delivery requirements – such as delivery on disk – should also be complied with. Under general contract law principles, there is probably only a limited window of opportunity here for the publisher either to reject the work on clear grounds as being unacceptable – not a sufficient performance of the contract by the author – or else expressly or impliedly accept it. Putting the work into production (or even editing, or marking up for house style) might well constitute implied acceptance, so that even if unacceptable defects were discovered later it might then be difficult for the publisher to reject the work as a whole. Accepting delivery of a work should therefore not merely be a process of passive collection, but should involve at some point a positive inspection and approval of what is delivered. For most works, the person to do this will be the commissioning publisher or in-house editor: for major works the approval of a general editor or section editor may be required. Whoever it is should be aware of the contractual significance of what they are doing – once a work is substantially accepted, then the publisher is to all intents and purposes probably stuck with it (apart from defects which may later come to light, such as libel).

As to what is or is not 'acceptable', this will be entirely governed by the publishing contract, whether written or informal. Where no written contract exists, or where the contract does not refer to any specification or acceptance criteria (it is surprising how many do not) then any reasonably competent work of approximately the right length in the subject area concerned would probably be sufficient to perform the contract. Most good publishing contracts, however, contain at least some acceptance criteria, ranging from a full detailed specification set out in an appendix – probably the clearest method – to generalised phrases such as 'of a standard which might reasonably be expected' or sometimes just the single, and wonderfully simple, word 'acceptable' (which, unless further defined, probably does not mean very much, but can give the publisher very wide discretion, particularly if 'in the Publisher's sole opinion').

Rejection

What happens if the work – or a substantial part of it – is not acceptable to the publisher? The general rule in law is that the contract will prevail; if the publisher has a wide discretion under the contract, or if what the author delivers cannot reasonably be regarded as fulfilling his or her obligations under the contract, then the publisher may well have the right to reject it and terminate the contract in accordance with any relevant termination provisions. An author commissioned to write a 300-page textbook who delivers instead a 50-page pamphlet (this has been known) is clearly not delivering the work contracted for. Similarly, an article or research study commissioned for inclusion in a post-graduate STM journal which turns out to have no references or footnotes and to be written at a much lower level would also be a fairly obvious candidate for rejection, provided that the requirement to write at post-graduate level had been clearly agreed. But what if the publisher simply does not like the work, or is disappointed by it?

If it complies with the contract, but just isn't as good as hoped for, then the publisher will probably not have the right to reject the work for that reason alone, unless the contract gives the publisher virtually complete discretion. In most cases, the publisher's only remedy will be to persuade the author to improve it (see below), and if that still does not produce the desired result, make the most of what was clearly a commissioning mistake.

Rejection, if it happens, should be in accordance with any procedures set out in the contract: the publisher may have the option either to reject at once, or to put the author on notice to make specified alterations or improvements to bring the work up to contract standard within a given timetable, and then to reject if this is not done. Where improvements are feasible, some contracts give the publisher a further option of commissioning a competent editor to make the necessary improvements and deduct the cost from the author's royalties or other earnings in due course (this would be subject to the author's moral rights, on which see further below).

Disputes

There are often disputes surrounding rejection of a work and termination of the contract may not always turn out to be as straightforward as the publisher might hope. Where the contract gives the publisher absolute discretion, and the work as delivered is obviously not in accordance with the contract terms, there should be little cause for dispute, but in other cases – particularly where alterations are involved – there may be considerable disagreement. If such disputes cannot be resolved amicably between the parties, many contracts provide arbitration clauses as a means of avoiding full-scale litigation. Arbitration clauses normally survive termination of the contract, and can usually be invoked unilaterally by either party, but formal arbitration is not always any quicker or cheaper than pursuing a claim in the High Court (see Chapter 4). It is still, therefore, comparatively rare in publishing disputes; most are settled one way or another between the parties.

In the event of rejection and termination it is important to confirm:

- what happens to the rights granted under the contract; and
- what happens to any advances, or other payments made.

In most cases the author will quite reasonably want his or her rights back, and most contracts provide for all rights granted to revert under such circumstances so that the author can still exploit the work, even if this will now have to be elsewhere. If the author assigned full copyright to the publisher (or someone else) under the contract, this may have to be formally re-assigned; to be effective, this should be in writing, and signed by or on behalf of the current copyright owner (see Chapter 4).

Advances, though always a fertile area for dispute, are either a matter for the contract or entirely at the publisher's discretion: where the publisher has paid an advance (or advances) the publisher will normally be entitled to ask for these to be repaid if the work is rejected unless they are clearly stated to be non-returnable.

SUMMARY CHECKLIST: DELIVERY

- Is time of the essence?
- Has the delivery schedule been revised (even impliedly)?
- Is the work delivered the work which was contracted for?
- Does it comply with any 'acceptance' criteria in the contract?
- Are there any grounds for rejection?
- Is there any rejection or disputes procedure?
- What happens to the rights and any advances?

EDITING AND ALTERATIONS

Once a work is accepted, it may be sent straight off for production as it is (particularly if it comes in on disk) but in the great majority of cases the publisher will want to edit it first, often via an outside editor. This mysterious process frequently leads to disputes, and horror stories abound of uncontrolled, demented editors mutilating what were previously perfectly publishable works. In reality, of course, editing varies widely from publisher to publisher, some doing little more than marking up to conform with agreed house style, and others adopting a more interventionist role. From a legal point of view, the position is fairly clear: subject to any agreement to the contrary, a publisher who contracts to publish an author's work is obliged to publish that work substantially as delivered by the author, and is not entitled to adapt (or 'improve') it without the author's consent. This is particularly so in light of the author's moral right of integrity and other moral rights in the UK under the 1988 Act. We will consider the implications of the right of integrity below.

AGREEMENT BY CONTRACT

As a general rule, authors will not be entitled in law to prevent editorial changes to which they have freely consented. Even their moral rights (see below) will not apply to anything done with their consent. Consent may be express (and set out, for example, in a contract) or implied – perhaps by conduct, or a previous course of dealing – but implied consent may be harder to prove. Most publishers will therefore seek the author's express consent in advance to the level of editorial changes they think they might need to make by including a specific clause to that effect in the publishing agreement. What changes may or may not be permitted will therefore become a question of interpreting the relevant wording of the contract.

Contracts, as we saw in Chapter 4, vary widely but most publishing agreements try to give the publisher some leeway at least to make necessary and reasonable alterations in accordance with any agreed specifications, and the relevant house style. Where a detailed house style book is available this should ideally be made available to the author well before the time the contract is signed and expressly referred to in the contract itself: you cannot generally incorporate express terms into a contract which have not been disclosed and agreed by the time the contract is signed.

In addition, many contracts give the publisher the right to make alterations on the advice of its legal advisers, for example to remove passages which might be libellous or infringe someone else's privacy, or which might otherwise be in breach of the author's warranties (see Chapter 4). Libel is a particular risk (see Chapter 7), and it may be advisable to have any suspect passages read for libel by a lawyer who specialises in this kind of work and knows what to look for; many publishers retain lawyers to do regular libel reading for them, since a legal opinion may often be required at short notice.

Any alterations beyond the level clearly provided for in the contract, or otherwise agreed by the author, are highly dangerous, and where they cause damage to the author or his or her reputation may entitle the author to bring an action for breach of contract, infringement of moral rights, or – in severe cases – for defamation. Editors who feel an author's work could be 'improved' should therefore keep any urge to rewrite it firmly under control.

NECESSARY CHANGES

A publisher might be entitled in an emergency to make last-minute deletions, or minor consequential amendments, in order to avoid publishing infringing or illegal material (such as defamatory matter) and the moral right of integrity in particular does not apply to anything done to avoid the commission of an offence or comply with a statutory duty. However, in the absence of a clear contractual right to make the changes concerned, changes the publisher considers 'necessary' may not always be entirely safe: if time allows, it is always advisable to consult the author, and ideally get the author to make the changes personally. Obtaining the author's participation, or at least express agreement, will give the greatest possible protection against future claims by the author, for example, of breach of contract, or defamation. In addition, anything done with the author's consent cannot infringe his or her moral rights.

IMPLIED CONSENT

An author's consent to alterations may be implied in some circumstances – by the author's conduct (in accepting previous changes, for example), or in some cases by the nature of the publication or the list itself: where an author submits a contribution to a periodical or a major work known to be edited to a certain standard, or submits a work to a series or list of titles with a distinctive house style of its own, then it is quite likely that he or she will be deemed to have consented to a reasonable level of editorial changes consistent with those standards or styles. Where the changes made go a significant way beyond what might reasonably be expected, however, an author may well have a cause of action, for example for breach of contract or infringement of moral rights (see below).

MORAL RIGHTS

As we saw in Chapter 3, authors have statutory moral rights in the UK. In the context of editorial alterations, the two moral rights most likely to be in issue are:

- the right of integrity – the right to object to derogatory treatment of the work; and
- the right to prevent false attribution – the right not to be wrongly described as the author of something in fact written by someone else.

The right of integrity

We considered this key moral right fully in Chapter 3; to recap briefly, section 80 of the 1988 Act gives the author of relevant copyright works (including both literary and artistic works) the right not to have those works subjected to 'derogatory treatment' – additions or deletions, alterations or adaptations which are so serious that they amount to distortion or mutilation of the work, or are otherwise prejudicial to the author's honour or reputation. The right lasts for as long as the work remains in copyright. Infringement of the right is actionable by the author as a breach of statutory duty, and the author may be entitled not only to appropriate damages but also to the grant of an injunction.

The right is, however, hedged about with limitations and restrictions under the 1988 Act, and may not apply in every case (for example, not to many collective works). The limitations are set out in full in Chapter 3.

The right to prevent false attribution

Under section 84 of the 1988 Act, authors (indeed any persons) have the right not to have material written by others falsely attributed to them (see Chapter 3).

Adding to the existing law of defamation, this statutory right is designed to protect authors' reputations from harmful association with work which they did not write, and over which they had no control, but which the publisher may try to pass off as theirs. Since it is a right protecting personal reputations, rather than the integrity of copyright works themselves, it lasts not for the full period of copyright but only for 20 years after the person's death. As with other moral rights, infringement of the right is actionable as a breach of statutory duty.

The right of paternity

Do not forget that the author is also likely to have a right of paternity – the right to be credited as the author in a clear and reasonably prominent way every time the work is published commercially. There are a number of exceptions to this right such as employee and collective works (for a full list, see Chapter 3), and at the time of writing the right also crucially depends on being asserted by the author. Where it applies, many contracts therefore provide for an assertion of the right to appear in a prominent position – usually together with the UCC copyright notice (see Chapter 4). Most publishers will have no difficulty about crediting their authors prominently on the works themselves, but it is important to remember that this is now a statutory right. It is also equally likely to apply to authors of copyright material other than text, such as artists, illustrators and photographers – subject of course to the same exceptions.

SUMMARY CHECKLIST: EDITING

- Are alterations really necessary?
- Has the author consented to alterations (for example, in the contract)?
- Do author's moral rights apply to this type of work, or does it fall under one of the exceptions?
- Has the author waived his or her moral rights?
- If not, can the author make any alterations personally, or at least be consulted?
- Is there any danger that the author's moral right of integrity may be infringed?
- Might there be a risk of false attribution?
- Has the right of paternity been complied with, and if necessary has it been asserted?

PERMISSIONS

Most published works contain extracts or quotations from other copyright works, and often reproductions of complete works such as illustrations, maps or photographs. If these works are still in copyright – older illustrations, for example, may by now be in the public domain – it will be an infringement of the owner's copyright to reproduce any substantial part of those works without permission. A court may award the copyright owner damages or an account of profits, delivery up or destruction of infringing stock, and in appropriate cases an injunction preventing publication (see Chapter 9).

It is therefore crucially important to check the copyright status of all such material as soon as possible and ensure that permission to reproduce it is obtained from the copyright owner well before the work goes into production – preferably before or soon after delivery. Most publishing contracts require the author to arrange (and sometimes pay) for all such permissions and indeed give a warranty and indemnity against any copyright infringement which may take place, but this of course does not help the author, and is not always sufficient to remove legal risk from the publisher, who is very likely to be joined as a co-defendant in any legal action. It will also not cover any copyright permissions necessary for material not included in the author's work itself, for example, an illustration or photograph selected by the publisher for advertising. Editors should therefore check as soon as possible:

- whether permissions have already been obtained by the author (preferably in writing);
- if not, which existing copyright works have been reproduced, at least in substantial part (if the author does not have a reliable list, the editor should compile one);
- whether they are still in copyright, or have fallen into the public domain (for duration of copyright, see Chapter 2). As a general rule, a literary or artistic work is still likely to be in copyright if the author died less than 70 years ago;
- whether they may be copied without permission under the fair dealing provisions of the 1988 Act: for example, limited extracts reproduced for the purpose of criticism or review, and accompanied by a sufficient acknowledgement (see Chapter 9).

This may remove the risk of copyright infringement from a number of extracts, but in all other cases permission should be sought from the copyright owner straightaway.

Who should arrange (and pay for) permissions is a matter for the author and publisher to agree, if they have not already agreed it in the contract. For large-scale works, such as dictionaries and encyclopaedias, or for multimedia works, clearing permissions might be a major undertaking, so whoever does it needs to allow plenty of time. It is worth remembering the following points:

- Owning copyright means being able to prevent others from copying your work, so the copyright owner may say 'no'. It is highly dangerous to write off a batch of letters and just assume that permission will be granted in due course – it may not be.
- The copyright owner may require a permissions fee, particularly if a print or transparency is supplied as well. Museums and galleries are raising increasing amounts of revenue from this source, even for works which are themselves long since out of copyright (since the authorised reproduction which is supplied is of course a new copyright work). These fees can mount up very quickly: it may therefore be necessary to reconsider some of the more expensive ones if

production budgets are tight. Give yourself time to consider all this, and if necessary select something else.

- If permission *is* given, check that the licence covers all formats, languages and territories in which the work is likely to be exploited (if permission is only granted for the UK, for example, including that extract or illustration in a French edition, or a digital version downloadable in France, would not be licensed).
- Bear in mind that some permissions may only be given for one edition at a time – for example, of a dictionary. If subsequent editions are planned, these permissions will need to be renewed.

What happens if you cannot find out who – if anyone – owns the copyright? In the case of extracts from a book, the obvious place to start is the publisher of the most recent published edition: even though copyright in the literary work may vest in the author, the publisher will normally handle permissions requests. If, however, the publisher is no longer in business, and the author cannot be traced personally (for example, via the Society of Authors, Public Lending Right Registrar, or simply via the telephone directory) then you will have to accept the risk that, if the work is still in copyright, and no copyright exception such as fair dealing applies, publishing a substantial part of it without express permission may well be infringing someone's copyright. If the owner subsequently appears (possibly after publication) then he or she may have a legitimate claim of copyright infringement. There is no absolutely secure protection against such a possibility, but evidence that the copyright owner was difficult to trace, and that you had made serious efforts in that direction – not merely sent off a single letter – would probably be taken into account by any court. So also would the fact that you had credited the copyright owner, via a suitable acknowledgement. Any sums you had set aside by way of royalty or fee, against the possibility the copyright owner may one day turn up, would also be convincing evidence of good faith. The only entirely safe course of action, however, is not to copy the material at all.

Where a rightsholder really cannot be found after diligent search, proposals in the UK and EU are under consideration at the time of writing to authorise limited licences to use such 'orphan works', probably with provision for due acknowledgment and reasonable remuneration for any returning rightsholder, and possibly notice and takedown. Limited protection (e.g. against a risk of statutory damages) is already available under US law. In the UK, provision for orphan works was included in the 2010 Digital Economy Bill, but failed to be included in the final Act (largely because of the contentious inclusion of Scandinavian-style Extended Collective Licensing). The EU Commission is expected to produce an Impact Assessment on orphan works, possibly recommending a fully fledged copyright exception, but more likely mutual recognition of national solutions, which would mean that any final UK solution would be recognised across Europe. A truly international solution may take some more time.

PRODUCTION AND PROOFS

Although it is a solidly established trade practice that publishers will supply the author with proofs of the work for correction before it is sent for press, there is no general legal obligation on them to do this, and in some cases there may simply not be time. However, most publishing contracts provide for proofs, which therefore gives the author a contractual entitlement to see and approve them, on the terms set out in the contract. These normally provide for proofs to be returned within a reasonably prompt schedule – 14 or 21 days is common. In many cases the publisher will retain the right to pass the proofs for press if the author does not return them on time, or cannot check them personally or arrange for someone else to (or simply cannot be contacted). Most contracts also make it clear that the supply of proofs is an opportunity to correct errors, not an open invitation to revise and rewrite sections over which the author may have had second thoughts (and which can be expensive). It is therefore common for an upper limit to be set on any author's corrections: 10 or 15 per cent of the cost of composition is fairly standard (although what the cost of 'composition' actually is where the author has supplied the work on disk might need to be separately agreed: 10 per cent of the cost of editorial revisions alone might not pay for very many corrections). Whatever the percentage, it is important to consider when signing the contract whether this is appropriate for the work concerned – in the case of a scientific, technical or professional text, for example, unforeseen new standards or legislation, or new research findings, may make corrections at proof stage essential if the work is not to be seriously inaccurate and misleading, and the contract should allow sufficient flexibility for this.

If an index is necessary, the contract should say so, and specify whether the author is to do this or whether it is the publisher's responsibility (and who pays).

Most other aspects of design, production, promotion and marketing are normally reserved to the publisher's sole discretion, and most publishing contracts reflect this. The price at which the work is sold, and the discounts and other terms of trade which would apply, are also normally entirely under the publisher's control. However, some agents' contracts provide for the author to be consulted on subjective matters of taste and style, such as design or the jacket.

OBLIGATIONS ON PUBLICATION

PRINTERS AND PUBLISHERS' DETAILS

Under what remains of the Newspapers, Printers and Reading Rooms Repeal Act 1869, it is a legal requirement in the UK for anyone who prints commercially 'any paper' (probably including a book):

- to 'carefully preserve and keep' at least one copy for at least six months, and
- to write or print on it 'in fair and legible characters' the name and address of the person commissioning the printing,

subject to a fine on summary conviction for failure to do so. In addition, subject to a similar penalty, printers of 'any paper or book whatsoever' intended to be 'published or dispersed' are required to print their own name and address on the first page (or on the front, if a single sheet only). It is unclear how far, if at all, these requirements apply to publications made available exclusively in digital or downloadable form, but it is probably wise to bear them in mind.

The requirement does not extend to Parliamentary papers, or to things published by public or local authorities, or to banknotes, and there are simplified requirements for the Oxford and Cambridge presses. The obligation was also further relaxed by the Printers' Imprint Act 1961, in order to exclude printed matter consisting only of:

- a greeting, invitation, 'or other message in a conventional form'; or
- a picture representing only a geometrical, floral or other design or a registered trademark (or any combination of these).

LEGAL DEPOSIT

Most countries have a legal deposit requirement of some kind, requiring deposit with the national library (or libraries) of one or more copies of most significant publications published in that country. In the UK, the requirement goes back at least 400 years, and is generally regarded as a necessary contribution to the national heritage, for the use of scholars, researchers and other authorised library users. Under the 1911 Copyright Act, publishers and distributors are still today legally obliged to supply to the British Library one copy of each publication issued or distributed to the public in the UK within one month of publishing it. This covers all publications, except that some categories need only be deposited on specific request by the British Library – these include trade advertisements, local railway timetables, calendars and appointment diaries, educational posters and examination papers. All other publications (except newspapers) should be sent to the Legal Deposit Office at the British Library in Boston Spa, West Yorkshire (the full address is set out in Appendix B).

In addition, five other legal deposit libraries are entitled to receive copies (but only on request). These are:

- the Bodleian Library, Oxford;
- the University Library, Cambridge;
- the National Library, Scotland;
- the National Library of Wales; and
- the Library of Trinity College Dublin.

These copies, if requested, should be sent to the Agency for the Legal Deposit Libraries, 100 Euston Street, London NW1 2HQ (further contact details, again, are in Appendix B).

Compliance with these requirements has been relatively straightforward for most publishers and deposit librarians, but following the Legal Deposit Libraries Act 2003 the Secretary of State for Culture, Media and Sport was authorised to issue Regulations extending the deposit requirements to electronic publications as well. This raises a number of important issues of definition: how wide is the category of 'publisher' in the online, Internet age, and what kind of electronic 'publication' is – or should be – liable to UK legal deposit? How do you deposit a website or an online database? Is everything downloadable and accessible in the UK liable to legal deposit here?

Publishers and deposit librarians have been discussing these issues in a Joint Committee on Legal Deposit (JCLD) for some time, and agreed a Voluntary Code of Practice in 2000 (re-issued in 2009) dealing with offline electronic publications such as CD-ROMs. A statutory Legal Deposit Advisory Panel was set up under the 2003 Act to advise the Secretary of State on suitable Regulations for further categories of online publications, including for example e-journals and harvesting of websites, and draft Regulations are expected by 2011.

Part IV
Publish and be damned

Defamation and other risks 7

DEFAMATION

LIES, DAMNED LIES AND DEFAMATION

Every publication which contains statements of fact or opinion runs the risk that some of them may be untrue, or unjustified. However hard authors and editors try, a certain number of inaccuracies will always slip through the net and get published. Some will not matter very much, or will simply look unfortunate. Some, more serious, mis-statements may raise allegations of negligence, and we will look at negligent mis-statement below (p. 193). There is a particular category of untruth, however, which publishers would be well advised to avoid at all costs, and that is any untrue statement which might be taken to impugn a person's reputation. In essence, this is what defamation is.

It is not necessarily illegal to publish untruths about someone: English law has considerable sympathy for the concepts of free speech and freedom of the press. These are now enshrined in the Human Rights Act 1998 which gives everyone the right to freedom of expression. However, at the same time, the law also seeks to protect citizens from the publication of false allegations which may harm their reputation. It is not always easy to balance these opposing needs. There usually comes a point, however, where a critical or disparaging comment becomes a recognisably more serious allegation of fact, or of unsupported opinion: at that point, if it or the facts on which it is based is untrue, the law may intervene and decide that it becomes libellous.

It may also become expensive, because ever since the Libel Act of 1792 it has been settled law in the UK that damages for defamation are not a matter for judges to settle, but are primarily for a jury to decide. The Court of Appeal has stated that 'the question whether someone's reputation has or has not been falsely discredited ought to be tried by other ordinary men and women and . . . it is the jury who are the people of England'. This remains a fundamental principle of English law for the time being (although Lord Lester's Private Member's Bill is, at the time of writing, being debated in Parliament which includes a clause which would reverse the presumption of trial by jury if enacted, so that the presumption would be trial by judge). Juries (and judges), however, can be unpredictable. In the libel case concerning allegations by the *Sun* newspaper that Bruce Grobbelaar took bribes for fixing football matches, the Court of Appeal overturned the jury's verdict which had been in the footballer's favour. The House of Lords overturned the Court of Appeal's decision on liability (finding that the *Sun* was liable) but reduced the jury's award of damages from £85,000 to £1.

The purpose of an award of 'general damages' by the court is to cover the following:

- Vindication – to show to the world at large that the allegations were false;
- Compensation for damage to reputation; and
- Compensation for injury to feelings (e.g. pain, suffering, humiliation and embarrassment). However, damages under this head cannot be recovered by corporate claimants (as companies do not have feelings).

Whatever they think the actual damage to the claimant's reputation was, a jury may also decide to punish a defendant for behaviour of which it disapproves, particularly if the defendant has repeated the libel or failed to take opportunities to apologise. They might not care for your defence, or think much of your witnesses. At a time when reports of six-figure advances and cheque-book journalism appear regularly in the media, they may have great sympathy for a lone individual fighting to clear his or her name against what they see as a wealthy publisher or newspaper, and may award substantial damages. For a publisher seeking to defend a defamation action, therefore, it means that the financial risks of losing a case – including the costs – are impossible to calculate with any certainty in advance and can be considerable.

Awards of general damages by English juries at one point reached levels in excess of £1 million – the record is still held by an award of £1.5 million to Lord Aldington for allegations of war crimes contained in a book by Count Tolstoy. Following a Court of Appeal decision in December 1995, however, in which the Court reduced an award of damages to Elton John against the publishers of the *Sunday Mirror* from £350,000 to £75,000, it is now open to judges to give much clearer guidelines to libel juries on what may or may not be appropriate damages, and most now do. These guidelines may take account, among other things, of the maximum sums normally available for personal injury awards. In the opinion of the Court:

> It was rightly offensive to public opinion that a defamation claimant should recover damages for injury to reputation greater, perhaps by a significant factor, than if that same claimant had been rendered a helpless cripple or an insensate vegetable.

In 1996, a jury awarded £45,000 to Victor Kiam (the businessman appearing in the Remington electric razor advertisements) for allegations of insolvency published in the *Sunday Times*. In another case in the same year, the Court of Appeal substituted an award of £40,000 in place of a jury's award of £100,000 for allegations that the claimant was a pimp and exposed men whom he introduced to prostitutes to the risk of blackmail by the KGB. The Court stated that it was difficult to imagine any defamation action where even the most severe damage to reputation, accompanied by maximum aggravation, would be comparable to physical injuries such as quadriplegia, total blindness and deafness, where top of the range awards were £130,000 (now about £200,000). The highest award made, at the time of writing, was to two individuals in 2002 following the publication of untrue allegations that they had physically, sexually and emotionally abused a number of children. Each claimant was awarded general damages of £200,000, the maximum amount of damages said to be available in libel proceedings, as the Court felt that they were entitled to be vindicated and recognised as innocent after such serious allegations.

It is unlikely now that there will be any further seven-figure general damages awards, but even at the new, more realistic, levels the financial risks can still be considerable. The losing party will frequently have to pay the winning party's legal costs if the matter proceeds to trial, which are often substantial (usually running into hundreds of thousands of pounds). We look at the important issue of legal costs below (p. 188).

If a successful claimant has suffered actual financial loss, which they are able to prove, then he or she may be able to recover 'special damages' in addition to an award of general damages. The claimant must, however, prove that the loss was suffered as a result of the defamatory publication and also that it was a reasonably foreseeable consequence of the publication. In 2004, the court struck out a special damages claim for £230 million pounds. Collins Stewart Limited, a stockbroker, sued for libel on an article published by the *Financial Times*. It claimed the meaning of the allegations was that they were guilty of gross impropriety in the way in which they carried on business, and had committed or acquiesced in serious criminal offences, in particular insider dealing. Collins Stewart sought special damages on the basis that the share price of the parent company had fallen relative to comparative companies but the court decided that this measure was too uncertain to be accepted as a legal basis on which to found a claim for special damages.

Coupled with the financial risks is the view that the UK has become the libel capital of the world with foreign claimants (such as Arnold Schwarzenegger) suing here to protect their reputations. Overseas litigants have also tried to use UK defamation laws against foreign publishers in the UK courts, sometimes based just on the fact that online articles can be downloaded in the UK. Where a claimant is not resident in the UK but can show a real or likely damage to his reputation here as a result of publication in the UK, he will generally be able to bring an action. This trend is due to a perception that English laws are more claimant-friendly than those in other countries such as the United States. For example, in the United States publishers have more extensive defences in relation to defamatory statements. Some commentators attribute the popularity of the UK to the following factors (among others):

- The presumption under English law that defamatory statements are false; and
- The costs regime (discussed below at p. 188) under which claimants are frequently represented on the basis of no-win-no-fee agreements, thereby exerting tremendous pressure on defendant publishers to settle.

WHAT IS DEFAMATION?

Any statement in a book or journal or newspaper, or any other published matter (an advertisement, e-mail or website, blog, message board for example), runs the risk of being defamatory if it contains an untrue allegation or imputation which disparages the reputation of another. All those elements must be present, before a statement can be libellous:

- It must have been published (or in the case of slander, spoken) to a third party.
- It must be understood to refer to the person complaining about it.
- The allegation must bear a defamatory meaning.

We shall look at each of these categories in turn. But first, a distinguishing note about libel and slander.

LIBEL AND SLANDER

Broadly speaking, libel is defamation in written or permanent form (such as a book or newspaper): slander uses the more transitory medium of face-to-face words and gestures. Traditionally, printed libel was felt to have a more serious long-term effect on a person's reputation than words spoken during an argument or at a public meeting. Spoken words might be forgotten, but words you had printed would still be there the next morning.

As a result, there is a distinction between libel and slander: in an action for libel, damage is regarded as self-evident, and does not have to be proved; in order to succeed in an action for slander, however, claimants must normally provide evidence that they have incurred a specific quantifiable loss. The only exceptions are:

- accusations of a crime punishable by imprisonment;
- allegations of contagious disease;
- imputations on a person's ability to carry on an office, business or profession, or on the reputation or credit of a trader;
- imputations of adultery or unchastity in women.

Technology has rendered this distinction between libel and slander increasingly out of date. The printed word is no longer the only permanent medium capable of inflicting damage, and words spoken on radio and TV, and via cable services and satellite broadcasts, are all now specifically treated as libels (since the Broadcasting Act 1990). Accessible or retrievable messages delivered via a computer network – such as the Internet – are also now regarded as libels 'permanent' enough for damage to be assumed. This is also true of e-mail as well as bulletin boards.

DEFAMATORY MEANING

Before an action for defamation can proceed, the trial judge must decide whether the words complained of are capable of bearing a 'defamatory meaning'. Because it is possible to defame a person's reputation in a number of different ways, there is no single test for defamation, but several. Judges have sought to remedy each category in a succession of cases since the seventeenth century. Generally speaking, a statement will be defamatory of a person today if it substantially affects in an adverse manner the attitude of other people towards him, or has a tendency to do so (*Dr Sarah Thornton v. Telegraph Media Group Limited*).

SUBSTANTIALLY AFFECTS THE ATTITUDE OF OTHER PEOPLE TOWARDS THEM

A statement may still defame you, even if it does not fall under any of the other categories, if the actions of right-thinking persons towards you are likely to be affected (so that they treat you unfavourably, or less favourably than they would otherwise have done). It would almost certainly be defamatory, for example, to say that you have a criminal record, but it may also defame you to say that you regularly drink and drive.

In the case of *Thornton v. Telegraph Media*, Mr Justice Tugendhat classifies defamatory statements into two categories: personal defamation and business defamation.

Personal defamation is where there are imputations as to the character or attributes of an individual. Business or professional defamation is where the imputation is as to an attribute of an individual, a corporation, a trade union, a charity, or similar body, and that imputation is as to the way the profession or business is conducted.

(i) Personal defamation comes in a number of sub-varieties including:

  (a) Imputations as to what is illegal, or unethical or immoral, or socially harmful;
  (b) Imputations as to something which is not voluntary, or the result of the claimant's conscious act or choice, but rather a misfortune for which no direct moral responsibility can be placed upon the claimant (such as disease);
  (c) Imputations which ridicule the claimant.

(ii) Business or professional defamation also comes in a number of sub-varieties:

  (a) Imputations upon a person, firm or other body who provides goods or services that the goods or services are below a required standard in some respect which is likely to cause adverse consequences to the customer, patient or client;

(b) Imputations upon a person, firm or body which may deter other people from providing any financial support that may be needed, or from accepting employment, or otherwise dealing with them.

In addition to these varieties, there is a distinction between sub-varieties of business defamation in which:

(a) The action is brought by an individual, where damage may include injury to feelings; and

(b) The action is brought by a corporation, where damage cannot include injury to feelings.

IMPUTATIONS UPON A PERSON OR ENTITY WHO PROVIDES GOODS OR SERVICES

You may defame someone not only in their personal or social capacity, but also at work, for example by alleging immorality or hypocrisy of a politician or a clergyman, professional misconduct or incompetence of a lawyer or doctor, plagiarism of an author, or fraud, false accounting or general lack of creditworthiness of an agent or publisher.

EXPOSES THEM TO RIDICULE

It was defamatory of a man in 1680 to allege that his wife beat him, and possibly still is. Anything which exposes someone to ridicule is actionable, particularly if they have a professional or social position to protect (even repeating a story they originally told as a joke against themselves). It is certainly defamatory to publish a statement causing someone to be despised – for example by falsely accusing them of child abuse, or even perhaps cowardice. In 1996 the actor, director and writer Stephen Berkoff sued over a film review which stated that 'film directors from Hitchcock to Berkoff are notoriously hideous-looking people'. The Court of Appeal held that the words were capable of exposing him to ridicule.

In a contrasting case in 1998, the defendant published an article about the opera singer Jessye Norman who had allegedly become stuck in swing doors. The article stated that when advised to release herself by turning sideways, the singer replied 'Honey, I ain't got no sideways'. The singer sued stating that the words, which she had not spoken, exposed her to ridicule as they conformed to a degrading racist stereotype of an African-American. The Court of Appeal held that in the context of the publication – which was affectionate rather than critical – the words were not capable of bearing a defamatory meaning.

CAUSES THEM TO BE SHUNNED OR AVOIDED

Even if an allegation inspires only sympathy, rather than contempt, it may still be defamatory if it has the effect of causing people to avoid you, or excluding you from the society in which you normally move. Imputations of insanity or serious disease (such as leprosy) often had this effect in the past, even though they implied no blame or discredit. In the *Berkoff* case mentioned above, the words in question were held not to be capable of causing people to shun or avoid the claimant.

SOCIAL CONTEXT

In deciding whether a particular set of words is capable of being defamatory or not, a judge will have to bear in mind two things: current social standards and what the 'ordinary reader', applying those standards, would think. These standards may change, of course (and do), and what the ordinary reader may have thought defamatory in our grandparents' day may not strike us as defamatory at all.

SOCIAL STANDARDS

It was defamatory to say of a man during the First World War that he was German, or to say someone was a Communist in the 1920s, and the word 'appeasement' was capable of being defamatory in the 1930s. However, it was not regarded as defamatory to say of someone in the 1920s that they had worked during a strike, even though they were active trade unionists, since ordinary, decent members of society then were clearly not expected to strike, or even belong to trade unions. The standard is of society generally, not of any particular group. So, to say of a person that they have given information to the police is not necessarily defamatory, since right-thinking members of society generally – even today – are expected to do their civic duty and assist the police, despite the fact that it may make you unpopular with your neighbours.

THE ORDINARY REASONABLE READER

The objective test for defamation is not what the writer intended or had in mind in writing the words complained of, but what an ordinary reader would have thought when he or she read them. This hypothetical ordinary reader is not merely a reasonable person of normal intelligence but also moves about in society, probably reads newspapers and watches TV, has a reasonable sense of humour and is fairly up to date with common linguistic usages, including current slang. As the House of Lords said in one case: 'The ordinary man does not live in an ivory tower. He can and does read between the lines in the light of his general knowledge and experience of worldly affairs.'

Thus, in the classic 1930 case of *Tolley* v. *Fry*, the depiction of a champion amateur golfer apparently advertising a Fry's chocolate bar was defamatory, since the ordinary reader would assume that he would have been paid for such sponsorship and had therefore prostituted his amateur status. The advertisement itself did not say that, but that is what the ordinary reader would have thought.

The ordinary reader is not, however, unduly suspicious or cynical. A 1964 case held that to say officers of the City of London Fraud Squad were inquiring into the affairs of a company did not mean the company was guilty of fraud: although some cynics might have thought so, the ordinary reader would not necessarily conclude that the company was guilty simply because an inquiry was under way. The article was capable of meaning that the company was suspected of fraud, which was a less serious, but still defamatory, meaning.

CONTEXT OF THE STATEMENT

The ordinary reader is taken not just to read headlines (which are often sensational in nature), but also to read the article accompanying the headline. In 1995, the House of Lords held that a prominent headline or a headline and photograph could not found a claim in libel in isolation from the related text of an accompanying article which was not defamatory when considered as a whole.

In that case, the actor and actress who played the characters Harold and Madge Bishop in the soap *Neighbours* sued when their faces were superimposed on to a photograph of a couple engaged in sexual intercourse. The headline read 'Strewth! What's Harold Up To With Our Madge?'. However, the body of the article discussed a computer game which superimposed the faces of celebrities on to the bodies of porn stars and stated that the celebrities had nothing to do with it. The single natural and ordinary meaning to be ascribed to the words of the allegedly defamatory publication was the meaning which the article taken as a whole conveyed to the mind of the ordinary, reasonable, fair-minded reader. Accordingly, the claimants could not rely on a defamatory meaning conveyed only to the limited category of readers who only read headlines. However, when considering the context of an article, material which can be accessed via a link included within the article does not form part of the article (*Islam Expo Limited* v. *The Spectator (1828) Ltd and Stephen Pollard*).

HIDDEN MEANINGS AND INNUENDOES

Words are normally to be construed in their 'natural and ordinary meaning' – might reasonable people understand those words in a defamatory sense? To call someone a thief or a murderer is fairly plainly defamatory. Remember, however, that the ordinary reader is also capable of reading between the lines. Words not so plainly defamatory in themselves may still carry a defamatory innuendo, when read in context, or when used against certain people. The classic example of innuendo meaning is *Tolley* v. *Fry* mentioned above. The special fact known by certain persons which made the advertisement defamatory was that the claimant was an amateur golfer. Similarly, to describe a person as voting Liberal Democrat is not defamatory per se, but it could be if the person concerned is a well-known Labour supporter, because it would imply the person was a hypocrite, or even a liar.

Even if the specific facts which you are describing are true, it is still dangerously easy to go beyond those specific facts and draw a more general inference which might not be true, and would therefore be defamatory. To say of a publishing company that they were once found to have committed a trading standards offence in their advertising would not be defamatory, if it was true, but it might become defamatory if you then go on to imply from that that they are the sort of publisher that regularly defrauds the public with misleading advertising. A tour operator might on one occasion have sent tourists to a non-existent hotel, but if you publish an inference that they habitually do so they might well have an action against you for defamation.

THE REPETITION RULE

Every re-publication of a libel is a new libel. It is not a defence to say that you are simply a commentator or reporter repeating a statement made by someone else: defamatory statements do not somehow come into the 'public domain' once published or uttered, so that the subject thereafter becomes fair game. A libel is a libel, and the more often it is repeated – even as a 'rumour' or as an attributed quote – the more damage it can do and the more libel writs it may provoke. Different newspapers repeating the same story can all therefore be sued (and often are), and a remainder merchant or bookshop re-publishing an old title as a remainder might well find that they are repeating an old libel.

Where a publisher repeats a statement made by somebody else then the publisher is treated as having made the statement. So, the statement that 'the BBC reported that X is a terrorist' means that 'X is a terrorist', not that the BBC reported it. This is known as the 'repetition rule'. Furthermore, when it comes to proving the truth of the allegation, the rule states that it is not sufficient simply to point to the fact that the BBC was accurately quoted. The publisher must prove the substance of the allegation, namely that X is a terrorist (which, in this example, is an extremely difficult thing to do).

LEVELS OF MEANING

According to the courts, a defamatory allegation will usually have one of three levels of meaning. The highest level is 'guilt' (level 1), so for example, the statement that 'X is a thief' has a level 1 meaning. In order to succeed in a defence of justification at this level, which we deal with below (p. 177), a publisher would have to prove that the claimant is in fact guilty of theft (e.g. by pointing to a criminal conviction). The second level of meaning is 'reasonable grounds to suspect'. Statements will be attributed this level of meaning if the imputation is that the claimant is or was under suspicion. To say that someone has been 'accused of' or is 'alleged' to have committed theft would usually bring it under this level of meaning. To justify this level 2 meaning, one would generally need to prove that the reasonable grounds to suspect existed at the time the statement was published (justification of this level of meaning is explained further below on p. 177). The third (and lowest) level of defamatory meaning is 'grounds to investigate'. Stating that someone has been or is currently being investigated of a wrong doing but denies the allegations is likely to convey this level 3 meaning. Such a statement could be justified by proof of the grounds on which the investigating body brought the investigation. However, such information may not always be available to the publisher.

IDENTIFICATION

Once you have established that a statement is defamatory, a claimant must still prove that he or she, personally, is identifiable as the target before he or she can succeed in a defamation action. The words must not only be defamatory, and be published, but they must also be published 'of the claimant': that is, the finger must point at him or her. Put another way, the words complained of must be capable of being understood by reasonable people to refer to the claimant, so that those who know him or her would think that they were the person referred to.

It is not necessary that you should actually be named. If you are well known as the head of a particular publishing house, or the leader of a religious cult, or even the headteacher of a school, then you may be sufficiently identifiable to have an action for defamation – on the grounds that you were known to be responsible at the time, or must at least have known what was going on. 'A wealthy benefactor of the Liberal Party' secured damages on one occasion on the grounds that there were so few wealthy benefactors of the Liberal Party that everyone knew the words referred to him. Authors and publishers should therefore take great care over 'fictionalised' accounts of real-life situations or events. However much the names are changed, if it would be clear to any reasonable person which actual people or companies are being described, those concerned might well have an action for defamation.

It would not be defamatory, however, to make generalised statements about all members of a broad group or class, such as members of the Garrick Club or the Groucho Club: the statement must be taken to refer to the claimant personally, or to an identifiable group. To say that 'all lawyers are thieves' is not defamatory (however shocking), but it may be defamatory to criticise a particular group of lawyers, or a particular jury: each of them would then have an action.

Authors, and their publishers, should be particularly careful how they select names of fictitious characters, particularly if they are planning to put those characters in compromising positions. A humorous article in which a fictitious character called Artemus Jones appeared on the Continent 'with a woman who is not his wife' was held to be defamatory in 1910, when a real Artemus Jones turned up with several witnesses, all of whom claimed they thought the article referred to him. It would be similarly dangerous to publish unflattering references to any fictitious, but named, character, for example a fat actress: a real actress who happened to have the same name and who was a little plump may be able to prove that her friends (and potential theatrical employers) thought the references were to her. Selecting names of wicked aristocrats, dissolute women or any other fictitious rogues or crooks, should therefore be undertaken with great care.

Nevertheless, in a 2001 case, the *Sunday Mirror* published, in five consecutive issues, a pornographic advertisement for an adult Internet service provider. The advertisement contained a photograph of a woman holding a telephone to her ear saying 'See me now at www.internet.com if you have access to the net, join on line now'. The claimant sued for defamation alleging that, as the photograph was the spitting image of her, people who knew her would believe she was appearing on a pornographic website as well as in the advertisement. In fact the photograph was of a glamour model who had consented to the publication.

The court held that the advertisement was objectively capable of referring to the claimant. Furthermore, it referred to the case involving Artemus Jones mentioned above and confirmed that innocence was no defence in such a case. Nevertheless, the court decided that Article 10 of the European Convention on Human Rights, which protects freedom of expression, prevented the law of defamation applying in the 'look alike' situation. The judge stated that it would impose an impossible burden on publishers if they were required to check if the true picture of someone resembled someone else who, because of the context of the picture, was defamed.

Nonetheless, the general rule is: if you think there is any risk you may be identifying a real person, do everything you reasonably can to check that no one of that name and description already exists, and if still in doubt, pick another name.

Finally, bear in mind the risk of juxtaposition of unconnected pieces of text or photographs. This can apply to any publication including advertisements. It is a risk particularly run by periodical and newspaper publishers. One extreme example of this was Jason Donovan's successful libel action in 1992 against *The Face* magazine, when his face was superimposed on to a photograph of someone else wearing a T-shirt which read 'Queer as Fuck'. It can be done quite innocently and accidentally, however: it is possible to defame someone simply by printing their photograph, or some other reference to them, next to quite unconnected text which is critical or unflattering of other people – a picture of a reputable literary agent next to an article on corruption or tax evasion, or of a happily married author next to a piece about prostitution or pornography. The fact that you did not intend any defamatory reference will not necessarily give you a defence, if the friends of those people would assume the piece referred to them. Those responsible for final page make-up should therefore be made well aware of the risks.

PUBLICATION

A statement in order to be libellous must be published to a third party. This means that any communication to someone other than the person being defamed counts as a publication. Most publications or information services put on to the market will, by definition, satisfy that requirement. It does not matter if the circulation of the publication is limited. In 2010, Mr Justice Tugendhat held that the claimant could proceed with a libel claim in respect of a publication read by 13 readers (*Underhill* v. *Corser and Watson*). Three points in particular should be noted.

LIABILITY FOR PUBLICATION

All those involved in a publication are *prima facie* liable for defamatory statements contained in it. This includes not only the original author of the words concerned, but everyone else who has taken part in publishing them. This could potentially include the author, editor, sub-editor, publishing director, publisher and proprietor. Responsibility can also extend to the printer, distributor, bookseller and even newspaper vendor. Nevertheless, anyone who is not the author, editor or publisher of the statement may have a defence if they can show that they took reasonable care in relation to the publication and did not know, and had no reason to believe, that what they did contributed to the defamation (see below). One of the most important issues is the liability of Internet service providers for defamatory remarks on sites which they host (as to which see the section on innocent dissemination at p. 185 below).

ONLINE PUBLICATION

In a case in December 2001, the Court of Appeal held that every time someone reads an article in a newspaper's online archive, the newspaper is considered to have made a fresh publication. This was confirmed as good law by the European Court of Human Rights in March 2009. Thus, the limitation period (which is one year) begins again for each communication. In theory, this means that a publisher can potentially be open to a libel suit forever.

JURISDICTION

For the purposes of English defamation law, publication takes place in the jurisdiction where the matter is viewed. So if a foreign publisher sells some copies to people in England or Wales (whether in hard copy or online form), it will be publishing in England.

Depending on where the claimant and the publisher are domiciled, the courts may need to consider whether the allegedly defamed person has a connection to the United Kingdom (e.g. by virtue of his reputation, family or business connections). The cases of *Don King* v. *Lennox Lewis* and *Richardson* v. *Schwarzenegger* make it clear that the English courts will not distinguish between those who deliberately publish in the UK and those who do so incidentally and without intending to target any particular jurisdiction. Generally, the greater the connection which the claimant has to England, the more likely it is that the English court will seize jurisdiction of the proceedings. Thus, if the claimant is an English citizen or has a significant reputation in England, it is likely that the court will refuse to stay the proceedings, even if the publisher is based in the US and most of the readers are in the US.

However, where the number of publications in England is so insignificant that there was no real or substantial tort, the English court is likely to strike out the claim as an abuse of process. In the case of *Dow Jones* v. *Jousef Jameel* (2005), the Court of Appeal struck out a claim against the *Wall Street Journal Online* as there had only been five subscribers to the publication in the jurisdiction. In the circumstances of the case, the costs of the litigation would have been out of all proportion to any damage which could have been suffered by the claimant.

DEFENCES

Once a claimant has proved that the words complained of were defamatory, that they refer to him or her, and that they were published by the particular publisher concerned (note that claimants do not need to prove that the words were false), then the burden of proof shifts to the publisher: they must then prove (if they can) that there is a valid defence. English law provides a number of possible defences to an action for defamation. We will look at them in turn, but the main defences are:

- truth or justification,
- fair comment,
- absolute or qualified privilege,
- innocent dissemination.

JUSTIFICATION

With one very limited statutory exception (below) it is an absolute defence to a charge of defamation to prove that the statement you published was true. It is not necessary to prove that every word of the statement is true, provided that it is substantially true. Minor errors of detail, which do not form the main substance, or essence, of the libel, will not prevent a defence of justification from succeeding.

What is the position, however, if the fact which turns out to be untrue is not some minor detail of time or place, but is also defamatory itself? It used to be the position that every defamatory statement of fact had to be separately justified, but under the Defamation Act 1952 this is no longer the case. Section 5 of the 1952 Act provides that a defence of justification will still succeed 'if the words not proved to be true do not materially injure the claimant's reputation, having regard to the truth of the remaining charges'.

Remember, however, that if you go beyond individual facts and make a much more serious general inference or innuendo which is not true, a defence of justification may not protect you. All material allegations must be substantially true.

It is no defence to claim afterwards that you were merely repeating rumours which genuinely existed, although the meaning may not be defamatory if you make it clear at the time of the statement that what you are saying is only a rumour. As a general rule, the truth you must prove is the truth of the sting of the article – not the fact that it was being rumoured. It is therefore important, if you are going to plead justification as a defence, to have reliable witnesses who will be prepared to testify in person as to the main fact on your behalf at a trial. If they are likely to become unreliable or disappear altogether, it may be in your interests to secure a witness statement from them, or at least ensure that they have kept a written note, or some other record such as a tape recording, but such evidence will not always be admissible.

The conduct rule

A publisher seeking to justify a statement which imputes a meaning of 'reasonable grounds to suspect' (a level 2 meaning) can generally only succeed by adducing convincing evidence relating to the conduct of the individual claimant. This is referred to as the 'conduct rule'. Evidence of existing credible allegations in the hands of a defendant publisher at the time of making the statement has been held by the courts not to be sufficient to justify such a meaning. For example, if the meaning of the publication is that there are reasonable grounds to suspect that X is a fraudster, it is not enough to prove that someone else (e.g. the police or the government) believes X is a fraudster. The publisher must prove that the conduct of X gave the publisher reasonable grounds for the suspicion (for example, that he used a false name when signing cheques). In summary, the conduct rule states that a defence will generally only succeed if the publisher is able to prove the level 2 meaning by concentrating on the conduct of the claimant which gave rise to the suspicion at the time of publication.

Spent convictions

The one exception to the general rule that truth is an absolute defence is the statutory provision relating to 'spent' convictions under the Rehabilitation of Offenders Act 1974. It is considered socially useful that relatively minor offences should be erased from the public memory after a certain period of time – the periods vary from three to ten years, depending on how serious the original offence was. After such convictions have become 'spent', evidence relating to them will not generally be admissible, but such evidence will be available in defamation actions to support a plea of justification, provided the original publication was not made with malice. We will deal more fully with 'malice' below, but for practical purposes here this is a very restricted exception.

HONEST COMMENT

English courts have long recognised a limited right of honest comment (previously known as fair comment but renamed by the Supreme Court in the case of *Spiller* v. *Joseph*), by accepting it as a valid defence to a charge of defamation. This does not protect every form of comment, but it does provide a real defence for honest opinions, based on real facts and honestly expressed, on matters of public interest. To succeed in an honest comment defence, the defendant must prove four things:

(1) The statement must be an opinion.
(2) The opinion must be honestly held.
(3) The facts on which it is based must be true.
(4) The comment must be on a matter of public interest.

Even if the defendant can prove these things, the defence will not succeed if the claimant can show that the publication was made maliciously. Here, malice means an improper dominant motive such as making the statement knowing it was false, being reckless about its truth or falsity, or making the statement deliberately to injure the claimant.

Honest comment must be based on true fact

The statement must clearly be recognisable as personal opinion, but it must be opinion on something. It is not honest comment simply to express random opinions on other people. So to say of a well-known entrepreneur that they are not fit to be a director of a British company, without any supporting facts, would not normally be regarded as honest comment. If, however, you said that in your opinion the person was unfit to be a director because they had just been convicted of specific crimes (and that was true), then your comment is likely to be held to be honest comment.

It is very important to separate opinion from statements of fact. Honest comment must be based on true facts (known at least in general terms to the commentator at the time of publication), but it is still recognisably comment. The facts must have existed at the time of publication and be referred to in the publication at least in general terms. If it consists merely of fresh, unsupported allegations of (untrue) fact, or is mixed up with such statements, it may not be defensible as 'fair comment' at all. Something that is clearly intended to be healthy, vigorous comment may still be found to be defamatory if it contains strong inferences of (untrue) fact. A book reviewer might run such a risk, if he or she significantly misdescribes the book being reviewed, for example in basing criticism on its irresponsible approach to some topic such as adultery or child abuse when in fact the book does not adopt that approach or even deal with those topics at all. If you impute to an author that they have written something which they have not in fact written, you are making an allegation of fact, not making a fair comment – and that allegation of fact might well be defamatory.

Reviewers and columnists are as much at risk from this as anyone else, even though they may think their copy is self-evidently honest comment. So too are biographers, and even those who write letters to the editor, if they make allegations of fact which are untrue. The House of Lords has held that the writer of a letter to a newspaper has a duty to take reasonable care to make clear that he is writing comment, and not making misrepresentations about the subject matter on which he is commenting.

If any passage of text which includes both fact and opinion is giving concern, therefore, it is a good idea to run the following tests:

- Are all the facts stated (and quotations) true and accurate – and can we prove it?
- Is any 'comment' honestly held and based on true facts?

If the answer to either of the above questions is 'no', a defence of fair comment may not succeed.

Honest comment and honest opinion

'Honest comment' may be profoundly biased and deeply unfair as long as it is an honest opinion. To succeed in a defence of honest comment, the defence need only establish that the statement was objectively capable of representing an honest opinion, or in other words that any person, however subjectively unreasonable, might honestly have held those views. The opinion need not be 'fair' in the colloquial sense of reasonable, fair-minded, balanced or even-handed. Commentators and critics are expected to express vigorous, often highly subjective, opinions. However, your defence may still fail if the claimant can show that you were not in that particular case being subjectively honest, and for example did not honestly hold those views yourself; or were motivated by some improper ulterior motive, such as malice.

'Malice', for these purposes, is any improper motive, including not only personal spite and ill-will but also any desire to cause injury, directly or indirectly – usually to the person who is defamed, but also including his or her family, or company, for example. Seeking a personal benefit without any desire to harm others can also be malice. Evidence that someone has gone ahead with publication of a statement, knowing it to be false, is *prima facie* proof of malice. A refusal to apologise, or offer any amends, once it has become clear that the statement is false or misleading, may also in some circumstances be regarded as malice. Similarly, a failure to give the other side a reasonable opportunity to state their own case, or comment on criticisms prior to publication, may be seen as malicious, especially if the allegations are likely to cause damage. Product reviews in trade journals which make imputations about a company may particularly be at risk from this. In the 1994 *Yachting World* case, a yacht was given a poor review and the manufacturers claimed the review implied that they had made dishonest representations about the yacht's performance. The review was held to be defamatory and malicious because the makers were not given an opportunity to comment on the review, which questioned the company's integrity in a way which was likely to cause serious damage.

Honest comment and public interest

Finally, honest comment must be comment on a matter of public interest. Nowadays, public interest is fairly widely defined to include any matters in which the public might have a legitimate interest, including (up to a point) the private lives of politicians or public officials. It covers, by definition, comment on all published works available to the public at large, such as books, plays, newspapers, theatrical or musical performances, exhibited paintings, or photographs. It would probably not include the private lives of authors, but it may well include their public activities and equally the public conduct of anyone else in a public role, such as doctors, teachers or company directors. The question is for the judge to decide, but few matters are now considered not to be of any public interest. However, at the less serious end of the spectrum, we do have some guidance from the House of Lords in the case of *Jameel* v. *Wall Street Journal*. Baroness Hale commented that 'the most vapid tittle-tattle about the activities of footballers' wives and girlfriends interests large sections of the public but no-one could claim any real public interest in our being told all about it.'

PRIVILEGE

English law regards some occasions as being self-evidently of public interest, and therefore protects statements made on those occasions from any actions for defamation. Such statements are said to be 'privileged'. The law will protect them, however untruthful they may turn out to be, in order to give the greatest possible freedom of speech to those who are regarded in the public interest as having a social or professional duty to speak freely.

Privilege comes in two kinds: absolute privilege, and a lesser form of conditional privilege known as qualified privilege.

Absolute privilege

As the name implies, statements carrying absolute privilege are completely protected from defamation actions, even though they may have been made maliciously or with reckless unconcern for the truth. Statements made by MPs or peers in Parliament are absolutely privileged, as are statements made in court, or during quasi-judicial proceedings, for example before tribunals, inquests or courts martial. Statements made by government ministers, senior civil servants or officers of the armed forces in the course of their official duty are absolutely privileged. So too are official Parliamentary or government reports such as Reports of Select Committees or White Papers.

In addition, the following reports are absolutely privileged:

1   *Hansard.* This is the official daily report of proceedings in Parliament.
2   Contemporaneous court reports. The Defamation Act 1996 provides that fair and accurate reports of proceedings in public before any court in the UK, the European Court of Justice, the European Court of Human Rights and any international criminal tribunal established by the United Nations are also protected by absolute privilege, provided they are published 'contemporaneously', that is in the next reasonably available issue or broadcast if in a newspaper or on the radio or TV.

Apart from the above two examples, second-hand reports of statements, for example in newspapers, are not generally protected by absolute privilege, although they may be given qualified privilege.

Qualified privilege

The essence of qualified privilege is the public interest for a particular recipient to receive frank and uninhibited communication of information from a particular source. Although only a conditional form of protection, qualified privilege still gives considerable protection to many statements even if they turn out to be untrue, made on matters of public interest, or in the context of a social or professional duty, provided that they are made without malice (as defined on p. 180 above in relation to the defence of fair comment). The publication must be in the public interest, not merely of interest to some of them.

The leading case on qualified privilege is *Reynolds* v. *Times Newspapers Limited*, where Albert Reynolds, the former Irish Taoiseach (prime minister) and leader of the Fianna Fáil party sued for defamation over an article, which he alleged meant that he had deliberately and dishonestly misled the Irish Dáil (Parliament). The article failed to give an account of Mr Reynolds's side of the story. The judge held that the newspaper could not rely on the defence of qualified privilege even though the reported matter was political in nature. This issue went all the way to the House of Lords, which rejected the argument by *The Times* that the law should recognise a generic qualified privilege for the publication by a newspaper of political information affecting the people of the United Kingdom.

The House of Lords held in 1999 that in order to succeed in the defence of qualified privilege for a statement published without malice, the publisher must be under a legal, social or moral duty to publish the statement to the recipients and the recipients must have a corresponding interest in receiving the statement ('the duty–interest test'). In applying this test, the court must have regard to all the relevant circumstances, such as:

(1) the seriousness of the allegation;
(2) the nature of the information and the extent to which the subject-matter was a matter of public concern;
(3) the source of the information;
(4) the steps taken to verify the information;
(5) the status of the information;
(6) the urgency of the matter;
(7) whether comment was sought from the claimant;
(8) whether the article contained the gist of the claimant's side of the story;
(9) the tone of the article; and
(10) the circumstances of the publication, including its timing.

The test for qualified privilege in the case of a publication to the world at large, for example in a newspaper, was whether the public were entitled to know the information and not whether a responsible journalist would publish it. It is important to note that a defendant cannot rely on facts of which it had been unaware at the date of publication, to support its defence of qualified privilege.

The courts have applied the *Reynolds* criteria in a number of cases since the House of Lords' decision in 1999. Notably, the House of Lords (now the Supreme Court) stressed in the *Jameel* v. *Wall Street Journal Europe* case that the *Reynolds* criteria are not tests which the publication has to pass but constitute a well-known nonexhaustive list of ten matters which should in suitable cases be taken into account.

However, in interpreting the criteria, the courts have made it clear that they will expect the defendant to demonstrate responsible journalism before the privilege can be established. In particular, the courts will expect:

- checks to be made by journalists to verify their stories;
- the journalist to approach the subject of any allegations and put the allegations which are to be published to the person and ask for comment, giving the subject adequate time to respond on all of the allegations. The graver the allegation, the greater the need to give an opportunity to the subject of the allegations to comment;
- the journalist/publisher to delay publication if more checks must be made to verify the story, unless the story is objectively of an urgent nature (which is rare);
- the journalist not to rely heavily on draft or interim reports but to point to a concluded investigation before identifying the subject of any allegation. If the journalist waits until the outcome of an investigation, the defence is more likely to succeed.

For example, in the case of *Flood* v. *Times Newspapers Ltd*, the Court of Appeal ruled that *The Times* could not rely on qualified privilege in relation to an article which went beyond reporting a brief police press statement, also reporting the nature of the allegations that had been made to the police about the claimant. The Court of Appeal held that the journalists should have done more to satisfy themselves that the allegations were true. In summary, the Court of Appeal expects the media to stick to fair and accurate reporting of police statements (and thereby rely on statutory qualified privilege – see section below) or, where they step outside statutory qualified privilege and report allegations that have been made to the police, journalists will need to make very real efforts to verify those allegations. In practice, this will often be difficult to achieve without mirroring the police investigation, with the result that the media will have to wait for the results of that investigation before a report can be made.

As far as the courts are concerned, the desire to be the first to deliver a scoop and/or editorial pressure are not relevant to the consideration of urgency. The courts will also consider if the urgency alleged is borne out of the way the journalist/publisher has conducted his affairs.

Even if a newspaper, for example, can rely on the defence of qualified privilege in relation to the original publication of a defamatory article, it may not be able to do so in relation to fresh publications of the article stored in its online archive (as mentioned above, there will be a new publication every time someone views the article online). Publishers therefore face the burden of continually checking their archived materials. This has recently been confirmed by the European Court of Human Rights in the case of *Times Newspapers Limited (Nos. 1 and 2)* v. *The United Kingdom* and most recently by the Court of Appeal in the *Flood* v. *Times Newspapers Limited* case (which at the time of writing is being appealed to the Supreme Court).

Book publishers may have particular difficulties in relying on qualified privilege. This is because the lead-in time for a book is so much longer than for newspapers that the author and publisher will probably be expected by the court to have thoroughly satisfied the ten *Reynolds* factors. So for example, the author will usually have to have carried out rigorous checks of the facts as well as put the allegations to the claimant and printed his or her side of the story. Furthermore, if the publisher is put on notice about false information but continues to publish the book, then this could amount to malice which defeats a qualified privilege defence. The general rule therefore is that book authors and publishers should work on the basis that they will have to justify all defamatory allegations contained in the book.

Statements to and from those with a common interest may also be protected by qualified privilege – for example, between doctor and patient, or solicitor and client, company shareholders, employers (sharing references), or even members of a club. They must, however, be on an actual topic of shared interest, and be made without any hint of malice.

Statutory qualified privilege

The 1996 Defamation Act specifically grants qualified privilege, in the absence of malice, for fair and accurate reports of proceedings in public of any legislature, court, official public inquiry or international organisation or conference in the world as well as copies or extracts from documents required by law to be open to public inspection or published by any court, government, legislature or international organisation or conference in the world. It also provides a further category of qualified privilege including the following fair and accurate reports, but 'subject to explanation and contradiction':

(1) A copy or extracts of matter:

   a.   issued from an EU legislature, government or authority performing govern-
        mental functions (including police functions), the European Parliament or
        Commission, or an international organisation or international conference
        (attended by at least two governments);
   b.   made available by any EU court or the European Court of Justice;

(2) Reports of any finding or decision of any EU associations promoting:

   a.   art, science, religion or learning;
   b.   any trade, business, industry or profession;
   c.   any game, sport or pastime;
   d.   charitable objects or other objects beneficial to the community;

(3) Reports of proceedings of any public meeting in the EU of a local authority,
    justice of the peace, official inquiry or held under a statutory provision;
(4) Reports of proceedings at any *bona fide* and lawful meeting in the EU concerning
    a matter of public concern;
(5) General Meetings of UK public companies.

However, this further category of qualified privilege will not be available if the claimant has requested a reply to be published and the defendant refuses or neglects to do so.

INNOCENT DISSEMINATION

A person who is not the author, editor or publisher of a statement complained of has a defence if he took reasonable care in relation to its publication and did not know, and had no reason to believe, that what he did caused the publication of a defamatory statement. Here 'publisher' means a commercial publisher, that is, a person whose business is issuing material to the public. A person is not considered to be an author, editor or publisher if he is only involved in the following:

(a) in printing, producing, distributing or selling printed material containing the statement;
(b) in processing, making copies of, distributing, exhibiting or selling a film or sound recording containing the statement;
(c) in processing, making copies of, distributing or selling any electronic medium in or on which the statement is recorded, or in operating or providing any equipment, system or service by means of which the statement is retrieved, copied, distributed or made available in electronic form;
(d) as the broadcaster of a live programme containing the statement in circumstances in which he has no effective control over the maker of the statement;
(e) as the operator of or provider of access to a communication system by means of which the statement is transmitted, or made available, by a person over whom he has no effective control.

This defence was tested in 1999 when a Dr Godfrey sued the Internet service provider (ISP) Demon Internet. In that case a defamatory article was posted on one of Demon's newsgroups. However, the posting was falsely stated to have been written by Dr Godfrey. He wrote to Demon requesting that the statement be removed. Demon did not take any steps to remove it and it remained in the newsgroup until the posting expired ten days later. Dr Godfrey sued for libel and the ISP sought to rely on the defence of innocent dissemination. The court held that although the ISP was not the author, editor or publisher (as it fell within (e) above), it failed to take reasonable care in relation to the statement and knew about the publication of the defamatory statement. Once Dr Godfrey had given the ISP notice of the defamatory statement, the ISP could no longer rely on the defence of innocent dissemination. Therefore, ISPs who have been given notice of defamatory statements on websites hosted by them should ensure that they take reasonable care in relation to these statements.

The innocent dissemination defence has also been tested in relation to bookshops. In 2002, the court decided that a bookshop could not rely on the defence following the sale of an anti-racist pamphlet which included a defamatory statement. The man to whom the statement related had written a letter of complaint to the bookshop and the bookshop continued to sell the pamphlet. The bookshop therefore could not establish that they had no reason to believe that what it did caused or contributed to the publication of the defamatory statement.

ISP LIABILITY

In addition to the innocent dissemination defence, Internet service providers were given further comfort under the Electronic Commerce (EC Directive) Regulations 2002. Regulation 17 provides that where a service consists of the transmission in a communication network of information provided by a recipient of the service, or the provision of access to a communication network, the service provider is not liable for the information transmitted, on condition that the provider:

- does not initiate the transmission;
- does not select the receiver of the transmission; and
- does not select or modify the information contained in the transmission.

Transmission and provision of access includes the automatic, intermediate and transient storage of the information transmitted, insofar as the sole purpose is the transmission and provided that the information is not stored longer than is reasonably necessary. Thus ISPs and intermediaries which are merely conduits will not be liable. (As mentioned below, the position is different where an ISP hosts a website.)

Furthermore, the Regulations also limit liability for ISPs which cache information, that is, store information more locally to make more efficient the transmission of the information. The service provider is not liable for caching, on condition that the provider does not modify the information and complies with certain industry rules. A further requirement is that the provider acts expeditiously to remove information upon obtaining actual knowledge that the information at the initial source of transmission has been removed or ordered by a court to be removed.

The Regulations also state that a provider of a service which consists of the storage of information provided by a recipient of the service, i.e. where an ISP hosts a website for someone, will not be liable for the information stored at the request of the recipient of the service. The conditions are that:

- the provider does not have actual knowledge of illegal activity or information; or
- the provider, upon obtaining such knowledge acts expeditiously to remove or disable access to the information.

In the United States, ISP immunity from defamation actions has generally been granted by section 230(c)(1) of the federal Communications Decency Act 1996. This is achieved by stating that ISPs, and indeed any provider or user of interactive computer services such as libraries and schools, are precluded from being treated as publishers of any information provided by another content provider. The US Court of Appeals, Fourth Circuit confirmed in 1997 that the section covered tort-based lawsuits, including defamation, and that it extended to 'distributors' of such material, as well as 'publication', protecting ISPs further.

OFFER OF AMENDS

Defamation proceedings can be long and expensive. Where a defendant has published a defamatory statement, there is a method of speedily resolving the matter which aims to reduce expense. In order to achieve this, a defendant may offer to make amends by publishing, in a reasonable manner, a suitable correction of the statement complained of and a suitable apology to the aggrieved party, and to pay compensation and costs as may be agreed or determined. Thus, if the compensation under an offer of amends cannot be agreed between the parties, the matter will be determined by a judge.

The offer to make amends must be made before the defence is served and so the defendant must act quickly. If the offer is accepted, the party accepting the offer may not bring or continue defamation proceedings in respect of the publication concerned. If the offer is not accepted, the fact that the offer was made shall be a defence, unless the person making the offer knew or had reason to believe that the statement complained of referred to the aggrieved party and was both false and defamatory of that party. In any event, an offer to make amends may be relied on when arguing the amount of damages which should be awarded, usually having a deflationary effect on damages. For example, in the case *Nail* v. *News Group Newspapers Ltd & Others*, the court held that, as there was a public interest in encouraging media defendants to make offers of amends, damages awards ought to be 'healthily discounted' in these sorts of cases and discounted the damages by 50 per cent.

OTHER DEFENCES

Consent

Evidence of consent to publication is a full defence – although often difficult to prove, without signed statements. If you participate in the publication, for example by joining in a radio or TV discussion to put your side of the story, or by publishing your own statement alongside the offending version, then you may be held to have consented to publication taking place. However, the mere consent to be interviewed does not imply consent to specific libels. Consent can only be deduced from some positive act: silence does not imply consent, nor does the time-honoured phrase 'no comment'.

Death of the claimant

Libel is a purely personal action under UK law, and since the dead cannot sue personally, it is normally a complete defence to a libel action to establish that the person defamed is now dead. Even if the claimant was alive when the libel was published, but dies before the case is tried (or even in mid-trial), the action instantly dies too, and cannot be continued by the claimant's relatives or heirs.

Limitation

It is a defence to an action for defamation to prove that it is out of time, or in other words has been started too late. Claimants must bring their actions within one year from the date of publication. However, if the court considers that it would be equitable to allow the claimant to sue even if he or she is outside this time limit, it has a discretion to allow the claim to proceed if it would not prejudice the parties. Publishers with online archives should note that the time period of one year does not start from the date on which an article is uploaded on to the archive. Each time an article is downloaded and read by a web user it counts as a fresh publication with a fresh limitation period. It is therefore important to monitor archived articles and to remove any which, although perhaps not defamatory at the time the original story was published, are later rendered so by the occurrence of new events.

COSTS

The legal costs of bringing or defending an action for defamation often run into hundreds of thousands of pounds (and sometimes even exceed the £1 million mark).

The general rule in the English courts is that the losing party has to pay a proportion of the winner's costs. As mentioned above, the maximum general damages awarded have been about £200,000. It therefore comes as no surprise that it is frequently the costs of an action that become the driving force of the dispute. This is especially so if the person bringing the claim is funding the action by way of a conditional fee agreement (CFA) with his or her lawyer.

Under a CFA, a claimant's solicitors will usually only recover their fees in the event that either the claim succeeds or the defendant admits liability (e.g. in a settlement). The solicitors' fees are recovered from the losing defendant. A CFA is a kind of no-win-no-fee system. If the claimant wins, his lawyer will be able to charge a 'success fee', which can be an additional 100 per cent of the actual costs that have been incurred. So, if the defendant is unsuccessful in defending the claim, he may be liable to pay not only his own costs but also the claimant's costs plus the success fee. For example, if both sides' costs are £300,000 and the claimant's lawyer is working on a 90 per cent success fee, a losing publisher could have to pay £756,000. This is made up of £300,000 paid to the publisher's own lawyer and £456,000 to the claimant's lawyer at a recovery rate on the base costs of 80 per cent. The calculation is 80 per cent × £300,000 = £240,000 for the claimant's base costs, plus 90 per cent × £240,000 = £216,000 for the success fee. Furthermore, even if the defendant is successful, he will sometimes be unable to recover his own costs from a claimant who is funded by a CFA because the claimant may have no money.

After-the-event insurance policies (ATEs) are sometimes available to provide cover for a claimant's liability for the defendant's costs if the claim is unsuccessful, but these are very unlikely to be available for claims where the chances of success are not favourable. Also, some policies will be invalid if the publisher successfully justifies the claim (since the insurance would have been premised on the fact of the claimant telling the truth to his or her insurer). At the time of writing, the government has indicated its intention to review and restructure the current costs regime in relation to publication proceedings.

LINKING

An issue relevant to many online publishers is linking to material published on other websites. The law in this area is largely untested. In certain circumstances, linking could well give rise to liability for defamation. The key issue is whether a linker is publishing, or participating in the publication of, the linked defamatory material. Publication at common law is a question of fact. It depends on the circumstances of each particular case whether or not publication has taken place. Publication requires a degree of 'knowing involvement' in the publication of the defamatory material (although it is not necessary for the publisher to know that the material is defamatory or even be aware of the defamatory material, as with, for example, the position of an editor and publisher of a newspaper who are responsible for its journalistic content). The linker would need to have had the necessary degree of knowing involvement in the publication. In assessing this, the court is likely to consider the linker's knowledge and intention in placing the link and the context of the link.

In the absence of case law on linking, the case which provides the closest analogy to linking is the 1894 libel case of *Hird* v. *Wood*. The defendant, Mr Wood, was sitting silently on a stool by the roadside and continually pointing at a nearby sign to attract the attention of passers by to it. The sign contained defamatory remarks about the claimant, Mr Hird. There was no evidence as to who had written the words on the sign or put it beside the road. The Court of Appeal found that, by drawing attention to the sign, there was evidence of publication.

Some caution is needed with the *Hird* v. *Wood* decision. While it is from the Court of Appeal, it predates the Internet by nearly a century and was a preliminary decision rather than final judgment following a trial. Nevertheless, it could be argued, by analogy, that a link resembles Mr Wood's pointing finger and the linked webpage resembles the sign, and so a link (by 'pointing' to content) would amount to publication of the linked defamatory material.

A linker could in certain circumstances be liable for linking to other types of unlawful material, such as content that infringes copyright, breaches privacy or confidentiality, is in contempt of court, incites racial or religious hatred, is obscene or encourages/induces acts of terrorism. While there is no English case law directly on this question, the analysis of when a linker could be held liable/guilty is likely to be the same as for defamation. If the main purpose of the link is to disseminate or refer readers to the unlawful material, then the linker is more likely to be found liable/guilty.

USER-GENERATED CONTENT ('UGC')

It is becoming increasingly common for online publishers to encourage readers to post content to their websites e.g. readers are permitted to upload comment on articles published online. However, this practice can expose publishers to the risk of liability for content over which they have no control.

The main areas of risk are defamation, privacy, copyright and contempt of court. If the website enables users to trade products via the site, trade mark law may also give rise to risks. Given that the content is generally provided by users over whom the website owner has no control, it will often be necessary for the website owner to establish the hosting defence offered by the Electronic Commerce (EC Directive) Regulations 2002 or the innocent dissemination defence available under the Defamation Act 1996, described above.

An online publisher which enables the public to post unmoderated content on its website is, on balance, likely to fall within the hosting defence vis-à-vis the UGC, as being an information society service that consists of the storage of information provided by a recipient of the service. However, this is untested. It is possible that the courts could limit the definition of a host to an ISP which merely enables individuals to set up their own websites and stores a recipient's data.

In relation to the innocent dissemination defence under the Defamation Act 1996, the English courts have not yet tested the argument that a commercial publisher, such as a newspaper with a website with news or other online editorial content, can ever avail itself of a section 1 innocent dissemination defence on the basis that it falls within the definition of a 'publisher'.

It is possible that an online publisher which has unmoderated UGC on its website, so far as the UGC is concerned, will fall within the definition of a person which is only operating a service by means of which the statement is made available in electronic form or by analogy with the broadcaster of a live programme. Certainly, the more the online publisher contributes to or provokes the website content, the more likely it will be deemed an editor or publisher.

If users write about 'active' legal proceedings, the content may interfere with the course of justice in those proceedings (e.g. because jurors may read it). Under English law, a person is guilty of strict liability contempt if he or she publishes material which creates a substantial risk that the course of justice in the proceedings will be seriously impeded or prejudiced, regardless of the publisher's intent. In general, the closer in time to the trial, the greater the risk (see p. 202).

If a publisher is aware of potentially prejudicial UGC on its website, the prudent thing is generally to take it down. In some cases, the publisher will be put on notice by the prosecution or defence. Strict liability contempt is particularly concerning for publishers of UGC.

The defences to contempt include innocent publication or distribution. The publisher of a UGC website would have to prove that:

- as the publisher, at the time of publication (having taken all reasonable care), he did not know and has no reason to suspect that relevant proceedings were active; or
- as the distributor, at the time of distribution (having taken all reasonable care), he did not know that it contained such matter and had no reason to suspect that it was likely to do so.

If the website owner had invited users to comment on particular legal proceedings or been put on notice of the proceedings by the prosecution or defence, the website owner would not be able to show that it had no reason to suspect that the proceedings were active.

Website owners who wish to control the content as much as possible and minimise the amount of potentially infringing material on their site before it is posted will generally pre-vet the UGC. The advantage is a cleaner site. The decision to moderate may be determined by a need for editorial integrity. It may also be determined by the amount of UGC on the site. Given that the interpretation of the law on liability for user-generated content is uncertain, a strategy of pre-vetting content may result in avoiding the risk of liability in the first place and thus avoid the need to rely on an uncertain area of law.

The main legal disadvantage of moderating is that the website owner is then in the position of a conventional editor or publisher. If potentially unlawful material is posted on to the website, the website owner will then almost certainly not be able to rely on the intermediary defences. A further disadvantage is that moderation can be costly. Not only would the moderators have to have adequate training, but also the most popular sites receive hundreds or thousands of posts per day. If effective procedures are put in place, the decision not to moderate may sometimes be the better option from a legal perspective. However, if a complaint comes in, the website owner has to take the chance that one of the Internet defences will succeed. Whether to moderate is ultimately a commercial decision.

SUMMARY CHECKLIST: DEFAMATION

Is it defamation at all?

- Is it a statement of fact, or an honest opinion?
- Has it been published yet? If not, is it too late to take it out, or tone it down?
- Is there any dangerous innuendo or inference?
- Does it refer to an identifiable individual?
- Does it lower their reputation?
- Have we checked any 'fictitious' character names (for example in relevant directories)?
- Might this be repeating an old libel?
- Do we have an effective warranty against libel or libel insurance?

Are there any defences?

- Is the statement (and any innuendo) substantially true? Can we prove it?
- Is this all 'fair comment', or are there (untrue) allegations of fact?
- Is this an honest opinion, or is there any malice?
- Is it comment on a matter of public interest?
- Is the statement privileged in any way?
- Was the defendant an ISP which was merely an information conduit or was merely caching or hosting information?
- Has there been or should we make an offer of amends?
- Is the person concerned still alive?
- Did they consent to publication?
- Is it too late to bring a libel action?

MALICIOUS FALSEHOOD

Some untruths may not, strictly speaking, be defamatory and (for example) lower you in the estimation of right-thinking members of society, but they may still cause you harm. To say of a publisher or a literary agent, for example, that they had retired from business and were therefore no longer looking for authors, would not be defamatory – people do retire occasionally. If it was untrue, however, it might cause them considerable financial harm, in the shape of lost business, and if it was said maliciously they may have an action for malicious falsehood.

In order to succeed in an action for malicious or injurious falsehood, a claimant must prove:

- that the statement is false;
- that it was published maliciously ('malice' here means that the defendant knew the statement was untrue, and made it intending to injure the claimant or made it with a reckless indifference as to whether harm may be caused to the interests of the claimant); and
- actual financial loss or that it is likely to cause financial loss in his or her office, profession, calling, trade or business at the time of publication (or if the statement is published in writing or other permanent form).

The action was used by the actor Gordon Kaye to prevent the *Sunday Sport* tabloid from publishing an interview he made whilst in hospital just after undergoing extensive surgery for head injuries. Journalists had gained unauthorised access to Mr Kaye's hospital room to interview him. The court prevented publication of the interview on the grounds of malicious falsehood. The article falsely stated that Mr Kaye had consented to the interview (when he was in no fit state to do so). It was published maliciously as it was apparent to the journalists that he was not able to consent. Furthermore, the article was likely to cause damage as Mr Kaye had a valuable right to sell his story. It should also be noted that at the time there was no actionable right of privacy in English law. Such an action can now be brought as a breach of confidence in the light of the Human Rights Act 1998 (see Chapter 8).

Most recently, the action is being used in the case of *Ajinomoto Sweeteners Europe SAS v. Asda Stores Ltd*. Ajinomoto, a leading supplier of the sweetener aspartame, is taking action against ASDA after the packaging of some of the supermarket's range of 'healthy' foods suggested that aspartame was a 'hidden nasty'. The goods in question were labelled with the slogan 'No hidden nasties' and also contained a note which typically read 'No artificial colours or flavours and no aspartame'.

The supplier is complaining that the meaning of the labelling was either that aspartame is especially harmful or unhealthy; potentially harmful or unhealthy; or a sweetener that customers concerned for their health would do well to avoid. On this basis, they brought an action for malicious falsehood. In a preliminary ruling, the Court of Appeal recognised that a statement can reasonably mean different things to different people and decided the case on the basis of a variety of meanings, including those more serious meanings pleaded by Ajinomoto. At the time of writing, the case continues and the Court of Appeals ruling is being appealed to the Supreme Court.

Since likely financial loss is an important element of actions for malicious falsehood, interim injunctions may often be more readily granted than they are in libel actions, and legal aid may also be available (when it is not for libel). However, the court must be convinced there is a serious risk of financial loss, and there must be a strong suggestion of malice.

NEGLIGENT MIS-STATEMENT

If a statement is not defamatory, or a malicious falsehood, or otherwise illegal, but nevertheless causes harm to people who rely on it, it might still expose the publisher to an action for damages if it was made negligently. Suppose that a leading medical textbook seriously mis-states a recommended drug dosage, or that a specialist financial journal gives a subscriber the wrong investment advice in its regular advice column. Would either of these mis-statements be negligent?

Negligence is a particular kind of civil wrong (known in English law as a tort). It consists, briefly, in the breach of a duty to take care in a way which causes damage to others. To prove negligent mis-statement, therefore, it is necessary to prove five things:

(1) the person making the statement owed the claimant a duty of care;
(2) the statement was incorrect;
(3) the maker did not take reasonable care, i.e. he or she breached that duty;
(4) the recipient relied on the statement and it was reasonable for him or her to rely on it; and
(5) loss or damage was suffered which was reasonably foreseeable and caused by that breach.

DUTY OF CARE

There is no general legal duty to the whole world not to be careless. For a mis-statement to be negligent, it must be more than merely careless: the maker of the statement – the author or the publisher – must at the time the statement was made have owed the reader a specific legal duty of care. Such legal duties of care are not always easy to prove. They may arise in the context of a clear professional relation-ship (such as that between doctor and patient), or they may sometimes be assumed or implied in strongly similar circumstances, where any reasonable publisher (for example) would have foreseen the risk of injury to that particular reader, and taken suitable precautions to avoid it.

In the leading case of *Hedley Byrne* v. *Heller* (1964), the House of Lords confirmed as a general rule that:

> if A assumes a responsibility to B to tender him deliberate advice, there could be a liability if the advice is negligently given.

The crucial word in that proposition is 'assumes'. In that particular case, an adver-tising agency was retained by a new client for a major advertising campaign, and took out space ads in national newspapers and booked TV advertising slots, all at the agency's own financial risk. Understandably, the agency sought financial references from the new client's bank, which the bank duly gave, but 'without responsibility'. The references turned out not to be reliable and the agency lost a large amount of money. The House of Lords held that a duty of care could exist where a 'special rela-tionship' was created, which might happen in the following circumstances:

- where the party seeking information or advice was 'trusting the other to exercise such a degree of care as the circumstances required';
- where that trust was reasonable; and
- where the other gave the information or advice 'when he knew or ought to know that the enquirer was relying on him'.

However, in that particular case, the bank had clearly given the advice 'without responsibility', and in the view of the House of Lords that disclaimer was sufficient to avoid liability – they had not 'assumed' responsibility.

In the case of a publisher who publishes statements for the whole world to read, it would be difficult to establish a specific legal duty of care unless it could be shown that there was a 'special relationship' with a particular reader, or group of readers. This is unlikely to exist in the circumstances of trade publishing, but it may pos-sibly exist in the case of some specialist, professional or STM publishers, who give information or advice to a limited, specific market knowing that those people might reasonably be expected to rely on it. This might particularly be so in the context of a specific advice service (or column) – the second of our two original examples – where answers to subscribers' queries are held out as being authoritative; a reader or subscriber relying (and known to be relying) on the skill and judgment apparently being offered might well – in the absence of any disclaimer – be able to prove that a sufficient duty of care existed, and claim damages for negligence if he or she suffered loss when the advice turned out to be wrong.

In the first of our two examples above, however – where a mis-statement is published in a textbook circulating generally to a wide readership – it is unlikely that any individual reader would be able to establish a similar duty of care, and negligence would be much harder to prove.

The same considerations would apply to mis-statements published on the Internet. Although statements made on a website will, by definition, be addressed to a very large audience (potentially, the whole world), there will also be instances where, for example, specialist advice is given to a particular individual or a group of Internet users, such that a duty of care could be established.

DISCLAIMERS

Some publishers seek to discourage negligence claims by printing general disclaimers of liability at the front of their books. Such disclaimers are usually unpopular with authors since they imply a lack of confidence in the text, and they are probably of limited legal effect. Even if it can be established that they formed part of the contract of sale (and disclaimers in small print tend not to be noticed at the time) they are still subject to the test of 'reasonableness' under the Unfair Contract Terms Act 1977 (see p. 298) or the Unfair Terms in Consumer Contracts Regulations 1999. A court might well find in all the circumstances that the disclaimer was unreasonable – particularly if the publisher could easily have insured against the risk.

A specific disclaimer given in circumstances similar to the *Hedley Byrne* case above, however, might be effective if it made it clear that no responsibility for the statement(s) was being assumed.

OBSCENITY

INTRODUCTION

It is not a crime for an author to write obscene material, but it is a crime for a publisher (or anyone else) to publish it. It is also an offence for anyone to have it in their possession, with a view to publication for profit. Although authors are often asked in their publishing contracts to warrant that the material they produce is in no way obscene or indecent, this only gives a limited contractual remedy to the publisher against the author: the criminal offence will still be committed by the publisher and, in some cases, by the distributor, and it is they who will be prosecuted and possibly fined or sent to prison. Publishers should therefore take every possible precaution themselves against publishing obscene or indecent material, however innocently. This applies as much to text as to photographs or other illustrations, and increasingly to computer images (for example, on the Internet) as much as to printed matter.

OBSCENE PUBLICATIONS

What is or is not 'obscene' has never been defined very clearly. The law is now largely contained in the Obscene Publications Act 1959, and the test of obscenity is now contained in section 1 of that Act. Section 1 provides that an article, or any distinct item contained in an article, is obscene:

> if its effect . . . is, if taken as a whole, such as to tend to deprave and corrupt persons who are likely, in all the circumstances, to read, see or hear the matter contained or embodied in it.

'Deprave' and 'corrupt' are strong words. They mean something considerably worse than simply shocking or disgusting, and one conviction (of the Oz 'School Kids' issue) was overturned in 1971 because the trial judge had wrongly directed the jury that obscenity could mean merely 'repulsive, filthy, loathsome, indecent or lewd'. An article is not obscene simply because it is repulsive or filthy. The prosecution must prove that its tendency is strong enough actually to deprave and corrupt a significant proportion of its likely audience; in other words, to pervert or corrupt their morals sufficiently for it to constitute a public menace. It is necessary for more than a negligible number of persons to see the material (see *R* v. *Perrin* below). Furthermore, the entire article 'taken as a whole' must have that tendency, not just one small bit of it.

It is important to note that obscenity is not just about sex. Anything tending to deprave or corrupt may be obscene, including material encouraging the taking of dangerous drugs or glorifying violence, particularly if it is expressly targeted at children or adolescents. However sex usually creeps in somewhere.

OBSCENITY OFFENCES

Publication

It is an offence under section 2 of the Obscene Publications Act 1959 to publish an obscene article. 'Publish' includes distribution, circulation, sale, hire or even free gift or loan. It also includes, where the matter is data stored electronically, transmitting that data. Publication therefore includes storing images on a computer and transferring them via the Internet. In *R* v. *Waddon* (2000), the Court of Appeal held that, even though the website in question was situated in the United States, publication took place in England because the defendant had transmitted the material to the website from England, which was then transmitted back to England when users there gained access to the website. However, the court left open the question of whether publication would take place in England if the website was not intended to be accessible there, and suggested that this would depend on issues of intention and causation in relation to where publication should take place. TV and broadcasting are also covered under the 1990 Broadcasting Act. In 2002, in a similar case involving a website depicting 'people covered in faeces, coprophilia or coprophagia, and men involved in fellatio', the Court of Appeal further held that the jury only had to be satisfied that there was a likelihood of vulnerable persons seeing the material, not that such persons had actually seen the material, and also that the Crown in such a case did not have to prove where the major steps to publication had taken place (*R v. Perrin*). In that case, there was sufficient evidence of publication in the UK for jurisdiction to be satisfied.

Possession

The 1964 Obscene Publications Act added a further offence of having an obscene article for publication for gain, which extends the threat of criminal penalties to printers, distributors, wholesalers, shopkeepers and booksellers. There may, however, be a defence of innocent dissemination where the person did not inspect the articles and had no reason to suspect they might be obscene (see below, p. 198).

Under section 85 of the Criminal Justice and Public Order Act 1994, publication of obscene matter is a serious arrestable offence, which means that a police superintendent may authorise the holding of suspects for up to 36 hours without access to legal advice or even notifying relatives. On conviction for either offence (publication or possession), a sentence of up to three years imprisonment, with an unlimited fine, may be imposed.

DEFENCES TO OBSCENITY

Public good

No defence of literary or artistic merit had existed prior to the 1959 Act. It is now a defence under section 4 of the Act to prove:

> that publication of the article in question is justified as being for the public good on the ground that it is in the interests of science, literature, art or learning, or of other objects of general concern.

'Other objects' includes sociological, ethical and educational merits, but must fall within the same general area as those listed. Mere therapeutic relief of sexual tension (seriously argued in one case) is not an object of sufficiently general concern.

The burden of proof is on the publishers, but they may call expert witnesses in their support. Penguin Books used the defence of public good successfully shortly after the Act was passed, in the 1961 trial of D.H. Lawrence's *Lady Chatterley's Lover*, and a succession of expert witnesses – including the Bishop of Woolwich – testified to the literary and sociological merit of the work 'taken as a whole'. Expert evidence may even be admitted to establish that a work, far from promoting or glorifying obscenity, deliberately shocks and disgusts so much that the likely audience will only be repelled: this defence was used (ultimately successfully) by Calder & Boyars Ltd in 1969 to defend the book *Last Exit to Brooklyn*, which contained graphic depictions of drug abuse, senseless violence and sexual perversion. It seems likely now that any serious work of literature will have a strong defence, however graphic its contents, and more recent works, such as Brett Easton Ellis's *American Psycho* (and its Hollywood film adaptation), have not even been prosecuted.

Indeed, the Crown Prosecution Service ('CPS') appears to be recognising the increasing difficulty of securing a jury conviction on the 1959 test. In 1997, the library of the University of Central England in Birmingham was raided by the West Midlands Police pornography squad who confiscated a book about Robert Mapplethorpe and his work, and threatened to imprison the University's Vice-Chancellor unless he agreed to the destruction of two photographs in the book that were said to be obscene. However, the University stood their ground and, after a year of uncertainty, the Crown Prosecution Service decided not to prosecute and the book was returned to the University's shelves. Equally, the CPS dropped their case on the day the trial was due to begin (June 2009) against a civil servant accused of publishing an allegedly obscene story entitled 'Girls (Scream) Aloud' focused on the rape, mutilation and murder of the popular group Girls Aloud.

Arguably, the Act is also at odds with the more liberal British Board of Film Classification guidelines. It must also be interpreted in line with the Human Rights Act 1998, which, as we saw in Chapter 1, has been in force since October 2000 and incorporates various important rights and freedoms set out in the European Convention on Human Rights: freedom of expression (Article 10) in particular. This freedom is, however, subject to such restrictions as are 'necessary in a democratic society', such as the protection of health or morals.

Innocent dissemination

Under section 2 of the 1959 Act and section 1 of the 1964 Act it is a defence for someone found in possession of an obscene article to prove that:

(1) they had not examined the article; and
(2) they had no reasonable cause to suspect it was obscene.

Both conditions must be satisfied – once a wholesaler or bookseller has actually examined (in other words, personally inspected) an article it will be no defence to claim that they did not realise that it was obscene. This defence is therefore more likely to protect printers and distributors than booksellers, most of whom 'examine' their stock at some point, even if only to look at the cover or read the blurb.

INDECENT PHOTOGRAPHS

Although something which is 'indecent' is by definition less offensive than something which is 'obscene', special considerations apply to publications containing indecent pictures of children. Under the Protection of Children Act 1978 it is an offence to take, permit to be taken, make (e.g. by downloading from the Internet), distribute or show, possess with a view to distribution, or advertise, any indecent photograph of a child under the age of 18. The age limit was increased from 16 as of 1 May 2004 under the Sex Offences Act 2003, subject to the defence discussed below regarding photographs of children aged 16 or 17. The Criminal Justice and Public Order Act 1994 extended the definition of 'photograph' for these purposes to include any 'pseudo-photograph', for example, a computer-generated image on the Internet (it has also made offences under the 1978 Act serious arrestable offences – see above, p. 197).

Whether or not a photograph is 'indecent' under the 1978 Act is to be decided by a jury according to 'the recognised standards of propriety'. These standards may of course change, which makes the task for publishers of illustrated or children's books of keeping within the law particularly difficult. Subject to the defences below, the circumstances of the photography or the publication, or the motivation of the photographer, are all irrelevant: in one 1988 case, despite the fact that the 14-year-old girl concerned had clearly consented to the photographs being taken (in order to further her fashion career), and was photographed in the presence of her family and boyfriend, two or three of the photographs – showing her lightly clad, in underwear only, and 'in a provocative pose' – were held by a jury to be indecent.

The American photographer Tierney Gearon sparked an uncomfortable controversy when images of her own children playing naked in front of adults, and sometimes urinating or dressed in animal heads, were exhibited at the Saatchi Gallery in Hampstead. Scotland Yard's obscene publications unit threatened to seize the photographs unless they were removed from the gallery, and also warned that thousands of copies of her book, *I Am a Camera*, should be withdrawn from bookshops by the publisher, or all concerned would face action under the 1978 Act. The Crown Prosecution Service lifted the threat of prosecution on the grounds that there was insufficient evidence to secure a conviction.

The Sex Offences Act 1993 offers a specific defence regarding photographs of children aged 16 or 17 where the following conditions are satisfied:

- at the time of the offence, the child and the defendant were married or civil partners of each other, or lived together as partners in an enduring family relationship;
- (in relation to the offences of taking or making indecent photographs, and possessing indecent photographs with a view to distribution only) the child consented to the photograph or the defendant reasonably believed that the child consented; and
- the photograph did not show a person other than the child and the defendant.

In order to reassure police officers and others (e.g. ISPs) involved in identifying and securing data for evidential and investigative purposes that they will not be prosecuted, the Act also creates a limited defence where a photograph is 'made' (i.e. usually, by computer download) for the purposes of the prevention, detection or investigation of crime, or for the purposes of criminal proceedings.

In spite of the outcome of cases like the Gearon photos, and the above defence relating to 16- and 17-year-olds, at times of public concern about Internet pornography, paedophile rings and child abuse, it would be wise to take advice before publishing photographs of children that a jury might feel were indecent, particularly if they are in any sense provocative or suggestive.

INDECENT IMAGES

Legislation came into force in 2010 making it a criminal offence for a person to be in possession of a prohibited image of a child. The legislation is targeted at criminalising possession of images (such as cartoons, computer-generated images or drawings) which depict sexual abuse of children. It has implications for any industry which may inadvertently take possession of material containing such images, for example publishers receiving unsolicited manuscripts or Internet intermediaries who may host such material.

There are three elements to the definition of 'prohibited image of a child', which are designed to set a high threshold:

(1) The image must be pornographic. The definition is tied to the assumed purpose behind producing the image: the purpose must be solely or principally for the purpose of sexual arousal. This implements the government's intention to avoid criminalising legitimate works of art, literature or science, news and documentary programmes.
(2) The image must portray an act of sexual abuse involving a child. There is a list of six such acts, which was introduced to provide 'clarity and precision'.
(3) The image has to be grossly offensive, disgusting or otherwise of an obscene character. This matches the test in the Obscene Publications Act, so that this legislation would not go beyond that Act.

It is likely that hosting images on a web page will count as possession. The government seemed to suggest in its consultation paper that 'those in the Internet industry who come across indecent photographs of children in the course of their work' could commit the offence, which is partly why certain defences were required.

Defences were introduced to meet the concerns expressed by broadcasters and those in the Internet industry to ensure that there are adequate defences to cover those who need to have contact with the material in the course of their legitimate work. Those with legitimate reasons to possess the images include law enforcers, broadcasters and those involved in the Internet industry (e.g. filter systems developers).

There is a defence if a person is in possession of an image but does not see it and was unaware of its nature. There is also a defence for a person who receives an image unsolicited or stumbles across it but does not keep it for an unreasonable time, i.e. acts quickly to delete it or otherwise get rid of it.

The information society services defences required by the E-Commerce Directive (i.e. those for mere conduits, caching and hosts) also apply, provided those roles are passive and conducted without knowledge of the offending material. To take advantage of the defence hosts must have no actual knowledge of the images and remove the material expeditiously on obtaining actual knowledge.

POSTING INDECENT OR OBSCENE MATTER

Under section 85 of the Postal Services Act 2000, it is an offence to send any indecent or obscene article by post. It is also an offence under section 4 of the Unsolicited Goods and Services Act 1971 to send unsolicited material describing human sexual techniques, or unsolicited advertisements for such material.

BLASPHEMY

After much campaigning by interested parties, the common law offences of blasphemy and blasphemous libel were abolished by section 79 of the Criminal Justice and Immigration Act 2008 which came into force in July 2008. Following this, section 73 of the Coroners and Justice Act 2009 came into force in January 2010. This section abolished the common law offences of sedition and seditious libel, criminal libel and obscene libel.

INCITEMENT TO RACIAL AND RELIGIOUS HATRED

Most public order offences, including race relations offences, are now dealt with under the Public Order Act 1986 and the Racial and Religious Hatred Act 2006 (which amended the 1986 Act). It is an offence to stir up racial hatred by, among other things, using threatening, abusive or insulting words or behaviour, publishing, displaying, distributing or possessing written material which is threatening, abusive or insulting, or distributing or showing or playing a recording of visual images which involves the use of threatening, abusive or insulting words or behaviour. Equally, it is an offence to incite hatred against a person on the grounds of their religion. Stirring up racial hatred may be punished on conviction by up to two years' imprisonment or an unlimited fine, or both. Acts intended to stir up religious hatred may be punished on conviction by up to seven years' imprisonment or a fine or both;

Note the requirement that the medium used should be 'threatening, abusive or insulting'. There must also be either:

- a positive intention to stir up racial hatred; or
- a likelihood that it will be stirred up.

'Racial hatred' is defined in the 1986 Act as meaning 'hatred against a group of persons defined by reference to colour, race, nationality (including citizenship) or ethnic or national origins' (the requirement that such a group be in Great Britain was repealed by the Anti-terrorism, Crime and Security Act 2001). In early 2005, the former talk-show host Robert Kilroy-Silk caused an uproar by referring to Arabs as 'suicide bombers' and 'limb-amputators' in an article in the *Sunday Express*, but the CPS declined to prosecute, having determined that he had not intended to stir up racial hatred, and nor were his actions likely to do so. Note that religious or other social groups are currently not included as such – the purpose behind the legislation is to prevent racial discrimination, not discrimination generally. It was held in 1983, however, that an attack on the long-established Sikh community could be considered an attack on an 'ethnic' rather than merely religious group and much the same might be said of an attack on Jews.

Religious hatred is defined as hatred against a group of persons by reference to religious belief or lack of religious belief. Among other things, it is an offence to use threatening words or behaviour, or display any written material which is threatening if you thereby intend to stir up religious hatred. It is also an offence to publish or distribute written material which is threatening if you thereby intend to stir up religious hatred.

CONTEMPT OF COURT

Publishing comments on cases which are currently being tried, or are due to be tried, can carry a risk of a fine or even imprisonment for contempt of court. The law is designed to protect the administration of justice by preventing the jury, judge and witnesses from being influenced by external factors, such as prejudicial media reporting.

Under the Contempt of Court Act 1981, a person will be guilty of contempt where the publication by that person creates a substantial risk that the course of justice of active court proceedings will be seriously impeded or prejudiced. This is known as 'the strict liability rule' and it is irrelevant whether or not the publisher intended to interfere with the course of justice.

Proceedings are 'active' from the moment a case is scheduled for a hearing, or an arrest is made. Note that there must be a substantial risk of serious prejudice. 'Substantial' here means more than remote and not minimal. The prejudice has to be so serious that it could alter the outcome of the trial. Thus, the more distant the trial or the more peripheral the material published the less likely that a contempt will have been committed.

The courts take into account a number of factors in deciding if there has been a substantial risk of serious prejudice, including

- The likelihood of the publication being read by a potential juror. It is worth finding out if the publication will circulate in the relevant jury catchment area and, if so, how many copies will circulate.

- The likely impact of the publication on an ordinary reader at time of publication. The more prominent, striking, memorable and novel the publication, the greater the risk that it would prejudice a juror. Mere discussion of the issues, particularly those already in the public domain, rather than specific allegations which could influence a jury's decision, are lower risk.
- The length of time between the publication and likely trial date. The longer the period, the lower the risk. This is known as 'the fade factor'. In a 1986 case relating to a *News of the World* article about cricketer Ian Botham's conduct on tour about which there was a libel trial, the court refused to grant an injunction against the newspaper because the trial was 10-11 months away.

In general, the highest risk cases relate to prejudicial publications about criminal proceedings which are soon to be heard before a jury. It is usually low risk for civil proceedings which are to be tried before a High Court or Court of Appeal judge.

The facts of *Attorney-General* v. *ITV Central* (2008) are a telling reminder, albeit in relating to a broadcast. During the morning of the first day of a murder trial, ITV had broadcast a 23-second news item stating:

Five men are due in court later charged with the murder of an amateur footballer. Kevin Noon's body was found near a pub . . . He was a drugs courier for a group affiliated with a notorious gang . . . One of the defendants [Mr X] is already serving life for the murder of a soldier three years ago.

As the court said, 'One of the first things that journalists involved in court reporting are told is that in circumstances such as these previous convictions should not be broadcast'. ITV was fined £25,000 and paid the Attorney-General's costs plus the £37,000 wasted costs caused by the postponement of the trial by two weeks. In mitigation over this 'blindingly obvious' error, ITV had promptly apologised, immediately offered to pay the costs due to the adjournment, dismissed staff, implemented a mandatory refresher course and changed their internal systems so that two people would always be involved in the pre-broadcast decision-making process.

As the *Sunday Mirror* found out to its detriment in the 2002 *Leeds United* case, contempt of court can arise by publishing an interview with a member of a victim's family. Jonathan Woodgate and Lee Bowyer were accused of attacking a student outside a nightclub. From the start of the trial, the prosecution and the judge emphasised to the jury that there was no evidence that the attack was racially motivated. About eight weeks into the trial of the footballers, the newspaper interviewed the victim's father giving an assurance that the interview, in which he said he believed the attack had been racially motivated, would not be published until after the trial. However, the paper went ahead and published the interview. The judge stopped the trial, ruling that there was a 'clear and substantial risk' that the case had been prejudiced by the publication of the interview. The first trial was estimated to have cost over £1 million (a subsequent (also very costly) retrial exonerated the two players). Although the Attorney-General decided that the paper's former editor, who had resigned over the affair, would not be prosecuted, the *Sunday Mirror* was fined £75,000 and ordered to pay the Attorney-General's costs of £54,000.

Two years later, the *Daily Star* was fined £60,000, plus costs, for failing to heed the Attorney-General's guidelines issued after the alleged rape of a 17-year-old girl at the Grosvenor Hotel by a gang of footballers, requesting the media not to publish any material that could prejudice the identification of the suspects by the complainant. The paper's clear identification of two players as potential defendants, at a time when the complainant had not clearly identified her alleged attackers and identification was a key issue, was held to create a substantial risk of serious prejudice. The players denied the allegations, and in the event no criminal charges were brought against them or anyone else.

Although liability is 'strict', there is a 'public interest' defence to contempt where:

- a publication was made as, or as part of, a discussion in good faith of public affairs (or other matters of public interest), and
- the risk of impediment or prejudice to the particular proceedings is merely incidental to the discussion.

The editor of the *Daily Mail* was able to rely on this defence in the 1982 case of *Attorney-General v. English*. The paper had published an article by Malcolm Muggeridge in support of a 'Pro-Life' candidate which spoke disparagingly of what was described as the common practice of doctors deliberately failing to keep deformed children alive. Contempt proceedings were instigated over alleged prejudice to the trial of a doctor who had allowed a Down's syndrome baby to die. Importantly, the article had been published during the trial. However, the court held that despite there being a substantial risk of serious prejudice, there was no contempt as the risk of prejudice was merely incidental to the main theme of the discussion, and the defence succeeded.

It should be noted that publishers are allowed to publish a fair and accurate report of legal proceedings held in public where the publication is contemporaneous and in good faith. Of course, a publisher must not publish details of a trial which is held in private or subject to reporting restrictions. Similarly, if a publisher becomes aware of a court order against a person or another publisher prohibiting the publication of certain e.g. confidential information, then the first publisher must not breach the injunction even if it is not a named party to the order. It is contempt to disobey a court order.

A key part of the justice system is the jury and the Contempt of Court Act protects jurors from feeling that what they say in the jury room might be exposed. It is contempt of court to obtain, disclose or solicit any particulars of statements made, opinions expressed or votes cast by members of a jury in the course of their deliberations.

Publishers should also be aware that it is contempt to use a tape recorder or similar device in court without the permission of the court, and publishing a recording by such a device is prohibited. Strictly speaking, it is also contempt to bring such devices into court but it will be interesting to see how this provision is interpreted given that many mobile phones now have a sound recording facility.

In this regard, the Lord Chief Justice has issued an Interim Practice Guidance note (20 December 2010) on the use of live text-based communications (such as mobile email and social media, for example Twitter) in court. An application can be made to the court to activate and use a mobile phone, small laptop or similar piece of equipment solely in order to make live text based communications of the proceedings. The court will decide if such use 'may interfere with the proper administration of justice'. The most obvious purpose of getting permission is to enable the media to pursue a fair and accurate report of the proceedings, in accordance with the principle of open justice. A consultation process is pending. There is an absolute prohibition on taking photographs in court.

SUMMARY CHECKLIST: OTHER RISKS

- Is this a malicious falsehood?
- Is it negligent to make this statement? Do we owe any duty of care to particular readers?
- Might this be obscene? Taken as a whole, would it deprave or corrupt?
- Are we publishing it, or in possession of it?
- Can it be justified as being for the public good (for example on grounds of literary merit)?
- Are we disseminating it innocently?
- Would a jury think this photograph was indecent?
- Is this an incitement to racial or religious hatred?
- Might this breach the Official Secrets Act, or any duty of government confidentiality?
- By publishing this now, would we be in contempt of court? Would publication by us seriously prejudice active court proceedings?

Confidentiality and privacy

8

INTRODUCTION

Publishers and others who wish to reveal sensitive commercial, governmental or private information should be aware that publication of such information may be unlawful. The law of confidence protects information which is confidential to a person or a company. The UK courts have also applied the law of confidence to prevent the disclosure of private information. The law in this area has developed rapidly since the enactment of the Human Rights Act 1998 which brought in the right of privacy and the right of freedom of expression into UK law. This chapter first addresses confidential information before discussing the expanding area of privacy.

CONFIDENTIAL INFORMATION

There is a general rule of equity in English law that a person who receives information in confidence has a duty to keep that confidence and not disclose the information to others. Lord Denning put it well in a 1969 case when he said:

> No person is permitted to divulge to the world information which he has received in confidence, unless he has just cause or excuse for doing so. Even if he comes by it innocently . . . once he gets to know that it was originally given in confidence, he can be restrained from breaking that confidence.

Are authors and publishers under a duty not to disclose or use information merely because it arrives on their desk in an envelope marked 'Confidential'? What if it is a completely unsolicited proposal – a fairly common publishing event – from someone they have never met? That will depend (in that particular case) on whether the information is indeed confidential and whether, in the circumstances, a duty of confidence arises. You do not make information confidential simply by stamping 'Confidential' on it (although this may often point towards the information being so). The law will prevent the disclosure of confidential information where:

(1) the information is confidential in nature;
(2) a duty of confidence arises; and
(3) there is no overriding public interest in disclosure.

INFORMATION OF A CONFIDENTIAL NATURE

Information may be of a confidential nature where it is available to one person (or a group of people) and not generally available to others, provided that the person (or group) who possesses the information does not intend that it should become available to others. In *Attorney-General* v. *Guardian Newspapers* (1988) the court refused an injunction preventing publication in the UK of Peter Wright's book *Spy-catcher* (the memoirs of a former MI5 officer), partly on the grounds that the book had already been published in Australia. The information should also be more than trivial.

Plots and scenarios

In some cases, a plot or scenario may be protected if it was revealed in confidential circumstances. W.S. Gilbert obtained an injunction in 1894 to prevent unauthorised publication of the plot of his new play *His Excellency*, which was then in rehearsal but had not opened, on the grounds that the people seeking to publish it knew it had been obtained in breach of confidence. Publishers and authors would similarly be prevented from re-using the key elements of a scenario – plot, characters, dramatic ideas – which had been submitted to them, but rejected, if it could be established that they had been submitted in confidence and accepted as such at the time. There may also be an action for breach of copyright in the case of more developed material.

Developed concepts

If an idea is less than a completed plot or scenario, how far must it be developed before it is protectable by the law of confidence? Hughie Green, in a famous case, failed to protect the general ideas and format behind his game show *Opportunity Knocks* because so little of his own format had actually been put into fixed or developed form, or even written down: there were, for example, no scripts as such. However, in the case of *Fraser* v. *Thames TV* (1983) a much more developed concept – a television series about a three-girl band – was successfully protected by an action for breach of confidence. In this case, the concept was clearly identifiable, commercially attractive, original (and was not, for example, public knowledge) and capable of being realised in actuality. In contrast, in *De Maudsley* v. *Palumbo* (1996), the claimant had an idea for a new nightclub which would open all night, have separate dance areas, an acoustic design and top DJs from around the world. The defendant subsequently opened the Ministry of Sound nightclub which had a number of these features. The claimant's idea was held by the court to have been too vague and generally not novel enough to give the information the necessary quality of confidence to be protected. In order for an idea to be confidential, it must go beyond the identification of a desirable goal and needs a considerable degree of particularity. Simple ideas can be protected but they must not be vague.

The dilemma for an author who wishes to disclose information to a potential publisher is that if he only discloses an outline of the plot (while holding back essential detail), the information may not be detailed enough to be confidential. On the other hand, the more detail the author discloses, the more he has to take a risk that the publisher could decide (whether deliberately or not) to commission another author to write a book with the same plot. Whether information is confidential is ultimately a question which can only be answered by taking all the circumstances into account. To minimise the uncertainties of the law, it is important that publishers and authors have clearly worded written agreements which specify what information is confidential and the circumstances in which it can be disclosed.

OTHER TYPES OF CONFIDENTIAL INFORMATION

Many other kinds of information may be confidential, including business proposals and reports, customer lists, interim reports from investigations, government and state secrets, ideas for new designs and technology and other trade secrets. In fact, a lot of financial and business information which has not been published is confidential.

Draft reports and opinions are obviously confidential. In *Sir Elton John* v. *Countess Joubeline* (2001), information from a confidential draft of a barrister's opinion, which had somehow been filched, was posted on a 'gossip' website. The opinion related to Elton John's court case against his accountants. The operator of the website created a link to the information from her home page. She was held liable for breach of confidence and the fact that the material was initially posted on the website without her knowledge was irrelevant once she became aware of it and allowed it to remain. She should have known that the information was confidential.

IS THERE A DUTY OF CONFIDENCE?

The circumstances in which a duty of confidence can arise are where:

- there is a relationship of confidence, as for example between husband and wife, or doctor and patient;
- there is a contractual duty of confidentiality, such as those included in many employment contracts or consultancy agreements; or
- the party receiving the information knows or ought to know that the information would be regarded as confidential by the party to whom the information relates.

CONFIDENTIAL RELATIONSHIPS

Clearly, there are some close relationships, such as that between husband and wife, which the law will automatically regard as relationships of trust: the Duchess of

Argyll found in a celebrated case in 1967 that information communicated confidentially to her by the Duke while they were married could not be published in later divorce proceedings. This duty of trust has been held to apply to secrets disclosed in other close or long-standing, personal, professional or business relationships of trust. Examples of such relationships include confessions made to a priest, information disclosed to doctors (although the courts have decided that there is no breach of confidentiality where doctors reveal prescription details without revealing the identity of the patients), solicitors or bankers and their clients, and secrets shared between an employer and employee (particularly where the employee is relatively senior and has regular access to the employer's trade secrets), partners of a firm or directors or shareholders of a company. It may well extend to ideas and other information disclosed by an author to his or her literary agent, but would not necessarily cover disclosures made to a publisher unless the author–publisher relationship was a fairly close or long-standing one. It would be unlikely to protect an unsolicited idea offered to a publisher by an author never previously dealt with: some other basis for protecting confidentiality would need to be found, such as a contractual agreement (see below).

CONTRACTUAL AGREEMENTS

Duties of confidence may be entered into contractually; for example, as part of a consultancy agreement, or disclosures of trade secrets made prior to a possible joint venture. Clearly, those seeking commercial backing for an exciting new idea will need to disclose at least some details of the idea in order to interest their potential partners, but they will only want to do so in circumstances of agreed confidentiality. A specific contract, usually known as an 'NDA' (non-disclosure agreement), is therefore often recommended – and is fairly common – in these circumstances.

The most common contractual obligations of confidentiality, however, arise out of contracts of employment. The general rule is that employees may not disclose confidential information acquired during the course of their employment, or use it for the benefit of others, either while they are employed or (usually more importantly) after they have left. For example, in HRH the Prince of Wales v. Associated Newspapers (2006), Prince Charles sought to stop the Mail on Sunday from publishing further extracts from his private journals from his overseas tours. They had been provided to the newspaper, via an intermediary, by one of Prince Charles' employees in breach of her employment contract. The Court of Appeal, in finding for the Prince, noted the strong public interest in preserving the confidentiality of private journals and communications within private offices.

The test most usually adopted is: would people of ordinary honesty and intelligence recognise the information as the property of their employers and not their own to do with as they like?

In the publishing context, the kind of information covered would include lists of customers, contacts or suppliers, advance price lists, pricing structures or mark-ups, contract terms, royalties or other financial information and future publishing plans.

Documents as well as more general information would be caught, but they need not be taken away in physical form – an employee who memorised a list of customers for use in a future job might still be prevented from disclosing that information later. These days, however, the most common breaches are where employees email the information to themselves or save the information on a disk or memory stick. All kinds of publishing employees may be covered, including editorial, marketing, production and finance staff, particularly those at senior levels. To reinforce the general rule, confidentiality clauses are often specifically written into employment contracts. A confidentiality clause was successfully used by Tony Blair and his wife Cherie Booth QC in 2000 in obtaining an injunction preventing the publication by the *Mail on Sunday* of extracts written about the Blairs' family life by their former nanny, Rosalind Mark. It is, however, possible that in some circumstances where a contract of employment has been terminated as a result of a breach by the employer, the employee may be discharged from obligations of confidentiality under that contract. This was recognised as at least arguable in *Campbell* v. *Frisbee* (2002) where information from a former employee of Naomi Campbell, including information about alleged sexual encounters between Miss Campbell and the actor Joseph Fiennes, was published in the *News of the World*. However, even if an expressly assumed duty of confidence is found to be discharged on a serious breach of the employment contract, it is likely that a non-contractual duty of confidence may nevertheless exist.

For many employers, the greatest risk of disclosure of trade secrets comes when senior employees – such as marketing or other directors – leave to go to other jobs, or to set up on their own. For this reason, employment contracts for such staff often include restrictive covenants preventing the use of the firm's confidential information in the future, or for a limited number of months. Such covenants restricting future behaviour need to be very carefully drafted: the wider and more restrictive their terms, the more likely it is that a court might find them to be void as being in restraint of trade (see Chapter 13). In the first place, the terms of such clauses will be strictly and narrowly construed against the person seeking to enforce them, so that, for example, an agreement not to 'disclose' company information will be just that, and may not prevent the employee from 'using' the information. Secondly, the information protected must truly amount to a trade secret of the firm. No employee can be prevented from using his or her general 'know-how' (often called 'life skills') in future jobs, even though that expertise will inevitably have been picked up in earlier employments. This is only reasonable – otherwise, as one judge put it, 'no servant could ever advance himself'.

REASONABLE EXPECTATION OF CONFIDENTIALITY

In the absence of a contract, a duty of confidentiality may be implied from particular circumstances, even if there is no relationship between the person whose confidential information it is and the recipient of the information. The question often asked is: would a reasonable person, standing in the shoes of the recipient of the information, realise on reasonable grounds that the information was being given to him or her in confidence? In the case of *Prince Albert* v. *Strange* in 1849, the Prince Consort was granted an injunction preventing the publication, by an employee of their chosen printer, of drawings and etchings which had been produced by him and Queen Victoria. The employee had been entrusted with the plates and other materials for a limited printing only, and clearly knew this – any further disclosure would have been a breach of trust. This would apply to any similar information improperly obtained, such as private letters (see the section on privacy below). In the Australian case of *Foster* v. *Mountford and Rigby Ltd* (1976), adopting English law principles, the same implied duty of trust and confidentiality was held to apply to aboriginal tribal secrets disclosed to an anthropologist in the course of his research. The tribal elders showed him sacred sites, paintings and other objects, and shared secrets known only to male members of the tribe, and obtained an injunction limiting his right to publish them later in a book. The outcome might have been different if it had been clear to them from the outset that he was researching the information for publication in a book, but then he might not have been given the information.

A duty of confidence may arise where a person:

- is given confidential information from a person in circumstances where he knows or ought to know that a duty of confidence arises; or
- even if he is not given the information, he obtains or chances upon clearly confidential information in circumstances where he knows or ought to know that the information belongs to someone who can reasonably expect his or her confidential information to be protected. In this latter case, the person may have used surreptitious methods (such as a telephoto lens or listening device) to obtain the information or may have found a document in the street or been sent it anonymously.

Where information is conveyed in a social setting it is unlikely, in the absence of other factors, to give rise to an obligation of confidence on the part of the confidant. In *De Maudsley* v. *Palumbo* (1996) (see above), the claimant's idea for a new nightclub was disclosed to a friend around the table at a dinner party. Nothing was said to change what was a social setting into an occasion where confidence could be expected to be maintained. Where it is expressly made clear that the information conveyed or to be conveyed is to be treated as confidential, an obligation of confidence is more likely to be created – even in a social setting.

The information itself and the circumstances in which the party comes by that information will be of relevance in determining whether the other party has a duty of confidence. Clearly labelling documents with words such as 'private and confidential' is also likely to point towards the information being so. In many circumstances in which someone finds or is the recipient of unsolicited information, it is obvious if the information is confidential. In *Imutran Ltd* v. *Uncaged Campaigns Ltd* (2001) the confidentiality of information regarding the claimant company's research into xenotransplantation (the replacement of human organs with those of animals), sent on CD-ROM to the director of an animal rights campaign company, was never in dispute. The documents comprised laboratory reports, minutes of meetings and correspondence. Interim injunctions preventing further disclosures of the information were granted pending trial.

THE PUBLIC INTEREST DEFENCE

It is important to be aware of the risks of publishing information which is potentially confidential. It is possible that an injunction may be granted to prevent publication and/or that an action for breach of confidence could be brought. Both have significant potential costs and damages implications – not to mention the possible embarrassment and inconvenience of having to recall a publication at the eleventh hour. However, it is a defence to an action for breach of confidence if the information is being published in the public interest.

Traditionally, the legal principle applied has been that there is 'no confidence in an iniquity'. This means that there is a public interest in the disclosure of crimes, misdeeds and fraud. However, the public interest defence only applies where the disclosure is to someone with a proper interest to receive the information.

In *Lion Laboratories* v. *Evans* (1984), former employees of the claimant gave information to the *Daily Express* newspaper that certain intoximeter devices were liable to error which was biased against motorists. The court refused to grant an injunction as it was in the public interest to know about this matter which was a serious question affecting the life and liberty of citizens. In contrast, where the *Daily Mirror* had obtained information by phone tapping that there were possible breaches of the jockey club rules by the jockey Johnny Francome, the court granted an interim injunction to prevent disclosure in the newspaper. It was held in *Francome* v. *Daily Mirror* (1984) that there was an arguable breach of confidence and although there might have been a public interest in disclosing the information to the jockey club or the police, there was no such interest in publishing the information in the media. What appealed to the public was not necessarily in the public interest.

Since the Human Rights Act 1998 has been in force, the right of freedom of expression is usually the starting point in considering the public interest defence.

ARTICLE 10 – FREEDOM OF EXPRESSION

Article 10 of the European Convention on Human Rights gives everyone the right of freedom of expression, including the right to impart information and ideas without interference from the state or public authorities (such as the courts). The right does, however, carry with it duties and responsibilities which make it subject to restrictions which are prescribed by law and necessary in a democratic society. One of these restrictions is for preventing the disclosure of information obtained in confidence, while another is to protect the interests of national security. It will therefore be up to the court to balance the right of those seeking to publish confidential information on the grounds that the disclosure is in the public interest against the right to stop such a publication under the law of confidence. The question is whether it is necessary in a democratic society to keep the information confidential or whether the public interest defence takes precedence. The court will ask whether the public interest in disclosure outweighs the public interest in keeping the information confidential.

PRIVATE INFORMATION

The UK courts have upheld people's rights of privacy by developing the tort of breach of confidence. Under the Human Rights Act 1998, the UK courts must not act incompatibly with the right of privacy enshrined in Article 8 of the European Convention on Human Rights. Article 8 gives everyone the right to respect for their private and family life, their home and correspondence.

There is an obvious potential for conflict between Articles 8 and 10 (the right to freedom of expression) and publishers and authors should be alert to the risks of an action for the misuse of private information.

The first question is whether the information is private. If it is, then the court must balance the right of freedom of expression against the right of privacy, bearing in mind the principle of proportionality (by which, the court should not go beyond what is necessary to achieve a reasonable and lawful result).

TYPES OF PRIVATE INFORMATION

To determine if information is 'private', the court will ask if the person in question can reasonably expect his or her privacy to be respected. The courts have noted that in many cases information is obviously 'private' in nature. This would include information relating to health, personal relationships and finances. Where the information is not 'clearly' private, the court may consider what a reasonable person of ordinary sensibilities would feel if he or she was placed in the same position as the person in question and faced with the same publicity. According to the European Court of Human Rights, private life includes a person's 'physical and psychological integrity'.

Relationships

Details of sexual relationships have been found to be a clear example of private information. In *Mosley v. News Group Newspapers* (2008), the court noted that anyone indulging in sexual activity is usually entitled to a degree of privacy, especially if it is on private property and between consenting adults (whether paid or unpaid).

Medical information

Medical information is private. This not only includes notes of and treatment by clinical practitioners but also non-clinical forms of therapy. In *Campbell v. MGN Ltd* (2004), Naomi Campbell's therapy sessions at Narcotics Anonymous were held to be private and no less worthy of protection than treatment carried out by medical practitioners.

Daily life, home life and correspondence

Princess Caroline of Monaco was photographed during many day-to-day activities, a number of which were in public places. For example, she was captured shopping on her own, on horseback, on a bicycle, at a market, playing tennis, in a restaurant, skiing and tripping over an obstacle and falling down at the Monte Carlo Beach Club dressed in a swimsuit. The European Court of Human Rights in *von Hannover* v. *Germany* (2004) held the publication of those photographs represented an invasion of her privacy. Princess Caroline seemed to have been pursued relentlessly for many years by the paparazzi wherever she was and whatever she was doing. Thus there was a climate of continual harassment. Since this case, the UK courts have tended to give increasing protection to a person's daily life. In *Murray* v. *Big Pictures* (2008), for example, the Court of Appeal noted that routine acts, such as a visit to a shop or a ride on a bus, could potentially attract a reasonable expectation of privacy, depending on the circumstances. In that case, the Court agreed that it was arguable that the writer J.K. Rowling's infant son had a reasonable expectation of privacy that photos of him being pushed by his father down a street in a buggy, with his mother walking alongside, would not be published in the media.

Home (and family) life and correspondence have been recognised as being areas subject to privacy, as identified in the wording of Article 8. 'Home' would include certain aspects of a person's business and professional premises and correspondence could include telephone calls made from business (and residential) premises. E-mails are also likely to be covered by the concept of 'correspondence'.

PRIVACY IN FALSE INFORMATION

The essence of a privacy claim is whether the information is private, not whether it is true or false. The Court of Appeal has held that a claimant can succeed in a claim for misuse of private information which is false: *McKennitt* v. *Ash* (2006).

CAN PRIVATE INFORMATION BE PUBLISHED?

Once it is established that the proposed publication contains private information, the next question is whether or not publication should be allowed. This is answered by the courts in weighing up the conflicting right of the individual to privacy under Article 8 against the right of freedom of expression under Article 10. The right of freedom of expression is not only the right of the publisher and author but also of the person who wishes to tell their story and the right of the public to receive the information. In a kiss-and-tell situation, the court must balance the right of the kisser (who is usually selling their story) with the privacy of the other party (who is usually a celebrity).

Neither human right takes precedence over the other and publication will be allowed only where the Article 10 right outweighs the Article 8 right. In striking the balance, the interference with either right must not be impaired more than is necessary and proportionate in a democratic society.

In analysing the competing rights, regard will be had to the 'public interest' in publishing (or not, as the case may be). This is distinct from information which may merely be interesting to the public. There are a number of factors which will be of relevance when considering what is in the public interest, including the degree of intrusion caused by the disclosure, the position of the claimant and whether the dis-closure reveals a wrongdoing which the public has a right to know about.

The claimant

The type of person the claimant is (in terms of their status) is of relevance because there is more likely to be a public interest in revealing private information about certain types of individuals. Information about political figures is more likely to be in the public interest than that about general celebrities, whilst information about celebrities is more likely to be of public interest than that about ordinary members of the public.

A distinction should also be made between those who actively seek publicity and those who do not. Those who seek publicity are less likely to be able to argue against publication of information of which they do not approve. In *von Hannover* v. *Germany* (2004), Princess Caroline, while undoubtedly a public figure, was not a person who had truly courted publicity and she did not fulfil a public function. Contrast this with celebrities such as the Beckhams, who can be said to have courted publicity. They failed to obtain an interim injunction to prevent the publication of the story of their former nanny, partly on the grounds that much information about them was already in the public domain and there was a public interest in publishing the information. In 2010, the footballer John Terry failed to obtain an interim injunc-tion to prevent the publication of details of an alleged extra-marital affair, in part because he had given an interview to a national newspaper in the past in which he made statements about other relationships in which he had been involved, and as a consequence the court considered it unlikely that he found the information at issue particularly sensitive.

Generally, publication of private information relating to children will not be in the public interest. In *Murray* v. *Big Pictures* (2008) (see facts described above), the court held that it was arguable that children have a right to privacy distinct to that of their parents. As a result, the child of a celebrity may have a reasonable expectation of privacy even where his or her celebrity parent does not.

Setting the record straight

Where the public have been either directly or indirectly misled as to the truth regard-ing an individual, the public is usually entitled to know the real truth. In *Campbell* v. *MGN Ltd* (2004), Naomi Campbell had previously indicated that, unlike other models, she did not take illegal drugs. This was in fact not the case and it later tran-spired that she was an addict. She could not complain, therefore, about publication necessary to correct the false image she had portrayed. However, in the court's view the newspaper in this case went beyond what was proportionate and necessary to set the record straight when it published additional details of the treatment she was receiving and photographs of her leaving a therapy session.

Subject-matter

The subject-matter of the publication is an important factor in determining whether private information can be lawfully disclosed or not. Different types of information are generally accorded different weight. Political expression (as distinct from merely personal information about a political figure) is regarded as the most important form of expression to protect in a democratic society. Educational expression is next on the scale of importance and then perhaps artistic expression. 'Gossip' and private information published merely for commercial profit fall below artistic expression in terms of the extent to which protection of it is important.

Matters of public debate will more likely be in the public interest. So, for example, if there is a contentious new law proposed, it is more likely that it is in the public interest to publish private information which is of relevance to that new law about a political figure involved in the debate over the new law. Such information might include the individual's policy in private where they have publicly stated something in apparent contradiction to support their party's policy. For example, if a politician is espousing the benefits of banning abortion and yet chooses to have an abortion herself, then it is more likely (but by no means certain) that the court may permit publication of the fact of the abortion. But publication of details about the abortion could be going too far. If it is an actress who has had the abortion, it is less clear why it is in the public interest for the fact of her abortion (private information) to have been revealed.

Photographs

Photographs represent a special category of information which the courts regard as particularly intrusive when published. As such, publication of photographs of a person in a private situation is likely to impair a person's right to privacy more than is necessary and proportionate. The reason behind this approach seems to be that photographs have a more immediate, intrusive and long-lasting impact than a verbal description. In the Princess Caroline case, the fact that the photographs showed her going about her ordinary daily life and perhaps the climate of continued harassment persuaded the European Court of Human Rights to hold that there had been an invasion of privacy.

In *Theakston v. MGN Ltd* (2002), the court held that there was no breach of confidence in the newspaper printing details of the claimant's activities in a brothel but an injunction would be granted to prevent publication of photographs of the activities since the photographs were particularly intrusive. In *Campbell v. MGN Ltd* (2004), the newspaper's publication of information, including photographs of the model leaving a therapy session for a drug addiction, was not necessary (words having adequately corrected her false public image). In *Douglas v. Hello!* (2005), which concerned unauthorised and surreptitiously taken photographs of the wedding of Michael Douglas and Catherine Zeta-Jones, it was recognised that a person viewing the photographs in *Hello!* magazine would be in a position of a spectator of the wedding or, as one member of the Court of Appeal remarked, 'in some cases voyeur would be the more appropriate noun'. In *Murray v. Big Pictures* (2008), the court took into account the fact that the photographs of famous author J.K. Rowling's infant son were taken deliberately, in secret and with a view to their subsequent publication, no doubt in the knowledge that the parents would have objected to them.

REMEDIES FOR BREACH OF CONFIDENCE AND PRIVACY

In actions for breach of confidence, including privacy cases, the claimant may be entitled to several forms of remedy.

INJUNCTIONS

An injunction will often be the most important remedy to the claimant as it could prevent publication (or re-publication) of information giving rise to the action. The injunction could even be broad enough to cover the whole world, as was the case in *Venables v. News Group Newspapers* (2001), where an injunction was imposed preventing the disclosure of information leading to the identity or future whereabouts of the killers of James Bulger. Injunctions are always discretionary. Before publication, a claimant may apply for an interim injunction pending trial. At trial, the claimant can apply for a permanent or final injunction. Section 12 of the Human Rights Act 1998 sets out that, when a court is considering whether to grant relief which might affect freedom of expression (such as an injunction), relief should not be granted to restrain publication before trial 'unless the court is satisfied that the applicant is likely to establish that publication should not be allowed'. Furthermore, section 12 expressly requires that the court must 'have particular regard to the importance of the Convention right to freedom of expression' and that, where the material is journalistic, literary or artistic, the court should have regard to the extent to which the material is, or will become, available to the public and any potential public interest in publication, together with any relevant privacy code. As one example in a publishing context, in 2010 the BBC was not granted an interim injunction blocking the publication of an autobiography by Ben Collins, the man who had played 'The Stig' on Top Gear. This was because Mr Collins' identity had already been revealed in the media and so it was no longer confidential information. The judge commented that, 'for all practical purposes, anyone who would have any interest in knowing the identity of The Stig now knows it', and in these circumstances publication of the autobiography would not cause any further harm to the BBC.

In practice, the Court of Appeal indicated in *Douglas v. Hello!* (2005) that, in future, pre-publication injunctions to prevent the disclosure of private information pending trial are more likely to be granted than had previously been the case in order to provide a claimant with an effective remedy, following the decisions in *Campbell* v. *MGN Ltd* and *von Hannover* v. *Germany*. This has generally proven to be the case, although there is no guarantee that a claimant will be awarded an interim injunction. In 2008 Max Mosley failed to get an interim injunction in relation to edited video footage of sexual activities in which he had been involved that were available on the *News of the World* website. This was primarily because the footage had been so widely viewed and disseminated that there was 'in practical terms, no longer anything which the law can protect' (the footage on the website was viewed approximately 1.4 million times in two days, and had been copied on to other websites). In 2010, the court refused to grant an interim injunction to the footballer John Terry over the publication of information about a personal relationship. This was, in part, because the court felt that the nub of the claim was to protect Mr Terry's reputation, in particular with sponsors, rather than his private life.

It is important to be aware of the risk of an injunction preventing a planned publication at the eleventh hour. This may have significant consequences financially and in terms of a publisher's reputation. Whilst newspapers and magazines may have a reserve article to use, the financial consequences for a book publisher are likely to be more severe as the book may have to be pulped.

DAMAGES

Damages for a tort, including breach of confidence, are to put the claimant in the position he or she would have been in had the tort not been committed. In 'classic' confidentiality cases, such as where a trade secret is revealed by a former employee, damages would reflect the loss to the employer caused by the disclosure of the secret, provided that damage was reasonably foreseeable.

In privacy cases, the calculation of the loss suffered by the claimant is often hard to quantify in monetary terms. Damages have, however, been awarded for distress caused by the invasion of the claimant's privacy, although this is generally a relatively small sum. In *Cornelius* v. *de Taranto* (2001), the disclosure of medical information about the claimant by a consultant psychiatrist to another psychiatrist and the claimant's GP and solicitor, resulted in damages of £3,750. The nature and detail of the information disclosed, the character of the recipients and the extent of the disclosure were said to be material factors in assessing the true degree of injury to the claimant's feelings.

In *Adeniji* v. *London Borough of Newham* (2001), photographs of a child (taken without parental consent) which were used in a brochure advertising services offered by the defendant gave rise to damages of £5,000. The photographs were used in relation to titles including 'The strategy for children and young people who are infected by HIV or AIDS' but the child was not herself infected with HIV or suffering from AIDS.

In cases of commercial publication of private information, one might expect damages to be much higher but this has not usually been the case. In *Campbell* v. *MGN Ltd*

(2004), Naomi Campbell was awarded £2,500 general damages plus £1,000 aggravated damages for distress and injury to feelings occasioned by the invasion of her privacy by the newspaper for publishing details of her treatment for drug addiction. In *Douglas* v. *Hello!* (2005), the award for distress caused by the invasion of privacy by unauthorised photographs of their wedding was £3,750 for each of the couple. They also received £7,000 jointly for the expenses and disruption caused by having to select the authorised photographs to be published in *OK!* (with whom they had an exclusive contract) ahead of the planned publication date, and nominal damages of £50 each for breach of the Data Protection Act 1998, making a total damages award to the Douglases of £14,600. However, *Hello!* magazine was ultimately ordered to pay *OK!* magazine £1 million for scooping the latter's exclusive, which was held by the House of Lords to be a breach of the confidentiality in the photographic images of the wedding. In *Mosley* v. *News Group Newspapers* (2008), Max Mosley was awarded £60,000 in damages to compensate him for the injury to feelings and the embarrassment and distress caused by the *News of the World*'s print and online publication of details and footage of sado-masochistic and sexual activities in which he had been involved. The judge in that case held that it would not be right to extend exemplary damages (i.e. an additional damages award to punish or deter the defendant) to privacy cases.

ACCOUNT OF PROFITS

Where the defendant has benefited from a breach of a duty of confidence or privacy, the claimant may elect to receive an account of the defendant's profits attributable to that breach as an alternative to damages. It is at the discretion of the court whether to award such an equitable remedy. An account of profits is more likely to be awarded where the defendant has not acted innocently (e.g. by deceptively obtaining the confidential information or deliberately taking a free ride on the confidential or private information to sell more copies). In *Douglas* v. *Hello!* (2005), the Court of Appeal indicated that had *Hello!* made a profit as a result of the breach of confidentiality, they would not have hesitated in awarding the couple an account of profits.

DELIVERY UP

At the court's discretion, material containing information in breach of confidence may be ordered to be delivered up or destroyed. Those involved in publishing should be aware of the costs and impracticalities involved.

COSTS

Although not strictly speaking a remedy for a breach of confidence or invasion of privacy, it is important to note that the loser in litigation is normally ordered to pay a contribution (usually about 50–80 per cent) of the winner's costs. In most recent cases, costs have significantly outweighed the damages awarded, with costs often running well into hundreds of thousands of pounds and sometimes into the millions.

Thus in financial terms, the risk to a publisher of fighting a privacy action often comes down to costs. Further risk to the defendant can arise where the claimant's solicitors work under a conditional fee agreement, whereby they may not charge their client any fees if the case is lost, but agree a percentage uplift (currently up to 100 per cent) of their fees for a 'successful' outcome. In rough terms, this is a no-win-no-fee agreement. Naomi Campbell's solicitors acted under a conditional fee agreement in her House of Lords appeal against the *Daily Mirror*. For more on conditional fee agreements see Chapter 7.

ONLINE ISSUES

PRIVACY AND CONFIDENTIALITY IN THE AGE OF SOCIAL MEDIA

The growth of the internet has brought privacy and confidentiality into sharp focus. Social media such as Facebook and Twitter (to name but two of the most well-known) and other online services like Google maps Street View have led to considerable debate in the media about an individual's right to privacy. They have also highlighted the inherent tension between the rights of privacy (including data protection law) and freedom of expression, the latter being, after all, one of the driving forces behind much online activity and social media.

The privacy and confidentiality principles regarding information on the internet are the same as set out above (see Chapter 12 for more on data protection law). For publishers, one particular issue to be aware of in an online context is a kind of court order called the Norwich Pharmacal order, named after a case of that name. This kind of order requires a respondent, such as a publisher, to disclose certain documents or information to the applicant. In an online context, the applicant will often want to know the identity of a particular anonymous poster or blogger who it believes is a wrongdoer. A publisher can generally decline any such request for disclosure until there is a court order in place. Indeed, disclosing the information other than in accordance with a court order could potentially give rise to privacy, confidentiality or data protection issues for the publisher.

LINKING

The potential risks with linking to defamatory content are discussed above (see p. 189). A linker could potentially, in certain circumstances, be liable for linking to material that breaches privacy or confidentiality. While there is no English case law directly on this issue, the analysis of when a linker could be held liable is likely to be the same as for defamation. If the main purpose of the link is to disseminate or refer readers to the unlawful material, then the linker is more likely to be found liable.

OFFICIAL SECRETS

The Freedom of Information Act 2000 (which came fully into force in 2005) allows individuals and businesses to access information held by public authorities and it can potentially represent a significant commercial opportunity for businesses to find out more about their competitors' tenders and contracts with public bodies. Similarly, it offers the media the chance to discover more information about decisions taken in government, as illustrated by the parliamentary expenses scandal in 2009 which was triggered by Freedom of Information Act requests. The Freedom of Information Act is discussed in more detail in Chapter 12.

However, in many respects we still live in a secret society. Civil servants are required under the Civil Service Management Code not to publish or broadcast personal memoirs reflecting their experience in government, or enter into commitments to do so, whilst in Crown employment. Upon leaving the service, permission from the head of the former civil servant's department and of the Home Civil Service must be sought before entering into commitments to publish such memoirs.

Under the Official Secrets Acts of 1911 and 1989 it is an offence to publish several categories of official government or state information if publication may be prejudicial or damaging to the safety or interests of the state. In practice, this tends to affect investigative newspaper and TV journalists more than book publishers, but memoirs of former civil servants, especially those involved with the security services and members of the armed services, can often run a serious risk of legal action. This may not only be prosecution under the Official Secrets Acts, but also civil action for breach of government confidentiality. These matters came to the fore in the Spycatcher saga in the 1980s, and in the David Shayler affair (both discussed below). It remains to be seen whether the activities of online 'leaks' websites, such as that operated by WikiLeaks, will be affected by the Official Secrets legislation.

THE 1911 ACT

Although intended to apply to the spying activities of foreign enemy agents, section 1 of the 1911 Official Secrets Act still makes it an offence if any person for any purpose prejudicial to the safety or interests of the State:

- approaches, inspects, passes over or is in the neighbourhood of, or enters any prohibited place within the meaning of the 1911 Act;
- makes any sketch, plan, model or note which is calculated to be or might be or is intended to be directly or indirectly useful to an enemy; or
- obtains, collects, records or publishes, or communicates to any other person any secret official code word, or password or any sketch, plan, model, article or note or other document or information which is calculated to be or might be or is intended to be directly or indirectly useful to an enemy.

A 'prohibited place' might include an aircraft, a vessel or a power station, as well as more obvious military establishments, and an 'enemy' may include potential as well as actual enemies of the UK. 'Any person' might in theory include internal saboteurs or even journalists and authors, but the section has not successfully been used against non-spies, and an attempt by the Attorney-General in 1978 in the 'ABC' case to prosecute Time Out journalists Duncan Campbell and Crispin Aubrey under section 1, for a story including security revelations by a former soldier, was thrown out by the trial judge as being 'oppressive' (they were given lighter sentences under section 2 – now replaced by the 1989 Act).

THE 1989 ACT

Section 2 of the 1911 Act, so widely drafted as to include almost anything, was replaced on the recommendation of the Franks Committee. Offences are largely broken down to those most likely to be committed by 'insiders' and those most likely to be committed by 'outsiders'. The latter category is of most relevance to publishers and authors. There are specific classes of restricted information in the 1989 Official Secrets Act. They include, among others:

* security and intelligence,
* defence,
* international relations,
* information which might facilitate a criminal offence.

In relation to 'outsiders', such as publishers, it is an offence to publish information which they know is protected by the 1989 Act and which originated from a Crown servant or government contractor. In most cases the prosecution will need to prove that the disclosure would be damaging to the security services or to the interests of the UK. Exactly what constitutes 'damaging' in this case will depend upon the type of information. The prosecution also needs to prove that the author or journalist knew or had reason to believe that publication would be 'damaging'.

There are a number of other offences under the 1989 act, including:

* Disclosure of any information, document or article that the defendant knows, or has reasonable cause to believe, has come into his or her possession as a result of a breach of section 1 of the 1911 Act;
* Failure to return or failure to prevent unauthorised disclosure of any document or article which it would be an offence to disclose; and
* Disclosure of any information, document or other article which can be used for the purposes of obtaining access to any information, document or other article protected against disclosure by the 1989 Act.

In 2002, the House of Lords, in upholding the decisions of Mr Justice Moses and the Court of Appeal, held in the David Shayler case that the provisions of the 1989 Act did not breach Article 10 (freedom of expression) of the European Convention on Human Rights, as enshrined in the Human Rights Act 1998. Shayler, a former MI5 officer, was charged with passing documents and information to the

Mail on Sunday in 1997, which disclosed, among other things, that the agency kept files on a number of Labour ministers. The judge held that the 1989 Act did not permit a defence that a disclosure was 'necessary in the public interest to avert damage to life or limb or serious damage to property'. The ban on disclosures by members or former members of the security and intelligence services was 'necessary in a democratic society, in the interests of national security', and was therefore compatible with Article 10.

In contrast, in 2000, the *Guardian* and the *Observer* successfully fought broad court disclosure orders obliging them to hand over e-mails sent to them by Shayler. In the absence of 'compelling evidence' that they were in the public interest, the High Court quashed the orders made by an Old Bailey judge, with Lord Justice Judge holding that they 'would have a devastating and stifling effect on the proper investigation of the Shayler story'. Interestingly, in the same month that the Court quashed the disclosure orders, the Home Office approved for publication Shayler's 'gritty thriller about spies, sex and football', *The Organisation*, written while in exile in France, without a word being cut.

BREACH OF GOVERNMENT CONFIDENTIALITY

Juries are not always as willing as governments would like to convict under the Official Secrets Acts, and where diaries or memoirs are concerned civil actions for breach of confidence have been used to try and stifle publication on the grounds that every minister or government employee has a duty not to reveal government secrets. The confidentiality principles covering government secrets are the same as those set out above. An injunction might be granted if there is still a risk to national security. However, Jonathan Cape Ltd was allowed to proceed with publication of the Crossman Diaries in 1975 on the grounds that by then the revelations were too old to be dangerous.

The Attorney-General was more determined in 1985 and 1986, however, when attempting to suppress publication of former MI5 officer Peter Wright's memoirs, *Spycatcher*. While proceedings for breach of confidentiality were under way in the Australian courts, several UK newspapers began to publish extracts. In a succession of actions, the government obtained interim injunctions against the *Guardian*, *Observer* and *Sunday Times* but meanwhile the book was published in Australia and became freely available throughout the rest of the world. The House of Lords finally lifted the injunctions in 1988 on the grounds that there could no longer be any public interest in suppressing 'secrets' that had become so widely public. As a final humiliation, the European Court of Human Rights later ruled that maintenance of the injunctions after general publication had taken place was an infringement of the right to freedom of expression contained in Article 10 of the European Convention (now encoded in the Human Rights Act 1998).

Where there has been a breach of an undertaking of confidentiality, the claimant (in these cases, the Crown) may be entitled to an account of profits in exceptional circumstances – rather than the more usual remedies of compensatory damages, specific performance and injunctions. In *Attorney-General* v. *Blake* (2000), the House of Lords held that the Attorney-General was entitled to the money that remained payable (around £90,000) by Jonathan Cape Ltd to former secret agent George Blake under their publishing agreement. The 'exceptional circumstances' in that case included the fact that Blake – who was described by Lord Nicholls as 'a notorious, self-confessed traitor' – had 'deliberately committed repeated breaches of his undertaking not to divulge official information gained as a result of his employment' and had 'caused untold and immeasurable damage to the public interests he had committed himself to serve'.

DA-NOTICES

The Defence, Press and Broadcasting Advisory Committee was set up after the 1911 Official Secrets Act to issue Defence Advisory notices, or DA-notices (previously called D-notices) to the media, to advise on both general policy matters (there are currently five) and on the security implications of particular pieces of information. The notices are for guidance only, and have no legal status or authority and proceedings are rarely initiated following publication in apparent breach of a Notice. Publishers and authors should not rely too heavily on indications by the Committee that a publication will not threaten national security: while perhaps unlikely, prosecution under the Official Secrets Act could nevertheless follow.

SUMMARY CHECKLIST: CONFIDENTIALITY AND PRIVACY

Confidential information

- Is it proposed that information of a confidential nature be published?
- Is the information generally available to the public?
- Does a duty of confidence exist in relation to that information:

    - by way of a relationship of confidence;
    - by way of contract; or
    - through the recipient's knowledge that the information would be regarded as confidential by the person to whom the information belongs (or where the recipient ought to know)?

- If so, is there an overriding public interest reason why the confidential information should be published?

Private information

- Is the information private? Consider:

    - Does the claimant have a reasonable expectation of privacy?

- Obviously private information includes health, personal relationships and sex life;
- How would a reasonable person of ordinary sensibilities feel if he or she was placed in the same position as the person in question and faced with the same publicity?

- If so, is the benefit of publication proportionate to the harm done by the violation of individual's right to privacy? Consider:

  - The type of individual to whom the information relates;
  - Whether publication would set the record straight;
  - The subject-matter of the publication (including whether it is a matter of public debate);
  - Whether the publication of photographs is necessary to convey the information.

- Finally, give thought to the practicality of having to withdraw and/or replace the publication if an injunction is granted, and to the potential costs involved in legal proceedings, should they arise.

Additional considerations:

- Could publication be an offence under the Official Secrets Acts?
- Are any DA-notices relevant in relation to a proposed publication?

Copyright infringement 9

We saw in Chapter 2 that copyright in the UK is not merely a personal licence to copy; its value lies primarily in the right to control (and if necessary, prevent) copying by others. In this chapter we will set out in detail exactly which activities a copyright owner may control in this way, and what remedies UK law provides against infringers. We will need to look in turn at the following:

- the primary 'restricted acts' under UK law, such as copying itself;
- secondary infringements such as possession or dealing with infringing copies;
- defences such as fair dealing, and the permitted acts which will not infringe;
- where infringement does occur, the civil and criminal remedies available in the UK against infringers;
- the legal protection available for UK works overseas and for foreign works here.

PRIMARY INFRINGEMENT

Section 16 of the 1988 Act provides that copyright owners have the exclusive right to do the following 'restricted acts' in relation to most copyright works in the UK (but not always artistic works):

(1) to copy the work;
(2) to issue copies of the work to the public;
(3) to rent or lend the work to the public;
(4) to perform, show or play the work in public;
(5) to communicate the work to the public;
(6) to make an adaptation of the work, or do any of the above things in relation to an adaptation.

Anyone who does any of the above restricted acts to a relevant work without the licence of the copyright owner will infringe copyright in the work, unless one of the exceptions applies (see below, p. 237).

The key restricted acts for publishing purposes are 1, 2, 5 and 6, but before we go on to consider these in more detail, two further general points need to be made.

TAKING A 'SUBSTANTIAL PART' MAY INFRINGE

Any of the acts listed above may infringe copyright if they are done either in relation to the work as a whole, or to any 'substantial part' of it. It is therefore not necessary for an infringer to copy (for example) the entire work, as long as a substantial part is copied. This of course rather begs the question: what is a substantial part?

The 1988 Act itself gives no guidance, but in a long line of decided cases the courts have held that what is substantial is a question of fact and degree in all the circumstances, and depends more on the *quality* of what is taken than the quantity. The courts have also held that each case is one of feel and impression. The test is, first, to identify the features found to have been copied from the original work and, second, to ask whether those features form a substantial part of that work. One or two lines of text taken from a 500-page textbook might not be significant enough to amount to a substantial part of the whole thing, but centrally important dramatic lines from a novel or play might well be. As little as four lines from Rudyard Kipling's poem 'If' constituted a sufficiently substantial part in the 1920s when used without consent in a Sanatogen advertisement, and one verse out of four copied in the Robbie Williams/Guy Fletcher song 'Jesus In A Camper Van' was a substantial part of the claimant's song. A few bars from the 'Colonel Bogey' march infringed even though the full march lasted over four minutes, as did five minutes in a feature-length film based on four pages in a 126-page novel.

A key issue is often whether the part taken is commonplace or insignificant or whether it includes some identifiable, distinctive flavour of the work.

In another case, IPC claimed that Highbury had infringed the artistic copyright in certain covers and articles in its *Ideal Home* publication. The court dismissed the case, referring to IPC's over-reliance on similarities common in the trade and on design elements which are not subject to copyright protection. The judge held copyright does not protect general themes, styles or ideas. The Court of Appeal in the *Da Vinci Code* case (see p. 19) also recently found that to the extent there was copying, this was of a general expression of facts and ideas and therefore copyright had not been infringed.

In the much-quoted words of one judge in 1916: 'What is worth copying is *prima facie* worth protecting.' If it is valuable enough to an infringer to be worth taking at all, it may well be important enough to be a substantial part.

INFRINGEMENT MAY BE INDIRECT

Any of the above infringing acts may be done indirectly as well as directly. Copying a copy (or a copy of a copy) may therefore infringe copyright just as much as copying directly from the original. In most cases of copying (for example from a book or journal) what is copied is not the author's original, but the authorised published edition, which is itself of course a copy.

Equally, copyright may be infringed by authorising (even impliedly) the infringement of others. There must, however, be a direct causal link between the 'authorisation' and the infringing act(s) which resulted. So the sale and supply of recording equipment with a copying feature expressly advertised as suitable for home copying might in some circumstances infringe, even though the infringements would actually be done by others, but the mere sale of blank DVDs by itself would probably not. Manufacturers of photocopying machines do not 'authorise' copyright infringement merely by selling and supplying their machines, but a university library or a business which installs a machine or a bank of machines and permits multiple copying, knowing that most if not all of the copying will infringe copyright and does nothing to prevent it, may well be held to have 'authorised' those infringements. In addition, unlike the restricted acts, which have to take place in the UK, authorisation can take place outside the UK and may still infringe UK copyright.

COPYING

Although anti-piracy slogans such as 'Copying is Theft' are not always strictly accurate, copying the work, or a substantial part of it, without permission and in the absence of one of the exemptions, is probably the most common primary infringement. It often accompanies other infringements such as issuing copies to the public; indeed it would usually be difficult to do some of the other restricted acts without someone having copied first. A copy may still infringe even if its making is transient or incidental to some other use of the work.

Copying is widely defined in the 1988 Act (section 17) to mean reproducing the work 'in any material form' and this is expressly stated to include storing the work in any medium by electronic means. Any reproduction of any work in physical or retrievable form can therefore be caught under the definition. One case held that the use of small-scale copies of a third party's photographs as icons and banners on a website designed for the purpose of selling antiques online infringed the third party's copyright. In the Scottish *Shetland Times* case, it was held at least arguable on an interim application for an injunction that the copying verbatim of headlines by one website operator from another web site operator infringed copyright under section 17 of the 1988 Act, copying being storing the works by electronic means.

Caching involves taking a snapshot of a webpage from a third party website and storing it. As such, a copy is made of any copyright works on the third party webpage. This may be done, for example, by a search engine in order to speed up the searching process. Such cached pages may also be made available to the search engine's users as a back-up in case the current live webpage is not available. In a Belgian case, the making of copies of extracts of articles from websites by caching was found to infringe the copyright of the rights owner. Although there are no UK cases on this question, this is likely to be *prima facie* infringement of copyright under UK law.

Scraping involves the extraction of information from third party websites by copying the whole or part of articles and/or images as they appear on those sites and subsequently displaying the information extracted on the 'scraper's' website. In July 2010 the ECJ held on a referral from the Danish courts that a data capture process used by a media monitoring business by which eleven-word extracts from newspaper articles were stored and printed out amounted to copying if the works copied were protected by copyright. It was also held that this was not temporary copying (see p. 239). The UK court followed this decision in late 2010. It held that customers of a media monitoring company who were sent reports of news articles including their search terms (the company scraped publishers' websites) would be infringing the publishers' copyright without a licence.

Whatever the medium, however, there must be some objective evidence that copying actually took place, and that the alleged infringing copy was derived directly or indirectly from the work in question. It will not often be possible to produce firsthand witness evidence of copying (unauthorised copying is not usually done in public), and a court will therefore in many cases be prepared to make a presumption that copying must have taken place where:

- there is sufficient objective similarity between the work and the alleged copy;
- the alleged infringer had access to or knew of the original;
- no (credible) counter-evidence is produced to suggest that the alleged copy might have resulted from independent skill and effort (or been taken from some other source).
- Under these circumstances there will be a strong inference that copying must have occurred, and in the absence of any defence (see below) this is likely to amount to copyright infringement.

Intention

It does not matter that the infringer did not consciously intend to copy; all the primary acts of copyright infringement are offences of strict liability, requiring no evidence of guilty knowledge or intent. An apparently innocent state of mind is no defence – neither is ignorance (for example, that the work in question was still in copyright, or even that it existed) and neither is honest mistake, such as a genuine belief that the copying in question was licensed by the copyright owner.

Evidence of this kind will of course be taken into account, and may provide a defence to any award of damages if there was no reason to believe the work was in copyright at all (see p. 257) but it will not otherwise prevent the acts concerned amounting to infringing acts. However blameless you think you are, if you in fact copy without permission you are very likely to infringe copyright.

In some cases, copyright infringement will occur even if the infringer does not consciously realise he or she is copying the work.

Plagiarism

There is a common misconception in some circles that copying someone else's work can somehow be legalised by the strategic alteration of a few words and phrases. This is entirely wrong, and highly dangerous. The mere fact that few passages are reproduced exactly, word for word, will not necessarily be sufficient to prevent what is copied from being a substantial part of the whole, particularly if the copying is extensive and blatant. It will also not give any protection against infringement of the separate copyright in the author's compilation of material, including the selection and arrangement of topics and headings. The question to be asked is very simple indeed: did copying actually take place? If it did – whether of the text, or the compilation – then no amount of subsequent tinkering with the wording or the arrangement will save the activity from being copyright infringement – provided that at least some substantial parts have been taken. The fact that all the material *could* have been obtained from elsewhere will also not alter the position if the infringer chose instead to save the time and effort and skill involved and copy from an existing compilation. In the 1985 case of *Geographia Ltd* v. *Penguin Books*, the selection and arrangement of map details including colours was accepted as protectable, although on the facts the copying was insufficiently substantial.

This is not to say of course that existing material and common sources cannot be relied upon in creating a new work – provided that they are not copied. It may also be permissible to reproduce limited extracts in the context of fair dealing for the purposes of criticism and review, but these must be accompanied by a sufficient acknowledgement (see below). There have often been borderline cases where there is a marked similarity between two works, and it is clear that much of the material in the new work has been derived from the thoughts and ideas in the existing one. Even without any acknowledgement this may be perfectly legal (if a little unprofessional). There is no copyright in ideas as the Court of Appeal stated in the *Da Vinci Code* case (see p. 19). However, over-reliance on any single existing work is generally inadvisable, and even though there may be no direct evidence of intentional copying, provided that sufficiently substantial parts have been taken a court may still be willing to infer that copying – however inadvertent– must have taken place.

Many publishers find it useful nowadays to use a plagiarism detection system such as CrossCheck and often notify authors on submission (particularly of peer-reviewed STM journal articles) that this system will be used.

Artistic works

The 1988 Act provides that the definition of copying in relation to an artistic work includes:

- making a three-dimensional copy of a two-dimensional work; and
- making a two-dimensional copy of a three-dimensional work.

A carving or sculpture which is copied from an original photograph may thus infringe copyright in the photograph even though the new work has added an extra dimension, and three-dimensional toys based on two-dimensional cartoon characters may similarly infringe copyright in the original graphic works. Conversely, a two-dimensional photograph or painting may infringe copyright in a three-dimensional work.

ISSUING COPIES TO THE PUBLIC

Under section 18 of the 1988 Act the issue to the public of copies of any copyright work is a restricted act. Copyright in the work will be infringed if it is done without the copyright owner's consent.

'Issue to the public' is defined as the putting into circulation of copies in the EEA which were not previously put into circulation in the EEA by the copyright owner or with his consent or the putting into circulation of copies outside the EEA which were not previously put into circulation in the EEA or elsewhere. Under the Act issue to the public specifically does *not* include:

- any subsequent distribution, sale, hiring or loan of copies already circulating; or
- any subsequent importation of those copies into the UK or another EEA state

but it does include putting into circulation in the EEA copies previously put into circulation outside the EEA.

Note that 'copies' are referred to in the plural, though there seems no particular reason why the issue to the public of a single copy should not also infringe copyright, in appropriate circumstances. However, it is likely that at least one physical copy of the work itself must actually be put into circulation, so that merely advertising or collecting orders will probably not of themselves amount to issue to the public.

RENTAL AND LENDING

Under section 18A of the 1988 Act the rental or lending of copies of certain works (including literary works) is a restricted act.

'Rental' is defined as making a copy of a work available for use, on terms that it will or may be returned, for direct or indirect economic or commercial advantage.

'Lending' is defined as making a copy of the work available for use on the terms that it will or may be returned, otherwise than for direct or indirect economic or commercial advantage, through an establishment which is accessible to the public.

'Rental' and 'lending' do not involve making a work available for on-the-spot reference use.

'Lending' excludes making available between establishments which are accessible to the public.

If the lending of a work results in a payment which covers the lender establishment's operating costs, there is no direct or indirect economic or commercial advantage.

In certain circumstances (principally the rental of sound recordings or films) authors who have transferred their rental rights are nevertheless entitled to claim equitable remuneration from the rental of their works.

However, some of these definitions were extended for the purposes of public lending right (PLR) in section 43 of the Digital Economy Act 2010, which provided for lending of audio and e-books on library premises but specifically not for remote download (for more on this, see Chapter 3). At the time of writing, these extended provisions had not been implemented, but publishers should note them for the future.

PERFORMING, SHOWING OR PLAYING IN PUBLIC

Performing, showing or playing most works (but not artistic works) in public is a restricted act, which will infringe copyright if done without permission. 'Performance' includes delivery of lectures, addresses, speeches and sermons and can include presentation via any method of sounds or images, including sound recording, films, or broadcast as well as live recital. The audience does not need to be large, but in order to be 'public' must consist of more than a purely domestic or private gathering.

The Act (section 19(4)) provides a limited exemption for those (such as TV companies) whose electronic media for transmitting sounds or images are used by others (such as publicans or club secretaries) for infringing performances: in such cases the person by whom the visual images or sounds are sent, and in the case of a performance the performers, shall not be regarded as responsible for the infringement. They may, however, be caught by other sections (see below).

COMMUNICATION TO THE PUBLIC

Communication to the public of most works is a restricted act. Communication means by electronic transmission and includes broadcasting and Internet transmission making a work available to the public in such a way that members of the public may access the work from a place and at a time they individually choose.

Cases have established that a link in a website to a work that is already available on the Internet is unlikely to be making that work available to the public. There may however be infringement if the link makes the linked work available to a new public that could not otherwise access it or could not access it so easily, for example, the link circumvents a paywall and allows non-subscribers to access subscriber-only content. In *Twentieth Century Fox* v. *NewzBin* (2010) the link allowed Internet users to access consolidated versions of films that had been posted in many different files which all had to be downloaded before the user could watch the film in question. NewzBin, the search service, was found liable for copyright infringement.

MAKING AN ADAPTATION

Making an adaptation of a literary, dramatic or musical work (not, incidentally, of an artistic work) is an act restricted by copyright. Doing it without the copyright owner's consent will amount to copyright infringement unless one of the exceptions (such as fair dealing – see below) applies.

However, adaptations for the purposes of copyright law are narrowly defined. What amounts to an 'adaptation' under UK law is defined in section 21 of the 1988 Act in relation to different kinds of works:

Literary and dramatic works

In relation to a literary or dramatic work (other than a computer program or computer database), an adaptation means one of the following:

- a translation (normally from one human language to another);
- a dramatisation of a non-dramatic work (turning a novel into a screenplay, for example) or the converse: a conversion of a dramatic work into a non-dramatic work;
- a picturisation (conveying the story or action by means of pictures, in a form suitable for reproduction in a book, newspaper, magazine or similar periodical).

Musical works

An adaptation in relation to a musical work means an arrangement or transcription of the work.

Computer programs

An adaptation means an arrangement or altered version of the program or a translation of it. A translation involves a version of the program in which it is converted into or out of a computer language or code or into a different computer language or code.

Computer databases

An adaptation means an arrangement or altered version of the database or a translation of it.

THE DIGITAL ECONOMY ACT

In April 2010 the Digital Economy Act (the 'DEA') received Royal Assent. The Act covers a wide range of issues facing the communications and creative industries that were raised initially in the *Digital Britain* Report of June 2009.

The DEA contains a number of provisions including measures designed to reduce online infringement. Perhaps the most controversial and high-profile part of the DEA relates to Internet Service Providers ('ISPs') and their obligations in relation to copyright material transmitted by end users. Measures include the requirement for ISPs to send notifications to their subscribers where they have received a report of copyright infringement by those subscribers from copyright owners. ISPs are also required to create records on the number of reports they receive against their subscribers and provide anonymised lists to copyright owners setting out, in relation to each copyright owner, which of the reports it has made relate to a subscriber who has reached a threshold number of notifications of alleged infringements. The ISP would then make subscribers' personal data available to the copyright owner on receipt of a court order so they can take action against those subscribers.

The DEA set out how telecoms regulator Ofcom should implement many elements of the measures but left the detail for other measures to be produced through a number of consultation processes. Ofcom was obliged under the DEA to draw up a code of practice called the Online Copyright Infringement Obligations Code (the 'Code') to effect these measures.

In May 2010 Ofcom published its draft of the Code which covers many different requirements that affect both ISPs and copyright owners. The Code will initially be limited to fixed ISPs who have a subscriber base of over 400,000 subscribers (in effect, seven major ISPs – carrying an obvious risk that infringers will migrate to smaller ISPs in due course).

Copyright Infringement Reports ('CIR') are the reports that 'qualifying rightsowners' may generate and send to ISPs. However, in order to qualify as a qualifying rightsowner, any rightsowner must estimate to the ISP in advance how many CIRs it proposes to submit each year, and pay any costs up front (which many consider to be a difficult if not impossible task, although trade associations such as the Publishers Association may qualify on members' behalf). Ofcom has also proposed that a minimum level of information must be included in a CIR such as the copyright owner's name and address, details of the work in which copyright is alleged to have been infringed, details of the apparent infringement, the time and date of the apparent infringement and the IP address associated with the infringement.

Following receipt of a CIR, an ISP must identify a subscriber from the information contained in it and operate a notification process to inform the subscriber of the reported incidence(s) of copyright infringement which they have been alleged to have committed. Effective technical systems must be implemented by the ISPs to match IP addresses to subscribers. Notifications must provide sufficient information on the nature of the allegations made against the subscriber and what actions they can take, including information about subscriber appeals to an independent appeals body and the grounds on which such appeals can be made.

Qualifying rightsowners will be able to request from ISPs Copyright Infringement Lists ('CILs'). These are anonymised. Ofcom is proposing that subscribers who receive three CIRs within 12 months may be included in a CIL requested by a copyright owner if such owner has made at least one CIR relating to that subscriber. Details of those subscribers appearing on a CIL may only be disclosed to a relevant rightsowner where the rightsowner obtains a court order.

Ofcom proposes to set up an independent appeals body for subscribers and in the Code sets out the powers that the appeals body will have along with a framework for conducting appeals. The government has proposed that the costs of the ISPs and Ofcom in relation to these initial obligations should be split, 75 per cent to be paid by the rightsowner and 25 per cent by the ISP – a highly contentious proposal which seems to many to be unreasonably weighted against rightsowners.

The Code includes provisions allowing Ofcom to enforce the requirements under the Code against ISPs and rightsowners and to resolve disputes between them. Penalties that can be imposed on an ISP or rightsowner which contravenes the DEA can be up to £250,000.

The government has said it will review the levels of online copyright infringement and may take further action to require ISPs to take technical measures (such as suspending or slowing a subscriber's connection) against those suspected of repeatedly engaging in infringement activity, though this would require further legislation to be passed. Thus, what was seen as the most controversial element of the DEA will be addressed at a later stage.

Before the Code can come into effect, approval from the European Union (Standards and Technical Regulations Committee) must be obtained. If approval is given, the Code will need final approval by the UK Parliament.

During its passage through Parliament, the (then) Digital Economy Bill also contained provision for orphan works licences, but the over-broad wording for these proved too controversial, and it was lost. However, extended provision for public lending rights, permitting audio and e-book lending under certain circumstances, survived, although not yet brought into force (see above, and Chapter 3).

The court has agreed to an application for judicial review of the infringement provisions of the Act.

SECONDARY INFRINGEMENT

As well as the key primary infringements of copyright set out above, sections 22 to 27 of the 1988 Act provide for further, secondary infringements. They include:

- importing an infringing copy;
- possessing or dealing with it;
- providing means for making it.

There are also secondary infringements of transmitting a work via a telecommunications system, permitting the use of premises for an infringing performance, and providing apparatus for infringing copyright by public performance of a work.

IMPORTING AN INFRINGING COPY

Section 22 provides that:

> the copyright in a work is infringed by a person who, without the licence of the copyright owner, imports into the UK otherwise than for his private and domestic use an article which is, and which he knows or has reason to believe is, an infringing copy of the work.

Guilty knowledge

Note that the person must *know* (or have reason to believe) that the article is an infringing copy – unlike primary infringements, which are all offences of strict liability (see above), it is an essential element of all secondary infringements that the alleged infringer should have known – or can be presumed to have known – the full significance of what he or she was doing. Proving – or inferring – such 'guilty knowledge' is a question of fact in each case: some defendants (such as rival publishers or experienced book importers) may be presumed to be more familiar with copyright transactions than others. Where there is some doubt whether importers have the necessary knowledge or not, it is usually advisable to remove any doubt by putting them on formal written notice that what they are doing is an infringing act. This is normally done by a letter before action – after receipt of such a letter it is not then open to them to claim that they had no idea that the copies concerned were infringing copies.

'Infringing copy'

An infringing copy is quite widely defined in section 27 of the Act to include as well as actual imports, copies that have not yet been, but are 'proposed to be', imported into the UK. Those copies may also include not only those which – if made in the UK – would have infringed the copyright itself, but also (under section 27(3)) those which would be in breach of an *exclusive licence* agreement relating to that work.

There is, however, a significant limitation on an exclusive UK licensee's rights to prevent parallel importation in section 27(5) of the Act, which makes it clear that any such rights will not be enforceable against imports from other member states of the EU.

> Nothing in sub-section (3) shall be construed as applying to an article which may lawfully be imported into the UK by virtue of any enforceable Community right within the meaning of section 2(1) of the European Communities Act 1972.

For more on parallel imports and Europe, see Chapter 13.

POSSESSING OR DEALING WITH AN INFRINGING COPY

Copyright may also be infringed by doing any of the following acts in relation to infringing copies without the consent of the copyright owner and (again) 'knowing or having reason to believe' that the copies are infringing:

- possessing them in the course of a business;
- selling or letting them for hire, or offering or exposing them for sale or hire;
- distributing them or publicly exhibiting them, both in the course of a business;
- distributing them other than in the course of a business, but still to such an extent as to affect prejudicially the copyright owner.

Possession must be 'in the course of a business' (which the Act defines to include a trade or profession). On the meaning of this phrase generally, see Chapter 11.

Note that sale or letting for hire need not be in the course of a business in order to infringe copyright. Neither need distribution if it is significant enough to affect the copyright owner prejudicially (so that handing out to a class of students course work books known to contain infringing copies of copyright text could well amount to infringement in itself, even though it is not in the course of business and the copying was done by someone else, if such distribution was likely – as it probably would be – to affect sales of the authorised editions prejudicially).

PROVIDING THE MEANS FOR MAKING INFRINGING COPIES

It is also an infringement of copyright in a work for a person, without the copyright owner's consent to:

- make;
- import into the UK;
- possess in the course of business; or
- sell or let for hire (or offer or expose for sale or hire).

an article specifically designed or adapted for making copies of that work, knowing (or having reason to believe) that it is to be used for making infringing copies. Specialised photocopying or recording equipment might be covered, but only if specifically designed or adapted for making copies of the particular work concerned: the section is more likely to cover unauthorised dealings with negatives or plates.

OTHER SECONDARY INFRINGEMENTS

It is also an infringement of copyright in a work to do the following acts without the copyright owner's consent:

- transmit it via a telecommunications system (other than by communication to the public) knowing or having reason to believe that infringing copies will be made as a result;
- permit the use of premises for an infringing performance (unless whoever gave the permission believed on reasonable grounds that the performance would not infringe copyright);
- supplying infringing apparatus (such as film or recording equipment) knowing or having reason to believe that the apparatus was likely to be used to infringe copyright.

PERMITTED ACTS AND OTHER DEFENCES

If one or more of the infringing acts listed above is alleged, a number of legal arguments may be produced by way of defence. Here is a checklist of the likeliest possible defences.

SUMMARY CHECKLIST: LIKELIEST POSSIBLE DEFENCES

- the work concerned is not a copyright work at all (for example it is not a literary or other work, or it lacks the necessary originality – see p. 19);
- it is not a qualifying work by reason of first (or simultaneous) publication in the UK or the author is not a qualifying person in the UK – see p. 34);
- it will not be protected under UK law for some other reason (for example, that it offends public sensibilities, or is fraudulent or otherwise unlawful – see below);
- although it was a copyright work, the period of copyright protection has now expired and/or at the relevant time the work was in the public domain (note that copyright in some public domain works revived following the EU's Duration Directive; on this and the term of copyright generally – see p. 37);
- the person alleging copyright infringement is not in fact the copyright owner (or the owner's licensee – see p. 251);
- no copying took place, and the work which allegedly infringes copyright was in fact the result of independent skill and effort – see p. 228);
- if copying did take place, the material copied is not significant or extensive enough to amount to a 'substantial part' of the copyright work concerned – see p. 227);
- the copying or other acts done were permitted acts, such as fair dealing (see below, p. 240);
- the copyright owner consented.

Most of the above defences are dealt with elsewhere in this book, but we will look below at public policy (briefly) and permitted acts (in some detail).

PUBLIC POLICY

Although the boundaries of copyright are primarily defined by statute in the UK, the 1988 Act contains a number of general saving provisions (at section 171) for other existing rights – for example that the rights and privileges of the Crown and Parliament will not be affected by any copyright, and that a similar exemption applies to:

- any rule of equity relating to breaches of trust or confidence; and
- any rule of law preventing or restricting the enforcement of copyright, on grounds of public interest or otherwise.

This last proviso leaves scope for the courts to refuse to enforce any copyright on grounds of public interest or public policy, if it conflicts with 'any rule of law'.

Although the old cases denying copyright protection to blasphemous or 'irreligious' works are unlikely to be followed nowadays, the proviso probably still gives judges sufficient grounds for denying copyright protection to a work which has already been held to be defamatory or obscene or where there is some other strong public interest argument against giving protection – but probably only if publication would actually be unlawful. It might also enable them to prevent a criminal from profiting from a crime, or from relying on copyright to protect a work which amounts to a fraud on the public (in one nineteenth-century case, an action against a book pirate failed because the religious work copied claimed to be a translation from an eminent German authority when in fact it was nothing of the kind).

The courts have held that this defence cannot be defined or categorised. It includes freedom of expression under the European Convention on Human Rights. It also includes:

- if the work is immoral, scandalous or contrary to family life;
- if the work is injurious to public life, public health and safety or the administration of justice; or
- if the work incites others to act in a way which would be so injurious.

PERMITTED ACTS

There are certain kinds of copying – generally non-commercial in nature – which may be done without infringing copyright if they come under the definition of one of the permitted acts set out in the 1988 Act. It would be a complete defence to any claim of copyright infringement to establish that the activity complained of was in fact a permitted act, although as we shall see motivation may be relevant too (for example in questions relating to fair dealing). The Act provides a long list of permitted acts, many of which are quite narrowly defined: we will consider below those of most relevance to publishing.

3-step test

Article 5.5 of the Directive provides, in wording taken from the Berne Convention, that any copyright exception must only be applied 'in certain special cases which do not conflict with a normal exploitation of the work or other subject matter and do not unreasonably prejudice the legitimate interests of the rightsholder'. This is likely to be a significant factor in interpretation by UK courts of 'fair dealing' and other exceptions.

Temporary copying

Section 28A provides that copyright in most works is not infringed by the making of a temporary copy which is transient or incidental, an integral and essential part of a technological process and the sole purpose of which is to enable either a transmission of the work in a network between third parties by an intermediary or a lawful use of the work. In addition, the temporary copy has to have no independent economic significance.

Fair dealing

Copyright will not be infringed:

(i)   by any 'fair dealing' with a literary, dramatic, musical or artistic work or a typographical arrangement for the purposes of research or private study
(ii) by any 'fair dealing' with any works for the purposes of criticism or review and
(iii) by any 'fair dealing' with any works (other than photographs) for reporting current events.

'Fair dealing' is not defined in the Act, but it is an essential prerequisite of all three of the above defences. It is not enough therefore merely to prove that copying (for example) was done for the purposes of research: it must have been *fair dealing* for the purposes of research. It will not succeed as a defence to a claim of copyright infringement otherwise. We will look at what is or is not 'fair' in the context of each individual activity. The test is an objective test. However, the intentions of the user are relevant to the question of whether the use is fair dealing. Other factors may include whether the original work has been published yet, and how extensive – and how important – are the extracts taken as a proportion of the whole (and in some circumstances how frequent). The difficult issue of fair dealing was dealt with, amongst other things, in Joint Guidelines on Copyright and Academic Research published in April 2008 by the British Academy and the Publishers Association.

Research or private study

Fair dealing for the purposes of research (for a non-commercial purpose) or private study is a permitted act and will be a defence to any claim of copyright infringement. In respect of research fair dealing has to be accompanied by a sufficient acknowledgement unless this is impossible for reasons of practicality or otherwise. The research or private study must genuinely constitute fair dealing, however. First and foremost, this probably limits the defence to personal activities (such as personal copying) rather than acts undertaken collectively. In the case of copying, as a general rule the person doing the copying must be the same person as the person doing the research or private study. He or she may possibly ask a friend or some other agent, such as a librarian, to do it for them, and there seems no reason why more than one copy cannot be made, as long as all the copying is for the personal research or private study of the individual concerned. It will *not* be fair dealing if a librarian or teacher makes multiple copies on behalf of an entire class of students – even if individually they are all engaged in private study: this was confirmed as long ago as 1916 in the leading case of *University of London Press Limited* v. *University Tutorial Press Limited*, where the clear motive was not individual or personal, but a collective motive to save the users (examination candidates) from having to buy the original works themselves. The 1988 Act also makes it clear (in section 29(3)(b)) that copying by someone other than the individual researcher or student will not be fair dealing if:

> the person doing the copying knows or has reason to believe that it will result in copies of substantially the same material being provided to more than one person at substantially the same time and for substantially the same purpose.

Research does not include commercial research. If the copying is by a commercial organisation for the purpose of commercial research, the use is not fair dealing.

Fair dealing for the purpose of research and private study specifically does not now include decompilation of a computer program – this is a separate permitted act (see below, p. 248).

Criticism or review

Section 30 of the Act provides that fair dealing with any work for the purpose of criticism or review (of that work, or another work, or of a performance of a work) does not infringe any copyright in the work, provided that it is accompanied by a sufficient acknowledgement and provided the work has been made available to the public.

As with fair dealing for the purpose of research or private study, there are a number of points to note:

- In order not to infringe, the acts done must not merely be for the purpose of criticism or review, but must constitute *fair dealing* for that purpose. Any improper motive – such as an obviously commercial motivation – will weaken any defence of fair dealing at the outset. It will be a question of fact and impression in every case: in the *University of London Press* case referred to above, very extensive extracts were reproduced, with little or no attempt at 'critical' commentary, and the primary motivation behind the copying was clearly not critical at all but commercial.
- Fair dealing may be for the purpose of criticism or review, even though the criticism or review concerned may be of the theories or philosophy behind the work rather than its actual literary content or style, or of a class of works, such as a style of journalism and, of course, the criticism or review need not be favourable. It must, however, have some significant element of genuine comment, or assessment.
- The term 'criticism or review' is interpreted liberally.
- The criticism or review must be accompanied by 'a sufficient acknowledgement'. This phrase is defined in section 178 of the Act to mean 'an acknowledgement identifying the work in question by its title or other description, and identifying the author' (unless the work is published anonymously, or is unpublished

and the author cannot be identified by reasonable inquiry). Crediting the title and the author will constitute sufficient acknowledgement, therefore. There is no requirement under the Act to credit the publisher or copyright owner (if different from the author). It is probably advisable to include as complete a credit as possible on each page or webpage where an extract appears, and a full copyright acknowledgement on at least one page or webpage, perhaps under the relevant acknowledgements section, or list of sources.

- In the case of *Fraser-Woodward* v. *BBC*, the claimant owned the copyright in a number of photographs of the Beckham family which were first published in various tabloid newspapers. An episode of a TV programme featured images of the newspaper pages on which the claimant's photographs appeared. The defendant claimed this was criticism and/or review of tabloid journalism and the methods by which the tabloid press and the Beckhams built and exploited stories to their advantage. The court stated that all that is needed is for there to be sufficient content to amount to criticism or review and gave the following guidelines:

  - What is the real objective of the person using the copyright work?
  - Excessive use can render use unfair.
  - What is the actual purpose of the defendant's work?
  - The amount of the work used can be relevant.
  - What type of work is reproduced and in which medium is it used?
  - Reproduction should not unreasonably prejudice the legitimate interests of the author or conflict with the normal exploitation of the work.

  It was held that the use of the photographs was fair dealing

- In *IPC Media* v. *News Group Newspapers* the use of the front cover of a claimant's magazine in an advertisement by a defendant which included the defendant's own magazine was not criticism or review. The court found that the defendant's uses of the claimant's work was to advance the sales of the defendant's products.

Reporting current events

Fair dealing with any work (other than a photograph) for the purpose of reporting current events does not infringe any copyright in it, provided that it is accompanied by a sufficient acknowledgement (see above). The requirement of a sufficient acknowledgement does not apply to non-print reporting via sound recording, film, or broadcast where this would be impossible for reasons of practicality or otherwise.

The events being reported must be current, but the work copied or otherwise used need not be: it may count as fair dealing to reproduce part of an existing literary work (such as a political study, or a scientific report) for example, if it becomes relevant in reporting future current events. The purpose must be the immediate one of 'reporting' those events, not some wider or more long-term editorial purpose. Moreover the term 'reporting current events' is also interpreted liberally. Even if an event may only be of limited interest, it is still a current event. It appears that the threshold for showing something is a current event is not high or difficult to surmount. The distinction between current events and events which are currently of interest can however become blurred.

In *Pro Sieben Media AG v. Carlton UK Television Limited* the pregnancy of Mandy Allwood, who became pregnant whilst undergoing a course of fertility treatment and was found to be carrying eight live embryos, was considered to be a 'current event' and the defendant's current affairs TV program relating to cheque book journalism, which featured an extract from the claimant's TV interview of Mandy Allwood, was deemed to be for the purpose of 'criticism or review'. The 1990 World Cup was also held to be a current event.

The Court of Appeal decision in *Hyde Park Residence Limited v. David Yelland and others* illustrates the subjective (and therefore unpredictable) operation of this fair dealing provision. The case involved an application for summary judgment by a security company owned by Mohammed Al Fayed on the basis of copyright infringement in respect of the publication of still photographs of Diana Princess of Wales and Dodi Al Fayed taken from security camera footage on a visit to the Villa Windsor in Paris. Al Fayed had alleged that this indicated that they planned to marry. At first instance, the court held that the use of the video stills was for the purpose of reporting current events and fair dealing in all the circumstances. The Court of Appeal disagreed and upheld the claimant's appeal. On a liberal interpretation, the media coverage of Al Fayed's allegations was a reporting of a current event. However, the dealing with the photographs had not been fair. Their use was excessive in all the circumstances and the point could have been conveyed by text. Also, no fair-minded and honest person would have paid for the dishonestly taken stills in all the circumstances. The Court of Appeal stated that the court must judge the fairness by the objective standard of whether a fair-minded and honest person would have dealt with the copyright work for the purpose of reporting the relevant current events in the manner that the defendant did.

Incidental inclusion of copyright material

Copyright in any work is not infringed by its incidental inclusion in an artistic work (such as a photograph), or in a sound recording, film, or broadcast. This is sometimes referred to as 'passing shot use'. The inclusion must, however, be truly 'incidental', which would probably exclude most deliberate acts designed specifically to add value, for example by dubbing in background music (deliberate inclusion of musical and allied works is expressly ruled out by section 31(3) of the Act). Some other deliberate uses (such as the quotation of a few lines of a literary work by a character in a film) might nevertheless still count as 'incidental inclusion' in some circumstances, provided they amount to no more than passing shots.

The inclusion of badges and logos in photographs of football players in the defendant's football album was found by a court not to be incidental inclusion.

Educational use

Sections 32 to 36 of the 1988 Act provide several somewhat limited exceptions to copyright infringement, designed to cover activities which are regarded as permissible under the general heading of 'education'. In the UK, these categories of permitted educational use are narrowly defined, so that much of the copying which goes on in schools and colleges (particularly if it is multiple copying) will not be permitted use under the 1988 Act and will still require the consent of the copyright owner. This can now be licensed under collective licensing schemes run by the Copyright Licensing Agency (see below, p. 245). This is in marked contrast to the copyright laws of some developing countries (at least, developing in the copyright sense) where 'educational use' has been notoriously widely defined to enable faculties – and the local photocopy shops – to reproduce entire text books more or less with impunity. This kind of educational piracy or wholesale copying (for example, of carol books for school choirs) is not possible in Britain under UK law, and what the law permits is strictly defined. The following acts are permitted.

Things done for the purposes of instruction or examination (section 32)

This is a very limited exception. In respect of literary works, the copying must be done in the actual course of instruction or preparation for it. It must be done by the teacher or student concerned, must not be via any reprographic process (such as photocopying or electronic copying), has to be accompanied by a sufficient acknowledgement and the instruction has to be for a non-commercial purpose. For literary works made available to the public, the instruction does not have to be for a non-commercial purpose but the copying has to be fair dealing with the work.

Actual examination use is also permitted, such as for the purpose of setting the questions, communicating them to the students or answering them if the questions are accompanied by a sufficient acknowledgement – this extends to reprographic copying but not of musical works. Any subsequent use of a permitted copy under this section (including selling or hiring it) will lose the protection – and will be treated as infringing use.

Anthologies for educational use

Again, this exception (in section 33) is extremely limited. The passage taken must be 'short', and must be in an anthology designed for educational use, which otherwise consists mainly of public domain material, and must be accompanied by a sufficient acknowledgement (see above). No more than two excerpts from the same author may be used in collections published by the same publisher within any five-year period.

Performing and recording by educational establishments

Section 34 provides that a performance of a literary, dramatic or musical work at an educational establishment (and in the course of its activities) by teachers or pupils will not count as a public performance for copyright infringement purposes, provided that the audience consists entirely of other teachers or pupils 'and other persons directly connected with the activities of the establishment' – this may include some parents, for example if they are also school governors, but not others: an 'open' audience of parents and other guests will almost certainly be a (potentially infringing) public performance.

The playing or showing of a sound recording, film, or broadcast before such an audience for the purposes of instruction would also not count as playing or showing the work concerned in public.

Section 35 provides that educational establishments may also record broadcasts, or copy such recordings under certain circumstances, without infringing copyright provided it is accompanied by a sufficient acknowledgement and the educational purposes are non-commercial; however, this exemption does not apply where there is a licensing scheme available, as there currently is, so licences would now be required from the Education Recording Agency (ERA).

Under proposals contained in the Gowers Review, it is likely that amending legislation will be introduced in early 2011 extending the section 35 provisions to distance learning via supervised intranets, but (as above) only to the extent that no licensing scheme exists. This will also extend to section 36 below and certain library provisions.

Reprographic copying

Section 36 of the Act provides that reprographic copies (which include copies made by electronic means as well as photocopies) may be made of passages from published literary, dramatic or musical works by an educational establishment for the purposes of instruction, but *only* if:

* not more than one per cent of any work is copied in any quarter;
* no licences are available for such copying (about which the person copying knew or ought to have been aware); and
* they are accompanied by a sufficient acknowledgement and the instruction is for a non-commercial purpose.

Any subsequent commercial dealings with a permitted copy under this section (including sale or hire) will be treated as infringing acts. Educational licences for hard-copy and electronic reprographic copying are currently available in the UK from the Copyright Licensing Agency, who regularly grants such licences on behalf of publishers and copyright owners. It would be difficult nowadays for any teacher or librarian to claim that they did not know, or have any reason to believe, that such licences were available. Details of the Copyright Licensing Agency are set out in Appendix B. The collective licences which it offers will cover multiple copying within defined limits depending on the terms of the particular licence. The licence will bring with it an indemnity from the Copyright Licensing Agency against any legal action by the relevant individual copyright owners, provided the terms of the licence are complied with. It is likely that these provisions will be extended in 2011 to cover distance learning (see section 35 above).

Library and archive copying

'Fair dealing', for example for the purposes of research or private study, may well not cover all the legitimate copying a librarian needs to do. Sections 37 to 44 of the 1988 Act therefore provide certain additional exemptions, for librarians of 'prescribed libraries'. For some purposes, this covers all libraries in the UK, but for others excludes any library 'conducted for profit'. Under the Copyright (Librarians and Archivists) (Copying of Copyright Material) Regulations 1989 made under the Act, this would exclude any library or archive which forms part of, or is administered by, a body established or conducted for profit. For those purposes, this would almost certainly rule out for example research libraries in major oil companies (or law libraries run by law firms).

Articles in periodicals

Librarians of prescribed libraries (see below) may copy an article in a periodical without infringing copyright in the text, or any illustrations, or the typographical copyright, provided the following conditions are met:

(1) the librarian must be satisfied that the copies are required for the purposes of research for a non-commercial purpose or private study, and will not be used for any other purpose;
(2) no person may be supplied with more than one copy of the same article (or with copies of more than one article from any single issue of a periodical);
(3) the user must be charged a sum not less than the cost of making the copies (including a contribution to the general expenses of the library).

Libraries 'conducted for profit' are not prescribed libraries for these purposes.

Parts of published works

A similar copyright exemption exists for copying of parts of published works other than articles in a periodical by librarians at prescribed libraries – again, libraries conducted for profit are excluded. The conditions are virtually identical to those set out above, applying to copying from periodicals, save that no person is to be supplied with a copy of 'more than a reasonable proportion' of any work (what is a reasonable proportion is not defined, but would clearly not include copying the whole work).

Public lending rights

Copyright is not infringed by the lending of a book by a public library if the loan is within the public lending right scheme, nor is it infringed by the lending of copies of a work by a prescribed library or archive (other than a public library) which is not conducted for profit. The UK public lending right scheme may well be extended to lending audio and e-books, under provisions contained in the Digital Economy Act 2010, but at the time of writing, these provisions have yet to be brought into force.

Supply of copies to other libraries

All UK librarians, whether their library is conducted for profit or not, may copy and supply to librarians of prescribed libraries an article from a periodical or the whole or part of any literary, dramatic or musical work, unless at the time of the request they knew ('or could by reasonable enquiry ascertain') the name and address of the copyright owner. Only single copies may be made.

Replacement copies

Librarians of prescribed libraries may copy items from their holdings in order to preserve or replace them, or to replace copies in the permanent collection of other libraries which have been lost, damaged or destroyed. This exemption does not, however, apply where it is reasonably practicable to purchase a copy of the item in question to fulfil that purpose. Under proposals contained in the Gowers Review, it is likely that this exception will be extended to format shifting in 2011, but solely and exclusively for archiving or preservation purposes.

Copying unpublished works

All UK librarians may copy unpublished works made on or after 1 August 1989 and deposited with them, such as letters or manuscripts, without infringing any copyright. The conditions are similar to those listed above. The exemption does not apply if the librarian is aware (or ought to be) that the work had been published before being deposited, or that the copyright owner has prohibited copying of the work.

It will be seen that these statutory library exemptions are all fairly limited in scope, even where the library concerned is a prescribed library. Permitted copying is almost always restricted to single copies (which would exclude multiple copying of newsletters or journals to students or other users). In addition, in many cases the librarian must be 'satisfied' about the purpose for which the copies are to be supplied. This probably means that the librarian is at least expected to make reasonable enquiries of users and be reasonably satisfied with the response. This may be achieved by asking the user, but where a librarian (or the librarian's employer) is concerned about the risks of legal liability for copying which turns out to infringe (since copyright is infringed by the person making the copies, not the person making the request), it may be advisable for the librarian to obtain a signed declaration from the user before the copying is done. There is provision in section 37(2) of the 1988 Act for a declaration, which may be relied on in situations where a librarian is required to be satisfied as to any matter, and which will have the effect of transferring legal liability to the user, unless the librarian is aware at the time the declaration is made that it is 'false in a material particular'. The 1989 Regulations contain a prescribed form of statutory declaration for these purposes.

It is therefore possible for a librarian to avoid legal liability for single copying which turns out to infringe copyright. It is not, however, generally possible to avoid the risk of legal action by copyright owners for multiple copying in breach of copyright unless permission for that copying has been obtained from the copyright owner or under a collective licensing scheme operated on the owner's behalf, such as those offered by the Copyright Licensing Agency (see above, p. 245).

Parliamentary and judicial proceedings

Section 45 of the Act provides that copyright is not infringed by anything done for the purposes of Parliamentary or judicial proceedings. The Act defines 'Parliamentary' to include not only the UK Parliament, the Northern Ireland Assembly, the Scottish Parliament and the Welsh Assembly but also the European Parliament. Judicial proceedings are also widely defined to include, for example, tribunals. However, the copying must be done for the *purposes* of those proceedings, so that a solicitor copying evidence as part of pleadings prior to a trial will be protected, but a teacher or librarian copying Parliamentary or case reports for information or teaching purposes might well not be.

Sections 46 to 50 provide further exceptions regarding the proceedings of Royal Commissions and statutory inquiries, public records and other material open to public inspection or on an official register, and certain copying done by the Crown or under statutory authority.

Lawful use of computer programs

The Copyright (Computer Programs) Regulations 1992 provided permitted acts in relation to computer programs, under which any 'lawful user' – who already had a right to use the program – may:

- make any necessary back-up copy of it;
- 'decompile' it, where necessary to create an independent program to run with it, or with some other program (not substantially similar to the program being decompiled);
- observe, study or test the functioning of a program in order to determine the ideas and principles which underline any element of the program, if he does so while performing any of the acts he is entitled to do; and

- copy or adapt it (for example, in order to correct errors) (sections 50A–50C of the 1988 Act respectively).

Databases

It is not an infringement of copyright in a database for a person with a right to use the database or a part of it to do, in the exercise of that right, anything which is necessary for the purposes of access to, and use of, the contents of the database or that part.

Designs and typefaces

Under sections 51 and 52, copyright in a design document or model (for anything other than an artistic work or typeface) is not infringed by making any (presumably three-dimensional) article to that design, or copying such an article, or (inter alia) issuing it to the public. Artistic works which have been exploited by or licensed by the copyright owner to be copied 'by an industrial process' and marketed (such as character illustrations licensed for merchandised goods), may be copied by making and exploiting similar goods without infringing copyright after a period of 25 years from the end of the year the original articles were first marketed. This section does not, however, permit copying or exploiting the artistic works concerned in any other way.

Under section 54, it is not an infringement of copyright in the design of a typeface (which is an artistic work) to do the following things:

- to use it in the ordinary course of typing, composing text, typesetting or printing;
- to possess an article for the purpose of such use; or
- to do anything in relation to material produced by that use.

This is despite the fact that such use may be based on an infringing copy. There may, however, still be a liability for secondary infringement, such as importing or possessing an infringing copy of the typeface design itself.

Transferring copies in electronic form

Where a copy of a work in electronic form such as a software program is purchased with an express or implied licence to copy or adapt it (for example, permitting a back-up copy), then where the purchaser is freely permitted to sell or transfer it to someone else, that someone else may also copy or adapt it in the same way, without infringing copyright. A right to make a back-up copy, or any other licensed copy, can be passed on from seller to purchaser without the need for further licensing. However, any additional copy retained by the seller after the transfer of the licensed copy has taken place will be treated as an infringing copy.

Copying anonymous or pseudonymous works

For works made after 1 August 1989, copyright will not be infringed by any acts done at a time when:

- it is not possible 'by reasonable inquiry' to identify the author; *and*
- it is reasonable to assume copyright has expired or that the author died at least 70 calendar years earlier.

Complex transitional provisions apply to pre-1989 works. In addition, the above does not apply to Crown copyright works or copyright works of certain international organisations.

Copying abstracts (section 60)

Section 60 of the Act permits the copying (or issuing to the public) of abstracts which accompany published periodical articles on scientific or technical subjects. Such abstracts are a common feature of medical and other scientific journals, and are frequently copied. The abstract must be primarily an abstract rather than anything more (such as an extended editorial): it must have the function of describing or summarising ('indicating') the contents of the article. The article must also have a 'scientific or technical' subject – although this sounds as if it might have rather a narrow scope, it may well be wide enough to cover abstracts of any similar specialist or professional articles, even in the social sciences or arts generally, provided they were pure abstracts accompanying the articles concerned.

The exception does not apply if there is a licensing scheme available for such use: there is not, at the time of writing.

Copying for visually impaired people

Blind and other visually impaired persons (VIPs) benefit from two statutory copyright exceptions introduced under the Copyright (Visually Impaired Persons) Act 2002:

- an individual/personal right for every VIP to make 'accessible copies' for his/her personal use; and
- a multiple copyright right for 'approved bodies' to make copies on behalf of their members.

The second, collective copying exception does not have effect if, and to the extent that, a suitable licensing scheme exists. There are a number of key provisos to these copyright exceptions:

(1) Both exceptions are subject to a requirement for copies to include a statement that they are made under the Copyright Act, and sufficient acknowledgement to the source.

(2) Copies must be made from lawful originals.

(3) There must be no accessible edition already commercially available.

(4) The accessible copy may not be transferred, sold, lent or hired, etc. without consent.

(5) In the case of multiple copies, copying may only be made by an approved body, which must notify rightsholders, keep records and allow reasonable audits.

Provision of 'accessible copies' to visually impaired people (and similar groups, such as dyslexics) has been the subject of much discussion in recent years, focusing on their expressed need for publishers' digital files as near to publication date as possible. At the time of writing, a Memorandum of Understanding has been signed in the EU between organisations representing visually impaired people and publishers, expressing the intention to move towards a system of mutual exchange of digital files under secure, and audited, conditions by Trusted Intermediaries (such as RNIB) in each member state. A Stakeholder Platform with a similar agenda has also been established in Geneva by the World Intellectual Property Organisation, WIPO.

Other permitted acts

Other permitted acts under the 1988 Act include the following:

- things done in reliance on a registered design (section 53);
- use of notes or recordings to report current events (section 58);
- public reading or recital of reasonable extracts (with a sufficient acknowledgement) (section 59);
- representation of certain artistic works on public display (section 62);
- copying an artistic work in order to advertise its sale (section 63);
- an author of an artistic work copying the work to make another artistic work (section 64);
- lending of works and playing of sound recordings (sections 66 and 67);
- incidental recording for the purposes of a broadcast (section 68);
- Recording for the purposes of time-shifting or private photographing of a broadcast (sections 70 to 71);
- reception and re-transmission of a wireless broadcast by cable (section 73).

CIVIL AND CRIMINAL REMEDIES IN THE UK

What do you do if someone infringes your copyright? Perhaps equally importantly: what might they (and a court) do to you if you infringe theirs? In this section we will look at who can sue, and who can be sued, in UK courts, what civil remedies (such as damages) might be available to them, and in what circumstances, and finally – but increasingly importantly – what criminal penalties might apply. The following section deals primarily with infringements in the UK – for international issues such as piracy and cybercrime, see later.

WHO CAN SUE?

The copyright owner

Perhaps self-evidently, all copyright infringements are actionable by the copyright owner. It must be the correct copyright owner, however – as we saw in Chapter 2, a typical publication such as a book or magazine might contain several different copyright works, and there may be several different copyright owners: in order to bring an action for infringement, the copyright owner must be the owner of the particular copyright which has been infringed. So, if an illustration has been copied without permission, the owner of the artistic copyright in that illustration may sue for infringement, but not, for example, the owner of literary copyright in the accompanying text – they are different copyrights, and may be owned by different people. The position would be the same with any separate, but associated, copyright such as a compilation of the book as a whole, or an underlying computer program. If the text (or compilation, or computer program) was copied too, of course, then the owners of copyright in these works may have actions, but not otherwise.

The owner must also own the copyright at the correct *time* (in fact, two separate times):

- at the actual time when the infringement occurred. A subsequent copyright owner (such as a beneficiary under a will, or an assignee) cannot sue for infringements which took place before he or she became the owner (unless the rights of action have been assigned); *and*
- when the claim form is issued: you will have no cause of action if you do not own legal (or at least equitable) title to the copyright.

Joint copyright owners

Although a joint copyright owner cannot exploit the copyright without the consent of the others, any joint copyright owner can take legal action for infringement of the relevant copyright without needing to join the others in the proceedings (although the others, of course, may wish to join in).

Exclusive licensees

Section 101 of the 1988 Act provides that an exclusive licensee has the same concurrent rights and remedies as the copyright owner and can therefore sue for copyright infringement in the same way. Any infringer can be sued, except the copyright owner themselves.

The infringement must have occurred after the licence was granted, and while it was in force. The infringement must also fall within the terms of the particular exclusive licence concerned, of course, so that an exclusive licensee of English-language volume rights may bring an action against an infringing English-language paperback, but not against an infringing Russian translation on a website.

Although an exclusive licensee may seek an injunction, once the action is under way the copyright owner must be joined as a claimant (or added as a defendant) unless the leave of the court is obtained. The same point applies if the copyright owner commences proceedings. The court will usually only grant leave in exceptional circumstances – as in 1972, for example, when Bodley Head were granted leave to pursue an action on their own since the copyright owner – Solzhenitsyn – could not do so in Russia where the book concerned was banned.

Non-exclusive licensees may bring an action for copyright infringement if the infringing act is directly connected to a prior licensed act of the licensee. In addition, the licence has to be in writing, signed by the copyright owner and expressly grant the non-exclusive licensee the right to bring an action.

Other parties, such as agents, have no right to take proceedings for copyright infringement in their own name.

Presumptions on title

With old publishing records hard evidence of copyright ownership may be difficult to come by. The court will assist claimants in such cases by making a number of presumptions, spelt out in sections 104 to 106 of the Act. In each case, unless the contrary is proved:

- anyone whose name appears as the author on published copies of a work will be presumed to be the author;
- any such author will be presumed not to have written the work in the course of employment, or subject to Crown or other copyrights;
- where no author is named, but a publisher is identified, that publisher will be deemed to be the copyright owner, provided that the work otherwise qualifies for UK copyright protection on the basis of its country of first publication;
- Where the author is dead or unknown (and cannot be ascertained by reasonable enquiry) it will be presumed that the work is original, and that the claimant's claims as to first publication are correct;
- where the work is a computer program, and is published bearing statements crediting a particular copyright owner, or relating to first publication in a particular country or issue to the public in a specified year, those statements will be presumed to be correct.

WHO CAN BE SUED?

Section 16(2) of the 1988 Act provides that copyright in a work is infringed by a person who, without the licence of the copyright owner, does, or authorises another to do, any of the acts restricted by copyright. As we saw above, these restricted acts may be primary infringements such as copying, or issuing copies to the public (above pp. 228 and 231), or secondary infringements such as importation or possession. Any 'person' who does, or authorises, any such acts, as defined, without permission, may thus be sued. This therefore includes the following.

Natural persons

This means human beings who do, or authorise, any of the restricted acts (on the meaning of 'authorise', see above, p. 228). In a publishing case, there may be several different infringements, such as copying, issuing copies to the public, importing, possessing, selling, hiring or distributing, and each person will be separately and personally liable for their own infringements. Several defendants may therefore be sued at once, including authors and publishers, printers, wholesalers and bookshop owners, even though the causes of action may be different.

Employees may be personally liable even if they were acting in the course of their employment (in that case *both* employee and employer may be liable) and so may directors and agents.

Legal persons (such as companies)

In the case of many small companies the one or two directors in charge to all intents and purposes *are* the company. So although many of the infringements would have been done by the company and it will therefore be necessary to sue the company, it may be advisable to sue the directors personally as well (since small companies may conveniently cease trading, whereas directors tend to survive).

Joint infringers (or joint tortfeasors)

A common, concerted design by two or more persons to infringe may lead to both or all of them being sued jointly (even if one of them is outside the UK).

WARNING LETTERS

The first step in many actions for copyright infringement – indeed actions of any kind – is the sending of a warning letter. This is normal practice, and may give both sides the opportunity to sort the matter out (fairly) amicably without having to resort to costly and time-consuming litigation. If a standard business letter does not produce the desired result, a more formal solicitor's letter, threatening specific legal action (and therefore called a letter before action) might concentrate minds sufficiently to stop the infringement and settle the matter on mutually acceptable terms. Whether or not a warning letter was sent may also have an impact on the question of costs later on: if there is time, such letters are therefore advisable. Courts may be less likely to award a successful claimant his or her costs if he or she did not send a letter before action, as litigation is now seen as a last resort and parties are encouraged to settle their dispute before commencing proceedings.

Where the infringement is a primary infringement – such as copying (see p. 228) there is no legal requirement to send a warning letter before commencing legal proceedings: indeed, there may be very strong reasons for *not* warning the infringer what is about to happen (see below, p. 255). With secondary infringements such as possession or dealing, however, it is necessary to establish that the infringer *knew* (or ought reasonably to have known) that the acts concerned were infringing acts (see p. 235), and for this reason it may be necessary to send a formal warning letter at the outset, putting the infringer on legal notice, which can then be produced at the trial as hard evidence of guilty knowledge.

Drafting warning letters requires some care: defamatory statements and malicious falsehoods must be avoided (see Chapter 7), and in the case of letters sent to third parties such as distributors, any unlawful interference with contractual relations must be avoided also.

A committee of some leading intellectual property practitioners have published a Code of Practice for pre-action conduct in intellectual property disputes. The Code's aim is to set out the steps which parties should follow where litigation is being considered. Although not binding, the Code represents the committee's assessment of what is reasonable pre-action behaviour in intellectual property law disputes. The Code lists various matters to be included in a letter before action and the defendant's letter of response.

From October 2010 a new procedure has become available in the English Patents County Court ('PCC') intended to permit more efficient and cost-effective IP litigation and to promote the PCC as a viable alternative to the High Court for disputes covering all types of IP including copyright. Claims will where possible be determined on the statements of case. Witness cross-examination will be strictly controlled. Parties will be able to recover a maximum of £50,000 for costs relating to liability. Costs for an enquiry as to damages or an account of profits will be limited to £25,000. This new procedure is a significant opportunity for rights owners to bring less complex cases to trial more quickly and cheaply than in the High Court.

INJUNCTIONS

An injunction is a discretionary court order, either commanding someone to do something or (more commonly) ordering someone to *stop* doing something and forbidding them from doing it in the future, or at least until the injunction is lifted. The latter, negative, version is often the most important and most urgent legal remedy a claimant will seek against a copyright infringer: once the infringement is discovered what the copyright owner usually wants most of all is for the defendant to be ordered to stop (or in some cases not to start: for example not to publish). Questions of financial compensation, though important, are usually less urgent and can be left to be dealt with by a suitable award of damages at the trial (see below, p. 256): an injunction, however, may be an urgent priority.

The criteria which a court should consider in deciding whether to grant an interim injunction are:

(1) The grant of an interlocutory injunction is a matter of discretion and depends on all the facts of the case.

(2) There are no fixed rules as to when an injunction should or should not be granted.
(3) The court should rarely attempt to resolve complex issues of disputed fact or law.
(4) Major factors the court can bear in mind are:

 (a) the extent to which damages are likely to be an adequate remedy for each party and the ability of the other party to pay;
 (b) the balance of convenience;
 (c) the maintenance of the status quo;
 (d) any clear view the court may reach as to the relative strength of the parties' cases.

Having weighed the above, the court may still refuse an injunction if it appears inequitable to grant one – for example if the claimant has delayed unreasonably. If an injunction is granted, a court will usually require as a condition of granting it that the claimant gives the defendant what is called a cross-undertaking as to damages. This will protect the defendant against any loss or damage incurred as a result of complying with the injunction – for example by taking a book off sale on the day before publication – should the claimant's claim turn out to have been unfounded when it is finally adjudicated on, at the trial. Where the claimant is unable to give a sufficient cross-undertaking, the court may refuse to grant the injunction.

DAMAGES

It is not necessary in order to win an action for copyright infringement to prove financial (or any other) loss. If copyright infringement is proved, some damage will be assumed. There is a general burden of proof on any claimant to prove any specific loss or damage, but apart from that a court will usually be willing to make a general award of damages to compensate the claimant for what has happened. The basic aim is to restore the claimant to the position he or she would have been in had the infringement not occurred.

Not surprisingly, it is not always easy to arrive at a scientific method of quantifying the claimant's loss, particularly in publishing actions. Any one or more of the following criteria may be adopted:

• *Loss of profits.* A court will take into account any reasonable expectation of profits, either based on evidence of previous publications or on reasonable commercial forecasts. Loss of likely subsidiary rights revenue (such as a US deal) will be as relevant as lost home sales, although a court will not compensate a claimant for possible future profits which are purely speculative. There is also a general duty on all claimants to take any reasonable steps to mitigate their loss where possible.
• A *fair licence fee.* Where the claimant normally grants licences for the use of the copyright material concerned, a more reasonable starting point for assessing

damages might be to calculate a fair licence fee which might have been levied had the defendant sought a licence in the usual way. Evidence of current levels of licence fees in the market concerned will be borne in mind: the court may still award a higher figure if this calculation does not seem to go far enough to compensate the claimant properly. The court rejected the notional licence fee approach in a recent case concerning a CD covermount including recordings of songs performed at a Jimi Hendrix Experience concert. The covermount was distributed with the *Sunday Times*. The court said the claimants were entitled to be compensated for damage suffered worldwide as a result of the delay in one year in launching their film which was to include recordings of the Hendrix concert. The court found the claimant would not have agreed to licence the CDs in question as it would have upset their own plans.

• Additional damages Under section 97(2) of the 1988 Act, a court may award additional damages, as the justice of the case may require – bearing in mind all the circumstances, but in particular, the flagrancy of the infringement, and any benefits gained by the defendant. Flagrancy involves deceitful conduct and intended infringement and also sufficiently serious carelessness. Benefit includes not just monetary benefit.

It is important to note that damages are not available in copyright actions where at the time of the infringement the defendant did not know, and had no reason to believe, that copyright subsisted (at all) in the work concerned (section 97(1)) – however, other remedies, such as injunctions or an account of profits, may still be available in the court's discretion.

OTHER REMEDIES

Account of profits

This is an equitable remedy, available only as an alternative to damages (you cannot have both) where it seems more appropriate – once the financial information is known – to assess the profit the defendant earned from the infringement. It is unlikely that a claimant would opt for an account of profits unless the known profits were considerably more substantial than the sum a court would be likely to award in damages.

Delivery up

Section 99 of the 1988 Act entitles a copyright owner to apply to the court for delivery up of infringing copies which someone has in their possession, custody or control in the course of their business (innocently or otherwise). Proof of guilty knowledge is only required in the case of articles – such as machinery – specifically designed or adapted for making (infringing) copies. Under section 114 of the Act, the copies may be forfeited to the copyright owner, or destroyed, or otherwise dealt with as the court thinks fit.

Seizure

Copies which are found 'exposed or otherwise immediately available for sale or hire' (section 100) may be seized by the copyright owner without the need for any court order – however, there are serious practical restrictions: the local police station must be notified before any such raid takes place, no force may be used, and nothing may be seized from the infringer's permanent or regular place of business (since the section is primarily aimed at market stalls selling bootleg copies).

Confiscation by customs

Under section 111 of the Act, owners of copyright in a published literary, dramatic or musical work may give written notice to the Commissioners of Customs & Excise to treat infringing printed copies as prohibited goods for up to five years. This gives some scope for customs seizures where a tip off is received well enough in advance, but only applies to such works in *printed* form (and not therefore to computer software). There are however parallel provisions covering sound recordings and films.

Imports from elsewhere in the European Economic Area may be immune from prohibition under the free movement of goods provisions of the Treaty of Rome (see Chapter 13).

Search orders

These are pre-trial court orders requiring a defendant to give immediate access to premises without notice and to allow property – such as incriminating documents – to be inspected and in some cases taken away by the claimant (generally the claimant's solicitor). Needless to say such an order (which is not just confined to copyright actions) is a drastic measure and its execution is closely regulated by the court. Generally speaking, such orders may be used only where such access is urgent and essential and where the claimant's case is very strong. There must also be a substantial risk that the defendant might destroy such evidence if given advance warning.

Freezing injunctions

Freezing injunctions may be granted in urgent circumstances by a court to prevent a defendant from removing assets (such as stock or money) out of the country – or otherwise putting them beyond the court's jurisdiction – in order to avoid judgment. The claimant must have a strong arguable case and there must be a significant risk that the assets concerned may be dispersed.

CRIMINAL PENALTIES FOR COPYRIGHT INFRINGEMENT

As well as the more familiar civil remedies which copyright owners may seek to obtain against infringers, such as injunctions and damages, the 1988 Act also provides *criminal* penalties of fines or imprisonment for a number of specific criminal offences. These are largely contained in section 107(1) of the Act. Under that section, a person commits an offence who, without the licence of the copyright owner, does any of the following acts in relation to an article which he or she knows (or has reason to believe) is an infringing copy of a copyright work:

(1) makes it for sale or hire;
(2) imports it into the UK, otherwise than for private or domestic use;
(3) possesses it in the course of a business with a view to committing any act infringing the copyright; or
(4) in the course of a business:

(a) sells it or lets it for hire;
(b) offers or exposes it for sale or hire;
(c) exhibits it in public;
(d) distributes it; or
(e) distributes it otherwise than in the course of a business to such an extent as to affect prejudicially the owner of the copyright.

There are also separate offences under section 107(2) of the Act, of:

(1) making or possessing an article specifically 'designed or adapted' for making copies of a work, knowing (or – again – having reason to believe) that the article is to be used to make infringing copies for sale or hire in the course of a business;
(2) communicating the work to the public either in the course of a business or otherwise than in the course of a business to such an extent as to affect prejudicially the copyright owner *and* in either case the defendant knows or has reason to believe that by doing so it is infringing copyright in the work; or
(3) the public performance of a literary, dramatic or musical work, or the playing or showing of a sound recording or film, where the person responsible knew (or had reason to believe) that copyright would be infringed.

Persons convicted of these offences are liable to criminal penalties including fines and terms of imprisonment ranging from up to six months (in the Magistrates' Court) to ten years (in the Crown Court). The Digital Economy Act has increased the maximum fines relating to infringing articles and illicit recordings to £50,000, and includes the possibility (as yet not implemented) of disconnection for repeat offenders.

Further, under section 110 of the Act, directors or other senior officers of a company may be prosecuted personally if a relevant offence by the company is proved to have been committed with their 'consent or connivance'. In all these cases, proof of actual guilty knowledge or intent is not always necessary: evidence that the accused had 'reason to believe' infringement was occurring or would take place may also secure a conviction. In many cases, this may be established simply by sending a warning letter (see above, p. 254). There are provisions in sections 108 and 109 for delivery up of infringing copies, and for police search warrants.

Criminal provisions did not initially attract a great deal of legal attention, being seen as more relevant to the activities of obvious pirates and market traders selling bootleg tapes and DVDs than to reputable individuals or companies. However, given the rapid increase in cybercrime (see below), the relative speed and cheapness of proceedings in the Magistrates' Court, and the significant criminal penalties available – potentially giving individuals as well as companies a criminal record – the criminal provisions of the 1988 Act and the Digital Economy Act 2010 may have considerable relevance to copyright owners seeking remedies against infringers, even where the alleged infringer may be a substantial and reputable company. The general trend seems to be a considerable increase in sentences passed. For more on all this, see below.

PIRACY

Piracy of books, e-books and journals, within the UK and internationally, via illegal copying or reprints, or unauthorised translations, has been an illicit trade causing serious harm to the publishing industry for many years, and is still very much in existence. It continues to cause significant losses to all the creative industries, including music, film and software, and is a long-standing feature of trade negotiations with a depressingly large number of countries, both bilateral and multilateral. UK publishers lobby regularly on piracy issues, including lax or over-broad foreign copyright laws, or exceptions, and enforcement (or lack of it), represented by the Publishers Association (PA) in London, the Federation of European Publishers (FEP) in Brussels, and the International Publishers Association (IPA) in Geneva, along with their counterparts from other national publishers associations (such as APP in the USA) and other creative industries. The UK government takes piracy of UK copyright seriously. DG Trade within the European Commission similarly maintains foreign desks for key 'third countries' where piracy is an issue, and often helps to apply diplomatic and trade pressure on EU rightsholders' behalf, particularly with countries which attach importance to trade with the EU, or may be candidates to join. The PA's International Board helps to co-ordinate funding and operation of anti-piracy actions on UK publishers' behalf in key piracy countries (currently including India, China, Pakistan, Nigeria and Turkey), involving the retention of local attorneys and investigators, and pressure on local police, customs and government agencies. The PA also publishes a Six-Step Guide to deal with copyright infringement.

All this has been going on for many years in relation to print-on-paper publishing, and will doubtless continue, but over the past few years piracy – like most things – has increasingly become an online activity as well. As the early Napster and Grokster litigation showed, illegal downloads of infringing material from peer-to-peer websites proved extremely popular and took time to convert to a licensed model, although more recent examples of cybercrime such as the Pirate Bay website have proved harder to stop (indeed, some of the Swedish founders were elected to the European Parliament as MEPs). Where website operators and internet service providers could argue (as many did) that they were totally unaware of infringing activity on their sites, they usually had a legal defence under the EU E-Commerce Directive of 2000 or a similar 'safe harbour' under the USA's Digital Millennium Copyright Act 1998, provided that they acted 'expeditiously' to take down the offending material, or disable access. Not surprisingly, offending sites often re-appeared shortly after takedown. Where a defence of ignorance fails, however, UK courts have proved willing to enforce copyright directly against the ISP. In the 2010 *NewzBin* case (see p. 232), the High Court found that the Usenet site Newzbin was itself liable for copyright infringement when it became clear that NewzBin (who had 250 editors) themselves combined sections of copies of films (some obviously made in cinemas with hand-held cameras), making these available for download as complete films by members of the site for substantial commercial profit.

Governments have also now started to intervene with ISPs to try to control cyber-crime of this kind. The French Parliament recently passed a '3 strikes and you're out' law, under which repeat infringers would not only be liable to legal action but may also be disconnected. In the UK, the position after the Digital Economy Act 2010 seems somewhat more modest (see p. 233) with a Code of Practice operated by telecoms regulator Ofcom under consultation at the time of writing, which makes no mention of disconnection and leaves (traditional) legal action to rightsowners, who are also expected to fund 75 per cent of the (unknown) costs in advance. Larger publishers with the capacity to maintain substantial in-house anti-piracy units may find this works as an effective deterrent, but smaller companies may well find that existing Notice and Takedown remedies (including the PA's own Portal) are more suitable and affordable.

INTERNATIONAL COPYRIGHT PROTECTION

UK copyright works are not only protected in the UK, under domestic UK law, but to a large extent internationally too. Equally, a great many foreign copyright works are protected here. This happy state of affairs is not the result of any all-embracing international copyright law, but has been arrived at piecemeal, over the years, by a combination of bilateral treaties between the major copyright nations, and, increasingly, multilateral conventions to which most of the significant trading nations of the world now belong. We will look at these treaties and conventions in more detail below. It is, however, essential to bear in mind from the outset that these arrangements are no more than treaties – in the case of many nations (including the UK) they may well have no legal effect unless and until the country concerned implements them as part of its own domestic law. Some countries are better – and quicker – than others about implementing their international treaty obligations; for example, despite being a founder signatory of the Berne Convention in 1886 (see below) the UK did not comply fully with its Berne obligations to protect moral rights of authors until the 1988 Act. So, whatever the treaties say, if you want to know what actual copyright protection is available in a particular country at any given time, the only way of finding out reliably is to look at their own domestic copyright law.

THE BERNE CONVENTION

The most important international copyright convention today is the Berne Convention. Signed in 1886 by a handful of mainly European states and still going strong over a hundred years later, it has now been acceded to by over 160 countries, including every EU member state and Russia, the USA and China. It has of course been revised over the years: the latest (Paris) Act dates from 1971. Not all members have yet acceded to the Paris Act: in cases of doubt, it is advisable to check with the World Intellectual Property Organisation (WIPO), which administers Berne and other intellectual property conventions (their address is set out in Appendix B).

The levels of copyright protection required by Berne were strongly endorsed by the final (Uruguay) Round of the General Agreement on Tariffs and Trade (GATT), in particular in the associated TRIPS agreement (dealing with the Trade Related aspects of Intellectual Property Rights) which has now been adopted as a minimum international copyright standard by GATT's successor body, the World Trade Organisation.

For those who belong, the Berne Convention has a number of fundamental principles:

- A wide range of original 'literary and artistic works' are protected, defined to include 'every production in the literary, artistic or scientific domain, whatever may be the mode or form of its expression' – dramatic and musical works, films and photographs are expressly included and most member states now also protect computer programs (usually under literary works). Translations, adaptations and compilations are also covered.
- It is open to member states to require (as the UK does) that protected works must have been fixed in some material form (see p. 22).
- Protection shall extend equally to works of authors who are *nationals* of a Berne member state, and to works of non-nationals which are *first published* in a member state. First publication includes simultaneous publication within 30 days (for the UK position, see p. 36).
- Authors shall enjoy, in Berne countries other than the country of origin, copyright protection for their works amounting to 'national treatment': in other words, the same rights which those other countries grant to their own nationals (and governed by the same domestic laws).
- Protection must not be subject to any formalities (such as registration) and must extend from the moment a work is created – or at least fixed in material form – for the rest of the life of the author and at least a further full calendar 50 years (within the EU this period was harmonised up to life plus 70 years as from July 1995: see p. 38). In the case of simultaneous publication in several Berne countries granting different terms of protection, the 'country of origin' shall be the one granting the *shortest* term;
- Authors shall have independent moral rights of paternity and integrity in their works (see Chapter 3, pp. 46 and 49).

Generally speaking, authors shall have the exclusive right of authorising reproduction (and translation) of their works, but certain copying, for example fair dealing in the UK (see p. 240) may be allowed provided it 'does not conflict with the normal exploitation of the work and does not unreasonably prejudice the legitimate interests of the author' (this wording appears verbatim in a number of member states' copyright laws, but is often widely interpreted to cover copying activities such as large-scale educational copying which would be regarded as flagrant infringement in the UK). There are further exemptions, set out in an Appendix to the Paris Act, allowing in certain circumstances 'developing countries' to apply compulsory translation licences for limited periods 'for the purpose of teaching, scholarship or research' for works not otherwise available in the local language: these have also been a source of much controversy. A developing country is one regarded as such 'in conformity with the established practice of the General Assembly of the United Nations', and the exemption has strict conditions including prior request for consent, due acknowledgement and reasonable remuneration, but these strict rules have often been somewhat stretched.

WIPO COPYRIGHT TREATIES 1996

Although the Berne Convention is periodically revised, usually via diplomatic conferences, it was by 1996 in serious need of updating to take full account of the digital environment. The member states met at a major session in December 1996, together with interested parties such as authors and publishers, users and intermediaries, and produced two major treaties: the WIPO Copyright Treaty and the WIPO Performances and Phonograms Treaty.

The 1996 WIPO Copyright Treaty has gone a long way towards meeting the need for a flexible right of reproduction, a workable right of communication to the public, including making available via digital networks, modern 'fair dealing' exceptions, and provision for liability (or not) of intermediaries such as telecommunications companies and service providers, together with some agreement on anti-circumvention measures and remedies generally. It has been implemented in the EU via the Copyright Directive 2001, and in the USA via the Digital Millennium Copyright Act 1998 (on which, see below).

THE TRIPS AGREEMENT

The TRIPS Treaty is particularly concerned with intellectual property remedies and sanctions, setting out minimum compliance standards for member states to achieve initially by January 2000 (although some developing or East European countries may be given more time). Key provisions include:

- Article 41, requiring 'effective action' to be enabled, with 'expeditious remedies'.
- Article 50, requiring 'prompt and effective' provisional measures (such as injunctions).

The WTO offers a dispute resolution system to resolve disputes between member states, which has already proved effective. TRIPS treaty requirements can therefore now be a serious agenda item in dealings with WTO members, and (particularly) those countries wishing to join.

THE UNIVERSAL COPYRIGHT CONVENTION (UCC)

At the end of the Second World War neither of the two new superpowers, the USA and Russia, belonged to the Berne Convention. The new United Nations, and its educational and cultural arm UNESCO, were keen to bring the US particularly within the international copyright community, but the relatively long copyright term of life plus 50 years, and the ban on any registration formalities, among other things, proved continuing obstacles to US accession to Berne. UNESCO therefore sponsored an alternative Convention, the UCC, which was signed in 1952 and which the US, the UK and a number of other major copyright nations joined (although the UK did not finally sign up until 1957).

There is one important formality, but on the whole the level of copyright protection required by the UCC is somewhat lower than under Berne:

- Works protected are broadly similar, and a similar 'national treatment' principle applies. Protection is again on the basis of either the author's nationality or the country of first (or simultaneous) publication.
- The minimum period of copyright protection is, however, the life of the author and 25 years only. In some cases this may be 25 years from first publication.
- Formalities (such as copyright registration) are permitted, but will be regarded as complied with if all published copies carry what has become known as the 'UCC copyright notice' – the copyright ©, the name of the copyright owner, and date of first publication – in no particular order, but 'placed in such manner and location as to give reasonable notice of claim of copyright' (Article Ill).
- There are developing country provisions similar to those in the Appendix to Berne.

Between 1952 and 1989 (when US accession to the Berne Convention came into effect) most UK published works carried the UCC copyright notice on their title pages, expressly in order to comply with UCC requirements and thereby secure effective copyright protection in the USA, a key English language market. Since US accession to Berne, such formalities should no longer be strictly necessary for the purposes of US protection (but registration may still be desirable, though – see p. 266), but there are still countries which subscribe to the UCC but not to the latest (Paris) Act of Berne and most publishers will therefore probably continue to print the UCC wording. It is normally set out thus:

© Hugh Jones and Christopher Benson 2011

The word 'copyright' is sometimes added before the ©, but is not strictly necessary.

COPYRIGHT PROTECTION IN THE USA

For most of the nineteenth century, the USA granted little or no copyright protection to the works of foreign authors (indeed, such foreign copyrights were not recognised at all until the Chace Act of 1891). As a result, the works of European authors and composers such as Dickens, and Gilbert and Sullivan, were freely and frequently pirated in America, despite personal lecture tours and simultaneous 'authorised' performances. The Chace Act did finally provide copyright protection for foreigners, but only to citizens of those countries which either granted national treatment to US works or granted reciprocal protection under an international (bilateral) treaty. Thereafter, UK works could be protected in the USA, but (until fairly recently) subject to registration and renewal formalities. US copyright protection is still a formidably complex area of law. It is impossible in a book of this scope to do more than provide a brief overview of the current position: it cannot be stressed too strongly that for reliable answers to specific queries it is highly advisable to seek the advice of a specialist attorney. US domestic copyright law was significantly revised by the passage of their current copyright law, the Copyright Act of 1976. The Act came into force on 1 January 1978: as a consequence, one of the first and most important questions to ask is whether the work concerned was created before or after 1978.

Works created before 1978

Before the 1976 Act came into effect, US copyright protection did not depend on the life of the author, but lasted for a fixed term of 28 years, calculated from the date of first publication, with a possible renewal for one further 28-year term, making 56 years in all. Protection also depended on compliance with a number of formalities (not as a prerequisite for copyright itself, but as requirements to institute litigation for infringement and obtain statutory (liquidated) damage and attorney's fees):

- an approved copyright notice (as in UCC above) printed on all copies published in the US;
- registration of the copyright at the Copyright Office;
- deposit of copies (a single copy in the case of foreign works);
- formal renewal at the end of the first 28-year term;
- compliance with the notorious 'manufacturing clause' (section 16 of the Copyright Revision Act 1909) which required that all copies published in the US should be typeset, printed and bound wholly within the limits of the US.

The last formal requirement in particular – a fairly blatant piece of protectionism – prevented many UK works from being protected at all in the USA, until the UK became a signatory to the UCC in 1957: from that point on, the only formality required in order to protect newly created UK works in the USA was the UCC copyright notice. On the whole, however, with one or two exceptions, existing UK works continued to be unprotected unless the full range of domestic formalities had been complied with.

Works created after 1978

For works created on or after 1 January 1978 (and for works created but not published before then), the 1976 Act provided a new term of copyright protection, in line with the UK and other Berne countries, of life plus 50 years (this was subsequently increased to match the new European period of life plus 70 years). For works which, as of 31 December 1977 were in either their original or renewal terms of 28 years, the 1976 Act provided that the second term of 28 years be extended by an extra 19 years, to 47 years – making a total of 75 years from first publication. Those copyrights already in their second, renewal, term at the time were automatically extended; those copyrights still in their first term had to be renewed in their twenty-eighth year in the normal way (but would automatically get the new 47-year renewal term). Special provisions applied to works of unknown authorship and works 'made for hire' (works made in the course of employment, or under certain commission arrangements). Copyright was not revived in pre-1978 public domain works. The term of copyright in work made for hire is now 95 years.

Certain registration formalities continued to exist, including the UCC copyright notice for foreign works, but the 'manufacturing clause' was considerably reduced in scope and finally expired in July 1986. Subsequent legislation has removed the requirement for registration of the renewal term for pre-1978 works.

US implementation of the Berne Convention and GATT

Following the Berne Convention Implementation Act of 1988, the USA finally acceded to the Berne Convention, with effect from 1 March 1989. Thereafter, in the spirit of Berne membership all formalities, at least as a prerequisite to copyright protection, were swept away, and even the basic UCC copyright notice was no longer required. It is likely however, that UK works will continue to bear the UCC notice for some time to come, since among other things it will continue to provide evidence against any defence of innocent infringement under US law (which might otherwise reduce any damages). Indeed, copyright registration itself is still advisable in some circumstances for evidential purposes, and is required to maximise available damages, and to secure attorneys' fees in actions for infringement. Registration fees currently range generally from $35 to $65.

The status of registered and unregistered works has recently received much attention in the Google book litigation draft settlement, where only those US works that are registered in the US Copyright Office were deemed to be works included under the draft settlement agreement (although non-US works were included whether or not they were registered). In the most recent settlement proposal (November 2009), still unapproved at the time of writing, the scope of the agreement had been reduced to include only unregistered works of certain countries including the UK along with other non-US registered works.

Registration practices generally can be technically challenging and consultations with counsel with practical experience is highly recommended. Recent questions involving collective registrations of photographs have, for example, raised questions about the extent to which each individual contributor or co-author must be identified in application forms. It is also easy to confuse deposit for purposes of responding to mandatory deposit requirements of the Library of Congress with deposit for purposes of copyright registration (the former does not automatically cover the latter).

Despite Berne membership, the USA did not immediately grant retrospective copyright protection to all existing works of other member states: this did not happen until 1 January 1996, following US adherence to the 1994 GATT/TRIPS agreements (see p. 263). As of 1 January 1996, foreign works of Berne or GATT member countries – which includes the UK – which were still then protected in their country of origin, but which had entered the public domain for failure to comply with formalities in the USA, were restored to copyright protection for whatever remained of their domestic copyright periods. In the case of UK and other EU works, this meant up to an additional 20 years. US protection for such 'Restored Copyrights' was secured until 31 December 1997 by filing a Notice of Intent to Enforce with the US Copyright Office and can now be obtained by serving a notice directly on those concerned: those US publishers previously exploiting the work in reliance on its (then) public domain status (called Reliance Parties) have a 12-month sell-off period in which to dispose of remaining stock.

Reproduction for blind or other disabled people

In 1997, US copyright law was amended to permit non-profit organisations or governmental agencies that provide specialised services to the blind and other disabled people to reproduce and distribute copies of previously-published, non-dramatic literary works in specialised formats (e.g. such as Braille, audio and digital text) exclusively for use by such people, without permission from (or payment to) the copyright owner. A similar copyright exception was introduced in the UK under the terms of the Copyright (Visually Impaired Persons) Act 2002 (on which see copyright exceptions, above).

The question of access for visually impaired people has become an international issue with consideration given at WIPO for a new potential treaty, or at least a Stakeholder Platform.

Publishers distributing textbooks in the USA should also be aware that many individual states, notably California, have adopted regulations that require that electronically formatted files of textbooks are provided to school systems or directly to blind or disabled students, to enable alternative-version materials to be made.

US term extension

With respect to copyright duration, the Sonny Bono Copyright Term Extension Act (October 27, 1998), named after the now deceased former singer-turned legislator, extended the term of works that were currently protected by copyright to life of the author plus 70 years (or 95 years after publication for anonymous works or works made for hire). Term extension was controversial in the USA, especially when combined with prior legislation which had restored some works to proprietary status from the public domain. The restored works clause has been subject to a series of court challenges on First Amendment-Constitutional grounds but consistently upheld, most notably in the *Eldred* v. *Ashcroft* decision by the US Supreme Court (2003) and most recently by the 10th Circuit Court of Appeals in *Golan* v. *Holder* (June 2010). In the *Golan* case, the Court noted that compliance with Berne was a 'substantial' government interest and importantly noted that 'copyright also serves authors' First Amendment interests'.

Digital Millennium Copyright Act

The Digital Millennium Copyright Act (October 28, 1998) (the 'DMCA') was the USA's implementation of the WIPO Copyright Treaty of 1996. The DMCA clarifies that a copyright work is protected regardless of media, and amends existing US copyright law to eliminate 'media-bias' (e.g. references to print). Controversial issues include the prohibition of the circumvention of copyright protection systems (given that the copying of some works in some circumstances might be fair use), proposals for the uncompensated use of digital materials for so-called 'distance education', and limitations on liability of online service providers for infringing materials being posted on their services. With respect to the latter, the service providers were given a 'safe harbour' if they took certain remedial steps 'expeditiously' upon being notified by a rightsholder of the infringement.

There is a 'red flags' concept in the DMCA beyond which the safe harbour is not supposed to apply, when the service provider has actual knowledge of illicit posting or is aware of 'facts or circumstances from which infringing activity is apparent'. This was tested recently in the trial court decision in *Viacom* v. *YouTube* (June 2010), where, despite evidence that there was general knowledge that much content on YouTube was illicit, the court held that this knowledge was not specific enough as to individual works to amount to actual knowledge, and that YouTube's efforts to respond quickly to rightholders' takedown requests concerning illicit content (including Viacom's) defeated the 'facts or circumstances' standard. The case is being appealed to the Second Circuit Court of Appeals at the time of writing, and will be intensely watched. Some commentators have asked whether *any* conduct would qualify as 'red flag' conduct if the trial court's rationale is applied.

TEACH Act 2002

The Technology Education and Copyright Harmonisation (TEACH) Act 2002 amended US copyright law to allow the use of copyright works in online instruction and for distance learning purposes, but subject to a number of provisos, including the following:

- Any copying must be from a lawfully acquired copy.
- The use must be in the context of mediated instructional activities analogous to live classroom teaching.
- The copying must be by, at the direction of, or under the supervision of, an instructor.
- The work copied should not be one primarily published for educational purposes.
- Technical protection measures must ensure access is limited to enrolled students, and to the relevant class session only.
- In addition, there are limited provisions for educational institutions to digitise relevant portions of works not yet in digital form, including a proviso that no digital version should already be, or become, available.

SECTION 108 REPORT

The US Copyright Office convened a working group in 2005 to consider whether and how the provisions of section 108 of the US Copyright Act, dealing with libraries and archival exceptions, should be updated for the digital environment. Although at the time of writing the Report (issued in March 2008) has not been taken up in legislative proposals, it seems likely that it will serve as the basis for legislative reform purposes. The Report contains a number of firm recommendations, the most relevant of which are:

- Libraries may 'outsource' to perform permitted activities on their behalf;
- The three-copy limit for replacement copying should be updated;
- Unpublished works may also be archived;
- Preservation activities may be initiated before the original works begin to 'deteriorate', and
- The addition of a new exception to permit the capture of publicly available online content for preservation purposes (where public access is not prohibited or permitted only under licence).

The Report noted that there are controversial issues remaining on which the working group could not reach consensus, including questions about whether provisions enabling the copying of works for 'interlibrary loan' purposes should include scanning and making works digitally available.

Trade marks and passing off

10

TRADE MARKS

INTRODUCTION

Although copyright can be a powerful form of legal protection for published (and unpublished) works, there may be some key words, names or phrases, or other distinguishing signs (such as a logo), which have an established goodwill or reputation of their own in the market place and which may be protected independently as trade marks under UK law. They may include titles of books or journals, names of authors (such as Wisden), or names of characters ranging from Peter Rabbit to Gandalf to Harry Potter. They have become increasingly important to the publishing trade in recent years as a means of protecting properties with merchandising potential, but it is important to recognise that they are not just a useful means of protecting characters in children's books, and licensing T-shirts and novelty soap, but may also be an extremely valuable form of protection for database, reference and general publishing and all kinds of distinctive publishing marks. Publishers, authors and agents should at all times consider the trade mark implications of the material they are handling, for two reasons:

- to protect as soon as possible names or other signs with valuable trade mark potential;
- to avoid infringing any existing trade marks.

WHAT IS A TRADE MARK?

Under section 1(1) of the Trade Marks Act 1994:

> A trade mark means any sign capable of being represented graphically which is capable of distinguishing goods or services of one undertaking from those of other undertakings.

- *'Any sign'*. Although 'sign' is not defined, section 1(1) of the 1994 Act goes on to specify that a trade mark may consist of 'words (including personal names), designs, letters, numerals or the shape of goods or their packaging'.

- '*Capable of being represented graphically*'. This includes not only two-dimensional marks, but three-dimensional shapes (such as the famous Coca-Cola bottle) and sounds capable of being reduced to musical notation, such as advertising jingles.
- '*Capable of distinguishing goods or services*'. This is a central requirement of any trade mark, and we will return to this later. For the present, note that the mark, in order to be registered, does not need to distinguish goods or services at the time of filing as long as it is capable of doing so. In addition, in the UK the proprietor has to have a bona fide intention to use the mark at the time the application is made.

WHAT MAY BE REGISTERED?

Under present UK law, all the following familiar publishing signs may be registrable as trade marks, provided the UK Intellectual Property Office is satisfied that they are capable of distinguishing the relevant goods or services from others:

- single letters, or sets of initials
- single words
- proper names
- names of authors
- names of characters
- titles
- phrases or slogans
- logos and other designs
- the distinctive shape or size of a publication.

Logos or designs (known as 'devices') are often more distinctive than ordinary words or phrases, and therefore easier to register: the first trade mark registered in the UK was the Bass triangle, and the Guinness harp was close behind.

As a general rule, words or other marks may not be registered if they are generic, or descriptive of the goods in question, and which consist exclusively of signs which (in the words of the 1994 Act):

- 'designate the kind, quality, quantity, intended purpose, value, geographical origin (or) time of production' of goods or services; or
- have become customary in the language or practices of the trade.

However, such objections may be overcome with sufficient evidence of distinctiveness through use.

WORDS AND PHRASES

Given the above guidelines, the words most likely to be capable of registration as trade marks are those with no obvious descriptive or generic link with the product.

The best trade marks are often invented words: meaningless but punchy and with no generic connection to anything at all, such as Kodak, Persil, Typhoo or Lego.

Known or existing words can be used, if completely unassociated with the product – 'Mars' for chocolate, for example. Composite words may also be registered successfully if 'invented', such as Coca-Cola and Starbucks. A common surname or a geographical name may be registered, but may require evidence of distinctiveness in the market place, and several years' continuous use.

It had been difficult to register slogans and taglines as they were regarded as promotional statements, not trade marks. However, when considering the Audi tagline VORSPRUNG DURCH TECHNIK the Community Trade Mark Office (see p. 277) held that the fact that a slogan may be perceived as a promotional statement does not mean it is not distinctive and cannot be a trade mark. The Office also stated that a slogan does not need to be imaginative or a play on words to be registrable as a trade mark.

TITLES

Although many titles may lack the necessary substance and originality to attract copyright protection, book, journal, or other titles may be registered as trade marks. However, whilst it may be difficult in the case of a single edition of a book to establish a sufficiently strong association or reputation in the market, serial publications such as directories, newspapers or magazines are more easily registered. *Hello!*, *OK!* and *Heat* are all UK-registered trade marks for publications or magazines. An application in 1986 for *Radio Times* proceeded to registration claiming use of over 60 years from 1923.

If no registration has been obtained (either because the application has failed or because none has been made) a title may still be protected by an action for 'passing off' (the closest English law has so far come to an unfair competition action). There must, however, be a real likelihood of confusion, and also actual or probable damage or loss, before a passing-off action will succeed against a rival title: for more on this see below, p. 277.

The difficulties of stopping third parties using titles if there are no registered trade marks are illustrated by the James Bond cases. The owner of the James Bond trade mark rights unsuccessfully opposed a UK trade mark application for FROM RUSSIA WITH LOVE for jewellery and watches. It did not have any relevant trade mark registrations and there was no misrepresentation necessary to succeed in passing off (see p. 277).

It also unsuccessfully opposed a Community trade mark (see p. 277) for DR NO covering software, vehicles, clothing and other goods as the authorities found it had not used DR NO as a trade mark.

These cases confirm that titles (and character names see p. 273) should generally be registered as trade marks as early as possible and that the titles and names should be used as trade marks (that is as an indication of origin) rather than descriptively.

AUTHORS' NAMES

It may be difficult to secure trade mark registration of an author's name unless there is very strong evidence that it has become accepted as distinctive in its own right. This normally only applies to serial publications or to established works which have run to several editions. Wisden or Roget would be good examples.

A nom-de-plume may also be difficult to register, but the established user may well have an action for passing off against others using the same name. Similarly a signature (of a cartoonist, for example) may be hard to register if the name is simple or common. It should not be forgotten that an author has a statutory moral right in some circumstances to prevent false attribution to him or her of work which the author did not write (see Chapter 3, p. 52). There may also in some circumstances be an action for defamation (see Chapter 7).

NAMES OF CHARACTERS

As Sir Arthur Conan Doyle found with Sherlock Holmes, there is no general right to prevent a fictional character's name being used by other authors in their own works. For example the character name NELLIE THE ELEPHANT was used in the title of a book but this was not regarded as trade mark use. The Court of Appeal refused to allow Elvis Presley Enterprises Inc., which carried on merchandising activities, to register the names Elvis, Elvis Presley and the Elvis Presley signature as trade marks, holding that members of the public bought Elvis Presley goods because they bore his name or image, not because they came from a particular source. The same points arose in respect of the UK trade mark applications for the words Diana, Princess of Wales.

The Trade Marks Registry have issued guidelines on registering famous names as trade marks: they will not automatically refuse applications for famous names but will consider whether the name is descriptive for the goods and services in question. Name of famous people or groups may be registrable for printed publications. However the Registry will not in general allow famous names to be registered for what they call 'mere image carriers', such as posters and photographs. The name of the famous person is not likely to be seen as an indication of origin but a description of the subject matter. The US rock group Linkin Park applied to register their name for a wide variety of goods, including image carriers. However, the Registry rejected the application for posters, poster books and other goods.

HOW TO REGISTER A TRADE MARK

Provided there is no significant opposition, it is possible to secure UK registration for a registered trade mark in six months to a year. It is normally advisable to seek advice from a specialist trade mark lawyer before commencing an application.

Applications should be made to the UK Intellectual Property Office, who will need the following information:

(1) details of the applicant (for example, whether an individual, partnership or company, and whether or not resident in the UK);

(2) the particular goods or services for which the applicant is seeking to register the trade mark (see below);

(3) if a particular typeface, or a logo/device is involved, a representation of the proposed mark;

(4) a statement that the applicant (or a third party with the applicant's consent) is already using the mark in relation to the specified goods or services, or intends to do so.

Classes of goods and services

The UK Trade Marks Registry is divided into classes of goods and services. There are 45 classes in all, ranging from chemicals and drugs to clothing, games and playthings and (of course), beer. Books are included in Class 16. Publications which are downloadable fall within Class 9 and publications which are non-downloadable fall within Class 41. It is possible to register a trade mark for certain online services and retail services including Internet and online shopping. One of the most important things to grasp about trade marks is that protection is given for specified goods or services. However, one application can be filed covering several (or all) of the 45 possible classes.

Advertisement and opposition

Once an application has been examined by the Trade Marks Registry, it is advertised online in the *Trade Marks Journal* in order to enable other interested parties to oppose it if they think it will conflict with an existing mark (or prior application) of theirs, or otherwise cause confusion. Opponents must oppose within two months of the date of advertisement (or within that period obtain an extension of time of one month to oppose). If the opposition cannot be settled the matter may be resolved at a hearing, at which both sides may be represented.

Assuming that there is no opposition, or that any opposition is defeated, registration will then be granted for the particular goods and services concerned. Trade mark registration lasts for 10 years initially, but may be renewed indefinitely upon payment of renewal fees. The most famous marks are renewed regularly. Unlike copyright, therefore, which expires 70 years after the end of the year of the author's death, trade mark protection may last forever – as long as your mark is used in relation to the goods and services it covers and is not challenged (for example, for becoming generic) and you remember to pay the renewal fees.

There is no legal requirement, incidentally, to use the ®, although most proprietors find it a useful warning that their mark has been registered. There is certainly no requirement on authors, or editors of dictionaries, to use the ® sign whenever the word occurs: such advertising is the responsibility of the proprietor. One often also sees the letters TM in a circle: this has no legal significance whatsoever and indicates that the person using the mark regards it as a 'trade mark' whether it is registered or not. It should be noted that it is a criminal offence to represent a mark as a registered trade mark in the UK if it is not.

PROTECTION OF TRADE MARKS

The proprietor of a trade mark is in a very strong commercial position. Once the mark is registered, the proprietor acquires what amount to virtual monopoly rights over exploitation for that particular mark applied to the particular goods or services concerned. There may, however, be provision for individual words, or other elements, of the registered mark to be disclaimed – so that while 'Peter Rabbit' may be registered as a single mark, the individual words 'Peter' and 'Rabbit' may need to be disclaimed since individually they are too common, and non-distinctive of the particular goods concerned, to be protected. The Registry cannot, however, now insist on disclaimers and they have to be offered voluntarily.

TRADE MARK INFRINGEMENT

Section 10(1) of the 1994 Trade Marks Act provides that:

> A person infringes a registered trade mark if he uses in the course of trade a sign that is identical with the trade mark in relation to goods or services which are identical with those for which it is registered.

Section 10(2) further provides that infringement may take place where the sign is identical with the trade mark and is used in relation to goods or services similar to those for which the mark is registered or the sign is similar to the trade mark and is used in relation to goods or services identical with or similar to those for which the mark is registered in relation to, but where in either case there nevertheless exists a likelihood of confusion on the part of the public, including the likelihood that the public will associate the infringing mark with the registered trade mark. If the sign merely brings the registered trade mark to mind, this is probably insufficient.

Under section 10(3), infringement can occur if the mark is used in a way that 'takes unfair advantage of' or is 'detrimental' to the mark where the trade mark has a reputation in the UK. Confusion is not necessary. For use of registered trade marks in comparative advertising, see Chapter 12.

Certain proprietors of trade marks are vigilant about any unauthorised use of their marks, and often write standard threatening letters to publishers when they spot 'their' word or other mark in, say, a book title. Care should be taken in writing such letters as in certain circumstances a person aggrieved by such a letter could bring an action in relation to the threat of proceedings being brought for registered trade mark infringement.

Infringement is unlikely to occur, however, if the use is purely descriptive

In the Scottish case of *Bravado Merchandising Services Limited* v. *Mainstream Publishing (Edinburgh) Limited*, the registered owners of the trade mark 'Wet Wet Wet' failed to prevent a publisher – Mainstream – from marketing a book entitled *A Sweet Little Mystery – Wet Wet Wet: The Inside Story* as this use of Wet Wet Wet did not infringe the trademark registration.

In another case, the judge referred to the *Wet Wet Wet* decision, stating: 'It would be fantastic if the . . . trade mark legislation had the effect of enabling quasi censorship of books about people or companies just because those people or companies had registered their names as trade marks for books.'

You may even succeed in having an existing registration revoked if you can establish that the word concerned has become a generic term in its own right (inclusion in *The Oxford English Dictionary* is useful evidence, despite the editorial disclaimers one sometimes sees in dictionaries).

Advertisers can purchase other businesses' trade marks as Internet search engine terms ('keywords') and so appear in the top-ranked 'sponsored links' in search engine results, linking Internet users to competing or even counterfeit product websites. The ECJ recently held that Google does not infringe the trade marks in question by selling the keywords to unauthorised advertisers or arranging their display as sponsored links on the basis Google is not making relevant use of those marks. Google (and other search engines) may be liable if it does not remove or disable infringing data once it has been put on notice or if it has more than a neutral role and is involved in the selection of infringing keywords or the drafting of the advertisement displayed with the sponsored link ('the ad text').

However trade mark owners will be entitled to challenge unauthorised advertisers, on a case-by-case basis, where ad text suggests that the advertiser is authorised by or otherwise connected with the trade mark owner, or is too vague for reasonably informed and attentive Internet users to determine whether there is such a connection.

Where trade mark infringement does take place, however, the normal legal remedies will apply, including:

- an injunction to restrain infringing acts;
- an award of damages, or an account of profits;
- provisions for delivery up of infringing goods, material or articles.

EU AND INTERNATIONAL TRADE MARK PROTECTION

Registration of a trade mark in the UK only gives protection within the United Kingdom. If trade mark protection in other territories – such as the USA – is required additional applications will have to be filed. For an international publishing business seeking worldwide protection, this can prove expensive; however, it is often worthwhile for distinctive international publishing marks, such as Encyclopaedia Britannica, and Grove's Dictionaries of Music, particularly as an added deterrent to piracy.

Community trade marks

It is possible to file one trade mark application to cover all the countries of the European Union including the UK via the Community Trade Mark Office in Alicante, Spain. Advertisement and opposition procedures are similar to those under UK law, and the period of protection is 10 years. The Community trade mark is an all or nothing mark and has to be available in all EU countries. If there are earlier rights in any one country, the Community application fails although it is possible to convert it into separate national applications.

The Community Trade Marks Office examines applications on absolute grounds only, that is, for example, if the application is distinctive. It does not refuse applications on the grounds of earlier conflicting rights. It is cheaper to register a trade mark as a community trade mark rather than filing national applications in each of the member countries. Infringement of a community trade mark may be pursued centrally in one national court rather than separately in each member state where infringement has occurred and it is possible to obtain an injunction covering all of the EU

International trade marks

It is possible for UK companies to file one single application at the World Intellectual Property Organisation (WIPO) under an agreement called the Madrid Protocol (to which the UK is a party) covering some or all of the over 80 countries who are signatories to the Madrid Protocol. Countries who have signed the Madrid Protocol include various European countries, the USA and Japan. Unlike the community trade mark, the Madrid Protocol system provides for a number of separate national trade marks and is a useful means of international trade mark protection as more countries sign the Madrid Protocol.

PASSING OFF

THE TORT OF 'PASSING OFF'

Even without a registered trade mark, it is still possible over a period of time to acquire goodwill in a distinctive name or title, or in the distinctive style, design or general physical appearance of goods (known as their 'get-up'). Under common law, such trading goodwill will be protected against rival traders who may seek to use it unfairly in order to enhance sales of their own (usually more recent) product. The general principle of law was stated as long ago as 1896 in the leading *Camel Hair Belting* case, as follows:

> The principle of law may be very plainly stated, that nobody has any right to represent his goods as the goods of somebody else.

Prior to that case, it might have been thought that 'Camel Hair Belting' was just about as generic a product description as it was possible to have, and that any rival trader seeking to start selling belting made out of camel hair could not legally be prevented from using the same generic description. However, 'Camel Hair Belting' had by the time of the action acquired such established goodwill, and such a distinctive reputation, in the market place that the action for passing off succeeded. Many publications, or lists, acquire a similar goodwill in their name or physical get-up – famous labels such as Puffin would be similarly protectable under the law of passing off. Such common-law protection is not ideal and many of our trading partners, in Europe and the USA, deal with the matter somewhat more logically under fully fledged unfair competition laws. If the evidence is strong enough, however, our action for passing off can be an effective way of preventing such unfair competition under both English and Scottish law.

In the *Advocaat* case, the court identified the following characteristics which must be present in order to succeed in passing off:

(1) A misrepresentation.
(2) Made by a trader in the course of trade.
(3) To prospective customers of his or ultimate consumers of goods or services supplied by him.
(4) Which is calculated to injure the business or goodwill of another (in the sense that this is a reasonably foreseeable consequence).
(5) Which causes actual damage to a business or goodwill of a trader by whom the action is brought or will probably do so.

Passing-off actions under English law, as a general rule, will not succeed unless there is a real likelihood of confusion in the market place – this can usually be established by market surveys, but these take time and are not always conclusive.

Passing-off cases include the following: the publishers of the *Daily Mail* secured an injunction against a new evening newspaper called the *London Evening Mail*. The publishers of a series of free newspapers including *Bedfordshire on Sunday*, *Milton Keynes on Sunday* and *Hertfordshire on Sunday* were granted an injunction to prevent the free newspaper *Northants on Sunday*.

The publishers of the well-established *What's New In . . .* series of magazines secured an injunction against *What's New In Training Personnel* since in that case the risks of confusion, to public and advertisers alike, were great.

On the other hand, an injunction was refused to the claimant in respect of the two magazines *BBC Gourmet Good Food* and *Gourmet* as the court found the public would not be confused. In another case, it was arguable that the public would think *Management Today* and *Security Management Today* were linked, although the injunction was refused.

The politician Alan Clark succeeded in a passing-off action against the *Evening Standard* for publishing a diary 'Alan Clark's Secret Political Diary'.

Most publishers, of course, go to considerable lengths to create and establish their own distinctive name and get-up, but there are always those who will seek to cut corners by linking their product unfairly to the goodwill established by someone else.

Any new publisher launching a weekly trade journal for booksellers and publishers in the UK under the title *The Bookseller*, particularly if it used a similar design and get-up to the established organ, would almost certainly face an action for passing off. There might equally be an action for passing off against a publisher who tried to launch a new publication called, for example, *The Electronic Bookseller*, if the get-up was confusingly similar and there was an implication – as there probably would be – that the new product was being launched by the publishers of *The Bookseller*, or under licence from them, and carried with it their considerable reputation and goodwill.

If there is a real likelihood of confusion, a passing-off action may well succeed. It is, however, a question of fact in every case.

Where there really is no credible risk of confusion in the market place, an action for passing off will fail: in the case of *Mothercare UK Limited* v. *Penguin Books Limited* a passing-off action to restrain the use of the words 'mother care' in the title of a book *Mother Care/Other Care* published by Penguin Books Limited failed. In the view of the Court of Appeal, the requirement for a successful passing-off action that there should have been a misrepresentation (see above, p. 278) had not been established and the Court 'was wholly unable to see any basis for saying that there was a misrepresentation in the title of the book. The book, taken as a whole, did not begin to suggest that the book had been issued or sponsored by, or was in any way associated with Mothercare.'

REMEDIES

Where passing off is established, the most effective remedy a claimant will usually seek is an injunction, and the usual considerations will apply (see above, p. 255). Damages, or an account of profits, will also be available in appropriate cases.

DOMAIN NAME DISPUTES

Domain names (.com, .co.uk etc.) are increasingly valuable and important. At the same time the number of domain name disputes continues to grow. This is particularly so as more domain name extensions and multi-lingual domain names are added to the Web.

There are two principal types of domain name disputes, both of which arise where the defendant registers a domain name that is identical or confusingly similar to the claimant's trade mark. The first occurs where the defendant registers the name fraudulently, and is known as 'cybersquatting' (or 'typosquatting', where likely misspellings of the mark are registered). The second kind of dispute is where the defendant registers the name innocently and uses it for a legitimate website, but in circumstances where Internet users are likely to be confused into believing that the website is the claimant's.

A third type of dispute is where a 'spoof' or 'gripe' website is set up. One case involved the website NatWestSucks.com.

Under English law, the registration and use of a domain name in the situations described above may amount to common law passing off and/or registered trade mark infringement. The following principles have emerged.

CYBERSQUATTING

The courts, starting with the High Court and the Court of Appeal in *Marks & Spencer v. One in a Million*, have shown a determination to stop cybersquatters. This has been on the basis that a cybersquatter registers a domain name as an 'instrument of fraud' and that this will inherently mislead Internet users as to the origin of the domain name or dilute the claimant's mark. It has been held that:

- The mere registration of a domain name will be unlawful where the name is identical or confusingly similar to a household mark that is exclusively distinctive of the claimant, even in the absence of attempted extortion or blackmail. The claimant will only succeed on this ground if the mark is very well known and distinctive, like the Marks & Spencer mark in the *One in a Million* case, such that consumers are inherently likely to be misled.
- The mere registration of a lesser-known mark, or of a mark which, although famous, is not exclusively distinctive of the claimant because it consists of a common or descriptive name, will be unlawful if coupled with attempted extortion or blackmail – e.g. the J Sainsbury mark in the *One in a Million* case.
- A 'pattern' of registering well-known marks as domain names will usually amount to good evidence of cybersquatting.

LEGITIMATE USE

Where the defendant is not a cybersquatter, the registration and use of the domain name will only be unlawful where traditional passing off or registered trade mark infringement principles apply. In broad terms, this requires the claimant to show that Internet users are likely to be confused into believing that the products or services offered through the defendant's website originate from or are otherwise connected with the claimant.

DOMAIN NAME DISPUTE RESOLUTION PROCEEDINGS

An alternative to bringing court proceedings is to file a complaint under the relevant domain name dispute resolution policy. ICANN (Internet Corporation for Assigned Names and Numbers) has established a Uniform Domain Name Dispute Resolution Policy (UDRP) in respect of .com, .net, .org and a limited number of country code domain names. A domain name can be either cancelled or transferred to the complainant. These proceedings are significantly cheaper and usually quicker than court proceedings. However, they generally only apply to cybersquatting or cases where 'bad faith' on the respondent's part can be shown. Damages cannot be awarded nor can costs. They also do not cover .uk country-code domain names. Nominet UK, the Registry for .uk domain names, has its own dispute resolution service which is very similar to the UDRP.

The three elements of UDRP

Complaints are decided by single- to three-member panels composed of legal practitioners from around the world. In order to succeed in the proceedings a complainant has to satisfy the following three elements.

The domain name must be identical or confusingly similar to a trade mark in which the complainant has rights

Decisions have protected registered trade names. Panels have also recognised that writers (such as Louis de Bernières, Margaret Drabble and Catherine Cookson), actors (such as Kevin Spacey and Tom Cruise), singers (e.g. Celine Dion) and sports stars (e.g. Venus and Serena Williams) can own unregistered rights in their names. (In contrast, as already seen, English courts have traditionally been somewhat reluctant to enforce personalities' rights in their names, on the basis that, in general, their reputations do not grant them rights that extend beyond their core activities.)

The respondent must have no rights or legitimate interests in respect of the domain name

Legitimate interest may be demonstrated where the respondent is making a legitimate non-commercial or fair use of the domain name, without intending misleadingly to divert Internet users or tarnish the complainant's trade mark. A respondent was able to rely on this ground in brucespringsteen.com where he was using the domain name in connection with an unofficial Bruce Springsteen website. This proviso is also relevant to 'gripe' websites for persons who have genuine grievances or wish to express criticisms. Such views on a website may, however, be subject to defamation and trade libel laws and can, in certain circumstances, be removed from the Internet if a complaint is made against the Internet service provider (ISP) hosting the site.

The domain name must have been registered and be used in bad faith

This may happen if, for example, the aim is to resell it to the complainant or to a competitor for a sum exceeding the respondent's out-of-pocket costs or registering the domain name to prevent the complainant from registering that domain name which contains its mark or to disrupt the complainant's business.

Part V
Sales and marketing

Sale of goods and consumer protection

11

SALE OF GOODS

INTRODUCTION

Publishing is all about selling – or so, at least, every marketing director would tell us. Many other topics with legal significance are involved in the publishing process, of course, as we have seen – copyright, for example – but in a very real sense the act of publishing is the act of selling. No one who has been to Frankfurt could ever be in any doubt about that. However, this chapter is not about selling rights (for this, see Chapter 5), but about selling the thing itself – the book, or the journal, or the online service. What happens in legal terms when X sells something to Y? Are any legal duties and obligations imposed on the seller, and are there any exceptions? Are there any specific duties owed to the public? What is the position of wholesalers and retailers?

Lawyers have traditionally called this area of law sale of goods, although for much of the high street or mail order selling which publishers do, consumer law is now a more helpful label. Even when the publication concerned is not 'sold' as such, but distributed free of charge (for example, a controlled-circulation newspaper paid for by advertising revenue) many of the same legal principles apply. We shall take a look at these basic principles in this chapter, and in the next chapter we will examine the special rules applying to advertising.

SALE OF GOODS AND CONSUMER RIGHTS

Although 'sale of goods' has a wonderfully Victorian ring to it, the law in this area has progressed significantly since that time. The first piece of legislation in this field was the Sale of Goods Act 1893, which was passed in an age when a man's word was his bond and merchants did not expect (or want) the law to interfere with free trade or freedom of contract. The law assumed, however, that the parties were dealing on more or less equal terms, and that in the case of contracts of sale there was a reasonably fair balance between the buyer and the seller

Before the 1893 Act, the balance had become heavily weighted in favour of the seller. The basic rule of mercantile law was *caveat emptor*: let the buyer beware. The law would not protect a buyer from a bad bargain unless there was some obvious impropriety, such as fraud or duress, and buyers were expected to satisfy themselves about the suitability or quality of goods they were buying before buying them. Once the deal was struck, that was that: they must abide by their contract, however bad. This was all very well in the days when buyers could go to market and inspect what were then relatively straightforward goods (like horses or produce) for themselves, but as the Industrial Revolution developed, two things happened:

(1) goods became more complex and their defects became less visible – so that buyers often found they had to rely on the seller's description of the goods; and
(2) goods were increasingly mass produced, so that buyers were no longer making individual contracts which they could negotiate with each seller, but forced to deal on industry-wide terms and conditions, drafted entirely from the seller's point of view.

The 1893 Act went a long way towards restoring a fair balance between buyers and sellers. In particular, it introduced into all contracts for the sale of goods certain implied terms – for example, implied conditions that the goods would be fit for their purpose and of 'merchantable quality'. Although the 1893 Act has now been entirely superseded and amended by more recent legislation, many of these implied terms still form an important part of modern UK law. We will look at all of them below, in their modern context.

In today's consumer society, therefore, the law no longer assumes that well-informed buyers go about striking arm's-length bargains with individual sellers. That may be the commercial reality in some cases (a sale of stock between two publishers, for example), but in others the buyer (of a computer, for example, or an online purchase from a US-based website) may be negotiating at a distinct disadvantage, and may need more protection. We will therefore need to consider two different kinds of sale:

(1) sales between businesses (where the contract will usually prevail, subject to some important provisos, which we will consider below); and
(2) sales to the public, or 'consumer sales' (where the 'contract' may be hard to identify, and different provisions may now apply).

Both are now highly regulated, but in different ways. The original Sale of Goods Act 1893 has itself been replaced by a more modern 1979 Act (which in turn has been amended by the Sale and Supply of Goods Act 1994 and others), and has been added to by (among others) the Misrepresentation Act 1967, the Unfair Contract Terms Act 1977, and the Consumer Protection Act 1987. Supporting it all is a highly consumer-orientated European Commission, which has been responsible in recent years for a steady flow of Directives and other measures from Brussels on topics such as product liability, data privacy and misleading advertising, all designed to protect the interests of consumers throughout the European Union.

Remedies for unsatisfied buyers, or consumers, may now therefore be found in a number of different places:

- in the terms of individual contracts;
- in civil liability for torts such as negligence or misrepresentation;
- (increasingly) in specific statutory duties, many of which are now duties of strict liability.

Let us start at the beginning, however, and consider what duties – and remedies – may exist under the contract of sale itself.

CONTRACTS OF SALE

What does the law understand by a sale? Consider some publishing examples:

- A publisher's rep visited a bookseller a couple of weeks ago, and the bookseller ordered several titles. The rep described one as being particularly suitable for a degree course taught at the local university, and the bookseller ordered 30 copies. The publisher has now supplied the books, but the bookseller has not yet paid for them.
- An online bookseller sells an electronic book (an 'e-book') to a customer (who owns the appropriate hardware) over the Internet. Before the sale the customer e-mailed the bookseller to say that the book is required to study modern history. The bookseller replied by e-mail and said that the e-book was suitable for that purpose, but in fact, the e-book is about medieval history.
- A publisher sells copies of a textbook on wholesale terms to an educational supplier. The supplier has its own standard terms and conditions.
- A UK publisher agrees to sell 20,000 copies of a new title to US co-publishers, in their imprint. The US publishers need the copies by a particular date, and make it clear that time is of the essence.
- An online e-publisher sells a novel to a customer who has paid by credit card. The novel contains a virus and is inaccessible.

In all these examples, the essence of the transaction is a contract for the sale of goods. But when is each contract complete, what are the terms and conditions of each one, and does the law imply any terms of its own? Equally importantly, if the buyer has any rights under the contract, against whom can those rights be enforced? In the case of the novel for example, is it the bookseller's fault that the e-book is defective: and does this mean that the bookseller is obliged to give a refund? Who is liable to whom, and when?

Contracts for the sale of goods

Some of these questions can be answered by first finding out whether a contract exists at all, and if so what kind. Contracts, as we saw in Chapter 4, are fundamental to the publishing business, but may also essentially be very simple things. They may be created whenever X makes a promise to Y, and Y promises something of value in return: on that basis, all the above examples would clearly be contracts. They are also contracts of *sale*, because in return for an agreed price, it is intended that the buyer will get not only physical possession of the goods, but also the legal ownership of the goods (what lawyers call the 'property' or 'title' to the goods).

They are therefore different from contracts of hire, or contracts for services only, for an important part of the bargain is that the buyer will become the new legal owner. In the words of section 2(1) of the 1979 Sale of Goods Act, they are contracts 'by which the seller transfers or agrees to transfer the property in goods to the buyer for a money consideration called the price'. They are therefore covered by the Sale of Goods Act, and this has a number of important results.

It is important to note that the Sale of Goods Act will apply equally to Internet sales. It is therefore essential to ensure that, especially where the buyer has to click through several online pages before a sale is made (e.g. payment details), both the seller and buyer are aware of the exact stage that a legal contract is made and all the terms of the contract are incorporated into the contract.

Contract terms

What are the terms of each contract? Do they have equal weight, or are some more important than others? Terms of a contract may be express, that is specifically set out and agreed by the parties at the time, or they may be implied, for example by a previous course of dealing between the parties, or by representations made by one party to the other, and on which the other party relied. Some terms may also be implied by statute: we will come to several important examples of these below.

Some terms may also be more important than others. A condition is a term which is fundamental to the bargain, which goes to the root of the whole contract. The price is often the best example, but terms relating to quantity and schedule might equally be conditions. Breach of a condition by a seller normally entitles the buyer to treat the whole contract as being revoked, reject the goods completely, and ask for his or her money back. A warranty, by contrast, is much less important. Despite the frequent appearance of the word 'warranty' in publishing contracts, in law a warranty is merely collateral to the main purpose of the contract. Breach of a warranty will – generally speaking – not entitle a buyer to rescind the contract entirely or reject the goods, but will merely provide an action for damages. This is not always the case, and illustrates the importance of looking at the meaning of a term rather than its label – a warranty that is clearly core to the purpose of the agreement may in fact be treated as a condition.

OWNERSHIP AND TITLE

In a contract for the sale of goods, perhaps the most fundamental condition is that the buyer will acquire good title to the goods – in other words, become the legal owner, unhindered by any rival claims from elsewhere. This assumes, of course, that the seller owns the goods in the first place (and has not, for example, stolen them or have them on hire purchase). The normal rule in such cases (known to lawyers as the *nemo dat* rule) is that you cannot give better title than you yourself possess (*nemo dat quod non habet*: one cannot give what one does not have). If you do not own goods, then a person buying them from you will not own them either. There are exceptions to this general rule: where, for example, the owner has consented to the sale or has impliedly authorised the sale by his conduct. Therefore, a sale by a commercial agent would normally pass good title.

A seller who remains in physical possession of goods with the buyer's consent after a sale is completed (for example to repair them, or warehouse them) might also be capable of passing good title by delivering them to a new, second buyer, as long as the new buyer received the goods in good faith and without knowledge of the first buyer's rights. So if a bookseller sells the last signed copy of a Booker prize-winning novel to buyer A, who pays the price but leaves it in the shop to be collected later and the bookseller meanwhile re-sells it and hands it over to buyer B, buyer B might well become the new owner. Buyer A would of course have an action for the return of his or her money and possibly a claim for other damages, but would not be entitled to claim ownership of the book itself.

Similarly, a publisher who in similar circumstances sold a particular consignment of stock twice over would effectively pass legal ownership to the innocent final customer to whom the stock was actually delivered. In both cases, the seller (however dishonest) was in possession with the owner's consent, and can therefore pass on good legal ownership to someone buying in good faith.

Although this has the effect of protecting innocent book-buyers, it may leave publishers at some risk if they deliver stock on sale or return to a retailer and the retailer either fails to pay, or – worse still – goes bankrupt. Many publishing distribution contracts therefore contain express terms, known as 'retention of title clauses', which clearly stipulate that, even after they are delivered to the retailer, legal ownership of the goods remains with the publisher until they are paid for (or, in some cases, all outstanding debts are paid). If a major chain of bookshops (for example) calls in the receivers, such clauses are designed to ensure that relevant unsold stock can be reclaimed from the bookshelves by the publishers concerned, and will not belong to the bookshop's creditors. Nevertheless there are often practical difficulties in claiming title to specific stocks when they have become mixed with other stocks on the buyer's premises (how do you identify those which are yours?) and it may prove difficult to rely on a retention of title clause unless it is very carefully drafted.

IMPLIED CONDITION OF GOOD TITLE

With one exception, which we deal with below, section 12(1) of the 1979 Sale of Goods Act provides that in every contract of sale there is:

> an implied term on the part of the seller that . . . he has a right to sell the goods.

This is so, whether the contract refers to the matter or not. There is a corresponding implied condition in contracts for future sales. Note that the 1979 Act implies a condition of good title into every such contract, not merely a warranty. This means that a buyer who does not get the legal title he or she bargained for may rescind the whole contract – understandably enough.

In addition to the condition of good title, section 12(2) also provides additional warranties that:

- the goods are (and will remain) free of any legal charges or 'encumbrances' which may restrict their use; and
- the buyer will enjoy 'quiet possession' of the goods.

What happens if you wish to sell the goods, but are genuinely uncertain as to whether you have the full legal right to do so? Can you sell 'such title as I may have'? Where there are difficulties in proving title, buyers may be quite willing to bear that risk as a commercial risk, particularly if you and they have dealt with each other regularly before. Section 12(3) of the 1979 Act provides for this situation, and provides specifically that the implied conditions and warranties above will not apply to such limited sales: there will in such cases only be limited warranties, for example that any charges and encumbrances which are known to the seller are disclosed to the buyer before the contract is made.

SUMMARY CHECKLIST: LEGAL OWNERSHIP IN SALES

To recap so far: to find out who owns particular goods, the questions to ask might be as follows:

- Does a contract of sale exist?
- Does the seller own the goods in the first place?
- If not, has the owner impliedly (or actually) authorised the sale?
- If not, does the seller possess the goods with the owner's consent, and does the buyer buy in good faith?
- Is there a valid retention of title clause?
- Is there any other restriction on title (for example, a sale of only 'such title as I may have')?

If we apply these criteria to our first contract of sale example (at p. 287 above), where the publisher has supplied the books, but the bookseller has not yet paid for them, it is likely that the publisher will have owned the books, and that a contract of sale exists. However, if there was a valid retention of title clause, the bookseller might not yet own the books. Even so, if (as is likely) the bookseller had physical possession of the books with the owner's consent, the bookseller might still effectively pass on legal ownership to a customer who bought one of them in good faith.

SALES BY DESCRIPTION

The seller's description of the goods may be such an important factor in the buyer's decision to buy, that it should in fairness be treated as a term of the contract.

Accordingly, under section 13(1) of the Sale of Goods Act 1979:

> Where there is a contract for the sale of goods by description, there is an implied term that the goods will correspond with the description.

Under section 13(1)(A), this term is a condition in England, Wales and Northern Ireland (a breach will entitle the buyer to reject the goods and get a full refund). Note that the implied condition applies only where the sale is by description, in other words where the description forms a significant part of the bargain, and is not merely incidental. So where a bookseller describes a text to a customer as being suitable for a certain syllabus, that might well be a sale by description. What if the jacket blurb carries a similar claim, but the bookseller, when asked, expresses no opinion on the subject? The customer's contract of sale is with the bookseller, not the publisher, so the description in the blurb would not become a term of the contract if the bookseller carefully remained distanced from it, or refused to endorse it. What if the book in question is simply selected, taken to the check-out till, and sold, without the printed description being referred to? This is a common situation in busy retail shops, particularly supermarkets. Probably, now, section 13(3) of the 1979 Act would apply, which provides that:

> a sale of goods is not prevented from being a sale by description by reason only that, being exposed for sale or hire, they are selected by the buyer.

Under such circumstances any description on the goods themselves would give rise to the implied condition under section 13(1), and if the goods did not comply with that description the buyer would be entitled to rescind the contract and reject the goods. The publisher might also be guilty of an unfair commercial practice under the Consumer Protection from Unfair Trading Regulations 2008 (see Chapter 12).

Equally, a description would also bind a publisher who sold direct to a customer by mail order or through the Internet, if it formed a significant part of the bargain. Quite apart from the Consumer Protection from Unfair Trading Regulations implications, it would also constitute an implied condition of the contract of sale itself.

In the second 'Contracts of Sale' example (see p. 287), there may have been a sale of goods not matching their description if the text attached to the online description of the e-book was inaccurate. It is more likely that the e-book was not fit for the purpose for which it was bought (i.e. the study of modern history), when that was clearly communicated to the bookseller (see Fitness for Purpose on p. 295).

Sales by description might also bind a publisher selling stock, for example to a bookseller or wholesaler. The buyer could reject the goods if they did not comply with the description, even if the buyer had suffered no loss. This would be so, even if the buyer had inspected a sample – under section 13(2) of the 1979 Act:

If the sale is by sample, as well as by description, it is not sufficient that the bulk of the goods corresponds with the sample if *the goods do not also correspond with the description* (our italics).

Finally, note that unlike the implied terms of satisfactory quality and fitness for purpose (see pp. 293 and 295), section 13 applies to private sales as well as those 'in the course of a business'. Therefore, although a publisher selling its company car (for example) to an individual probably would not be subject to the satisfactory quality and fitness for purpose provisions, it would still have to ensure the car corresponded with its description.

MISREPRESENTATION

If a description cannot be incorporated as an implied term into the contract of sale itself, a seller might still be liable under the general law of tort for any misrepresentations made to the buyer, if the buyer relied on them and suffered loss or damage as a result.

Misrepresentations may be fraudulent, negligent or innocent:

- *Fraudulent misrepresentation.* It is well-established law that sellers will be guilty of fraud (strictly speaking, the tort of deceit) if they cause loss or damage to buyers by intentionally misleading them with statements of fact knowing them to be untrue or not caring whether they are true or false. Not surprisingly, most of the cases involve used cars. In most cases, where fraud can be proved, the buyer may rescind the contract (so as to be restored to his or her original position), or alternatively claim damages.
- *Negligent misrepresentation.* Even in the absence of actual fraud, the Misrepresentation Act 1967, section 2(1), provides that a buyer will still be entitled to damages, or to rescind the contract, if a misrepresentation was made negligently. Negligence, however, implies a duty of care, and may be difficult to prove: on negligence generally, see p. 193.
- *Innocent misrepresentation.* In the absence of either fraud or negligence, where the misrepresentation was entirely innocent, the buyer's only remedy would normally be to rescind the contract. However, if this was no longer possible – for example, because the goods had been destroyed – a court may award damages in lieu, under section 2(2) of the 1967 Act.

SUMMARY CHECKLIST: DESCRIPTIONS, AND MISREPRESENTATION

- Is there a sale by description?
- Do the goods correspond with that description?
- Has there been any misrepresentation?

In our first contract of sale example (p. 287) the sales rep described one book as particularly suitable for a local degree course, and the bookseller ordered on that basis: the sale would probably therefore be a sale by description, and if the books did not correspond with the description the bookseller could rescind the contract (for breach of an implied condition) and return the books.

MERCHANTABILITY AND SATISFACTORY QUALITY

Under section 14 of the 1979 Sale of Goods Act (as amended) all sellers of goods who sell in the course of their business are bound by an implied condition that those goods should be of 'satisfactory quality' (formerly 'merchantable quality'). Prior to 1994, when the wording changed, there was considerable argument in the courts over what was or was not 'merchantable' (because the implied term was a condition entitling the buyer to reject the goods). The factors which might be taken into account clearly included fundamental defects in quality, such as exploding 'Coalite' (in one case) and a plastic catapult which broke and blinded a boy in one eye (in another case), but minor and less obvious defects were less clear, particularly if they were aesthetic rather than purely functional. Although the definition of 'merchantable quality' provided an objective standard of sorts, following the introduction of the Sale and Supply of Goods Act 1994 the test now is one of 'satisfactory quality', with clearer guidance as to the factors which may be taken into account.

Implied terms of satisfactory quality

Section 14(2) of the 1979 Act, as amended by the 1994 Act, now provides as follows:

(2)   Where the seller sells goods in the course of a business, there is an implied term that the goods supplied under the contract are of satisfactory quality.

(2A) . . . goods are of satisfactory quality if they meet the standard that a reasonable person would regard as satisfactory, taking account of any description of the goods, the price (if relevant) and all the other relevant circumstances.

Note that, for the 1979 Act (as amended) to apply, the seller must be selling 'in the course of a business'. The implied term will not apply to purely private sales. For most publishers, booksellers and distributors most of their sales transactions will clearly be in the course of a business. This applies equally to sales of stock between publishers, consumer sales in bookshops, or mail order sales. However, it is not necessarily enough to establish that the seller is a business – the sale itself must be 'in the course of' that business. It may be necessary to examine the transaction more carefully in borderline cases, for example when a publisher sells off a company car or a bookseller disposes of a computer. Arguably, neither of those transactions would be in the course of the seller's particular business (although they would be still subject to section 13 – sale by description). In the case of the car, this might particularly be so if it were a private car only occasionally used on company business. It will be necessary to look at all the relevant factors – particularly, perhaps, whether the sale appears in the accounts (and tax return) of the business concerned.

'Satisfactory quality'

Under the 1994 Act, quality factors which may specifically be taken into account (among others) include the following:

- fitness for all the purposes for which goods of the kind in question are commonly supplied;
- appearance and finish;
- freedom from minor defects;
- safety; and
- durability.

Any one or more of these factors may be relevant in deciding whether a reasonable person would regard the goods as satisfactory. Clearly, the first category is potentially the broadest, covering all the purposes 'for which goods of the kind in question are commonly supplied' – note, however, that the relevant purpose must be one for which such goods are commonly supplied, not some special or esoteric purpose not normally associated with the goods in question (for fitness for a special purpose, see below, p. 295). A scientific or technical textbook with vital instructions missing so that it could not be used in teaching, or a cookery book without key ingredients or with the wrong quantities and therefore useless for cooking, would probably not be fit for all the purposes for which such books are commonly supplied, and since this would breach the implied condition that the goods would be of satisfactory quality the buyer would be entitled to rescind the contract, return the goods and ask for his or her money back.

'Appearance and finish' and 'freedom from minor defects' now appear for the first time, confirming the result of a 1988 case where a string of minor defects in an expensive Range Rover were held to make it unmerchantable (although it was still basically roadworthy). The buyer of a Rolls-Royce or a Range Rover is entitled to have higher expectations than the buyer of, say, a second-hand car whose only concern might be to get (relatively) safely from A to B. This flexible definition of what is or is not satisfactory quality must apply equally to publications. A buyer of an expensive multi-volume encyclopaedia might well be entitled to claim that it was not of satisfactory quality under the Act if the gold blocking on the spines came off after two weeks, whereas the buyer of a cheap paperback classic might be glad if the jacket stayed on at all.

'Safety' and 'durability' may be of vital concern to consumers, and so were expressly included in the 1979 Act by the 1994 Act. 'Durability' probably only implies durability for a reasonable time and depends on what is a reasonable duration time for those particular goods (in a 1987 case involving merchantable quality, a second-hand Jaguar which was purchased from a motor dealer that seized up three weeks after purchase was not fit for its purpose). 'Safety' here probably only implies safety for reasonable or normal use – in one case involving pork chops which contained a harmful parasite, the buyer failed to prove that the chops did not reach the (then) standard of merchantable quality since the chops were only partially cooked, and normal cooking would have killed the parasite and made them perfectly safe to eat. Safety is clearly relevant for cars or electrical goods such as computer equipment – an e-book containing a virus might not now be considered sufficiently safe to be of 'satisfactory quality'. Sellers also have statutory duties relating to safety under the Consumer Protection Act 1987 (see below, p. 303).

Exceptions

The implied term of satisfactory quality will not apply in the following circumstances:

- where the defect is specifically drawn to the buyer's attention before the contract is made;
- where the buyer examines the goods before the contract is made (and that examination ought to have revealed the defect); and
- where the sale was by sample, and the defect would have been apparent on a reasonable examination of the sample.

Note that the vital revelation, or inspection, must have taken place before the contract was made. In the case of sales by sample, section 15 of the 1979 Act provides similar implied terms that the bulk will correspond in quality to the sample, and will be of satisfactory quality except for defects apparent on examination.

SUMMARY CHECKLIST: SATISFACTORY QUALITY

- Is the sale in the course of the seller's business?
- Would a reasonable person regard the goods as satisfactory?
- Are they fit for all the purposes for which goods of that kind are commonly supplied?
- Is their appearance and finish satisfactory?
- Are they free from minor defects?
- Are they reasonably safe and durable?
- Was the defect brought to the buyer's attention before the contract was made?
- Did the buyer examine the goods before the contract was made? Ought that to have revealed the defect?
- Was the sale by sample, and would the defect have been reasonably apparent?

FITNESS FOR PURPOSE

In addition to the implied term that goods will be of satisfactory quality, there is a further implied condition imposed on the seller that goods will be reasonably fit for any particular purpose made known by the buyer. This implied condition is contained in section 14(3) of the 1979 Act, which provides as follows:

> Where the seller sells goods in the course of a business and the buyer, expressly or by implication, makes known . . . to the seller . . . any particular purpose for which the goods are being bought, there is an implied condition that the goods supplied under the contract are reasonably fit for that purpose.

This will apply to any purpose (even if unusual), provided that the buyer has made that particular purpose known to the seller. The House of Lords (Scotland) in *Slater* v. *Finning* (1996) has clarified this by stating that there will be no breach of the implied condition of fitness where the failure of the goods to meet the intended purpose arose from an abnormal feature or idiosyncrasy, not made known to the seller, in the buyer or in the circumstances of use by the buyer. It is not relevant whether or not the buyer is aware of that feature. For example, if a publisher contractually agrees to provide textbooks suitable for 15-year-olds, it is unlikely that there would be a breach of section 14 if a 15-year-old recipient had learning difficulties, and actually needed simpler material.

The purpose may be made known expressly, or by implication, but it must be clearly made known, so that the seller is in no doubt that that is the purpose for which the buyer requires the goods, and for which he or she is paying the price. Where the circumstances of the sale indicate otherwise, the implied condition of fitness for that purpose will not apply. For example, where the buyer would have made the purchase anyway, and was clearly not relying on the seller's professional advice – or where it would have been unreasonable to do so – any statement by the seller about fitness for purpose will probably be regarded as merely ancillary, and will not form part of the contract. So where a student goes into a campus bookstore with a reading list, and selects a textbook on the list and buys it at the till, the purchase is clearly being made in reliance on the reading list, not on any extra encouraging remarks which the bookseller may add. In those circumstances if the book turns out to be unsuitable, the student's remedy – if he or she has one at all – would be against the lecturer who drew up the reading list, not the bookseller who sold the book, or the publisher who published it.

Suppose, however, that the student is clearly in some doubt, expressly asks the bookseller's advice as to whether the text is suitable for a specific course, and is advised that it is? In those circumstances, where the student clearly relies on the bookseller's skill and judgment, the bookseller will almost certainly be bound by an implied condition that the book is fit for that purpose.

An interesting question is whether a supply of software might be considered to be a supply of goods for these purposes, so that the same implied condition of fitness for purpose would apply. The Court of Appeal (1996) has decided that it may do. In that case a bespoke software package ordered by St Albans City Council to calculate the basis of the community charge in its area, and which miscalculated the population in a way which led to revenue and funding losses of £1.3 million (not all of which were awarded as damages by the Court of Appeal), was held not to be reasonably fit for the purpose for which it had been ordered, and was thus in breach of contract. The Court drew a distinction between a computer disk (which is 'goods') and a computer program (the code), which is not 'goods'. The Court decided that if a disk is sold containing a defective computer program, so that the program will not instruct or enable the computer to carry out the intended purpose, the seller will be in breach of the terms as to quality and fitness implied by section 14.

On the facts of the case, an employee of the seller went directly to the offices of St Albans City Council and loaded the defective code straight on to their computers from his disk. Will the statutory implied terms still apply? The Court said that they do not (because the program is not 'goods') but decided in favour of the buyer by implying a common law duty in the contract (because of the particular factual scenario) that the program was reasonably capable of achieving its purpose (see above, p. 348). Whenever a software package is required that is not 'bought off the shelf' (e.g. a specially tailored program for calculating royalties) it is important to include express provisions in the agreement between the parties covering the standard of work required (in case the statutory terms are not implied).

Since the council was forced to deal on the computer company's standard terms and conditions, there was also an Unfair Contract Terms Act issue – see below, p. 298.

Publishers supplying goods or software direct would equally be bound in such circumstances, for example where a purchaser ordered a textbook, or a set of multiple-choice exam questions by mail order, making it clear to the publisher that it was required for a specified course. If the wrong book or set of questions is supplied, even though it may in all other respects be of 'satisfactory quality', there will be a breach of the implied condition of fitness for purpose and the buyer will be entitled to reject the goods. Equally, a publisher selling stock to a retailer or wholesaler, knowing that it is required for further distribution or re-sale, would probably be bound by a similar condition if the goods for some reason turn out to be impossible to re-sell.

The only way for the seller to avoid such liability would be to establish:

(1) that no particular purpose was specified or implied (and was not already obvious, such as the 'purpose' of an umbrella or a hot water bottle);
(2) that no opinion was expressed as to the fitness for that purpose of the goods in question; or
(3) that any unfitness which did appear stemmed from some other special circumstances unique to the buyer and not disclosed to the seller (or otherwise obvious) at the time – for example (as in one case) a perfectly good Harris Tweed coat which caused dermatitis to a lady buyer who did not disclose that she had abnormally sensitive skin.

SUMMARY CHECKLIST: FITNESS FOR PURPOSE

- Is the sale in the course of the seller's business?
- Has the buyer clearly made known a particular purpose?

- Was the buyer relying on the seller's professional advice or opinion?
- Did the unfitness stem from any other special circumstances, not disclosed at the time?

EXCLUSION AND LIMITATION CLAUSES

Is it possible to avoid or limit liability under such implied terms (of satisfactory quality etc.), for example by putting a clause in the contract in small print somewhere which specifically excludes or limits it? In most cases now, the answer is no – particularly where the exclusion clause attempts to avoid liability to consumers. However, some may still be permitted if they pass a test of 'reasonableness'. For disclaimers of liability for negligent mis-statements, see Chapter 7, p. 195.

Exclusion clauses (sometimes called exemption clauses) were once widely used (and abused) in standard form contracts, and some of the more notorious examples would attempt total, blanket avoidance of any liability to consumers for any loss, damage or injury, and even for death. In many cases judges have refused to enforce such clauses if they were not properly brought to the notice of the consumer at the time of the contract (as in the infamous phrase 'for conditions see timetable'), or were unduly onerous or exorbitant (such as a £3,783.50 time penalty charged by a photographic library for a two-week delay in returning transparencies). In addition, because exclusion clauses were so destructive of the consumer's rights, they have generally been interpreted narrowly by the courts against the party trying to enforce them – so that a clause excluding liability for a breach of warranty, for example, would not avoid liability for any breach of a condition. This is known in English law as the 'contra proferentem' rule, but even with this ammunition, courts have not always been able to prevent sellers from using exclusion clauses to avoid their proper obligations.

The Unfair Contract Terms Act 1977 was therefore passed to regulate the scope of exclusion clauses and other unfair terms by statute. The Act only applies to 'business liability' (generally in relation to acts done in the course of a business). Purely private transactions are outside the scope of the Act (with the exception of section 6, in relation to clauses that seek to exclude or restrict the statutory implied terms under the Sale of Goods Act 1979, which applies to all contracts). Also, importantly, under section 26, the Act does not apply to international supply contracts. This means exclusion or limitation clauses in a contract for the sale of goods made between parties whose 'habitual residences' are in different states will not be subject to the Act. Therefore, exclusion clauses in a publisher's contract for sale of 50,000 educational books to a US supplier would not be subject to the Act, but theoretically may be caught by equivalent US law.

Some liabilities – for example, for death or personal injury – may now never be excluded and others may only be excluded in certain circumstances. These largely depend on whether the purchaser is buying as a consumer, or negotiating freely in the course of a business (such as a publisher buying stock from another publisher). The following rules may apply.

Liabilities which may never be excluded

Any clause attempting to exclude liability for the following will be void and unenforceable:

- death or personal injury resulting from negligence;
- breach of the implied condition of good title (see p. 289).

Where the purchaser buys as a consumer

Stricter liability applies in the most common consumer situations where the seller is dealing in the course of a business but the buyer is not. A consumer is someone who does not make the contract in the course of a business and does not hold himself out as doing so. Under section 3 of the 1977 Act, any clause in a contract attempting to permit performance 'substantially different from that which was reasonably expected', or no performance at all (such as a *'force majeure'* clause) will only be allowed if it satisfies a requirement of 'reasonableness'. What is or is not 'reasonable' depends on all the circumstances, including customs of the trade, the intention and knowledge of the parties and the relative strengths (or weaknesses) of their bargaining positions.

Section 3 also applies where the buyer (even though a business buyer) is obliged to deal on the seller's standard terms of business. Those companies whose negotiating strength means that buyers in effect have no choice but to deal on their standard terms should therefore bear in mind that those terms and conditions will now be open to legal challenge unless they are reasonable. This might apply to publishers, printers, or any other commercial suppliers, including computer corporations: in the 1996 case discussed above (p. 296), where bespoke software for a local council was held not to be fit for its intended purpose, the Court of Appeal upheld the original decision that an exclusion clause limiting liability to £100,000 (losses were £1.3 million) was unreasonable under the circumstances. The local council was under severe time pressure, had a limited choice of suppliers (all of whom dealt on similar terms), and at the time the computer company concerned had product liability insurance of £50 million.

Under section 2, liability for any loss or damage (except death or personal injury) may be excluded, but again only if reasonable.

Equally importantly, under section 6, the main implied conditions under the Sale of Goods Acts – that the goods will correspond with any description, will be of satisfactory quality and fit for their purpose, and correspond with any sample – can never be excluded where the buyer deals as a consumer.

Where the purchaser buys in the course of business

This covers the case of businesses contracting at arm's-length, as in co-publishing deals, or contracts with printers, agents or distributors. Here, where the bargaining positions are deemed to be somewhat better balanced (and insurance cover is more likely on both sides), more liabilities may be excluded. Liability for loss or damage (other than death or personal injury) may be excluded, but only if reasonable, and all the Sale of Goods Act implied conditions listed above (except the implied condition of good title) may be excluded, but again only if the relevant clause satisfies the test of reasonableness.

Finally, the Unfair Contract Terms Act 1977 does not apply to contracts relating to the creation, transfer or termination of a right or interest in any intellectual property (including copyright). It would therefore not apply to most author–publisher agreements.

The Unfair Terms in Consumer Contracts Regulations 1994, which implemented the EC Directive on unfair terms in consumer contracts, have been repealed and replaced by the Unfair Terms in Consumer Contracts Regulations 1999 (as amended by the Unfair Terms in Consumer Contracts (Amendment) Regulations 2001). The 1999 Regulations are not confined to exclusion clauses, and may apply to the majority of terms in particular contracts. They will also apply to contracts for the supply of services as well as goods.

The 1999 Regulations apply to 'consumers' who deal with 'sellers or suppliers'. A 'consumer' is a natural person who is acting for purposes outside his trade, business or profession. Only transactions by sellers or suppliers acting in the course of their business come within the Regulations.

The Regulations regulate the clarity of language in contracts and the fairness of terms. By Regulation 7, written terms of contracts must be 'expressed in plain, intelligible language'. Where there is any doubt as to the meaning of a written term, the interpretation most favourable to the consumer will prevail.

The 'fairness' provisions are the most significant because any unfair terms in contracts between suppliers and consumers are not binding on consumers. Two types of terms are excluded from the fairness test under Regulation 6(2): 'the definition of the main subject matter of the contract' and 'the adequacy of the price or remuneration, as against the goods or services supplied in exchange'.

For the other qualifying terms, a term will be unfair if it:

- is contrary to good faith;
- causes a significant imbalance in the parties' rights and obligations under the contract;
- is to the detriment of the consumer.

All three requirements must be satisfied before a term is unfair. In considering the test, all the circumstances must be taken into account (e.g. other terms, nature of the goods or services involved).

Although the Regulations can be used by consumers to make claims in relation to individual contracts, consumers can also make complaints to the Director General of Fair Trading, who can seek injunctions to prevent the use of a term in a contract.

Additionally, the Regulations give a number of public bodies certain powers (e.g. to investigate and bring proceedings under the Regulations). That number includes the Information Commissioner, the Rail Regulator and the Financial Services Authority. The Regulations also give power to named private consumer organisations to apply for injunctions. At present, the only private consumer organisation given this power is Which? (the Consumers Association). We deal below with the wider use of injunctions for the protection of consumers' interests.

CONSUMER PROTECTION

NEGLIGENCE AND DUTIES OF CARE

So far, we have considered the remedies which a buyer of goods might have against a seller under a contract of sale. Some will be provided by the terms of the contract itself, and others under implied terms included by the Sale of Goods Acts, such as the implied terms of fitness for purpose or satisfactory quality. However, all these remedies depend on the contract of sale between the buyer and the seller. They will not protect anyone who is not a party to that contract. What happens if the defective goods cause loss or damage not to the buyer but to someone else – to the buyer's family or friends, colleagues at work, or even next-door neighbours? If the seller is not liable under the contract itself, does the manufacturer owe any general duty of care to such people, or to the public at large?

We have seen that, as well as contractual remedies, there may also be remedies in tort, for example for negligent mis-statement (above, p. 193) or for fraudulent or negligent misrepresentation (above, p. 292), where a duty of care can be shown to exist. Duties of care already exist between skilled or professional people such as lawyers and their clients, or between doctor and patient, and breach of such duties could well amount to negligence, but they were not generally regarded as existing between manufacturers and the general public. Not, that is, until 1932 and what is possibly the most famous case in English (and Scottish) law: *Donoghue v. Stevenson.*

A shop assistant, Miss Donoghue, went with a friend of hers to a cafe in Paisley. The friend (not Miss Donoghue, notice) ordered ice cream for both of them, and ginger beer in a brown bottle. They had the ice cream, and drank half of the ginger beer, but hidden at the bottom of the ginger beer bottle were the decomposing remains of a snail. These remains came floating out with the latter half of the ginger beer at an inappropriate moment and – quite understandably – caused Miss Donoghue severe shock and gastroenteritis.

Miss Donoghue had no action for damages against the cafe proprietor under the contract of sale, because the contract of sale was with her friend, not with her. The House of Lords held that, even so, the manufacturer owed a general duty of care to her as the ultimate consumer of the goods. In the immortal words of Lord Atkin:

> The rule that you are to love your neighbour becomes in law – you must not injure your neighbour; and the lawyer's question, Who is my neighbour? receives a restricted reply. You must take reasonable care to avoid acts or omissions which you can reasonably foresee would be likely to injure your neighbour. Who, then,

in law is my neighbour? The answer seems to be – persons who are so closely and directly affected by my act that I ought reasonably to have them in contemplation as being so affected when I am directing my mind to the acts or omissions which are called in question.

This duty of care is particularly strong when the goods are sold direct to the public in pre-sealed form such as canned or bottled goods – or perhaps today shrink-wrapped books or CDs – which cannot realistically be checked once they have left the manufacturer's warehouse. As Lord Atkin put it:

> A manufacturer of products, which he sells in such a form as to show that he intends them to reach the ultimate consumer in the form in which they left him with no reasonable possibility of intermediate examination, and with the knowledge that the absence of reasonable care in the putting up of the products will result in an injury to the consumer's life or property, owes a duty to the consumer to take that reasonable care. It is a proposition which I venture to say no-one in Scotland or England who is not a lawyer would for one moment doubt.

In cases since 1932, this duty has been extended to friends, family, guests, borrowers, employees and even bystanders. However, it is up to the person injured to prove that such a duty of care exists, and that – where it does – the manufacturer is negligent in failing to comply with it. In cases involving self-evident defects such as snails in ginger beer bottles, this may be relatively easy particularly now, but in other circumstances negligence on the part of the manufacturer may be harder to prove. It may require evidence of a failure in the production process, a design flaw, or defective instructions for use (where instructions are appropriate) and in many cases such evidence will be hard to obtain.

There may also be some difficulty in establishing negligence where the loss or injury is caused not by manufactured goods but by a statement of advice or assurance, even where the recipient has acted in reliance on that advice and suffered loss as a result: the difficulty will lie in proving that a duty of care already existed, or was assumed. Where a responsibility already exists, for example between professionals and their own clients, this will be fairly clear, and responsibility has been deemed to be assumed in some recent cases, for example involving negligent house surveys. But a business reference (such as a banker's or employer's reference) given to a third party, particularly with a disclaimer, might well not create a sufficient duty of care: there might perhaps be a general duty in such circumstances not to be dishonest or not to make statements which are known to be untrue, but otherwise it may be difficult to establish negligence based on a duty of care if the advice or opinion given turns out to be wrong. (On negligent mis-statement generally, see Chapter 7, p. 193.)

For these reasons, some duties of care are now imposed on manufacturers directly by statute. There is also scope for certain enforcement bodies to obtain injunctions against traders who fail to carry out a service with reasonable care and skill (for further comment on this, see p. 304).

LIABILITY FOR DEFECTIVE GOODS

In one particular respect – that of product safety – the liability of producers and manufacturers for their products has increased dramatically in the UK and throughout Europe since the mid-1980s. Following the EC Directive on Product Liability of 1985, the UK passed the Consumer Protection Act 1987, which now imposes on producers and others considerably stricter liability for damage or injury caused by defective goods, without any need for the consumer to establish liability under a contract of sale, or to prove negligence or any other fault. Such strict liability is, of course, chiefly designed to cover those consumer goods with the greatest inherent dangers, such as cars, electrical goods, and – because of the risks to children – toys, but could equally well apply to software containing a virus, or even defective ink or paper if they were proved to have some harmful chemical side-effect.

Those liable under the Act include:

- producers of products (or extractors or refiners of natural products such as natural gas or oil);
- those who import products into the European Union; or
- those who sell goods under their own brand name (such as supermarkets).

Suppliers may also be liable as well as producers where they have supplied the defective goods to the producer (perhaps in the form of defective components) or to the final consumer (such as a retailer, if the producer is not readily identifiable).

What is 'defective'? A product is defective under section 3(1) of the 1987 Act:

if the safety of the product is not such as persons generally are entitled to expect.

'Safety' includes not only the physical safety of the consumer, but also covers any damage to property, although not loss of or damage to the defective product itself – if software causes damage to your data (for example corrupts your hard drive), you may claim for the loss of your computer, but not for the cost of the software itself.

Under section 5 of the 1987 Act, 'damage' means death or personal injury or loss of or damage to any property (including land). However, there is no liability imposed in the case of loss or damage to property that is not ordinarily intended for private use and occupation. Note also that no damages will be awarded if the value of loss or damage (to property) would not exceed £275. Section 4 provides a number of defences. The strict liability under the Act may be avoided if:

- the defect was caused by compliance with any statutory or EU requirement;
- the defendant was not the actual supplier;
- the defective product was supplied privately and not for profit (for example, at a private dinner);
- the defect was not present when the product was supplied; or
- the state of scientific and technical knowledge at the time would not have enabled the producer to discover the defect.

In addition to these defences a producer of a defective product may also plead 'contributory negligence' on the part of the consumer – in other words, that the consumer's own negligence in using the product was at least partly to blame for the damage caused or injury suffered, and the damages awarded may be reduced accordingly.

SUPPLYING UNSAFE CONSUMER GOODS

As well as imposing strict liability for defective products on producers, the Consumer Protection Act 1987 (in Part II of the Act as amended by the General Product Safety Regulations 2005 which came into force on 1 October 2005 and please see below) also imposes criminal liability on suppliers of consumer goods which are not safe. It is an offence, punishable by fine or imprisonment, to supply, offer or agree to supply, or expose or possess for supply, any consumer goods which are not reasonably safe (having regard to all the circumstances). 'Reasonably safe' means that there must either be no risk of death or personal injury, or at most a risk 'reduced to a minimum'. The Secretary of State may make safety regulations and issue notices covering specific goods from time to time. It is extremely unlikely that these would affect publications such as books and periodicals, which in themselves are unlikely to be unsafe, although they might become unsafe if, for example, they were sold to children with accompanying toys, games or other free gifts. It is also quite conceivable that an educational software product might contain unsafe items, particularly if aimed at young children.

Innocent retailers have a defence where they were unaware that particular goods were unsafe, or can establish that they took reasonable precautions and acted with due diligence (for example, by conducting random safety checks).

The European Commission is in the process of reviewing the EU General Product Safety Directive 2001/95/EC. It seems likely that a proposal will be published in the second half of 2011.

THE USE OF INJUNCTIONS FOR THE PROTECTION OF CONSUMERS' INTERESTS

Over more recent years, developments in consumer law have added to the weaponry available to the Office of Fair Trading (OFT) and other enforcement agencies. For example, under the Enterprise Act 2002, the OFT, trading standards authorities, 'sectoral' regulators and other 'designated enforcement bodies' (which we will refer to collectively as 'Enforcers') can apply to the court for orders to stop traders that they consider to be infringing the consumer protection legislation and where such infringements harm the 'collective interests of consumers'. The orders are known as 'Stop Now Orders'.

In addition to being available in the case of an infringement of the consumer protection legislation, Enforcers can also obtain Stop Now Orders against traders who fail to run their businesses (in relation to consumers) with reasonable care and skill.

The 2002 Act provides for three types of Enforcers:

- General Enforcers: essentially, the OFT and trading standards officers;
- Designated Enforcers: public or private bodies which are empowered by the Secretary of State by way of Statutory Instrument. The following bodies have been designated:
  - The Civil Aviation Authority
  - The Director General of Electricity supply for Northern Ireland
  - The Director General of Gas for Northern Ireland
  - OFCOM
  - The Director General of Water Services Regulation Authority
  - The Gas and Electricity Markets Authority
  - The Information Commissioner
  - The Office of Rail Regulation
  - The Financial Services Authority
  - (Which?) (The Consumers' Association);

- Community Enforcers: entities from other European Economic Area (EEA) States that are published in the EU *Official Journal*.

A breach of a Stop Now Order would be a contempt of court and punishable by fine and/or imprisonment.

SUMMARY CHECKLIST: CONSUMER PROTECTION

- Does a duty of care exist?
- If so, does breach of that duty amount to negligence?
- Might the goods be defective goods?
- Is their safety such as the public is entitled to expect?
- Have unsafe consumer goods been supplied?
- Do any of the available defences apply?

Advertising

12

INTRODUCTION

There is a school of thought that if you invent a better mousetrap, the world will beat a path to your door. This may be true of mousetraps, and (perhaps) some essential professional texts, but as a general rule most publishers find it pays to advertise. As a result, as anyone who picks up a copy of *The Bookseller* will know, advertising is as prominent a feature of the publishing world as it is of any other major industry – perhaps more so – and can range from the modestly factual to the glossiest forms of hype. It is not, however, without its legal risks. We considered some of the general risks, which accompany all published text, such as defamation and malicious falsehood, in Chapter 7. In this chapter we will take a look at the laws which particularly apply to advertising and promotional techniques, and which govern what you say in advertisements, and how you say it.

All advertisers sooner or later face the same universal temptation: to overstate the value of the thing being sold. You know the sort of thing: brilliant author, uniquely authoritative (or hysterically funny/thrilling/raunchy) work, miraculously good value at this never-to-be-repeated pre-publication offer. In a world increasingly dominated by the media, consumers are probably immune to much of this, and most of it is harmless enough. If it is no more than generalised hype, the law treats it, rather crushingly, as a 'mere puff', and gives it no particular legal significance. But beware: look again at the above blurbs. Are you simply throwing in the adjective 'authoritative' (for example) as a mere puff or are you actually stating – or implying – that your author or publication has specific authority (such as that of an examining board or Royal College)? Similarly, are you merely describing your product as being 'good value', or are you making a specific pre-publication offer? The difference could be highly significant. Where statements are made which mislead the consumer into buying something which he or she would not otherwise have bought, publishers may find themselves breaking the law. The criminal law is often involved in this area of publishing, with fines and even imprisonment for those who infringe. It is therefore very much in publishers' interests to take care how they describe their publications.

UNFAIR COMMERCIAL PRACTICES

As we trailed in the third edition, member states were required to apply the Unfair Commercial Practices Directive 2005/99 at national level by 12 December 2007. Perhaps not surprisingly, given the range of the existing legislation affected, the UK failed to achieve this. However, the directive was implemented in the UK on 26 May 2008 by the Consumer Protection from Unfair Trading Regulations 2008.

The aim of the directive is to harmonise member states' unfair trading laws – it introduces a general prohibition on traders treating consumers unfairly.

The 2008 Regulations cut a swath through the existing legislation with some statutes being repealed or revoked in whole and others in part. Some of the repeals and revocations likely to be of relevance to the reader of this work are: key provisions of the Trade Descriptions Act 1968 and the Consumer Protection Act 1987 and the whole of the Control of Misleading Advertising Regulations 1988 (as amended). One notable victim of this cull was the Fraudulent Mediums Act 1951 (and we assume that only the genuine ones would have seen that coming).

With the introduction of the 2008 Regulations there is a new language applied to this aspect of trading law, with, in effect, a 'commercial practice' replacing a 'trade description'. A commercial practice is defined as:

> any act, omission, course of conduct, representation or commercial communication (including advertising and marketing) by a trader, which is directly connected with the promotion, sale or supply of a product to or from consumers whether occurring during or after a commercial transaction (if any) in relation to a product.

A commercial practice is unfair if:

(a) it contravenes the requirements of professional diligence; and
(b) it materially distorts or is likely to materially distort the economic behaviour of the average consumer with regard to the product.

This new term 'professional diligence' means the standard of special skill and care which a trader may reasonably be expected to exercise towards consumers which is commensurate with either:

(a) honest market practice in the trader's field of activity; or
(b) the general principle of good faith in the trader's field of activity.

'Materially distorts the economic behaviour' means, in relation to an average consumer, appreciably to impair the average consumer's ability to make an informed decision thereby causing him to take a transactional decision that he would not have taken otherwise.

A commercial practice will be unfair if:

(a) it is a misleading action;
(b) it is a misleading omission;
(c) it is aggressive; or
(d) it is on a blacklist contained in Schedule 1 of the Regulations.

A MISLEADING ACTION

A commercial practice is a misleading action if it contains false information and is therefore untruthful e.g. in relation to the main characteristics of the product – such as the availability of the product, benefits of the product or composition of the product, or if its overall presentation in any way deceives or is likely to deceive the average consumer and it causes or is likely to cause the average consumer to purchase it.

A MISLEADING OMISSION

A commercial practice is a misleading omission if, for example, it omits material information or provides material information in a manner which is unclear, unintelligible, ambiguous or untimely, and as a result it causes or is likely to cause the average consumer to purchase it.

AGGRESSIVE COMMERCIAL PRACTICE

A commercial practice is aggressive if it significantly impairs or is likely to significantly impair the average consumer's freedom of choice in relation to the product concerned through the use of harassment, coercion or undue influence; and it thereby causes or is likely to cause him to purchase it.

Coercion, in this context, includes using physical force. Undue influence means the exploitation of a position of power over the consumer.

COMMERCIAL PRACTICES WHICH ARE IN ALL CIRCUMSTANCES CONSIDERED UNFAIR: SCHEDULE 1 OF THE REGULATIONS

Schedule 1 of the Regulations contains a list of 31 practices which are, in all circumstances, considered unfair. The list includes:

1. Claiming that a trader (including his commercial practices) or a product has been approved, endorsed or authorised by a public or private body when the trader, the commercial practices or the product have not, or making such a claim without complying with the terms of the approval, endorsement or authorisation.
   An example of this would be a plumber who claims to be a 'Corgi' approved gas fitter when he is not so approved.
2. Making an invitation to purchase products at a specified price without disclosing the existence of any reasonable grounds the trader may have for believing

that he will not be able to offer for supply, or to procure another trader to supply, those products or equivalent products at that price for a period that is, and in quantities that are, reasonable having regard to the product, the scale of advertising of the product and the price offered (bait advertising).

This is the practice of advertising a product at a low price but where the business has such a small stock of the product that there is no prospect of meeting the demand.

3. Making an invitation to purchase products at a specified price and then:

    (a) refusing to show the advertised item to consumers;
    (b) refusing to take orders for it or deliver it within a reasonable time; or
    (c) demonstrating a defective sample of it, with the intention of promoting a different product (bait and switch).

4. Falsely stating that a product will only be available for a very limited time, or that it will only be available on particular terms for a very limited time, in order to elicit an immediate decision and deprive consumers of sufficient opportunity or time to make an informed choice.

5. Using editorial content in the media to promote a product where a trader has paid for the promotion without making that clear in the content or by images or sounds clearly identifiable by the consumer (advertorial).

    Publishers need to ensure that there is no confusion between adverts and editorial content and that advertorials are clearly identified as adverts.

6. Promoting a product similar to a product made by a particular manufacturer in such a manner as deliberately to mislead the consumer into believing that the product is made by that same manufacturer when it is not.

    In effect, a form of passing off. For further discussion on passing off, see p. 277 and Chapter 10.

7. Establishing, operating or promoting a pyramid promotional scheme where a consumer gives consideration for the opportunity to receive compensation that is derived primarily from the introduction of other consumers into the scheme rather than from the sale or consumption of products.

8. Falsely claiming that a product is able to cure illness, dysfunction or malformations.

9. Claiming in a commercial practice to offer a competition or prize promotion without awarding the prizes described or a reasonable equivalent.

    An example of this might be an on-pack promotion involving a prize (such as a large cash payment) where there are 'winning' codes but in reality, none of the codes corresponds to the prize.

10. Describing a product as 'gratis', 'free', 'without charge' or similar if the consumer has to pay anything other than the unavoidable cost of responding to the commercial practice and collecting or paying for delivery of the item.

11. Including in marketing material an invoice or similar document seeking payment which gives the consumer the impression that he has already ordered the marketed product when he has not.

12. Creating the impression that the consumer cannot leave the premises until a contract is formed.

13. Conducting personal visits to the consumer's home ignoring the consumer's request to leave or not to return, except in circumstances and to the extent justified to enforce a contractual obligation.

    This would cover the classic scenario of the encyclopaedia salesman with his foot in the door and not heeding the consumer's entreaty to go away.

14. Demanding immediate or deferred payment for or the return or safekeeping of products supplied by the trader, but not solicited by the consumer, except where the product is a substitute supplied in accordance with regulation 19(7) of the Consumer Protection (Distance Selling) Regulations 2000 (inertia selling).

    This type of activity became quite prevalent some years ago. Businesses send goods out unsolicited and then try to extract payment. This is now an offence. The consumer can keep the goods and does not have to pay for them.

15. Creating the false impression that the consumer has already won, will win, or will on doing a particular act win, a prize or other equivalent benefit, when in fact either:

    (a) there is no prize or other equivalent benefit; or
    (b) taking any action in relation to claiming the prize or other equivalent benefit is subject to the consumer paying money or incurring a cost.

In our view (b) above is likely to catch some of the scratch cards that, for example are included in newspapers and magazines. The consumer is led to think that they have won a prize but is then required to incur the cost of a premium rate phone call to have the chance of receiving the prize.

ENFORCEMENT

In most cases the Regulations are in enforced by trading standards offices although where the alleged infringement is serious and/or widespread, the Office of Fair Trading (OFT) may get involved. The Regulations can be enforced either by using the civil injunctive power (provided by the Enterprise Act 2002) or by way of criminal prosecution. The OFT has published guidance (September 2010) on when it will use criminal enforcement measures under the Regulations. In addition to applying the basic tests laid down by the Code for Crown Prosecutors (in short; (i) is there a realistic prospect of conviction and (ii) is prosecution in the public interest) the OFT will consider issues such as:

(i) is the (unfair) practice widespread;
(ii) is there a risk of the practice becoming widespread and causing consumer detriment;
(iii) is the trader deliberately or recklessly engaged in misleading or aggressive practices.

PENALTIES

Offences under the Regulations are punishable, on summary conviction, by a fine not exceeding the statutory maximum (currently £5,000) or, on conviction on indictment, to a fine or imprisonment for up to two years, or both.

DEFENCES

There are various defences to offences committed under the Regulations including where it can be proved that the offence was due to a mistake or to the act or default of someone else. However, this is a two-pronged defence, requiring in addition that the trader must be able to demonstrate that he 'took all reasonable precautions and exercised all due diligence' to avoid committing the offence (including by any person under his control).

As with the Trade Descriptions Act there is an 'innocent publication of advertisement' defence for those whose business it is to publish advertisements. However, a person in this position would also need to be able to show that he did not know and had no reason to suspect that publication of the advertisement would amount to an offence.

BUSINESS PROTECTION FROM MISLEADING ADVERTISING

As covered above in relation to unfair commercial practices, the Consumer Protection from Unfair Trading Regulations 2008 revoked the Control of Misleading Advertising Regulations 1988.

Directive 2006/114/EC concerning misleading and comparative advertising was implemented in the UK by the Business Protection from Misleading Marketing Regulations 2008.

The Regulations prohibit advertising that misleads traders. In other words, it covers business to business relationships. However, it also affords some protection to consumers.

COMPARATIVE ADVERTISING

The Regulations allow comparative advertising which is defined as: 'advertising which in any way, either explicitly or by implication, identifies a competitor or a product offered by a competitor'. However, for a comparative advertisement to be permitted, there are nine conditions that must be met. These are:

(a) it must not be misleading (under the Regulations);
(b) it must not be a 'misleading action' or 'misleading omission' under the Consumer Protection from Unfair Trading Regulations 2008;
(c) it must compare products meeting the same needs or intended for the same purpose;

(d) it must objectively compare one or more material, relevant, verifiable and representative features of those products (which may include the price);

(e) it must not create confusion among traders, i.e. between the advertiser and a competitor or between the trade marks, trade names, or other distinguishing marks or products of the advertiser and those of a competitor;

(f) it must not discredit or denigrate the trade marks, trade names, other distinguishing marks, products, activities or circumstances of a competitor;

(g) for products with a designation of origin, it must relate in each case to products with the same designation;

(h) it must not take unfair advantage of the reputation of the trade marks, trade names or other distinguishing marks of the competitor; and

(i) it must not present products as imitations or replicas of products bearing a protected trade mark or trade name.

OFFENCES

The Regulations make it a strict liability offence for a trader to breach the prohibition on misleading advertising.

On summary conviction the offence is punishable by a fine not exceeding the statutory maximum (currently £5,000) and on conviction on indictment to a fine or up to two years imprisonment, or both.

ENFORCEMENT

In the main, the Regulations are enforced by local weights and measures authorities. There is provision for an enforcement authority, when determining how to comply with its duty of enforcement, to have regard to the 'desirability of encouraging control of advertising' by 'such established means as it considers appropriate'. This allows for an informal approach in the resolution of disputes between traders and, for example, a case may be referred to the Advertising Standards Authority (ASA) for a ruling under the terms of the appropriate code. For further commentary on this, please see below under the heading British Codes of Advertising and Sales Promotion.

In the Government's consultation process a number of brand owners and organisations representing the interests of brand owners and the holders of IP rights pressed for the inclusion in the Regulations of specific powers for businesses to take civil (injunctive) enforcement action to stop look-alike packaging. The government rejected this request, taking the view that the existing enforcement arrangements are adequate. However, the government agreed to keep this issue under review, with a formal review scheduled for three years from when the Regulations came into force (i.e. around mid-2011)

DEFENCES

As with the Consumer Protection from Unfair Trading Regulations (see above) there are various defences including due diligence (mistake), the act or default of a third party and innocent publication.

TRADE MARK INFRINGEMENT

If your advertisement uses a rival's registered trade mark, you may be infringing that trade mark unless the advertisement complies with the Business Protection from Misleading Marketing Regulations (see above). On trade marks generally, see Chapter 10.

COPYRIGHT INFRINGEMENT

If you reproduce a substantial part of a rival's copyright work – for example, packaging design, a title or logo, or distinctive typeface – in an advertisement without their permission, you may infringe their copyright in that work, and (subject to defences such as incidental inclusion, for example in a film) they would have the usual remedies for infringement (see Chapter 9).

MALICIOUS FALSEHOOD

If you publish an untrue statement, motivated by malice (or some other improper motive), and thereby cause loss or damage to someone else, you may be guilty of publishing a malicious falsehood or a trade libel (on this generally, see Chapter 7, p. 192). The injured party may sue for damages and apply for an injunction: in one case between two computer companies, Compaq and Dell, the plaintiffs, Compaq, succeeded in obtaining an interim injunction on these grounds which prevented Dell from making untrue and misleading comparisons (particularly on dealer price) between the computer products of both companies.

PASSING OFF

Although most comparative advertising seeks to distinguish one product from another, it is possible to refer to a rival's product in advertising in such a way that the public is given the impression that they are somehow approving or endorsing your own product, or that the products are linked, with the result that their own goodwill would be diluted and confusion would be caused. A good example of this was the 1985 case between McDonald's Hamburgers and Burger King, where McDonald's took action to prevent advertisements being displayed by Burger King bearing the words 'It's Not Just Big, Mac.' Although McDonald's failed on the ground of malicious falsehood, they succeeded in obtaining an injunction to prevent passing off: on the grounds that potential customers would be misled into thinking that there was an association between McDonald's successful Big Mac hamburger and Burger King, and that they could get a Big Mac at Burger King establishments. (For further treatment of passing off; see Chapter 10, p. 277.)

Publishers would therefore be well advised to do all they can to make absolutely certain that statements made in comparative advertisements are fair comparisons, comparing like with like, that the quoted facts are true at the time of the advertisement, that they do not infringe any copyright or registered trade mark owned by rivals, and do not indulge in any form of passing off or in any other way mislead or confuse the public.

BRITISH CODES OF ADVERTISING AND SALES PROMOTION

In addition to the various legal controls mentioned above, the advertising industry has developed a parallel system of self-regulation, monitored and enforced by the Advertising Standards Authority (ASA). The ASA attempts to ensure that advertisements do not mislead, and are in the public interest, and may investigate complaints, publish findings and make references to the Office of Fair Trading, requesting the Office of Fair Trading to seek injunctions preventing offending advertisements. The ASA may also request newspapers and other publishers not to accept particular advertisements. In addition, the ASA's Committee of Advertising has issued a Code of Practice (the last edition came into force on 1 September 2010) called the UK Code of Non-Broadcast Advertising Sales Promotion and Direct Marketing. There are separate Codes covering TV advertising and radio advertising although the ASA has assumed powers over advertising in this media from the communications regulator Ofcom.

For some years now the ASA's remit has covered online paid-for advertising (such as pop-up adverts). From March 2011 this remit will be extended to cover marketing communications (advertising) on advertisers' own websites.

The first principle of the Advertising Code has become famous ('All marketing communications should be legal, decent, honest and truthful') but there are many other provisions covering, among other things, safety, personal privacy, prices, free offers, guarantees, and comparisons with rival products (see above, p. 313).

The Codes have no independent legal force, and are written in fairly general terms, but evidence that an advertiser has not complied with one or other of the Codes is likely to be taken into account in any court proceedings. Also, an adverse adjudication by the ASA can lead to negative publicity. It is therefore very much in publishers' interests to do all they can to see that their advertising complies with the Codes, and that copies of the Codes – which are usually available free of charge from the ASA website – are on every marketing and advertising department's shelves.

The Committee of Advertising Practice (CAP) has prepared a range of guidance notes – 'Help Notes' – including one on the marketing of publications. This can be accessed on-line from CAP at www.cap.org.uk.

We give below an example of the 'key' points in the Help Note:

- All factual claims must be substantiated.
- Unproven claims contained in the title of a publication must be put in inverted commas.
- The first reference to the title should be followed by the author's name.

- Marketers offering 'new' publications should ensure that those publications have been available for no longer than a year.
- Marketers should not misleadingly describe pamphlets and the like as 'books'.

JURISDICTION

The number of consumers and businesses using the Internet continues to increase at a fast rate, as does the number of those providing and utilising online advertising and buying/selling capability ('e-commerce'). Such an increase poses an interesting question about how the law governs such transactions, given that a website of one country is accessible from any country in the world.

One case where the problems of the worldwide web were exposed involved the huge US online web portal company Yahoo!. Yahoo! sold Nazi memorabilia (via online auction) on its US-based website (yahoo.com) presumably for the benefit of US citizens only. The items were not available on the Yahoo sites of other jurisdictions for obvious reasons (for example, the sale or promotion of Nazi-related items is prohibited by French law). However, as the website was accessible in France (even though France has its own French version of Yahoo! which did not have access to the material), an anti-racism group took Yahoo! to court in France to prevent sales of the paraphernalia to French citizens. The French court ordered Yahoo! to block the sale of Nazi items to French citizens or face fines of £10,000 per day. This was somewhat of a shock outcome not least because experts appointed by the court acknowledged that it was not, in practice, possible for Yahoo! to block all French users. However, Yahoo! sought and obtained a declaration from the US federal courts that the French ruling is unenforceable against Yahoo! in the US. Whilst national courts have often taken a pragmatic approach and generally only ruled against foreign sites that are actually targeted at users in the country in question, the significance of the French ruling should not be underestimated, and online advertisers and retailers should be wary of similar claims.

Another interesting question is how the law governs Internet transactions from the point of view of consumers. For example, if an individual, who resides in the UK, purchases a new bestselling novel (in the US) from Amazon.com or equivalent US-based online retailer using a laptop while on holiday in France, in which country does the buyer seek a remedy if the book is not delivered and the retailer denies responsibility? Would it be his home courts (UK), those of the country where the purchase was made (France) or the country where the website is based (USA)?

Assistance has been provided by a binding EU Regulation on Jurisdiction, Recognition and Enforcement to ensure that rules of jurisdiction and enforcement of judgments are dealt with consistently in the EU. The Regulation broadly confirms the 'country of origin' principle that persons (including companies) domiciled in member states must be sued in their own courts. However, this is subject to certain exceptions. For example, in contracts for the sale of goods or delivery of services (including website services), consumers may sue in the courts of the place of performance of the contract. This will usually be in their home courts in a sale of goods case (place of performance is deemed to be where the goods were or should have been delivered). The same will probably apply in a provision of services case (place of performance is deemed to be where the services were or should have been provided).

SUMMARY CHECKLIST: ADVERTISING

- Are our claims legal, decent, honest and truthful?
- Is it an unfair commercial practice (a misleading action or omission including as to price)?
- Might we have a defence, if we took all reasonable precautions, and used all due diligence?
- Is this an 'Advertorial'? If so, this must be made clear on the advertisement.
- Do we hold documentary evidence substantiating all claims which are capable of objective substantiation?
- Are we indulging in comparative advertising?
- Are we infringing any trade marks or copyrights (or using a well-known personality for implied endorsement without their consent)?
- Have we advertised online, and, if so, have we considered the impact this may have in countries where the site is accessible?
- Does the advertisement contain anything that might cause serious or widespread offence, such as on the grounds of race, religion, sex or sexual orientation.

UNSOLICITED GOODS AND SERVICES

One of the more notorious promotional techniques of the 1960s was 'inertia selling', an aggressive system of sending products – and invoices – out to people who had not ordered them in the hope that some at least would be passive or compliant (or intimidated) enough to buy them. The public outcry that resulted led to the passing of the Unsolicited Goods and Services Act 1971 (which has been amended by the Unsolicited Goods and Services Act 1971 (Electronic Commerce) (Amendment) Regulations 2005 and the Regulatory Reform (Unsolicited Goods and Services Act 1971) (Directories Entries and Demands for Payment) Order 2005) which now, together with other legislation (including the Consumer Protection from Unfair Trading Regulations 2008), severely restricts such practices.

Under section 2 of the 1971 Act, it is a criminal offence, punishable by fine, for anyone in the course of a trade or business to make a demand for payment for goods when:

- they know that the goods are unsolicited;
- they sent goods to another for the purpose of them acquiring them for their trade or business; and
- they have no reasonable cause to believe they have any right to payment.

Similarly, under Regulation 24 of the Consumer Protection (Distance Selling) Regulations 2000 (which repealed section 1 of the 1971 Act and was amended by the Consumer Protection from Unfair Trading Regulations 2008), it is a criminal offence for anyone, in the course of a trade or business, to make a demand for payment of goods or services when:

- they know that the goods or services are unsolicited;
- they are sent to another person with a view to his acquiring them for purposes other than those of his business.

It is also a criminal offence (which is confirmed by section 24(5) of the 2000 Distance Selling Regulations) under such circumstances to make threats of legal proceedings for non-payment, or threaten any other sanctions, such as unfavourable credit listings.

DISTANCE SELLING

Distance selling (like distance learning) is less exotic than the name implies: it simply means contracts negotiated at a distance (rather than face to face), and includes Internet and mail order sales (whether or not based on direct mail campaigns or telephone 'cold calling'). In the European Commission's view the development of new technology such as teleshopping and the 'Internet' required increased consumer protection within the EU, particularly for personal privacy, and so an EU Distance Selling Directive (1997) was enacted.

THE UK DISTANCE SELLING REGULATIONS

The Distance Selling Directive was implemented into UK law by the Consumer Protection (Distance Selling) Regulations 2000 (as subsequently amended). The scope of the Regulations is very broad, covering goods and services, where the contract is made without any face-to-face contact between supplier and consumer. It does not, however, apply to business to business transactions (only business to consumer).

Distance contract

A distance contract is defined as:

> any contract concerning goods or services concluded between a supplier and a consumer under an organised distance sales or service-provision scheme run by the supplier who, for the purpose of the contract, makes exclusive use of one or more means of distance communication up to and including the moment at which the contract is concluded.

As the Regulations only apply to 'organised' distance-sales or service provision schemes, it is probable that they do not apply if a business:

- does not normally sell to consumers in response to letters, phone calls, faxes or e-mails (i.e. if a business conducts a one-off sales request, then it would not need to comply but if a business regularly deals with one-off requests and has the facilities to do so, then it would need to comply); and
- the business does not operate an interactive shopping website.

Key features

The Regulations may apply to any business that sells goods or services to consumers:

- on the Internet or digital television;
- by mail order, including catalogue shopping;
- by phone or fax.

In summary, the key features of the Regulations are:

- the consumer must be given (in good time before the conclusion of the contract) clear information about the goods or services offered;
- the consumer must be sent a confirmation by the supplier after making a purchase (in writing, including by email);
- the consumer has a seven-day cooling off period during which they can cancel the contract (but this can extend by up to three months and seven days where the consumer is not properly informed of the right of cancellation).

Consumer information

The information that the consumer must be given includes:

- the identity and address (if payment is made in advance) of the supplier and his commercial purpose;
- a clear description of the goods or services;
- the price of the goods or services (including taxes) and delivery costs (where appropriate);
- information on the arrangement for payment, delivery or performance;
- the existence of the right of cancellation;
- the period that the offer or price remains valid.

In the case of telephone communication, the identity of the supplier and the commercial purpose must be made clear at the start of the conversation with the consumer.

Consumer's right to cancel

If within seven days after delivery of the goods (in fact seven days from the day after delivery), the consumer gives a notice of cancellation to the supplier, the contract will be cancelled. The notice of cancellation must be in writing or other durable form (as mentioned above, this probably includes e-mail). In contracts for services, the cancellation period can even exist after the service is commenced.

Unless the parties agree otherwise, the consumer does not have a right to cancel in respect of certain contracts, including:

- for the supply of newspapers, periodicals or magazines (but not for the supply of books, for example from a book club);
- for gaming or betting services.
- for the supply of audio or video recordings or computer software if they are unsealed by the consumer (although it is not clear whether this covers downloading computer software);
- personalised or specially made goods.

Once the contract is cancelled, it is treated as if it has not been made and the supplier must (as soon as possible and in any event within 30 days) reimburse any sums paid by the consumer under that contract (including delivery charges).

These Regulations need to be borne in mind, especially with the growth of e-commerce and the increase of availability of online publications. For businesses conducting 'distance selling', it is important that the information to be provided to the consumer is clearly displayed.

DATA PROTECTION

Most businesses maintain a certain amount of information about individuals. For example, as advertising and marketing models become more sophisticated, business reliance on information about customers and subscribers increases, and the type of information collected and used becomes more detailed. Also, a business involved with publishing, like any other business, will hold and use personal information about its employees, and other people with whom it deals including authors. It may also, of course, publish information that identifies individuals.

Use of information which relates to individuals is regulated in the UK by the Data Protection Act 1998 ('the 1998 Act'). The 1998 Act was brought into force to implement a 1995 European Commission Directive and provides the framework for the UK's data protection regime, with the detail being filled in by way of separate secondary legislation or regulations. It is important to note that contravention of the 1998 Act can be a criminal offence and directors and officers involved can also be held personally (and criminally) liable.

THE DATA PROTECTION ACT 1998

What does the 1998 Act cover?

The 1998 Act, which is enforced by the UK Information Commissioner, governs the 'processing' of information about individuals ('personal data') in the UK. Any business, person or company that 'processes' 'personal data' is known as a 'data controller' (except where that processing only takes place on behalf of and purely in accordance with the instructions of someone else in which case they will be known as a 'data processor').

- 'Data' is defined as information that is processed automatically (i.e. held on a computer) and information held in certain organised paper records (a 'relevant filing system'). In order for information held in a relevant filing system to be covered, that filing system must be structured by reference to individuals or to criteria enabling the user to readily access specific information relating to that individual. 'Personal data' is data that relates to individuals which can be identified from the data, or from the data and other information which is in, or is likely to come into, the possession of the data controller. Personal data can include expressions of opinion about the data subject and indications of the intentions of the data controller or any other person in respect of the data subject.
- 'Processing' is defined extremely widely and essentially includes any use of data from the collection and recording of data, the holding of data and the carrying out of any operation on data, to the data's subsequent disclosure and eventual destruction. The UK Information Commissioner has made it clear that the term will be interpreted broadly to include any conceivable operation on data.

In the case of *Durant* v. *Financial Services Authority* (2003) the Court of Appeal considered the definitions of personal data and relevant filing system in the 1998 Act. In terms of 'personal data', it took the view that incidental reference to a person's name will not necessarily be personal data about the named person. For the data to be 'personal data' it must affect an individual's privacy in some way, for example, the information has personal connotations or has the individual at its focus, rather than being a mere reference not associated with any other personal information.

The Court of Appeal also took the view that paper records would only qualify as a 'relevant filing system' where they are of 'sufficient sophistication to provide the same or similar ready accessibility as a computerised filing system'. In other words the files would need to be structured in such a way that it would be clear from the outset of a search whether specific information amounting to personal data is held and the structure of the files is so sophisticated to mean that specific criteria or information about a particular individual can be easily located.

The judgment was considered to narrow the interpretation previously placed on the term personal data and exclude all but the most organised of paper records from the scope of the 1998 Act. In view of the importance of this decision, the Information Commissioner published guidance on the implications of the case, followed in 2007 by a technical guidance on determining what is personal data. The technical guidance goes beyond the decision in *Durant* by giving more examples of when data might be regarded as relating to an individual, whilst attempting to reconcile the broader interpretation placed on the concept of personal data by the Article 29

Working Party – a European Commission advisory committee composed of representatives of the different national data protection authorities. The result is a definition that is a little wider than that adopted by the Court of Appeal.

The guidance focuses on whether a living individual can be identified, in other words, whether a person can be distinguished from other individuals. This might be through the presence of their name along with other contact information. However name is not critical, as identification may still be achieved because a person can be distinguished from others, perhaps because of physical characteristics or because they are recognised as living in a certain property.

Where an individual is identifiable then the data must also relate to them. In other words the data is processed to learn, record or decide something about that person or has an impact on them.

What must be done before personal data may be processed?

Notification

If someone is a data controller processing personal data, generally speaking (there are some exemptions), they must notify the Office of the Information Commissioner that they are doing so.

Under the 1998 Act, notification must take place annually. A notification involves giving certain information to the Office of the Information Commissioner including the data controller's name and address, a description of the personal data being processed, the purposes for which those data are processed and any recipients of the personal data and a description of any intended destination countries. The details of the notification will then appear on a publicly accessible register. Failure to notify or to notify the details of any material changes to personal data processing within 28 days of the change is an offence under the Act. A fee is paid on making a notification and each year on renewal of the notification entry. The level of fee to be paid is now tiered. As of 1 October 2009 a fee of £500 must be paid by any data controller with an annual turnover of £25.9 million or more and 250 employees, or by a public authority with 250 or more employees. All others who are required to notify, pay a lower fee of £35.

Compliance

The Act is based on eight 'Data Protection Principles' which must be observed by all data controllers whenever any personal data is collected and subsequently processed and can be viewed as enforceable, common sense standards that govern the handling of personal data. These are summarised below.

- *Principle 1.* Personal data must be processed fairly and lawfully and, in particular, shall not be processed unless at least one of a specified list of pre-conditions is met (for example, the data subject has given his consent or the processing is necessary for the performance of a contract to which the data subject is a party).

- *Principle 2.* Personal data shall be obtained only for one or more specified and lawful purposes, and shall not be used in any manner incompatible with that purpose or those purposes.
- *Principle 3.* Personal data shall be adequate, relevant and not excessive in relation to the purpose or purposes for which it is processed.
- *Principle 4.* Personal data shall be accurate and, where necessary, kept up to date.
- *Principle 5.* Personal data shall not be kept for longer than is necessary considering the purpose for which they are used.
- *Principle 6.* Personal data shall be processed in accordance with the rights of data subjects under the 1998 Act (see below).
- *Principle 7.* Appropriate technical and organisational measures shall be taken against unauthorised or unlawful processing of personal data and against accidental loss or destruction of, or damage to, personal data.
- *Principle 8.* Personal data shall not be transferred to a country or territory outside the EEA unless that country or territory ensures an adequate level of protection for the rights and freedoms of data subjects in relation to the processing of personal data (see below for further comment on this principle).

Compliance with the first principle is viewed as important as it deals with transparency and fairness in the collection and use of personal data by ensuring data subjects know what data will be held about them, what use will be made of it and how it might be shared – often (not always) it is necessary to obtain consent from the data subjects to use their personal data in the way intended by the person collecting the data. 'Consent' is not defined in the Act but it is accepted that it must be specific, informed and freely given.

Other principles focus on the quality and appropriateness of data processing and the rights individuals have in relation to their data.

In recent years the importance of compliance with the seventh security principle has been thrown into the spotlight by an increasing number of high-profile security breaches involving personal data, many of which have made front page news. Most significant among these are the incidents involving HM Revenue and Customs ('HMRC') and the Ministry of Defence ('MOD').

HMRC

In November 2007, HMRC lost two unencrypted compact discs holding child benefit records and in particular, the personal data of up to 25 million individuals. The discs were being sent by HMRC to the National Audit Office ('NAO') in response to a request for audit information. The package containing the discs (which was not recorded or registered) was lost in transit to the NAO.

MOD

In January 2008 a Royal Navy recruiter's laptop computer was stolen from a car that had been left overnight in a car park in Birmingham. The stolen laptop was not encrypted and held personal data of up to 1 million individuals. This data included the personal data of approximately 600,000 recruits or potential recruits, along with personal data of 400,000 individuals who were either referees, parents or guardians of the recruits.

In both cases the scale of the loss could have been avoided had both HMRC and the MOD not held excessive amounts of personal data (beyond that required for the immediate purpose of the processing) and had taken steps to securely encrypt the data.

Both incidents resulted in the Information Commissioner taking formal enforcement action requiring both to implement specified improvements to their data protection compliance.

Sensitive personal data

The Act treats processing of certain kinds of personal data ('sensitive personal data') more strictly. For example, in order to comply with principle 1 in the case of sensitive personal data, at least one of an additional set of pre-conditions must also be satisfied which include obtaining 'explicit consent' from the data subject rather than mere 'consent'.

'Sensitive personal data' are personal data containing information relating to racial or ethnic origin, political opinions, religious or other beliefs, trade union membership, physical or mental health or condition, sex life, offences committed or alleged to have been committed by the individual and proceedings in respect of offences.

Rights of data subjects

The 1998 Act confers a number of rights on individuals in respect of their personal data. For example, individuals:

- may make written requests to those who process personal data about them (known as 'subject information requests') for a copy of the data including information as to what that data are used for, the recipients to whom it is or may be disclosed and the source of the personal data;
- have rights to prevent processing likely to cause substantial damage or substantial distress to them or to another;
- have the right to object to the processing of personal data about them for direct marketing; and
- are entitled to take action through the courts for compensation from data controllers for breaches of the 1998 Act.

How does the 1998 Act affect the publishing trade?

The 1998 Act may apply in a number of situations:

- For example, as mentioned above, it may be necessary, as with any customer-focused business, to collect and use personal information about customers. This may take the form of a mailing list of individuals or (possibly more likely in the case of a publisher) a list of individuals within customer organisations such as retailers. Any use of this information must comply with the 1998 Act. The most simple example is marketing – if the publisher want to contact a database of customers to try to sell a book, then it will be necessary to comply with the relevant provisions of the 1998 Act. This is likely to involve obtaining the consent of each person whose details are held for direct marketing, and giving them the right to opt out of direct marketing.
- Also, like any other data controller, the personal data must be held securely from unauthorised access. This will involve investing in up-to-date technology as well as training staff and taking obvious steps such as locking filing cabinets that contain personal information.
- It is important to comply with all provisions of the 1998 Act in relation to data held about employees and any other data held about individuals.
- The content of some publications may also be affected by the 1998 Act. For example, a publisher may publish a directory of experts in a certain field (both online and offline) along with comments about each expert. It will have been necessary to obtain clear consent from each person included in order to use their information in this way (although it is appreciated that good practice would probably dictate that this procedure was followed anyway).

Journalism, literature and art

The 1998 Act contains a number of exemptions (covered generally below) which include an exemption relating to use of personal data for the purposes of journalism, literature and art. Personal data that are processed only for journalism, artistic purposes or literary purposes, are exempt from many provisions of the 1998 Act including many of the rights of individuals and the data protection principles (but are not exempt from the seventh data protection principle that relates to security measures, which continues to apply). The exemption only applies if:

- the processing is undertaken with a view to the publication of any journalistic, literary or artistic material; and
- the data controller reasonably believes that, having regard to the special importance of the public interest in freedom of expression, publication would be in the public interest; and
- the data controller reasonably believes that, in all the circumstances, compliance with the provisions covered by the exemption is incompatible with the purposes of publication.

When considering whether to publish the personal data, it is important to be able to satisfy each of the conditions and, in particular, take into account any relevant codes of practice in deciding whether a belief that publication would be in the public interest is reasonable. Relevant codes of practice include, for example, the code of practice issued by the Press Complaints Commission.

Human Rights Act 1998

When considering the application of the above exemption relating to journalism, literature and art, and also when processing personal data generally, the application of the Human Rights Act 1998 will need to be taken into account. The Act only directly applies to public authorities and to acts of a public nature. However this does also extend to cover the judicial functions of courts or tribunals and provides that other legislation (including the Data Protection Act 1998) should be interpreted in a way that is compatible with the rights provided by the European Convention on Human Rights. As mentioned in Chapter 8, Article 8 of the Convention provides that:

Everyone has the right to respect for his private and family life, his home and his correspondence.

Article 10(1) of the Convention provides that:

Everyone has the right to freedom of expression.

Although the Data Protection Act 1998 merely regulates the processing of personal information about individuals rather than offering statutory protection for individuals privacy rights, the effect of the Human Rights Act is that the courts considering a case concerning the publication of any information about an individual, will also need to balance these rights. This is particularly relevant to journalism, an area where there has been some significant case-law, generally, each case turning on its facts. The process of balancing the conflicting rights set out above as well as interpreting other legislation in a way that is compatible with the Convention rights is, at present, a delicate and often unpredictable exercise. The overriding consideration is that the Human Rights Act must be considered when interpreting any legislation, including the Data Protection Act 1998.

More specific information about the approach of the courts to issues of privacy and confidence since the Human Rights Act and the relevance of recent case law to publishers can be found in Chapter 8.

International sharing of personal data

Generally speaking, transfers of personal data to countries outside the EEA will only be allowed if the third country in question ensures an 'adequate' level of protection. Very few countries outside the EEA are deemed by the European Commission to have adequate protection. In the context of the US, certain measures have been put in place under which transfers of personal data can be made to US businesses who have signed up to a set of privacy principles similar to the data protection principles under the 1998 Act (because the measures will lead to a presumption of adequacy).

If the destination country outside the EEA does not have adequate data protection laws in place then the transfer will only be permitted in one of certain specified circumstances, such as where the data subject has consented, the transfer is necessary for the performance of a contract with the data subject or the rights of the data subject are protected by a contract based on European approved terms between the sender and the recipient of the data. It is also possible for multinational organisations to adopt binding corporate codes of conduct to ensure adequacy of protection for transfers of personal data to other group companies based outside the EEA. European guidance in the form of a checklist for the content of a binding corporate code, a procedure for making applications and a standard application form for approval of a set of binding corporate codes are available. However, the process for approval is complex and costly. So far, it has remained a process that only a handful of large multinational organisations have been prepared to consider.

Why comply?

Many breaches of the 1998 Act are criminal offences under which directors or other officers can be personally liable, aside from breaches giving rise to other civil issues. Criminal offences can arise where personal data is processed in a way not described by a data controllers, notification entry or in a way that contravenes an enforcement notice issued against a data controller by the Information Commissioner.

More significantly an offence can also arise where there has been unlawful obtaining, disclosure or procuring of personal data or the offering for sale of personal data that has been unlawfully obtained, disclosed or procured. The offence is particularly relevant to our media hungry society, where ever-increasing demands for information, often driven by publishing or journalistic interests has led individuals such as private investigators to use deception to obtain information often for financial gain. The use of an agent or middleman to obtain an unlawful disclosure of personal data is equally unlawful unless the procurer could show that he acted in the reasonable belief that he had the right in law to do so or that the consent of the data controller would have been forthcoming had they known the circumstances of it or that what the procurer did was in the particular circumstances, in the public interest.

Operation Motorman

This relates to an investigation conducted by the Office of the Information Commissioner which began in November 2002 and led to the home of a private investigator. Evidence seized from the property revealed a clear picture of an illegal trade in personal information. Among the different types of information seized were criminal records, vehicle ownership details, ex-directory telephone numbers, itemised phone bills and financial transactions. The records included account books detailing who had requested personal information, including records showing information being passed to 305 journalists working for a wide range of different national newspapers.

A government consultation on introducing custodial sentences of up to two years on indictment for those found guilty of an offence of unlawful obtaining, disclosure, procuring or offering for sale of unlawfully obtained, disclosed or procured data ran up until the beginning of 2010. The consultation included a proposal for a defence where it could be shown that the defendant acted for the purposes of journalism, literature and art, with a view to publication of journalistic, literary or artistic material and in the reasonable belief that, in the particular circumstances, the action was justified as being in the public interest.

A decision on the consultation was postponed on account of the national election in Spring 2010. It remains to be seen at the time of writing whether custodial sentences will be introduced.

To force compliance, the Information Commissioner may also serve enforcement and information notices, the latter requiring a controller to provide information to assist the Commissioner in determining whether the data protection principles have been broken. Going even further, the Commissioner may in certain circumstances apply to the court for an entry and inspection warrant.

As of April 2010 the Information Commissioner has had the power to issue fines of up to £500,000 for serious, deliberate or reckless breaches of the data protection principles of the 1998 Act. At the time of writing, two organisations have received fines. In the first case, a fine of £60,000 was issued against a company for the loss of sensitive personal data on an unencrypted laptop. In the second case, a fine of £100,000 was levied against a council for two separate incidents where council employees faxed highly sensitive personal information to the wrong recipients. One fax involved a child sex abuse case and the other details of care proceedings.

Finally the inconvenience factor of a breach of the 1998 Act should not be overlooked. The administrative costs of having to deal with complaints and, ultimately investigations by the Office of the Information Commissioner can be very high, in addition to the negative publicity that complaints or successful prosecutions entail.

Other exemptions

The 1998 Act contains a number of exemptions from some or all of the data protection principles and the other provisions such as:

- where national security is involved;
- where processing concerns the detection of crime or the assessment of taxation;
- where information must be made public by law;

- where the disclosure is made in connection with legal proceedings, or pursuant to a court order;
- for the purposes of research, history and statistics; and
- for processing for purely domestic purposes.

Achieving and maintaining compliance

Being compliant means having an up-to-date notification in place and internal procedures sufficient to ensure that in practice the organisation processes personal data in accordance with its notification and with applicable data protection law.

Generally, it is important to assess (and revise where appropriate) all data processing activities on a regular basis. Data protection notification must reflect the data processing activities in practice from time to time and relevant staff need to be aware of the impact of the Act and be appropriately trained. There should be suitable internal procedures in place to ensure the continuing compliance of the above and the effective handling of enquiries and complaints by individuals. This may involve appointing a data protection officer.

Finally, anyone publishing materials from which individuals can be identified should be extra careful to comply with the 1998 Act as well as the plethora of other laws covered by this book.

OTHER LAWS

Recent years have seen a number of other very significant items of legislation in this area, much of which has emanated from Europe. These laws have implications beyond the field of data protection but also have implications for data protection.

First, there are the Privacy and Electronic Communications (EC Directive) Regulations 2003 (the '2003 Regulations') which came into force in December 2003. The 2003 Regulations apply, among other things, to those sending electronic direct marketing communications such as by telephone, fax, e-mail or mobile text messages (SMS). In the case of marketing by e-mail or SMS, the default requirement is that it is only possible to send unsolicited communications in this way if the recipient has positively consented. There is an exception to this rule where a business is sending e-mail offers of its own similar goods or services to its existing customers who were offered an opt-out at the time their details were collected and at each time their details were subsequently used.

The 2003 Regulations also include rules relating to the use of cookies. These devices are regularly used by online publishers or advertising networks working with online publishers who look to monetise sites using cookie-based online ad-serving models. The 2003 Regulations currently require that computer users are given clear and comprehensive information about the use of cookies or similar devices, such as when they visit a website and are given the opportunity to refuse their use. At the end of 2009 the European Union and the European Parliament agreed various telecom reforms including amendments to the EC Directive on which the 2003 Regulations are based:

these amendments must be implemented by all member states by May 2011. In the UK this will probably mean that the 2003 Regulations will need to be replaced.

One of the amendments is relevant to the use of cookies and equivalent devices that can be placed on a user's computer. In particular it appears likely that a more positive indication of consent will be required from computer users by brand owners and publishers to the use of cookies to deliver, among other things, tailored advertising or content rather than the inferred consent based upon having been given information and an opportunity to object under the 2003 Regulations. It is anticipated that draft statutory instruments implementing the amendments contained in the revised Directive into UK law will be available in the first quarter of 2011.

Second, under the Electronic Commerce (EC Directive) Regulations 2002, people sending commercial communications (including about promotions and discounts) must ensure that those communications are labelled as such as soon as they are received by the recipient and that they clearly identify the sender.

The Regulation of Investigatory Powers Act 2000 regulates, among other matters, the interception and monitoring of communications on networks including private lines such as the internal telephone network of a business. Monitoring is allowed only if the controller of the network has obtained a warrant, if both parties to the call consent, or if the purpose of the monitoring falls within the Lawful Business Practice Regulations 2000. These separate Regulations permit the monitoring of communications, for example to ascertain compliance with regulatory or self-regulatory business practices, to ascertain or demonstrate the standards achieved by those using the system for work or to detect or investigate unauthorised use of the employer's system. It is also possible to monitor (but not record) communications in order to establish whether a communication is work related. However, for any of the exceptions to apply, the business must first have taken all reasonable efforts to inform staff that monitoring takes place.

Finally, the Freedom of Information Act 2000 is likely to be of interest to publishing and related trades, not because they are likely to be directly regulated by the provisions of the legislation (which generally speaking places obligations on public authorities such as government or other public bodies), but because the legislation provides for general rights of access to recorded information public authorities hold. The Act offers the opportunity for anyone to make a written request for information held by a public authority, providing authors and journalists among others with wider opportunities to access previously unavailable information. Extensive use has been made of the access rights since these came into force in January 2005. This has in turn fostered high profile public debates on issues of real significance, including the importance of public transparency and accountability – most notably in connection with the recent publicity surrounding the obtaining of access to MPs' expenses.

SUMMARY CHECKLIST: PROMOTION AND DATA PROTECTION

- Are we promoting unsolicited goods or services?
- If so, do we have reasonable cause to believe we are entitled to payment?

- Are we engaged in distance selling?
- If so, have we provided all the relevant information to the consumer?
- Are we using personal data in any way?
- If so, do we need to put in place notification with the UK Information Commissioner?
- To the extent we need it, do we have the consent of the individual?
- Are we using any 'sensitive personal data'?
- If so, do we have explicit consent from the relevant individuals?
- Do we have procedures in place to ensure compliance and to handle complaints or subject information requests?
- Are we sending unsolicited communications?
- Do we make any transfers of personal data outside the EEA?
- If so, can we meet the requirement for adequacy of protection of the transfers?
- Are all relevant staff trained to understand the impact of the 1998 Act on their particular area?
- Do we have in place procedures to ensure ongoing compliance with data protection laws?

Distribution and export   13

INTRODUCTION

We looked in Chapters 11 and 12 at the contracts which normally govern the sale of finished books and other manufactured products in the UK, and at the general law affecting consumer protection and advertising. We have seen that the law still attaches great importance to individual contracts, but increasingly regulates trading behaviour in the UK by means of statutory liability, especially where consumers are concerned. We have also seen how many of the statutes and other regulations now originate, not from Westminster, but from Brussels. In this final chapter, we shall turn a lot more of our attention to Europe. Distribution and the free movement of goods and services are key concerns of the European Union. So, also, are the goals of free, unrestricted, competition, and the famous 'level playing field'. Any publisher selling or distributing in the UK and Europe needs to bear these economic priorities very much in mind: agreements or trading behaviour which are found to be contrary to EU or UK competition rules, for example because they amount to the abuse of a dominant position or are otherwise anti-competitive, may be heavily penalised. This may affect distribution agreements, purchasing agreements, sales agency agreements, and potentially all commercial licensing of intellectual property, both within the UK and throughout Europe.

TRADE AND COMPETITION

Competition is a natural, some would say an essential, feature of healthy markets, and publishing is often highly competitive. Small publishers have a way of turning into larger publishers, however – or of being acquired by them (a process which may in itself require merger clearance, outside the scope of this book) – and large publishers may be able in time to influence, or even dominate, their particular market either by themselves, or as one of a group. Such groups can wield considerable market power. This is not in itself a bad thing: market power can encourage healthy rationalisation, and can benefit the consumer in many ways (by improving distribution, for example). It can cause legal difficulties, however, if it is used in an anti-competitive way.

Publishers must also be careful to avoid what are known as 'anti-competitive practices'. Anti-competitive practices can start quite informally, for example, over lunches between marketing directors, and may at first be nothing more than a (fairly) innocent exchange of views and gossip. When competitors have lunch, however, economists (and lawyers) start to feel nervous. From such humble beginnings, price-fixing agreements may result, or divisions of local territories or market sectors, agreements on discounts or other terms of trade or other measures designed to restrict competition. Agreements or practices which restrict competition are very likely to be prohibited under UK and EU competition law, and are very likely to be unenforceable. They may even lead to large fines.

In these circumstances, great care needs to be taken when entering into commercial agreements, not only 'horizontal' agreements between companies competing at the same level, but also where there are 'vertical' arrangements operating at different levels up and down the distribution chain, for example between suppliers and agents or exclusive licensees.

We will look first at UK common law rules on what is known as restraint of trade, and then consider the UK and EU competition rules.

RESTRAINT OF TRADE

Since the early fifteenth century, the courts have refused to enforce contracts which are in unreasonable restraint of trade. Any such contract is *prima facie* void under English law. Each contract, of course, 'restrains' trade in some way, since it limits what one or both of the parties may do in the future, but it is only unreasonable restraints which will not be enforced. These most often occur in the context of restrictive covenants, for example when seeking to control rival activity by former employees or proprietors of a publishing business, and may also occur with exclusive distribution or purchasing agreements.

An attempt to restrain a former marketing director from working in the same capacity for any comparable publishing company for the next five years would almost certainly be in unreasonable restraint of trade, for example – not only because of the breadth of the restriction (which would rule out a large proportion of the director's future job options) but also because of the unreasonably long time during which the ban would operate. A restraint on working for any direct competitor for 12 months, on the other hand, might be regarded as reasonable, and therefore enforceable. Any attempt to impose a wide-ranging ban over a long period may well be difficult to enforce, particularly if it would significantly limit the capacity of the person concerned to earn a living at all.

Anyone wishing to enforce a restraint of trade will need to prove three things:

- that he or she has a legitimate interest worthy of protection (protecting the goodwill of the business, for example);
- that the restraint is reasonable between the parties themselves (and does not, for

example, last for an unreasonable length of time or restrict too wide an area of activity); and

- that it is reasonable in the public interest.

Even if an individual contract may be enforceable between the parties, however, any business activity resulting from it which affects competition may still be caught by UK and EU competition rules. In fact, these currently impose a rather shorter duration (two or three years) on such restraints in the context of the sale of a business than the law on restraint of trade.

The scope of the principle has been considerably reduced by the modernisation of EU competition law in 2004, discussed below. Essentially, the common law rules may no longer be relied upon to avoid contractual obligations, at least as between businesses, in situations where there is no infringement of the EU competition rules.

EU AND UK COMPETITION RULES

The last few years have seen a significant convergence of EU and UK competition law, as a result of two key developments.

The first was the entry into force of the Competition Act 1998 (the 'Competition Act'), which introduced prohibitions on anti-competitive agreements (Chapter I) and abuses of a dominant position (Chapter II) that are worded in almost identical terms to those in Articles 101 and 102 of the Treaty on the Functioning of the European Union ('TFEU') (formerly known as Article 81 and 82 of the EC Treaty, respectively). Questions arising under the Competition Act are interpreted in accordance with principles laid down in EU case-law. This is intended to ensure consistency and, most importantly for businesses, commercial certainty.

The second was the so-called 'modernisation', or decentralisation of the enforcement of the EU competition rules, under which the UK authorities and courts, in common with other member states, are required to apply national and EU law in parallel; where there is an inconsistency in the approach the EU rules enjoy priority.

The UK and EU competition rules can, therefore, now be considered together. In each case, the principles and powers of enforcement are broadly similar. The key difference between the UK and EU rules is simply that whereas the UK rules apply to activities affecting trade within the UK (whether or not they also have a wider impact), the EU rules apply only to activities affecting trade between EU member states. A few differences of approach and procedure are highlighted where relevant.

The substantive prohibitions on anti-competitive agreements and abuses of dominance are addressed in turn.

ANTI-COMPETITIVE AGREEMENTS

Scope of the prohibition

Article 101 of the TFEU, and the Chapter I prohibition of the Competition Act, apply to:

- *agreements between undertakings*. An 'agreement' includes a non-binding 'gentlemen's agreement'. An 'undertaking' is defined as anyone carrying on a commercial activity, so potentially includes an author, commercial arms of government bodies such as HMSO and the Ordnance Survey, as well as the more obvious examples such as publishing houses. Agreements between members of the same group of companies are generally not caught, because they are considered to be within the same undertaking;
- *decisions of trade associations*. This includes their rules, resolutions of their members or management and recommendations to their members, even if not intended to be binding or not fully put into effect; and
- *concerted practices*. This is where, without expressly entering into an agreement, undertakings knowingly co-operate rather than compete, typically by informing a competitor of the action they propose to take with the object or effect of influencing the competitor's own activities.

These agreements, trade association decisions and concerted practices (which we will refer to collectively as agreements, in the interests of brevity) are prohibited if they have the object or effect of restricting competition and affect trade within the UK (in the case of the UK rules) or between EU member states (in the case of the EU rules).

The effect on trade between member states is relatively easily demonstrated: all that is required is that the agreement may have an influence, direct or indirect, actual or potential, on the pattern of trade between member states. This effect may be shown even in the case of an agreement between two UK businesses, for example if the agreement is likely to make it more difficult for foreign businesses to enter the UK market.

The rules give an illustrative list of prohibited restrictions of competition, and include those which:

- directly or indirectly fix purchase or selling prices or any other trading conditions. This covers both horizontal price-fixing agreements – cartels – and vertical resale price maintenance, discussed below. Exchanges of information on prices and terms of trade, are also very likely to infringe;
- limit or control production, markets, technical development or investment;
- share markets or sources of supply. This includes agreements only to sell in certain geographic markets or areas, or not to sell outside a designated territory (for example, in distribution agreements);
- apply dissimilar conditions to equivalent transactions with other parties, thereby placing them at a competitive disadvantage. Discrimination usually takes the form of the operation of differential pricing or discount policies, favouring one customer or category of customers over another. The mere fact of unilaterally charging different prices to different customers is not of itself prohibited; or
- make the conclusion of contracts subject to acceptance, by the other parties, of supplementary obligations which, by their nature or according to commercial

usage, have no connection with the subject matter of the such contracts. Tying or forcing customers to stock a complete range of products of a particular brand may therefore be prohibited.

Appreciability

In order to fall foul of the prohibition, the restriction of competition and the effect on trade must both be appreciable. The Office of Fair Trading ('OFT') and the European Commission ('Commission') take the view that:

- an agreement will generally have no appreciable effect on competition if the parties' combined market share does not exceed 15 per cent in the case of agreements between non-competitors, and 10 per cent in the case of agreements between competitors; but
- agreements containing 'hard-core' restrictions, such as price-fixing and market sharing, are likely to have an appreciable effect on competition irrespective of market share, as are agreements forming part of a wider network of agreements (such as a distribution network), the overall effect of which is to restrict competition.

The assessment of appreciability depends on understanding the market shares of the parties. In turn, market shares depend on the correct definition of the relevant market. This is considered briefly in relation to the prohibition on abuses of dominance below.

Exemption

Where the benefits of the agreement outweigh its anti-competitive effects, it may be exempted from the prohibition contained in Article 101 of the TFEU or the Chapter I prohibition. Following the modernisation of competition enforcement outlined above, it is no longer possible to notify the agreement to the OFT or Commission for individual exemption. Instead, the criteria for exemption are examined as part of any overall assessment by a court or competition authority after the event. An agreement may be exempted if it:

- contributes to improving production or distribution, or promoting technical or economic progress; and
- allows consumers a fair share of the resulting benefit and does not impose on the parties restrictions which are not indispensable (as opposed to merely desirable) for achieving those objectives; and
- does not make it possible for the parties to eliminate competition in respect of a substantial part of the product market.

Rather than attempt to conduct the complex balancing exercise required to determine whether an agreement is individually exempt, it is generally preferable, where possible, to draft an agreement so as to fall within the terms of one of a series of 'block exemptions' adopted by the Commission. An agreement satisfying the conditions set out in a block exemption regulation is automatically exempted from the prohibitions.

While there is a block exemption for so-called 'technology transfer agreements' (patents and know-how licences) there is no block exemption for copyright licences or assignments. In practice, the most common approach, where there is a possibility that the agreement will have an appreciable effect on competition, is to draft it in accordance with the general principles set out in the other block exemptions, so as to secure some degree of comfort by analogy.

Vertical agreements

For our purposes, the most important block exemption is the EU block exemption for vertical agreements. The block exemption theoretically adopts an economics-based approach. However, a close examination of the block exemption, and of the accompanying 46-page guidelines published by the Commission, reveals a large number of traps for the unwary. Drafting a distribution or other supply agreement requires expert advice if the pitfalls are to be avoided. The key features of the regime, as it applies to re-seller agreements, can be summed up as follows:

- The block exemption applies to agreements for the purchase, sale or resale of goods, together with related licences or assignments of intellectual property rights, provided that those rights are not the primary object of the agreement. This means that the block exemption will not apply to a simple copyright assignment or licence unrelated to the sale of goods.
- Both the supplier's and the re-seller's market share must be less than 30 per cent.
- Above these figures, the agreement is not automatically exempt, but will not necessarily be prohibited: its exemptibility will require an individual assessment and an economic analysis of the market and of the parties' position on it.
- The re-seller must not be restricted in the customers to whom, or the territories in which, it can supply, except that it may be prohibited from soliciting business outside its territory or customer group where it has been appointed as the exclusive distributor to that territory or group, and other exclusive distributors have been appointed to those other territories or groups or the supplier has reserved them to itself. However, the distributor must always be free to respond to unsolicited orders from other territories and customer groups (known as 'passive sales'). Re-sellers must also be free to supply over the Internet: the supplier cannot reserve this sales channel to itself or to a specialist seller. Recent revisal of the block exemption and the accompanying guidelines by the Commission has seen further clarification of the hard-core restrictions aimed at tackling attempts by a supplier to limit the ability of a reseller to make sales on the Internet. The aim remains to reinforce the principles of a free and open market within

the EEA. Resale restrictions are probably the most important area of the block exemption, and one of the easiest to get wrong when drafting.

- If the re-seller is prohibited from dealing in competing products, or is obliged to buy more than 80 per cent of its requirements of the products from the supplier, the agreement will only benefit from the block exemption for a maximum of five years. Thereafter, the agreement will need to be assessed in order to determine its effect on competition, and any attempt to tacitly extend or renew the agreement beyond the five year period will not be covered by the block exemption.

An agreement which is exempt under Article 101 is also automatically exempt from the Chapter I prohibition. There is provision for UK specific block exemptions under the Competition Act, but there are none relevant to the publishing sector.

Resale price maintenance

Following the collapse of the Net Book Agreement in 1995, and the ruling of the Restrictive Practices Court in March 1997 that resale price maintenance for books was no longer in the public interest, resale price maintenance is prohibited in the publishing sector as it is in other industries.

Notwithstanding this, the Commission does not take action against purely national systems of fixed book prices as long as they have no appreciable effect on trade between member states. In July 2001 the Commission initiated proceedings against German publishers who had extended a national book pricing scheme to cross-border book sales by refusing to supply Internet booksellers based in Belgium and Austria who wanted to sell books to German consumers at reduced prices; however, the Commission accepted an undertaking to desist, instead of imposing any penalty.

In contrast, the OFT takes particularly vigorous action against resale price maintenance, with some of its highest profile cases to date being directed at agreements to fix resale prices.

Agency

There is no block exemption as such for agency agreements. This is because an agreement which is regarded as a true agency agreement will generally fall outside the scope of the competition rules.

For the purposes of applying Article 101, an agency agreement will only be considered a true agency agreement if the

'agent does not bear any, or bears only insignificant, risks in relation to the contracts concluded and/or negotiated on behalf of the principal, in relation to market-specific investments for that field of activity, and in relation to other activities required by the principal to be undertaken on the same product market.'

That is, the agent accepts no commercial or financial risk in performing their transaction, and under competition law the agent and principal together can be considered to be one party rather than two separate individuals.

Labels can be deceptive. As in other aspects of EU competition law it is the economic effect of the agreement that is important, and not the label that is attached to it. A personal agency agreement – as, for example, between an author and a literary agent – will not be regarded in itself as anti-competitive or objectionable under Article 101 since it will have no effect on competition: in economic terms, one person is simply stepping into the shoes of another. In legal terms, true agents in any particular transaction, act only for the people they are appointed to represent (their 'principals'). They may, for example, seek out and pass on orders for their principals' products, but the customers are at all times their principals' customers, not their own, and their role is purely that of an intermediary.

However, agreements where 'agents' do more than simply represent their principals, and also operate on their own account as independent traders, might well have competition implications and might be caught by Article 101 or the Chapter I prohibition. In such cases, the 'agent' may not be regarded as an agent for the purposes of the competition rules and the agent and principal will be two separate parties.

The problem is that an agent's activities are generally controlled to a far greater extent than a distributor's – including by imposing sales prices, territories and customers. These restrictions, which are acceptable in a true agency agreement, would be viewed as serious 'hard-core' restrictions if they were included in a distribution agreement.

The key factor which will determine whether an agreement is a true agency agreement for the purposes of competition law, or is a more arm's-length commercial arrangement between two separate business entities liable to have competition law implications, is the degree of financial or commercial risk borne by the agent. Relevant considerations will include the following:

- Does property in the goods vest in the 'agent'?
- Is the 'agent' required to contribute to the cost of sales promotion?
- Is the 'agent' required to contribute to stocking and transport costs?
- Does the 'agent' provide an independent customer service?
- Is the 'agent' responsible for non-performance of the sales contract by customers?
- Is the 'agent' required to make market-specific investments (i.e. which cannot be recovered on leaving the market)?

If the answer to any of the above questions is 'yes', it is likely that the agreement is not a true agency agreement for the purposes of EU and UK competition law and might well have competition law implications.

It should also be noted that even where there is a true agency situation, Article 101(1) or the Chapter I prohibition may still apply, where it facilitates collusion. An example of this may be when a number of principals use the same agent or agents and the agents are used to collude on marketing strategy or to exchange sensitive market information between the principals.

If there is no genuine agency relationship between the parties for the purpose of competition law, then Article 101 may apply to the 'agency' agreement. However so long as certain criteria are met, the vertical agreements block exemption will ensure that the agreements do not infringe competition law. It will be necessary to ensure that the agreements contain no:

- restriction on the 'agent's' ability to make passive sales;
- prohibition on the 'agent' offering customers a rebate or discount out of his commission;
- excessive non-compete clauses. Such clauses should generally be limited to five years or less; or
- excessive post-termination obligations on the 'agent'. Such obligations will only be justifiable where they are indispensable to protect know-how, limited to the point of sale from which the agent has operated during the contract period, limited to a maximum period of one year.

Although not part of competition law, it is worth noting that throughout the EEA, there is now legislation regulating commercial agents. For this purpose a commercial agent is a person who has continuing authority to negotiate or accept orders for the sale or purchase of goods on behalf of, and in the name of, his or her principal. These rules are implemented in the UK in the shape of the Commercial Agents (Council Directive) Regulations 1993. The Regulations contain provisions governing remuneration, such as terms of commission and also minimum terms of appointment and (in particular) termination, including mandatory compensation payable on termination. It should be noted that a number of European countries have legislation which is more extensive than that in the UK, often extending to services provided by an agent. In most cases the law of the country in which the agent is based does not allow contracting out.

ABUSES OF DOMINANCE

Article 102 of the TFEU and the Chapter II prohibition of the Competition Act prohibit abuses of a dominant position on a market. In the case of the EU rules, the abuse must affect trade between member states, a concept which we have considered above.

Market definition

The key to these prohibitions is market definition. The relevant market is defined by reference to product and geographic scope.

The relevant product market is traditionally defined as the market for 'all those products or services which are regarded as interchangeable or substitutable by the consumer, by reason of the products' characteristics, their prices and their intended use'. This demand substitutability is the most important factor in market definition. A secondary defining factor is supply substitutability: the ability of suppliers of one type of product to switch to production of another (for example, the ability of a publisher of one type of book to publish another type within a short period).

The relevant geographic market is the area in which 'the undertakings concerned are involved in the supply and demand of products or services, in which the conditions of competition are sufficiently homogeneous and which can be distinguished from neighboring areas because the conditions of competition are appreciably different in those areas'.

Market definition in the publishing sector follows these same principles. A key question will be the extent to which customers view one type of book as substitutable for another. However, this is tempered by supply substitutability – focusing entirely on demand substitutability would lead to the absurd situation of a separate product market for each book or author. A few guidelines can be drawn from the rather limited case-law:

- There are likely to be distinct product markets for the acquisition of content and rights, and for the supply of books to re-sellers. There are likely to be distinct markets for different types of book, for example paperback fiction and illustrated reference works. There may also be separate markets according to the sales channel;
- Geographic markets will generally be world-wide in the acquisition of content and rights, national in book publishing (except in the case of scientific and technical publishing, where they may be world-wide), national in magazine publishing and possibly even narrower (regional) in the case of daily newspaper publishing.

Dominance

Once a relevant market has been defined, it is necessary to assess dominance on that market. Dominance is 'a position of economic strength enjoyed by an undertaking which enables it to hinder the maintenance of effective competition by allowing it to behave to an appreciable extent independently of its competitors and customers and ultimately of consumers'.

No single factor indicates dominance, but market share is an important one. A rule of thumb for likely dominance being a market share of more than 40 per cent. Market shares are at best a proxy for market power and are not conclusive of dominance; specifically they must be interpreted in light of market conditions. This is even more the case in innovative markets where the dynamics are subject to rapid changes. Generally a minimum of two years' stability in the market is required for market shares to be established. Other factors, such as the ease of entry on to the market, will also be relevant in deciding whether a high market share is sufficient to confer dominance.

In the publishing sector, market share can be calculated on the basis of the value of sales, or of the number of titles produced. However, changes to traditional business models and the advent of e-books and digital distribution chains means market shares in the publishing sector can be difficult to ascertain.

The Article 102/Chapter II prohibition also applies to conduct of undertakings which are collectively or jointly dominant, by virtue of links between them such that they adopt uniform conduct on the market.

Abuses generally

It is important to note that it is not dominance itself which is prohibited, but abuse of that dominance. Dominant undertakings have a special responsibility not to allow their conduct to impair competition, and a dominant undertaking may be unable to indulge in business practices which would be perfectly acceptable if carried out by a company without market power. The abuse need not make its effects felt on the market in which the company is dominant. Using dominance in a particular publishing market to strengthen one's position in a related media content market, for example, might be an abuse.

The two prohibitions set out an illustrative list of abuses:

- directly or indirectly imposing unfair purchase or selling prices or other unfair trading conditions. This includes both excessive pricing and predatory pricing below cost, in order to drive competitors out of the market;
- limiting production, markets or technical development to the prejudice of consumers;
- applying dissimilar conditions to equivalent transactions with other trading parties, thereby placing them at competitive disadvantage. This includes charging different prices to customers in the same circumstances without justification, or charging uniform prices to customers whose circumstances are different. Discounts which are not related to cost savings to the supplier, or intended to secure customer loyalty, may infringe the prohibitions if applied by a dominant supplier; or
- making the conclusion of contracts subject to acceptance by the other parties of supplementary obligations which, by their nature or according to commercial usage, have no connection with the subject of the contracts. The practice of tying the purchase of one product or service to the purchase of another, where the tie is not objectively justified (for example, on technical grounds) is similarly likely to be abusive.

To this list can be added conduct such as refusals to supply without objective justification: in short, anything which exploits the dominance or excludes competition still further. The UK and EU prohibitions on abuses of dominance contain no provision for exemption, because the concept of abuse provides sufficient scope for a similar weighing-up of benefits and anti-competitive effects.

Abuses of copyright ownership

There is invariably a tension between intellectual property rights and competition law: intellectual property rights grant the rightsholder a monopoly over their intellectual property, and one of the functions of competition law is to regulate the way in which monopolies are operated.

It is important to note that the mere ownership of copyright (or any other intellectual property right) does not in itself create a dominant position, neither will it necessarily define the relevant market. It is necessary to identify the relevant product market in which the company concerned may be dominant.

Refusals to license are a particularly complex area. It is relatively common for copyright owners to face complaints that they have abused their dominant position by refusing to license their copyright to an applicant, or have agreed to license only on unreasonable terms.

In the *Magill TV* listings case, a refusal by the dominant Irish State TV and radio company RTE and others (who held the copyright in TV listings) to supply details of the basic information on programme scheduling to a new market entrant which wished to publish a weekly TV guide, was held to be an abuse. This was despite the fact that RTE owned the copyright in its programme listings, and the strong argument that it was under no obligation to license them.

The Court of First Instance (now the General Court) and the full European Court of Justice ('ECJ') both decided that RTE's behaviour 'clearly went beyond what was necessary to fulfil the essential function of copyright as permitted in Community law' – which the ECJ defined somewhat narrowly as being 'to protect the moral rights in the work and ensure a reward for creative effort, while respecting the aims of, in particular, Article 86 (now Article 102)'. Important features of this case were that Magill was seeking to enter a market for which the Court found that there was clearly a demand and in which RTE was already present through its subsidiary. RTE, which owned the copyright in the TV listings, was attempting to use that copyright to protect its position in the downstream market of weekly TV guides, by refusing access to the raw material which was indispensable to new entrants for the compilation for a weekly TV guide.

All this supports – and extends – an important principle of EU law which is that while the ownership of restrictive intellectual property rights does not of itself create a dominant position and is not in itself anti-competitive (it is usually protected, along with other forms of 'industrial and commercial property' in Articles 36 and 345 TFEU), the use of those rights may be.

Magill, trumpeted at the time as imposing a duty to license, alarmed many copyright owners. However, it was clear that *Magill* turned on its facts and, since then, a series of further judgments of the ECJ and the General Court, have clarified the scope of the duty.

In the 1997 *Tiercé Ladbroke* case, concerning the refusal to license the copyright in recordings and broadcasts of horse races, the Court of First Instance ('CFI') held that a refusal to license did not fall within Article 102 unless it concerned a product or service which was:

- essential for the exercise of the activity in question, in that there was no real or potential substitute; or
- a new product whose introduction might be prevented, despite specific, constant and regular potential demand by consumers.

In one of the highest profile Commission cases to date Microsoft were fined €497 million (approximately £342 million) for abuses that included a refusal to license. The Commission held that Microsoft had abused its dominant position in the market for work group server operating system software by refusing to license to Sun Microsystems and others, the interface information required in order to allow their third party server software to communicate effectively with client PCs running Windows. Microsoft then appealed to the Court of First Instance and requested an interim suspension of the Commission's orders.

Shortly after the Commission issued its decision in Microsoft, the ECJ gave judgment in a further refusal to license case. This involved the refusal by IMS Health, a supplier of pharmaceutical sales data, to license its '1860 brick structure' (a format for dividing the German territory into geographic areas) to its competitor NDC.

The ECJ held that the refusal by a dominant undertaking to license an intellectual property right that is indispensable to operation on a downstream market constitutes an abuse of a dominant position where:

- the undertaking which requested the licence does not intend merely to duplicate the goods or services already offered by the intellectual property owner, but intends to produce new goods or services;
- the refusal is not justified by objective considerations; and
- the refusal eliminates all competition on that downstream market.

It was at this point that Microsoft's application for interim suspension of the compulsory licence of the interface information came before the CFI. A key argument of Microsoft was that its refusal was not an abuse according to the test set out in IMS, because Sun Microsystems did not intend to provide a new product, but merely server operating systems competing squarely with Microsoft's own products.

It was found that Microsoft's competitors had no interest in merely 'cloning' Microsoft's server operating systems and were offering products that had other features, ones which consumers valued. The CFI took the view that technical development, particularly in light of Microsoft's overwhelming market power and the pace at which technology was progressing, was becoming increasingly important in consumer demand and was thus in need of protection.

Interestingly, the CFI also noted that Microsoft's secret interface information, involving significant innovation, was fundamentally different in nature from the published TV listings data in *Magill* and the 1860 brick structure, which had been developed in consultation with the industry, in the case of IMS. There might therefore be a higher threshold for ordering a compulsory licence of intellectual property rights which reflect greater original creative effort than in cases involving 'commercial' information (the TV listings, the 1860 brick structure and the racing broadcasts). The European courts seem to view such commercial copyright as inherently less valuable than creative copyright and this may have influenced their decisions. The common theme in these cases is that the copyright material acted as the gateway to a particular product or service market.

ENFORCEMENT

Investigation and enforcement

The competition authorities have extensive powers of investigation, including the power to request information and the less frequently exercised but rather more draconian power to conduct on-site investigations or 'dawn raids'. These investigations require careful handling and a rapid response. Failure to comply with the investigators' requirements may be a criminal offence, and may result in a prison sentence for directors and managers.

A key development in recent years is the increasing reliance of the authorities on evidence from whistle-blowers. The first member of a horizontal cartel or a price fixing agreement to come forward with evidence of the infringement will, if certain conditions are met, be entitled to 100 per cent immunity from penalty. A business discovering an infringement to which it has been a party therefore needs to act quickly to ensure that it does not miss this opportunity.

Consequences of infringement

The consequences of infringing the competition prohibitions are as follows:

- the parties are exposed to enforcement action by the competition authorities, possibly resulting in orders to terminate the agreement and, in the case of very serious infringements such as price-fixing and attempts to prevent exports, the imposition of fines of up to 10 per cent of the annual world-wide group turnover of each of the parties;
- the anti-competitive provisions of the agreement are void and unenforceable, although it may be possible to separate them out from the remainder of the agreement; and
- those who suffer loss as a result of the infringement can bring civil action in the national courts for damages and/or an injunction.

It should also be noted that individuals who dishonestly enter into horizontal cartel agreements by which competitors fix prices, share markets, limit supply or rig bids may be guilty of the cartel offence, introduced by the Enterprise Act 2002. Penalties include individual fines and imprisonment.

ARTICLE 34: FREE MOVEMENT OF GOODS

Just as copyright ownership or licensing – though protected as such – must not be exercised in an anti-competitive way, or in abuse of a dominant position, so it must also not be allowed to interfere with the free movement of goods. The free movement of goods provisions of the TFEU are contained in Articles 34 to 36 (formerly Articles 28 to 30), and prohibit any 'quantitative restrictions' on imports or exports between member states. Put another way, there must be no internal barriers in the single common market, and there must be free movement of goods within Europe (and, equally, free movement of services and information). Goods lawfully on sale in one member state may not be prevented from entering any other member state. This clearly outlaws quantitative restrictions imposed by states themselves, but it equally restricts geographical market divisions within Europe imposed by individual rights owners. This is of considerable significance to UK publishers, particularly in relation to English-language co-editions which will be on sale not only in the UK but elsewhere in Europe.

There is a clear conflict between the enforcement of national intellectual property rights and the principles of free movement. In a number of recent decisions of the ECJ, national copyright protection and the exercise of intellectual property rights generally have increasingly given way to the overriding free movement of goods provisions of Article 34. Despite the fact that Article 36 specifically exempts 'the protection of industrial and commercial property' from the full effect of Article 34, this is subject to the proviso that any measures taken to protect an intellectual property right must not amount to 'a means of arbitrary discrimination or a disguised restriction on trade between member states'.

TERRITORIES IN EUROPE

Under co-publishing deals between, say, a UK and US publisher (see Chapter 5), a schedule of world territories would normally be agreed: some would be exclusive to either side, and the rest would be 'open' markets where either edition may sell. Traditionally in this case, the US publisher would have wanted exclusive rights to publish in North America, the UK publisher might have asked for exclusivity in the UK and other territories of the former Commonwealth, with all other European member states regarded as 'open markets'.

In view of the free movement of goods provisions of Article 34, and the rapid development of e-book licensing (see below), such an arrangement is now highly unsafe, and the UK exclusivity would almost certainly be unenforceable against parallel importation of US (or any other) editions lawfully on sale in any other European member state.

Once the US edition is lawfully on sale in another 'open market' member state, the provisions of Article 34 restrict the ability of a UK publisher to prevent its importation into the UK. The UK's own Copyright, Designs and Patents Act 1988, in fact, expressly guarantees this under section 27(5) – nothing in that Act will prevent the importation of any article 'which may lawfully be imported into the UK by virtue of any enforceable community right.'

If UK co-publishers wish to achieve effective exclusivity for their own edition in the UK, therefore, they will now need to consider negotiating exclusive rights to the whole of the EU and EEA. Such agreements will still of course need to be permissible generally under EU competition law.

EXHAUSTION OF RIGHTS

'Exhaustion of rights' is an important issue when considering the impact of competition law on an agreement. In essence, once an intellectual property rightsholder has consented to placing goods on the market, it cannot object to the subsequent sale of those goods, that is its rights to do so are said to be 'exhausted' and they expire.

Exhaustion of rights affects a copyright holder's exclusive rights of distribution but no other rights, and comes in a variety of shapes and sizes:

- International exhaustion – meaning that the distribution right is exhausted if the work is put on sale with the consent of the rights owner anywhere in the world
- National exhaustion – where the distribution right is only exhausted if the work is put on sale with the rightsholder's consent in that country
- Regional exhaustion (the EU model) – where the right is exhausted if the work is put on sale with consent anywhere within a regional (e.g. 'single') market.

Within the UK, the free movement of goods provisions of Article 34 apply to goods lawfully on sale in any member state, but in the case of copyright goods such as books it might previously have been possible under Article 36 to argue that books licensed by the copyright owner for territory B only, but then re-imported via parallel importation back into territory A without the owner's consent, would be infringing copies in territory A and could still be excluded. However, in a leading 1971 case involving Deutsche Grammophon, the ECJ decided that once copyright goods have been put on the market in any EC member state by the copyright owner or licensor, or with their consent, then their intellectual property rights restricting the distribution or circulation of those goods are 'exhausted'. The works are still copyright works, and other exclusive rights (such as the making available right) remain intact, but the distribution right is exhausted. Local, national, copyright cannot thereafter be used to prevent parallel importation from one member state to another. It is superseded by Article 36.

EU exhaustion in relation to copyright only applies within the EU, however, and where the owner has consented – there is no exhaustion of rights if goods are marketed outside the EU (for example, in a third country such as the USA) and then imported into the EU. Similarly, if goods are released onto the market inside the EU without the owner's consent – for example via a compulsory licence in one member state – the rights will probably not be exhausted. In the case of *EMI* v. *Patricia* in 1989, the ECJ held that records lawfully marketed in Denmark, not with the consent of the copyright owner but purely because the term of local copyright protection expired, could be prevented from entering the German market, where copyright protection still remained in force. If the Danish recordings had been produced with the owner's consent, however, their rights would have been exhausted.

More recent case-law on international trade mark exhaustion has not fundamentally altered the basic position outlined above. In a case involving Silhouette spectacles, the ECJ held that member states were not permitted to adopt rules providing for international trade mark exhaustion, i.e. to provide for exhaustion where goods were not placed on the market within the EEA by the trade mark owner or with his consent. The English High Court, in a case concerning Davidoff fragrances, rather undermined this principle when the judge held that the trade mark owner could be argued to have consented to the placing on the market within the EEA when he had not imposed constraints on their further sale, including possible sales within the EEA, following their first placing on the market outside the EEA. When the case was referred to Luxembourg, the ECJ ruled in November 2001 that the trade mark owner's consent to the placing on the market within the EEA must be given 'unequivocally'. This consent could be express or could be implied from the circumstances surrounding the placing of the goods on the market outside the EEA. Consent cannot be inferred from the silence of the trade mark owner, nor from the fact that it did not reserve its rights or expressly prohibit the placing of the goods on the market within the EEA.

RECENT DEVELOPMENTS

E-BOOKS

Digital media are dramatically changing the face of publishing. Online distribution has the potential to reach a much greater audience than could ever have been expected by many publishing houses. It represents an unrivalled opportunity to promote to a wider readership. However, online distribution may also mean online piracy, and uncertainty about the above exhaustion principles, and represents a major challenge to the industry.

The use of digital rights management (DRM) and other technological measures to thwart online piracy can lead to territorial restrictions and raise difficult questions about ownership and exhaustion. In addition, e-books have raised various legal issues that remain unresolved. For example, whether e-books are sold to consumers or whether they are merely licensed is unclear. Although it might be appealing for a publisher to characterise the distribution of e-books as licensing (particularly in order to maintain its position in relation to the first sale doctrine of copyright exhaustion in the US), consumers are likely to find this difficult to reconcile, as many consider e-books to be equivalent to their paper counterparts and therefore to be 'bought and sold' when downloaded.

These issues have been considered in the EU and the US, although the position has not yet been resolved.

- In the EU, the Commission has stated that 'the rights of authors and publishers should be duly protected and secured when their works are digitised and made available through online services'; however, the extent that protection can be justified has yet to be addressed. The principles of exhaustion of rights only apply to tangible goods, and electronic delivery of a work has been found not to be analogous to the physical supply or delivery of goods. This might well be held to mean in due course that the sale of e-books in the EU is not currently subject to the rules of exhaustion, and authors and publishers might theoretically be able to prevent, for example, e-books intended for one EU member state being placed on the market in another member state.
- In the US, there is a body of case-law which suggests that new e-books are 'sold' even when publishers and copyright owners claim simply to have licensed them. However, at the time of writing the position is still evolving. A 2010 decision in the US Court of Appeal's Ninth Circuit in a long-running case determined whether the first sale doctrine applied to computer software that was being resold on eBay. In *Vernor v. Autodesk*, the developer and copyright owner argued that the first sale doctrine did not apply as the original software was not sold, but was merely licensed and those licences were non-transferable. The terms of the licence stated that a licensee could not rent, sell, or lease the software to anyone else and that if the software was upgraded, the older version should be destroyed. The Court of Appeal considered this issue and laid out a test in order to determine whether it is a 'license' or a 'sale'. In short, a software user is a licensee rather than the owner of a copy where: the copyright owner specifies that the user is granted a licence; the user's ability to transfer the software is significantly restricted; and notable use restrictions are imposed.

The effect of *Vernor v. Autodesk* could potentially be far reaching, particularly in the digital media market. For example, Amazon licenses its Kindle e-books and places restrictions on consumers as to the transferability and use of the products, as do the publishers who control publishing rights in the e-book content itself. In addition, other digital media are licensed and this case seems to suggest that simply adding in the word 'licence' into an agreement, combined with a number of restrictions, will be sufficient for publishers to ensure that consumers are forbidden from renting, lending or selling the products and software by virtue of the terms of the licence.

Publishers and authors might at least learn from the difficulties experienced by the film, television and particularly the music industries, so that the legal issues involved in online access can perhaps be circumnavigated, at least in so far as e-books and the second-hand market are concerned.

DIGITAL DISTRIBUTION: THE GOOGLE BOOKS SETTLEMENT

In 2005 the giant search engine Google launched its 'Google Book Search' service. This was the culmination of a mammoth project undertaken by Google to create an online library, digitising whole collections from well-known (mainly US) libraries and academic institutions by scanning some eighteen million books. This process included the digitisation of orphan works and rare out-of-print works. It also involved often the full text of millions of works still in copyright being scanned and 'snippets' being made available to the public without the rightsowners' consent. Google claimed that despite the commercial circumstances such copying counted as 'Fair Use' under US law. Perhaps not surprisingly, this led to Google being sued by a number of publishers and copyright trade associations in the US, most notably, the Authors' Guild of America and the Association of American Publishers.

In 2008 Google agreed to settle for $125 million to resolve the outstanding copyright claims, and a draft Settlement was presented to the South Manhattan District Court. After concerns expressed by the US Department of Justice, on competition grounds, and the Copyright Office, on constitutional grounds, a revised Settlement was agreed. At the time of writing this still awaits the court's approval (although whatever the result is, it is likely to be appealed). However, there are still many opponents to the Google project, not least because of Google's possible monopoly over orphan works and the impact that this may have on academic publishers. Google's approach has also caused concern to other companies offering similar digital content, such as Amazon, who do seek permission from copyright holders to scan works for the Kindle reader. Rivals are also worried that Google's expansion in this area could lead to further dominance by the company in areas such as online advertising. These concerns would only be exacerbated if Google were to launch its own e-book.

This type of digital distribution clearly has far-reaching repercussions for the publishing world but exactly what the competition consequences will be remains to be seen.

E-PUBLISHING ISSUES

Meanwhile, even in the present-day world of e-publishing, a number of points still need to be made:

- The distribution right to sell a product 'as new' may be exhausted, although a right to sell 'second hand' may still remain.
- The right to sell in one territory will usually be a contract (licence) right, so that parallel importation from one (licensed) territory to another (unlicensed) territory is likely to lack the required rightsholder consent. In the UK, re-importation (from outside the EU) might well mean that the works are 'infringing editions' (and therefore illegal).
- Retailers or aggregators who sell, or make available, e-books will usually also be bound by licence terms of sale, governing the territories in which (and into

which) sales can be made. This will also govern whether or not sales are made with consent (without which the distribution rights are not exhausted).

- Physical delivery of goods (or e-files), even DRM-free, into a market does not of itself imply exhaustion of the distribution rights in those goods. It is not always clear whether supply to an intermediary or aggregator will in fact amount to 'putting on sale', or 'putting on the market' with rightsholder consent in that market. The key is still usually to be found in the relevant licence or contract terms under which the goods or files were delivered.
- It is clear therefore that delivery to retailers or aggregators should only be done under very clear conditions relating to sales and licences, and territories covered, to avoid inadvertently giving the impression that more distribution rights are being exhausted than actually intended.

SUMMARY CHECKLIST: COMPETITION

- What is the relevant market?
- Are we dominant in it?
- Are we abusing our dominance?
- Do we have a sufficiently strong position in the market that any agreement into which we enter is likely to have an appreciable effect on competition?
- Is there an agreement between undertakings (or a concerted practice or trade association decision)?
- Does it affect trade within the UK, or trade between EU member states?
- Does it restrict competition?
- Is it automatically excluded or exempt?
- Is it likely to be eligible for individual exemption?
- Are we within the free movement provisions of Article 34?
- Should we be seeking exclusivity across the whole EU?
- Have we exhausted our rights?

Appendix A
A to Z glossary of legal terms

Action A legal action in a court of law, normally commenced by the issue of a Claim Form. A 'letter before action' (or 'cease and desist letter') is often designed to avoid the need for this.

Applicable law The law which applies, for example to a contract, and which will govern any dispute arising under it.

Assignee Person to whom rights are assigned.

Assignment Formal transfer of ownership, for example in copyright. Assignments of copyright must be in writing and signed by or on behalf of the copyright owner.

Assignor Person assigning rights to another who is called the assignee.

CIF (Cost Insurance and Freight) Delivery terms under which the price includes delivery to the buyer's own designated port of entry (but not normally all the way to the buyer's own warehouse) (compare FOB).

Claimant The complaining party who seeks a remedy via a court action. The party being complained about is called the Defendant. If the case goes to appeal, the party appealing is the Appellant and the party resisting is the Respondent.

Claim Form Issue of a Claim Form is the normal method of commencing an action (usually accompanied by Particulars of Claim).

Common Law A body of English law based on decided cases and developed by the judges over many centuries. Actions for breach of contract or negligence are common-law actions. It is no longer the primary source of new law in the UK, which largely now arises from statutes.

Condition Fundamental term of a contract, which goes to the root of the whole contract. Breach of a condition by one party normally entitles the other party to terminate the contract.

Consideration Something of value, usually given in return for a promise or undertaking: to be legally binding, most contracts must be supported by some valuable consideration.

Covenant A binding undertaking, often limiting future activity (such as a restrictive covenant).

Damages Remedy normally available to a successful Claimant. Awards of damages may be liquidated, to compensate for specific losses, or general, or sometimes punitive if the Defendant's behaviour has been particularly blameworthy.

Defamation The law covering libel and slander.

Defamatory Statement A statement the meaning of which tends to make people think the worse of someone.

Defendant The party being complained about in a legal action; they must defend themselves against one or more Claimants (see above).

Directive An EU law adopted by the EU Council of Ministers following circulation of a draft or proposed Directive by the EU Commission. Directives do not as a rule have direct effect as law in member states but member states are required to implement them within a specified time limit.

EEA The European Union countries together with Norway, Iceland and Liechtenstein.

Equity A traditional body of law developed over the centuries by English judges, parallel to the common law concentrating less on formal procedure and more on fairness and justice to the parties. Injunctions are mainly equitable remedies. An equitable interest or other entitlement may arise where legal ownership has not formally been transferred (via an assignment, for example) but where it is clear that it was intended to create an interest or it is fair to do so (perhaps where the price or part of it has already been paid).

Estate Means of holding and administering property (for example, an author's, including any copyrights) after death: any property is normally vested initially in executors, for the benefit of any beneficiaries: if there are no designated beneficiaries, there are complex statutory rules on entitlement to any assets.

Exclusive Licence Licence where the person granting the licence undertakes not only that there will be no other licensees but also that there will be no rival exploitation by the licensor itself. Exclusive licences must be in writing and signed by or on behalf of the copyright owner.

FOB (Free On Board) Delivery terms under which the price paid does not normally include freight or insurance costs of transport to the buyer's warehouse or port of entry (compare CIF) but is normally based on delivery to the buyer's agent or shipper at the seller's port of shipment: traditionally legal title to the goods, and risk in them, was not transferred from the seller to the buyer until the goods 'passed the ship's rail'.

Grantor One who grants, for example, a publishing licence or sub-licence.

Indemnity A term in a contract under which the party giving it agrees to bear all the risks arising out of any breach of specified warranties and to compensate the other party fully for any losses, damage, costs or expenses which may be incurred.

Indictment Formal criminal charge before a Crown Court.

Injunction A Court Order, either ordering someone to do something or ordering them to stop (or not to start).

Insolvency The condition of being unable to pay current or outstanding debts as they fall due. Insolvency of individuals (as opposed to companies) is commonly referred to as bankruptcy.

Libel A defamatory statement published in written or permanent form.

Licence A grant of rights, normally limited to a specific period of time (or limited in other ways, for example, territorially or to particular languages or formats or subject to other conditions). Licences may be sole, exclusive or non-exclusive. Licences may normally be revoked, for example for breach of their terms.

Minor Person under the age of 18. Contracts entered into by minors may be voidable under some circumstances.

Novation Fresh execution of contracts (for example, where a new owner of a publishing business wishes to re-confirm existing author contracts).

Prima Facie At first sight, or on the face of it.

Reversion Rights granted (for example, under a licence) may revert to the person granting them if a specified term comes to an end, or if the terms are breached.

Slander A defamatory statement made verbally, and not in permanent (for example, printed) form.

Sole licence A licence in which the person granting the licence (the licensor) agrees that there will be no other licensees, but that the licensor itself reserves the right to exploit the rights concerned (compare Exclusive Licence).

Specific performance A court may in some circumstances make an order of specific performance ordering one party to perform one or more of their obligations under a contract, for example ordering a publisher to publish a book. The courts are reluctant to oversee the performance of contracts in such a direct way, where damages are an alternative.

Statutes Acts of Parliament: now the primary source of UK law (compare Common Law above). Statutory measures may include Statutory Instruments (SIs) and other orders made under Acts of Parliament.

Summary Conviction Conviction for a criminal offence by a magistrates' court. Penalties are normally lower than those following conviction on indictment before a Crown Court.

Title Legal ownership, for example of specific goods or property.

Tort A civil wrong (as opposed to a criminal wrong which is a crime). Examples of torts include negligence, defamation or passing off. Actions for tort may be commenced in the civil courts by the aggrieved parties (unlike crimes which are prosecuted by the authorities through the criminal courts). The most common remedy sought is an award of damages: in appropriate circumstances injunctions may also be granted.

Ultra Vires Beyond the given authority – an agent or an employee acting *ultra vires* is acting beyond his or her authority and the actions concerned may be challenged or declared void later (although authority may be implied in some circumstances).

Void Of no legal effect.

Voidable Liable to be declared void.

Warranty A term of a contract under which the party making the warranty gives certain guarantees, for example, that the subject of the contract (for example, a manuscript) is not defamatory or does not infringe any copyright or is not oth-erwise illegal. Breach of a warranty usually gives rise to an action for damages, and may sometimes entitle the other party to terminate the contract.

Work A literary, artistic or other creation, such as a novel or a photograph or a computer program. Most, but not all, original works of UK citizens, or first published in the UK, will qualify for copyright protection in the UK.

Appendix B
Useful addresses

Advertising Standards Authority
Mid City Place
71 High Holborn
London WC1V 6QY

Agency for the Legal Deposit Libraries
161 Causeway Side
Edinburgh EH9 1PH
publisher.enquiries@legaldeposit.org.uk

Association of Authors' Agents
Watson Little Ltd
48–56 Bayham Place
London NW1 0EU

Authors' Licensing and Collective
Society Ltd (ALCS)
The Writers' House
13 Haydon Street
London EC3N 1DB

British Copyright Council
Copyright House
29–33 Berners Street
London W1T 3AB

Copyright Directorate
21 Bloomsbury Street
London WC1B 3HF

Copyright Licensing Agency
Saffron House
6–10 Kirby Street
London EC1N 8TS

Copyright Tribunal
21 Bloomsbury Street
London WC1B 3HF

Design and Artists Copyright Society
(DACS)
33 Great Sutton Street
London EC1V 0DX

The Directory and Database Publishers
Association
Queen's House
28 Kingsway
London WC2B 6JR

Educational Recording Agency Ltd
(ERA)
New Premier House
150 Southampton Row
London WC1B 5AL

The Independent Publishers Guild
(IPG)
PO Box 12
Llain
Whitland SA34 0WU

Information Commissioner
Wycliffe House
Water Lane
Wilmslow
Cheshire SK9 5AF

Intellectual Property Office and
The Patent Office
Concept House
Cardiff Road
Newport
South Wales NP10 8QQ

The Legal Deposit Office
The British Library
Boston Spa
Wetherby
W. Yorkshire LS23 7BY
legal-deposit-books@bl.uk

Office of Fair Trading
Fleetbank House
2–6 Salisbury Square
London EC4Y 8JX

Office of Public Sector Information
(OPSI)
The National Archives
Kew
Richmond
Surrey TW9 4DU
www.opsi.gov.uk

Performing Right Society
Copyright House
29–33 Berners Street
London W1T 3AB

The Publishers Association
29B Montague Street
London WC1B 5BW

Publishers Licensing Society Ltd (PLS)
37–41 Gower Street
London WC1E 6HH

Registrar of Public Lending Right
Richard House
Sorbonne Close
Stockton-on-Tees TS17 6DA

Society of Authors
84 Drayton Gardens
London SW10 9SB

UNESCO
7 Place de Fontenoy
75700 Paris 07SP
France
(UCC Convention)

US Copyright Office
Register of Copyrights
Library of Congress
101 Independence Avenue SE
Washington DC 20559
USA

World Intellectual Property
Organisation (WIPO)
34 Chemin des Colombettes
1211 Geneva 20
Switzerland
(Berne Convention)

Writers Guild of Great Britain
40 Roseberry Avenue
London EC1R 4RX

Appendix C
Further reading and sources

FURTHER READING

Sheila Bone (ed.), *Osborn's Concise Law Dictionary*, 11th edition (Sweet & Maxwell, 2009).

J.M. Cavendish and Kate Pool, *A Handbook of Copyright in British Publishing Practice*, 3rd edition (Cassell, 1993).

Michael Flint, *A User's Guide to Copyright*, 4th edition (Butterworths, 1997).

Denis de Freitas, *The Law of Copyright and Rights in Performances*, 2nd edition (British Copyright Council, 1998).

Lynette Owen, *Selling Rights*, 5th edition (Routledge, 2010).

Lynette Owen (ed.), *Clark's Publishing Agreements*, 8th edition (Butterworths, 2010).

SOURCES

BIS www.bisgov.uk

British Copyright Council www.britishcopyright.org

British Library (Legal Deposit) www.bl.uk

DCMS www.culture.gov.uk

EU Commission (Directives and other information) www.europe.eu.int/comm/index_en/htm

EU intellectual property information europa.eu.int/scadplus/leg/en/S06020.htm

European Union (general site) www.europa.eu.int

Home Office (libel and other legislation) www.homeoffice.gov.uk

IPO www.ipo.gov.uk

Law Society (solicitors) info.service@lawsociety.org.uk

Patent Office (copyright information, trade marks and patents) www.patent.gov.uk

Public Lending Right www.plr.uk.com

Society of Authors www.societyofauthors.org

The Publishers Association www.publishers.org.uk

UK Parliament (legislation) www.publications.parliament.uk

World Intellectual Property Organisation (WIPO) (Berne Convention) www.wipo.int

Index

abstracts, copying 250
abuse of a dominant position 339–41
acceptance on delivery 152
account of profits 219
acquired rights, in revived copyrights 40–1
adaptation, making an 232–3
advances, publisher's duty to give 88–9
agency agreements 99, 337–9
agents' agreements 146–7
aggregator agreements 144
anonymous and pseudonymous works:
    copying 250; duration of copyright in 41
anti-competitive agreements
    (Article 81) 333–7
anti-competitive practices 332
applicable law and jurisdiction 101–2
arbitration, provision in authors'
    contracts 100
Article 34: free movement of goods 345
Article 81: anti-competitive
    agreements 333
Article 82: abuse of a dominant
    position 339–41
artistic craftsmanship, works of 22–3
artistic works: copyright protection for
    21–3; summary checklist 23
artist's resale right (*droit de suite*) 59–60
artwork, copyright distinct from physical
    ownership 34, 113
assertion, of right of paternity 47–8
assignment of copyright 74–5
assigns, and assignment of contracts 74–5
authorising copyright infringement 227–8
author–publisher agreements 72–102
authors and joint authors 30; warranties
    and indemnities by 81–5

bankrupts, contracts by 71

Berne Convention 4, 262–3; '3-step test',
    see three step test
blasphemy 201
block exemptions 336
book club rights 120–1; licensing
    points 121
breach of confidence, actions for and
    defences to 217
British codes of advertising 314–15
broadcasts 26; authors of 26

cable programmes and cable programme
    services 26; authors of 32
champerty 69
co-editions 121–6
collective works, authors of 30
'commercial publication' for right of
    paternity 47
commissioned works: copyright ownership
    in 32, 111; moral rights in 112
common law 5
communication/making available to the
    public right 16, 232
comparative advertising 311–12
competing works, by authors 81
Competition Act 1980 333
competition rules 333
compilations, as literary works 17
computer programs: as literary works 18;
    authors of 30; lawful use of 248
computer-generated works, as literary
    works 18; copyright ownership 30
concepts, developed, confidentiality in 207
concordat between book clubs 120
conditions, in contracts 288
confidence, actions for breach of 217
confidence, relationships of 208–9
confidential information 206; kinds of 207–8

confidentiality: agreements 209–10;
    government 223–4
consideration, necessary for contracts 65–6
Consumer Protection Act 1987 303
contempt of court 202–5
contract terms 288
contract, what makes a 7, 63–8
contracts of sale 287
copying 228–30
copyright: assignment of 74–5, 95–6;
    duration of 37–44; history of 11–12;
    intellectual property and 10–11;
    ownership 29–35; qualification for 34–5;
    works 15–29
copyright directive, 2001 12–14
copyright infringement: criminal
    penalties for 258; defences, summary
    checklist 238; indirect 227–8;
    primary 227; secondary 235; who can be
    sued 253; who can sue 252
copyright owner, what to do if you can't
    find 159
creative common licences 73
crown copyright, duration of copyright
    in 43
customs confiscation 258
cybersquatting 280

damages 218
DA-notices 224
data protection 319
database directive 54
database right 54
databases 17–18; lawful use of 249
deal memos 68
defamation: absolute privilege 181;
    consent, as a defence to 187; death of
    plaintiff, kills the action 187; 'defamatory
    meaning' 169–73; fair comment, as a
    defence to 178–81; ISP liability 186;
    identification, need for 174–5;
    innocent dissemination 185–6;
    innuendo and hidden meanings 172–3;
    justification (truth) as a defence
    to 177–8; juxtaposition, risks of 175;
    libel damages 166–7; limitation of
    actions 188; malice, defeats a defence of
    fair comment 180; 'offer of amends' 187;
    publication, liability for 175–6; qualified
    privilege 181–4; requirements for 168;
    social context, importance of 171–2;
    summary checklist 191–2
defective goods, liability for 303

delivery, authors' responsibility for 80–1,
    151–2
delivery up 219
derogatory treatment, and right of
    integrity 49–51
design material for computer programs,
    copyright protection for 18
designs and typefaces, permitted use of
    249
Digital Economy Act 233–6
Digital Millennium Copyright Act 268
Directives, EU 5
disclaimers, of liability for negligence
    claims 195
distance selling 317–19
distribution right 13
domain name disputes 279–81
'dominant position' in markets 339
dramatic works, as copyright works 23–4
DRM (Digital Rights Management) 347
droit de suite, see artist's resale right
droit moral, see moral rights
drunkards, contracts entered into by 70
duration of copyright 37–44; duration
    directive and EU harmonization
    38–41; 1995 UK regulations 38–41;
    in individual works 41–4; summary
    checklist 44

e-book agreements 142–4
editorial alterations 154–7
educational use 244–6
electronic copies, transferring 249
electronic licensing and joint ventures
    139–40
electronic rights 93, 136–8
employee works, copyright ownership
    in 32–4
employees, apparent authority to
    contract 71
European Court of Human Rights 4
European Court of Justice 5, 7
European Parliament 4
exclusion and limitation clauses 298–301
exclusive licences, meaning of 77
exemptions and block exemptions 335–7
exhaustion of rights, in Europe 346–7
extensions of copyright, following duration
    directive 39

fair dealing: criticism or review 241–2;
    reporting current events 242–3; research
    or private study 240–1

false attribution, moral right to prevent 52–3
film and TV rights 133–5
films 25–6; authors and copyright ownership 31; duration of copyright in 42–3; single frames of 22; sound tracks 25; underlying rights 25, 133
first publication, qualifying for copyright 35–6
fitness for purpose, implied condition of 295–8
formats 78–9
free movement of goods (Article 34) 345
freezing injunctions 258

GATT 12, 262, 266
ghost writers, as authors 29–30
government confidentiality, breach of 223–4
Gowers Review 14, 245
graphic works, as artistic works 21–2

honest comment see defamation
human rights and privacy 212–13

ideas: no copyright in 9; illegality, contracts unenforceable for 69
incidental inclusion 243
indecent photographs 198–200
indemnities 85
indexes: providing for 160; tired authors not always best at 86–7
infringing copy: importing an 235–6; possessing or dealing with an 236–7; providing the means for making 237
injunctions 255–6
innuendoes, see defamation
integrity, moral right of 49–52; derogatory treatment and 50–1; exceptions to 51–2; summary checklist 52
intellectual property, copyright as form of 10–11
international copyright protection 261–9
international court of justice 4
international law 3
internet transmissions, copyright in 26–7
Internet, legal risks of 136–40
issuing copies to the public 231

joint authors 30
joint ventures: co-editions 124–6; electronic licensing 139–40
judicial proceedings, permitted copying for 248

jurisdiction, provision in authors' contracts 101–2

'key man' clause, in merchandising agreements 132
'know-how', not normally confidential 210

legal capacity, to make contracts 68–72
legal deposit 161–2
letter before action 254–5
libel: authors' warranty against 83–4; damages for 165–7; different from slander 168; repeating a 173; see also defamation
library and archive copying 246
licences of right, in revived copyright works 39
linking 189
literary works 16–20; summary checklist 21

Malcolm v. OUP, and verbal publishing agreements 66–8
malice, see defamation
malicious falsehood 192–3
manuscripts, copyright distinct from physical ownership 34
Mareva Injunctions, see freezing injunctions
mental patients, capacity to contract 70
merchandising rights 129–32
merchantability and satisfactory quality 293–5
minors, capacity to contract 69
misleading advertisements 307, 311
misrepresentation 292–3
moral rights of authors 45–54; editorial alterations and 50; remedies for infringement 55; waivers of 48–9
multimedia, see electronic rights
musical works 24

'national treatment', under Berne Convention 262–2
negligence, and duties of care 194, 301–2
negligent mis-statement 193
non-delivery or late delivery 151–2
'novation' of contracts 75

obscene publications 196
obscenity: authors' warranty against 84; defences to 189–90; obscene articles, defined 196; offences 196–7
offer and acceptance in contracts 64–5

'offer of amends', *see* defamation
official secrets 220–3
online access licences 140–2
open access agreements 73
option clauses, not always enforceable 98
options, for film rights 133
originality, required for literary works 19–20
orphan works 87, 159, 235, 349
ownership and title, in goods 288–90

painting, must be on a fixed surface 22
paperback rights 117–20
parallel imports 346
parliamentary and judicial proceedings, permitted copying for 248
parliamentary copyright, duration of 43
passing off 277–9
paternity, moral right of 46–9; assertion of 47–8; summary checklist 49; waiver of 48–9; works excluded 48
performing, showing or playing in public 232
permissions, importance of 86–7, 157–9
permitted acts 239–51
'personal data' 320
Peter Pan, copyright in 44
photographs: as artistic works 22; authors of 31, commissioned, copyright in 32, 112; indecent 198–200
piracy 260–1
plagiarism 230
plots or scenarios, as confidential 207
post mortem auctoris (pma), duration of copyright 37
printers' and publishers' details, obligation to print 160–1
privacy, limited moral right to 54; UK law of 206–25
privilege, *see* defamation
procuring a breach of contract 69
proofs 87–8, 160
public lending right 58, 247
public policy, reasons for refusing copyright protection 238
publication right, in previously unpublished works 57–8
publication, qualifying for copyright 34–5
publishers' lunches, limited alcoholic effect of 70
publishers' responsibility to publish 85–6

qualifying authors/'qualifying persons' 35–6, 83

qualifying works, summary checklist 36
quitclaims 134

racial and religious hatred, incitement to 201
regulations, EU 5
Rehabilitation of Offenders Act 1974 178
rejection on delivery 153
remainders, provision in author contracts 97
rental 231–2
reproduction right 13
reprographic copying 245
resale price maintenance 337
restraint of trade 332–3
retention of title clauses 289
reversion of rights 98
reversion of rights to authors under 1911 Act 37–8
revision of the work, authors' duty 97
revivals of copyright, following duration directive 39
rights, granted by author contracts 75–80
royalties and advances, in author contracts 88–90
royalty statements, publishers' duty to provide 95

sale by description 291–2
sale of goods and consumer rights 285–7
'satisfactory quality', implied term of 293
search orders 258
seditious libel 84, 201
seizure of infringing articles 258
serious arrestable offences 196–8
simultaneous publication, qualifying for copyright 36
site licences, in electronic licensing 130–40
software, copyright ownership 31
sole and exclusive licences 77–8
sound recordings 24; authors and copyright ownership 24; duration of copyright in 31
'spent' convictions, *see* Rehabilitation of Offenders Act 1974
stamp duty, in author contracts 102
Statute of Anne 1709 11
statutes 6–7
statutory declarations, librarians for 247–8
statutory instruments 6–7
'stop now' orders 304
subsidiary rights, in author contracts 90–4
'substantial part' 227

'sufficient acknowledgement', in criticism or review 241–2
'sweat of the brow' in US works 18

tables and compilations, as literary works 17
term directive, *see* duration directive
termination, of authors' contracts 98
territories in Europe 345–6
third parties, contracts may be enforceable by 71–2
three step test 14
title: implied condition of good 289–90; presumptions on 253
torts 7–8
Trade Descriptions Act 1968 8, 307, 311
trade marks 270–7; infringement 275; registering 273
translation rights 93
translations: copyright in 115; moral rights in 115
treatment, derogatory 49–50
TRIPS agreement 4, 263
typographical arrangements of published editions 27
typographical arrangements, copyright ownership of 31

UCC copyright notice 95–6

UGC 190–1
UK law 5–6
Ultra Vires, contracts by those acting 70–1
underlying rights, for film 25, 133
unfair commercial practices 307
Unfair Contract Terms Act 1977 298
Universal Copyright Convention (UCC) 12, 95, 264
universities copyright, duration of 44
unpublished works, duration of copyright in 42
unsafe consumer goods, supplying 304
unsolicited goods and services 316
US copyright protection 265–9

verbal contracts 66–8
vertical agreements 336
visually impaired people, copying for 250–1
volume rights, meaning of 78

waivers, of moral rights 48, 92
warning letters, letters before action 254–5
warranties and indemnities, by authors 81–5
warranties, meaning of 288
WIPO 262
WIPO Copyright Treaties 1996 263
'works for hire' in USA, copyright in 112
World Trade Organisation 11, 262
writing, contracts which need 68